MW00606665

KISS and SELL

KISS and SELL

THE MAKING OF A SUPERGROUP

C. K. Lendt

BillboardBooks

New York

To my parents

Senior Editor: Bob Nirkind
Editor: Sylvia Warren
Book and cover design: Jay Anning
Production Manager: Ellen Greene

First published in 1997 in the United States by Billboard Books,
an Imprint of Watson-Guptill Publications, a division of BPI
Communications, Inc. 1515 Broadway, New York, NY 10036

Library of Congress Cataloging-in-Publication Data
Lendt, C.K.
    Kiss and sell: the making of a supergroup/ C.K. Lendt
        p.   cm.
Includes index.
ISBN 0-8230-7604-0 (hardcover)
ISBN 0-8230-7551-6 (paperback)
1. Kiss (Musical group) 2. Rock musicians—United States—Biography. I. Title.
ML421.K57L46 1997
782.42166′092′2—dc21
                                     96-52637
                                       CIP
                                      MN

Manufactured in the United States of America

First printing, 1997

2 3 4 5 6 7 8 9 / 99 98 97

CONTENTS

Foreword

I started work on *Kiss and Sell* knowing exactly where it would begin and end. What I didn't know was how quickly the shifting sands of the music business and the sea change in the world of Kiss would provide such a fascinating and satisfying conclusion to this story.

My twelve years of involvement with the band was a roller-coaster ride—turbulent, topsy-turvy, and terrifically enjoyable for the most part, but interspersed with moments of panic, uncertainty, and high anxiety. I have compressed a lengthy time span—eons in this business—into a relative handful of anecdotes, incidents, and events which shaped the making of Kiss and help to explain the phenomenon that they created.

An unusual alchemy of personalities, emotions, and money fuel the business of music and an insider needs to reveal how these ingredients are mixed. Having had a ringside seat gave me a unique perspective on Kiss's sharp upward trajectory in the '70s and how they faltered in the '80s. Now the cycle is being repeated as a new generation taps into the Kiss experience, re-created in its original incarnation with the identical formula that was so astoundingly successful two decades earlier.

The flesh and blood of what goes on inside the music business and the world of rock is far more compelling than the hype, hoopla, and ballyhoo that are perpetually regurgitated in the media. And the story behind the story of superstar artists is invariably more illuminating than the official story, especially how the money is made--and frequently lost. Lifeless accounts, sanitized by authorized chroniclers, seldom veer from a preordained path of pleasantries and puffery. But that is hardly what the music business--or the artists who drive it--is about. Creating an illusion is central to the world of music, and with Kiss, the illusion was both the source of their success and a cause of its unraveling.

Friedrich Nietzsche said a century ago that "Success has always been a great liar." Changing times and a different environment have done nothing to invalidate that observation.

Many people were immensely helpful in providing their insights and encouragement to me in writing *Kiss and Sell*. They need to be acknowledged: Mark Adelman, Ken Anderson, Lee Aronsohn, William Aucoin, Susan Cohen, Martin Cornbluth, Lydia Criss, Carol Ross-Durborow, Marilyn Ford, Jeffrey Franklin, Lee Friedman, John Harte, Isabel Ismael, M. William Krasilovsky, Henrietta Lendt, Harley Lewin, Al Lieberman, Ben Liss, Marvin Mann, Tom Marzullo, William McManus, Bob Nirkind, Michael Perlstein, Mark Phillips, Fritz Postlethwaite, Jeff Rowland, Ken Sharp, Rosanne Shelnutt, William Skrzyniarz, F. Robert Stein, Jeffrey Suhs, Richard Weidenbaum, and Linda West. And special thanks to my agent, Linda Konner.

C. K. LENDT
New York
February 1996

8

Initiation and Odyssey

On record, they sound like four accidents in search of a thud. But in concert they sound like the thud—and they look like bats on the lam, with their garish white make-up and their black sequined outfits and their fire-breathing bassist and their onstage explosions and their 60-foot curtain of flame. The effect is like Batman in quadruplicate, exploding in front of your face.

"Kitsch Me Deadly," *Village Voice*, February 16, 1976.

My introduction to Kiss and my initiation into the world of rock 'n' roll both came on July 10, 1976. I had just been hired as on-the-road liaison for Kiss's new business managers, the co-owners of a New York-based company called Glickman/Marks Management Corporation. It all seemed so incongruous and weird. I hadn't the slightest idea how this was supposed to work. Four heavy metal rock stars called Kiss who were a cross between the Bowery Boys and a Marvel Comics special edition; two middle-aged businessmen from Cleveland in suits and ties; and me, a freshly minted M.B.A. graduate starting his first job at 24 and a babe in the woods as far as this business was concerned.

This was my first real job since graduating from business school a year earlier, and I was Glickman/Marks's first employee. The economy was mired in recession, and job opportunities had dried up even for recent B-school grads. As I was about to find out, there was no recession in the world of Kiss. After nearly a year of chasing after job openings and trying to bluff my way through interviews, I was going to work for a rock group on tour. I was either totally out of my mind or I had no idea what I was getting into. The latter was probably closer to the truth.

My two bosses, Carl Glickman and Howard Marks, wanted to introduce me to their new client, signed only a few months earlier. Kiss was on tour, and the most convenient location for this formality was backstage here, at their only show in the New York area. I was a little nervous about what to expect, but Carl and Howard were such conservative, button-down business types, their demeanor allayed any fears I might have had. The way they described Kiss and the scope of their business activities made it all sound very matter-of-fact, even humdrum. Our job was simply to handle the money and advise them on financial matters.

The site for our introductory rendezvous, Roosevelt Stadium in Jersey City, New Jersey, was smack in the middle of a marshy bog, treeless and peopleless like a lunar surface. Dirt roads led from the nearby state highway into the facility. Roosevelt's half-oval grandstand, which could hold upwards of 30,000, had seen better days in the 1940s and 1950s when it was the venue for minor league baseball and high school sports events. Now, apart from summer rock concerts, it was little used. Why anyone would want to see a show in a ramshackle firetrap like this, a remote frontier post situated on a flat expanse of fetid swampland, was a mystery to me. Why anyone would want to put on a show in this eyesore was even more of an enigma. But I was new to this world.

By twilight, an endless stream of cars were clogging the main arteries which circled the stadium and funneled traffic into several parking fields that formed an apron around the grounds. People were coming in droves, undeterred by the oppressive summer heat of the New Jersey marshlands and the stadium's isolated location. They were determined to see a Kiss show no matter how arduous the journey.

Howard Marks was sitting in one of several small Winnebago-type trailers that had been set up backstage for the use of Kiss's guests and the show's promotion staff. I had seen Howard arrive earlier in a royal blue Cadillac limo with a white canvas top, his personal limo. All of this was new and impressive to me. I felt somehow privileged to be working for a man who could afford his own limo and chauffeur. Carl Glickman wasn't present. He lived in Cleveland and came to New York during the week for business meetings. I joined Howard in the trailer, and a few minutes later a man of refrigerator proportions with a black T-shirt seemingly glued to his back from perspiration barged into the doorway, unannounced. The shirt looked ready to rip apart, barely restraining a sagging gut that hung over a belt buckle. He was a bodyguard for the band. He told us in a muffled sort of growl that it was "okay to go in" to Kiss's dressing room trailer.

It was now around 7:30 p.m. Kiss would take the stage around 9:30 p.m., and they had to begin getting into makeup and costumes about an hour in advance. Business meetings would have to take place well before then since they had so many friends, relatives, and guests at Roosevelt Stadium. The bodyguard grunted something and Howard and I left our trailer.

As I would come to learn, bodyguards in the rock 'n' roll world were the gatekeepers and clock-watchers who controlled access to the Kiss members.

They were also enormous—hulking, overstuffed giants who looked as if they ingested steroids for breakfast. I did whatever they told me. The bodyguard led us the short distance to the nearby Kiss trailer. By the time Howard and I entered and found chairs, the tiny trailer was already crowded. It was getting close to when Kiss would have to begin preparing their makeup, a ritual which they performed themselves. A last-minute change due to a pre-concert photo session dictated an earlier start than usual. Howard would have to get on with business. After engaging in some banter with the group, now assembled at makeup tables and staring at themselves in front of illuminated mirrors with small white bulbs lining the edges, Howard spoke. "Fellas, this is Chris Lendt, the new Account Executive for Glickman/Marks Management. He'll be traveling with you on tour as our representative. Think of him as an extension of Carl and me. Whatever you want from us, talk with Chris. He's to be our eyes and ears on the road." I sat stone-faced and expressionless in my small chair while Howard delivered his buildup.

Sitting next to Howard in a collapsible deck chair was Bill Aucoin (pronounced (OH-coin), Kiss's discoverer and creative manager. I had first met Bill earlier in the week, when, after a brief interview, he had approved me as the business manager's liaison. An energetic man, he was obviously junior to Howard in both age and temperament. Grinning widely, Bill said, "Chris will be around until either the groupies wipe him out or the band drives him crazy, whichever comes first." It must have been funny because everyone was chuckling, but I had no idea what he was talking about.

Directly in front of me were four seemingly gigantic young men, most of them about my age in their mid-twenties. Each one was wearing platform boots which elevated their height by nearly a foot. All of the Kiss members had various pieces of black spandex-type material draped around their bodies. Some wore studded metal pieces and others had belts and capes. One was wearing what looked like a breastplate. Another wore a triangular shaped colored foam piece which, with his large silver-painted platform boots, created a space uniform look. He had a silver band circling his waist. The four of them were applying a carefully outlined makeup design to their faces, creating a bizarre Kabuki-style image with clown white greasepaint, powder, lipstick, mascara, and black and silver eyeliner. Dozens of tubes, brushes, Q-tips, and bottles were messily strewn out in front of their makeup table. I thought that I had just walked into a foldout from some fantastic science fiction and horror comic book. The final effect was certain to be both shocking and intimidating—which, of course, was the intent.

I shook hands with each and was acknowledged diffidently for the most part. None of this seemed very important to them. They were absorbed in getting themselves ready for the show and trading jokes with each other. Peter

Criss, the drummer, grumbled something unintelligible. Large, stylized cat whiskers were painted on his cheeks with a silver tip at the end of his nose and wide, black pockets all around his eyes. He appeared to be older than the others, with a long mane of graying hair, and wore a pendant. Ace Frehley (pronounced FRAY-lee), the lead guitarist and spaceman character, hardly looked at me while extending a limp handshake. He was as stringy as beef jerky. An elaborate zigzagging design in silver greasepaint formed a mask over his eyes, and his lips were painted black. Paul Stanley, the lead singer and rhythm guitarist, wore a black star painted over his right eye and had lips that were ruby red. His black, body-hugging outfit was cut wide open in front, exposing a furry chest and abdomen. Lots of silver sequins and stars were embroidered on it, and a large cluster of sequins formed around his crotch. Paul had a huge head of jet black hair that he kept teasing up and spraying. He was pleasantly cordial and courteous. Gene Simmons, the bass guitarist and also a singer, tried to come across as fierce at first but then retreated and made a good-natured quip. Gene's monster makeup and Grand Guignol persona made him by far the most extreme and menacing in appearance. His costume resembled simulated armor. He had a codpiece worthy of Priapus and what looked like flaps of silver protruding out from a plate around his chest and midsection. All of these intricately assembled multiple pieces must have weighed a ton, especially the knee-high platform boots. They were covered with reptile-like scales and featured a demon's mouth with fangs at the toe.

Slightly confused and disoriented, I managed to mumble a few words before their attention had completely turned elsewhere. I mentioned something mundane about the royalty checks that had recently arrived at our office, hoping to impress them. Seconds later, the meeting was adjourned and Howard and I left the trailer. I sensed that Kiss met lots of people in various capacities on a regular basis who remained with them for brief periods of time. No doubt, they regarded me as just another disposable item who wouldn't be around for very long. The rigors of the road and the frenetic pace and wild lifestyle of Kiss on tour would soon claim me as an early casualty, they probably thought. After all, I hardly looked like the rock 'n' roll touring type in my *écru* cotton suit and linen tie. Howard and Carl had instructed me always to appear in business attire whenever I was around the band. To Kiss, I probably came across as a man from Mars.

Howard and I left the trailer and waited for Kiss to take the stage. It was now dark. We watched the show from a gated area on the side of the stage, cordoned off from the crowd. Swarms of fans surged toward the stage as a glimmering haze of guitar chords and feedback ricocheted off the bleachers and the concrete retaining walls of the stadium. Kiss emerged on stage in a blaze of flickering strobe lights as sepulchral clouds of smoke swirled around them, blowing out of a battery of dry ice and fog machines. Once the concert started, I knew what Kiss was all about and what made it work. Kiss was an ear-shattering, blinding, total assault on the senses.

Fireworks, explosions, and pyrotechnics detonated on cue, synchronized to the beats of the music. Flash pots exploded with a searing intensity. Sirens wailed and huge emergency landing lights flashed like beacons on stage. A towering electric sign with a gigantic Kiss logo pulsed with blinding effectiveness throughout the show. Fire-breathing, blood-spitting, blankets of smoke and fog, bombs bursting on stage, and spectacular circus-style acrobatics by Paul whipped the crowd into a state of frenzy. Paul, shrieking in a high-pitched wail, took command of the stage, swaggering and pumping his hips, while Gene snapped his head sharply from left to right as if on a swivel, sneering at the crush of fans spread out in front of the 80-foot width of the stage. Some fans tried scaling the barricade until guards pushed them back.

Kiss stood 7 feet tall on stage in their giant platform boots, dwarfing the throngs of young fans who had ringed the barricades. Gene was clearly the main event, attacking his bass guitar and marching across the stage like a monster hunting for prey while he flicked his tongue and dribbled fake blood. In the final moments of "Firehouse," he swished kerosene in his mouth and held a lighted torch in his hand, spraying the kerosene into the flame and creating the illusion of breathing fire.

Ace swayed back and forth as his guitar appeared to catch on fire and erupt in a dense cloud of white smoke and orange sparks. Peter sat atop an enormous drum riser, cranking itself higher and higher until it was almost scraping the overhead lighting truss. A driving beat as unceasing as a drill punch kept pounding as Peter slowly rose above the stage. The deafening sound from the huge speaker bins stacked 10 feet high and butted from one side of the stage to the other roared like a jumbo jet taking off. The music wasn't exactly memorable, but who cared? It was plenty loud and there was such a frenzy on stage, anything else would have been a distraction.

Seeing Kiss for the first time was like watching a musical Armageddon with the stage as a battlefield. The music seemed to merge with the sound effects. An unending bombardment of noises kept pouring out—grinding guitars, electronically amplified drumbeats, caterwauling screams, sudden bursts of fire and gunpowder, and the deep rumbling of heavy-bottomed bass that sounded like a tremor was about to rip open the earth. It was strangely exhilarating in its own way. It may have had the subtlety of a steamroller, but it was obvious to me that Kiss was creating a visceral experience for their audience to feel as much as to see and hear.

The Kiss stage featured a painted cyclorama as a backdrop, evoking the look of a destroyed city's smoking ruins. The urban decay theme was in keeping with the cover artwork of their current album, *Destroyer*. A Broadway designer, Jules Fisher, had created the sprawling stage set. The city appeared to have been devastated by some sort of apocalyptic conflagration. A wall of amplifiers stretched across the stage and above them were platforms, catwalks, and stairways that the Kiss members tore up and down throughout the show. Paul made the most use of these and seemed to possess an inexhaustible energy source. Props filled the corners of the stage including a huge dragon next to Gene and torches resembling Bunsen burners that shot jets of fire straight up from the stage about ten feet or so, creating a hot blast that whooshed across the front rows of the audience. While Kiss was belting out a song called "Hotter Than Hell," I felt like a blowtorch had been pushed into my face.

Beyond the gates and the security guards which protected our backstage enclave hovered the fans, separated from us by a chain link fence which served as a buffer between the backstage area and the crowd. Here was the real world of Kiss, the fans who stood for hours in the wilting afternoon heat to enter the stadium and pick their spot on the turf to see the show up close. Thousands and thousands of them, swarming all over the grubby dirt surface of Roosevelt Stadium, spilling out of the grandstand and crowding the eight-foot-high stage. The truly hard-core fans positioned themselves in front of the speaker bins—a few would actually crawl inside the ducts—the better to feel the thundering, 120-decibel power of the bass beat. Several light towers filled with floodlamps bathed the stadium grounds in a bright glow, silhouetting the rickety structure against the night sky.

The fans were mostly teens and college-age, and a few younger ones. They all looked remarkably alike, male and female, in unisex style, although males clearly predominated. Long hair, T-shirts, tattered jeans, leather jackets edged in nailheads, boots, studded belts, and tattoos were the norm. Some of the girls wore tank tops, mostly cheesy nylon things clinging to their breasts, and many wore Kiss T-shirts. They looked like a truck stop crowd or bikers-in-training, downscale and beer-chugging, but not necessarily threatening. Many of them were scrawny-looking, even gamey in appearance. Some came dressed as Kiss, wearing identical costumes and makeup as the group's. They weaved through the masses of people now pouring all over the stadium's grounds and out of the tunnels that led from the parking area, being cheered and saluted like honorees at a parade. The thick, muggy humidity of the marshlands melted their makeup beyond recognition, but no one seemed to care. With all of Kiss's on-stage gyrations and sprinting back and forth, they were sweating buckets. The fans went wild each time Paul or Gene threw out a sweat-soaked towel from the front of the stage. It was bedlam.

From my backstage vantage point, people filling the stadium seemed like caged animals, shielded from us by iron gates and fencing. Here a privileged few could enjoy the festivities of the Kiss spectacle in a kind of *sanctum sanctorum*. There was a surreal, dreamlike quality to all of this. Fistfights broke out during the night in the stadium's bleachers and people were carried on stretchers or dragged out by the police through our backstage area. These intrusions were tolerated—in fact, they were hardly noticed—provided the victims were quickly removed from the immediate vicinity to a first aid tent that had been set up on the outer perimeter of the grounds. Nothing was to disturb the guests or interfere with their enjoyment of the Roman circus that was taking place.

As I would come to learn, first aid stations are a standard feature of all rock concerts. This is where the walking wounded and the casualties of drug overdoses and drunkenness are routinely treated and dispatched. Kiss had just launched into "Cold Gin," a song about hard drinking, and a wave of approval roared from the crowd as a punchy set of guitar chords boomed through the amps. Paul and Ace kept thrashing at their guitars as speakers started rumbling and blowing apart from the peaking volume. A team of technicians in black Kiss T-shirts leaped across the stage from behind the mountains of Marshall amps to attempt damage control and remove the blown speakers and fuses. Flashes of fire were shooting out of flash pots. Girls were tossing bras and panties onto the stage and guys were delirious as Gene exhorted the fans shoehorned in front of the stage barrier. The black and white greasepaint on his face was running down the sides of his neck and beads of sweat were flying in all directions as he marched to the edge of the stage.

The fans had stampeded from the back area of the stadium grounds to get as close to the front of the stage as they could push and shove themselves. Down in the trenches in front, they were packed in like locusts, screaming and cheering as Kiss played and Paul engaged them in a call-and-response rap. A throng of security guards in white T-shirts with red piping kept the more zealous and overwrought fans from jumping onto the stage. The atmosphere was now supercharged with excitement and the noise from the crowd was nearly as overpowering as the sound from the stage. The volume had become painful for me, so loud I couldn't hear anything except a maddening ringing noise in my ears that wouldn't stop. But I couldn't turn away, either. It was like witnessing a bizarre ritual, where thousands of faithful followers congregated to experience a spectacle of overwhelming power, leaving them in a trancelike state of ecstasy and delirium. I was mesmerized. Security guards and uniformed police ringed the stadium to prevent a melee. Even though I was safely ensconced backstage, the fear of being trampled by a wild pack of fans on the loose was palpable. This was a fierce crowd and Ace's blistering guitar solo had them worked up to a fever pitch.

My mind flashed to Altamont, the speedway in Northern California where the Rolling Stones performed in 1969 and where four people had died. I had the jittery feeling that if only one skirmish or scuffle couldn't be controlled, the chain reaction would ignite this crowd like a tinderbox. But I was new to all of this and still uninitiated. Maybe I was overreacting.

Kiss raged on, tearing up the stage, spinning, jumping, hair waving, inciting the crowd to their feet, and bombarding the huddled masses in front of the stage with bursts of confetti. Bolts of blue and white lightning flashed from behind the cyclorama as a massive confetti shower shot out from small cannons on stage. Fireworks began flaring out from the stage and across the sky like tracers, leaving an orange-colored trail of smoke and powder flashes. "Black Diamond," one of their signature songs, was in full throttle, guitars unwinding in a fury as the show raced to a close. It didn't seem as loud to me as when they started but that's because after nearly ninety minutes, my ears were numb and my senses deadened. My head was aching terribly now, as if it had been stuck in a vise and the screws tightened. Fourth of July pinwheels shot off and thousands of yellow and amber sparkles rained all over the stage as the bomb blasts sent a shattering shockwave rippling through the audience. There were plenty of people around me gasping from all of the smoke. I thought about the kids who'd stationed themselves inside the monstrous speaker bins—their heads must have felt as if they'd been cracked open like coconuts and their brains pulverized. The kids in front who were caught in a pelting rain of confetti and sparks from the fireworks that fell to the ground like flaming cinders were literally reeling from the excitement.

I started to drift away from the debris-covered stage, my eyes watery and singed from the acrid fumes of spent gunpowder. My brain felt flooded from this sensory overload. The blood-curdling screech of what sounded like metal being ripped apart erupted from the stage, and then came a final thunderclap and a salvo of rockets streaking overhead like shooting stars, signaling the end. Paul screamed, "Good night, New Jersey, we lovvvvvvvvvv youuuuuuuuuu," and the band ran off stage. I was shell-shocked. The audience stood nearly motionless for a few seconds, stunned and dazed.

✢

If any band typified the excesses and extremes of the '70s, it was Kiss. Their brand of crash and burn, head-banging rock 'n' roll won as many fans as it did detractors. The flamboyant stage show and theatrics were routinely described in the press as "spectacular," "outrageous," "mind-boggling," "gross," "crass," "sensational," "overpowering," and "overcommercial." Nonetheless, Kiss was the band that the critics loved to hate. They had reached the crest of fame and popularity through hyperbolic excess and the triumph of style over substance. Not surprisingly, the press reveled in taking swipes at the group's primal approach. Hype and more hype pumped up the Kiss image and energized their ardent fans throughout the country. Kiss thrived on this sentiment and manipulated it to their advantage. They championed themselves as "the people's band" and offered their own unique brand of escapism while the critics panned their music as "mindless." *Rolling Stone* compared Kiss's music to "buffalo farts." In *Rolling Stone*'s April 7, 1977, story on the group, Kiss was equally blunt in describing their appeal. Gene talked about what he thought Kiss did best:

> We're not a great band. The musicianship is average, maybe even below, but in a year we're going to be the biggest band in the world. Two hundred million Americans out there don't appreciate subtleties. They want to be sledgehammered over the head....

Kiss called their music "thunder rock," intended to be played at peak volume. They couldn't count on radio airplay to be successful. They earned their following by criss-crossing the country for years, performing at every hall available, from high school auditoriums to dingy clubs, starting as an opening act for any group that would have them, building a grassroots following, and quickly graduating to headliner status. This was accomplished in spite of minimal airplay as well as slow album sales in the early years until the highly successful double album, *Alive!*, a live recording of a Kiss show, was released in 1975. It became a multimillion seller. *Alive!* had sent Kiss skyrocketing to the top of the charts and their fortunes were on the rise as one of the major concert acts in the United States.

Kiss released their next album, *Destroyer*, in March 1976 and began a tour of Europe and England in May. Appearing overseas for the first time, the results were nearly a disaster. Kiss wasn't yet a well-established act outside their home turf. A German group, Scorpions, just starting to get noticed in Europe, was the opening act. The turnouts for the shows had been sparse in many countries. The promoters put them in old, dilapidated venues, and drug-related craziness plagued the tour.

The overall comfort level was far less than the regal standards to which Kiss had only recently become accustomed. Second-class, older European hotels and a backbreaking travel schedule which included trains, planes, and buses made everything worse. They couldn't wait to get home. A major summer U.S. tour was planned.

The tour got off to a rocky start, despite the fact that the *Destroyer* album jumped into the Top Twenty in the *Billboard* charts within weeks of its release. But the lack of a strong single meant that the top rock radio stations in major markets wouldn't play anything from the album, limiting its staying power in the charts. Kiss always had a problem with airplay, owing to their extreme visual image and the grating, blaring sound of their early records. They were an anathema to radio programmers.

Roosevelt Stadium was an early stop on the tour. Promoters thought that Kiss would sell out the stadium, located as it was near the New Jersey suburbs, not far from the bridges and tunnels which connect the many communities along the Palisades with New York. Special shuttle buses were arranged from New York's Port Authority Terminal to take fans from the city to Jersey City and back after the show. The metropolitan area was a region where Kiss's legions of fans were found in the greatest numbers—everyone in the band hailed from New York—and it was assumed that a Saturday night Kiss concert with a few well-known opening acts had to be a success.

18

The assumptions were wrong. Less than 7,000 tickets were sold in advance. The promoter, John Scher, was frantic. He was looking at a huge financial loss for the show and convinced Bill Aucoin to get Kiss to pay for half the cost of a full-page ad in the Sunday, July 4, 1976, edition of *The New York Times* Arts & Leisure section. This was an enormous ad for a rock show, but Scher and Aucoin justified the expense as evidence that they had tried to do everything possible to salvage the show for Kiss, including spending big dollars on advertising. It was also important to save face in front of Kiss, who would blame them if the turnout for the show was embarrassingly low. As additional insurance, another opening act was added, Bob Seger, who would join the J. Geils Band and Point Blank. Everyone was banking on a big walk-up on the day of the show by last-minute ticket buyers. By the first week of July, *Destroyer* had sunk to #80 in *Billboard* and so had everyone's hope for a smashing success at Kiss's only New York show that summer.

And there was an even more serious problem to deal with. Three weeks prior to the Kiss concert on July 10, a 16-year-old had been stabbed to death at Roosevelt Stadium during a show by the rock group Yes. Jersey City's mayor threatened to cancel all remaining rock concerts that season, and Scher went to court to be allowed to continue the shows he'd already booked. The fight went on for weeks before it was decided that the remaining shows on the schedule at Roosevelt Stadium, including Kiss, would be permitted.

I'd been told that lavish backstage parties were *de rigueur* for big time rock groups and that I wouldn't be disappointed with what was planned for this concert. Sure enough, shaping up backstage was a small-scale version of Mulberry Street's Feast of San Gennaro festival. Special guests of Kiss that July night were given laminated plastic passes with the Kiss logo plastered on them to allow entry to the backstage festivities. I was glad that I had one.

Large striped tents were pitched in a corner of the backstage area, far from the rear of the stage. A guard was posted in a makeshift kiosk to control access to the party area, and when I brandished my plastic pass, he waved me through to a specially outfitted VIP hospitality area for guests, decorated with Kiss posters, streamers, and black and silver bunting, the Kiss color scheme. It was a carnival atmosphere. Food stands featuring Ferrara's pastries from Little Italy, clams from Umberto's, sausages, calzone, zeppole, German draft beer, chianti in wicker-wrapped bottles, anisette and sambuca, Perugina candies, were all available in prodigious quantities. I went through several food lines as waiters heaped piles of Italian specialties on my plate. A roving accordionist played Italian folk songs and standards while strolling through the crowd.

Brightly lit neon and electric signs had been erected above the food stands, standing out in sharp relief against the darkness. As the tents began filling with people, the party began to look even more like the street festival it was intended to resemble. An arcade of pinball, video, and electronic games had been set up in an adjacent stand under a separate circus tent. Strings of colored lights were hung all around the tents and over the awnings. Money appeared to be no object in this world, I thought, as I grabbed another cannoli.

By 11:00 p.m., well over 200 people were in the hospitality area including friends, family, performers from the opening acts, business people, record company executives, employees of Kiss, relatives, assorted hangers-on, and, most likely, gate-crashers, all dressed in various modes. People kept streaming in, and the guard in the kiosk had to hold up the long line that formed to make sure each person's pass was carefully inspected. Beyond the line of party-goers queuing up—at least another hundred—were five or six luxury sightseeing buses with big bay windows, the kind that cruise New York on city tours. I'd been told they were rented for the night to ferry guests of "the Kiss organization" to and from Roosevelt Stadium out of New York. I mulled over what the price tag must have been for all this.

The party was jammed and everyone was clutching plastic drink cups and juggling plates of hot food. The noise level was steadily rising as guests greeted each other with cheery hellos and welcoming whoops amid the clatter of servers dishing out food and collecting dirty plates. It was a mixed bag of people, some in suits and others in the type of attire you would wear to the beach. There were girls in striped T-shirts, girls in culottes, and girls in hot pants. Many wore lace-up boots, and a few were decked out in platform shoes painted with glittery colors. A couple of girls were in maxicoat-style shirtdresses with their heads wrapped in paisley scarves. There were plenty of girls in their twenties, attractive and giggly, who were obviously very excited about being backstage at a party for Kiss.

A young girl in a canary-colored body stocking and girdle-tight denim shorts wandered around in an apparent daze. A frizzy mass of reddish-brown hair appeared to explode from her head. She was clutching a fistful of roach clips and looked to be strung out on something, but no one seemed to give her more than a passing glance as she drifted aimlessly through the crowd. As I came to learn, there were always lots of girls more or less like this one around at Kiss shows.

I circulated through the tents, past the chafing dishes of fried clams and manicotti drenched in marinara sauce, and found my way to one of the bars busily dispensing drinks. A small crowd was stationed at the bar near a large fan that was sending a breeze through the tent to provide some relief from the stagnant, stifling heat. Still more girls were pouring into the party—girls in skin-tight Lycra outfits and fishnet stockings, girls wearing so much purplish mascara that it seemed to be leaking from the corners of their eyes, girls with breasts bulging out of low-neckline minidresses that were practically hiked to the hips. Jewelry came in heaps—necklaces, pendants, chains, trinkets, turquoise pieces, gold charms, Indian artifacts, silver amulets—all dangling around peoples' necks, onto their limbs, and on their wrists and fingers. Long hair was the common denominator at this gathering—straight, kinky, fluffy, wavy, curly, layered, swept back, braided, blow-dried, and dried-out—a hodgepodge of styles.

As I milled through the huge crowd, my ears still ringing from the numbing impact of the percussion bombs, I ran into Bill and Howard. While Howard was getting a refill of Cutty Sark, Bill told me that the show had sold just under 14,000 tickets. It wasn't the unmitigated disaster everyone had feared a week earlier, but the take hadn't been nearly enough for the promoter to break even on his costs of producing the show, particularly with the major outlays for advertising, the additional acts booked for Kiss, and the extra security.

Bill said in a strained voice that Scher was angry about taking such a big loss. I later learned that Bill hated confrontations. He preferred to let underlings deal with promoters and settle the show's finances and contractual payments. Howard told Bill we would review the show's P&L statement and then take it up with him. Bill nodded his approval and then darted off to another tent where some of Kiss's friends and relatives were seated at a large round table. He quickly became animated and jovial, embracing them affectionately. He seemed to be quite the social gadabout as many other guests flocked to exchange greetings and shake hands. Bill was taking great pains to mingle with everyone, especially the record company people, to bolster their spirits and keep them excited about the future for Kiss. I would learn that salesmanship is one of the keys to success in the music business and Bill was doing a masterful job of exuding unalloyed enthusiasm.

After midnight, Gene, Paul, Ace, and Peter sauntered into the party. Without makeup and dressed in jeans, T-shirts, and leather, they were visibly drained from what had to have been a particularly exhausting performance given the crushing humidity. As they drifted into the tent area, the partygoers perked up, clapping and cheering, and formed a small ring around them. I stood off to the side, not yet comfortable to be more than an observer, unaware that what was to come in the months and years ahead would make this night's Saturnalia seem like a minor side show by comparison.

❖

My odyssey into the world of rock 'n' roll followed a fruitless job search in L.A. I graduated from the University of Southern California with a B.A. in Telecommunications and then went on to get an M.B.A. When no job turned up by graduation, I migrated back to my home in White Plains, New York. My luck finally changed in June 1976 when I spotted a small ad in *The New York Times*. It was inconspicuous, but there was something about it that grabbed my attention. A new company was looking for an account executive to be the liaison with their "star account," an undisclosed rock group. Having managed a rock band for a couple of years in high school, it sounded like something that I might enjoy. I spent several hours drafting one of the most hard-selling letters of my career.

It worked. An interview took place shortly thereafter. Howard Marks, 47, was the company president. His principal business at the time was an advertising agency located in a modest warren of offices on 75 East 55th Street in a small, oldish building. The space was cramped, and there were apparently not enough desks for the many employees circulating through the corridors. Howard's office was quite spacious, though, and well-appointed despite the rather loud tartan plaid carpeting. He did have a private bathroom.

Sitting behind a large oval desk, Howard projected the image of the quintessential American advertising man. Conservatively attired in a dark suit, white shirt, cuff links, and striped regimental tie, he was glib and cordial at the same time. Howard had a kind of midwestern plain-spoken quality. He spoke in a calm and measured manner and projected confidence. His striking resemblance to Tom Bosley of the TV series *Happy Days* gave him an avuncular appearance. I felt comfortable in his presence. A succession of Kent cigarettes lit with an elegant desk lighter from Mark Cross punctuated his conversation. Howard had an expansive style. He seemed to be a person who liked to be involved in big things.

Howard had always been in advertising, starting as a copywriter in Cleveland. Over the years, he'd been involved in producing many TV commercials and through his work, he'd met Bill Aucoin. Bill had worked in TV production and directed commercials and programs. In 1973, Bill was approached by a rock group called Kiss whose chief claim to fame was wild makeup, outlandish costumes, and stage antics including fire breathing, bombs, and smoke.

As Howard explained to me, Kiss had offered Bill the job of manager on the condition that he must get them a record deal within two weeks' time. He succeeded by signing the group to Casablanca Records, a fledgling label distributed by Warner Bros. Records, which had just been started by former record promoter Neil Bogart. Neil had recently left Buddah Records, where he'd practically invented the "bubblegum music" fad of the early '70s. He saw Kiss as the next big thing in rock.

It was this chain of events that eventually led to the creation of my job. By 1976 Kiss had begun to earn substantial sums of money, and Bill's talents weren't in financial management. He was a brilliant force who had masterminded the success of Kiss and who had a solid understanding of the marketing and promotional side of the music business. But Kiss was becoming increasingly concerned about where all of the money was going now that so much was coming in. They wanted a separate business manager. Howard had by this time ingratiated himself with Kiss and Bill through his advertising agency's work with Casablanca on album cover designs and promotional campaigns. He was nominated for the job. It also helped that Bill had borrowed an office from Howard. He and the group were frequently commuting in and out of the East 55th Street location.

It seemed odd to me that an ad man would become the business manager for a rock group but as I found out later, Howard had proven adept as a negotiator and mediator between Neil and Bill. When a large audit claim of Kiss's came to light following the release of the *Alive!* double album at a time when their career was taking off, the dispute over royalties due them from Casablanca was threatening to wreck the Kiss-Aucoin-Bogart relationship.

It could have been a crisis point in their career but Howard stepped in to engineer a settlement and prevent tempers from flaring up. His credentials as a shrewd businessman had been established and the royalty dispute was resolved.

Howard wanted an account executive to travel with the group and act as a liaison between them and the company. The job was similar to an ad agency account executive—daily contact with the client, follow-through on administrative and financial details, and maintaining good communications between Kiss and the company. Extensive travel would be required since Kiss spent much of their time on tour. I was admonished that if I took the job, "there would be a lot of booze and broads around," which, of course, I should avoid. It sounded fine to me. I hadn't had much of either since getting out of school. Besides, I was really keen on the travel part of the job. Howard didn't ask many questions but I felt the interview went well. He told me to come back the following week to meet his partner, Carl Glickman, who lived in Cleveland and would be in town for meetings.

What was even odder than how Howard entered the picture was how Carl fit in. When I returned for my interview with Carl, I waited patiently in the reception area for nearly an hour. Finally, I was ushered in and I shook hands with Carl in a nondescript office he shared with a bookkeeper. At 50, Carl was a few years older than Howard, and his stern visage and owlish appearance were somewhat unsettling at first. The thick, horn-rimmed glasses and clipped, frequently blunt tone of voice took a while to get used to. A bit wooden, he looked like the banker from the midwest that he was. But he impressed me as being straightforward and sincere, unruffled by the showbiz environment in which he was now involved.

Carl was a wealthy private investor in real estate who had been an adviser or director at a number of financial companies and banks. He had become friendly with Howard when they both lived in Cleveland and Howard rented an office in one of Carl's downtown properties. Carl had a reputation as a financial whiz, earning millions from turning around bankrupt companies and investing in commercial property. As Carl explained to me, Howard took on the job as business manager for Kiss after Carl had agreed to be his partner, providing the necessary financial expertise.

Carl said that my job would be, in part, "a policeman." I wasn't exactly sure what he meant. I didn't think I would be much of a success as Kiss's overseer on the road. He explained that what he wanted was to know how things were being run and to make sure the money was being handled properly on tour. The job was really to monitor the finances. After about five minutes, we agreed on a small starting salary for me. In other words, I had the job. I did have to clear one final hurdle and that was to pass the interview with Bill Aucoin. At that point, Carl picked up the telephone and dialed Bill's office, barking into the mouthpiece that he was "sending someone over to meet you right now, Fred Lendt." I politely interjected that my name was Chris, not Fred. He apologized, wished me well with my interview, and said, "goodbye, Steve." Carl's carelessness with names wasn't limited to mine. It would take him more than a year to get the names straight of everyone in Kiss.

I walked out of the building and up Madison Avenue to 645 Madison at 60th Street. This was quite a contrast to the building that the Glickman/Marks Management offices were in. Bill had only recently moved into this modern, new luxury building, impressively emblazoned with the name Pan Ocean Building.

When I got off the elevator at the fifteenth floor, I stepped into a gleaming lobby and reception area. Aucoin Management, Inc., Bill's new corporate moniker which had replaced the considerably less formal-sounding Rock Steady Inc., its predecessor, occupied the entire floor. There was a lot of glass and chrome and the carpeting was a slightly hypnotic geometric design in brown and gold, all of which might be described as Miami Beach modern. Still, it was impressive.

After announcing myself to the receptionist, I sunk into a leather couch next to several young guys with shoulder-length hair who looked to be in a band. They eyed me a bit suspiciously, as if I was a narc. A few minutes passed before an elegantly dressed, attractive young blonde woman walked assertively into the reception area and greeted me enthusiastically. Identifying herself as Linda West, Bill's executive assistant, she told me that "Bill was ready for your meeting." The guys on the couch seemed impressed. I was whisked away down a long corridor toward Bill's corner office. I felt important. There seemed to be no shortage of nubile, young girls in this office, sprinkled around conspicuously to give the place a very hip, appealing style.

Bill's office commanded a panoramic cityscape of upper Madison Avenue. Gold and platinum albums filled one wall, and an oversized custom-built cabinet crammed with audio and video equipment and a bank of TV monitors faced his desk which was catty-cornered to the windows. Bill sat behind a large rectangular rosewood table with stainless steel trim, flanked by a set of five hand-crafted marionettes, each about two feet high. Four of them were painted to look like the Kiss members. A fifth marionette, which looked like Bill, was depicted, naturally, as the one pulling the strings of the others. His desktop was fashionably uncluttered, holding only a sleek, black electronic calculator, a ten-button phone, and one small stack of papers. No Tin Pan Alley setting this, but rather an amalgam of big business and show business. Steps away from his office was an executive bathroom. The door was open and I could see a shower along with towels to match the office decor and a telephone with rows of flashing buttons next to the sink. It was all a bit dizzying. Rain started to drizzle down the floor-to-ceiling windows.

Bill looked to be the master of ceremonies of this rock 'n' roll enterprise. Nattily dressed in a blue blazer, checked shirt, and taupe trousers secured with a narrow calfskin belt, Bill projected a natural charisma. Stylish and reed thin, he looked the picture of success. A carefully trimmed mustache gave him the distinctive touch of an impresario and his slightly jutting jaw lent a touch of authority. Bill was from the Boston area, and his voice still carried traces of a Boston accent. He had longish light brown hair, swept back from his forehead where it had started to thin. He had a well-manicured appearance and looked to be a perfectionist. Bill was 32.

We quickly exchanged pleasantries and I mentioned something about a previous summer job I had in Washington at the U.S. Information Agency in the Motion Picture and Television Service. I thought this would be a plus in my favor since Bill's background was in TV. A steady stream of phone calls poured in, and I knew that with all the unavoidable interruptions, my time would be limited. He didn't ask too many questions, but like Howard, he seemed to be interested in gauging my personality. We shook hands and he told me to go back to the Glickman/Marks Management offices. One of his secretaries would arrange the details of when and where I would join the Kiss tour, then in progress. He also asked me to plan on coming to Roosevelt Stadium the following weekend to be introduced to "the guys."

⁘

Things kicked in for Kiss not long after Roosevelt Stadium. Another single was released from *Destroyer,* a syrupy ballad called "Beth." It featured Peter singing the lead vocal in a raspy voice with a lush orchestration of violins swelling in the background. It was hardly a typical Kiss song and an even less likely choice for a single, but it worked wonders. "Beth" climbed to #7 in *Billboard* and revived a tour that had started to stall. The song got extensive radio airplay on stations around the country, both rock and middle-of-the-road pop stations. Airplay begets ticket sales, and the tour had a much-needed shot in the arm.

Roosevelt Stadium was also the beginning of an upturn for me—the first benchmark of the years I would spend with Kiss in the volatile world of rock concerts, promoters, agents, managers, attorneys, and record companies. I was excited that I finally had a job, and an unusual one at that. My corporate training program would include rock shows, groupies, sharpshooting promoters, huge sums of cash, round-the-clock phone calls, and manic fans, hell bent for leather and chrome. I wasn't exactly sure what I was getting into, but after seeing Kiss at Roosevelt Stadium, I was seduced. The Tuesday following the show, I boarded the Metroliner for Baltimore, where Kiss was playing that night, and started my job.

Larger Than Life

We get our fans to jump past the thinking process because that's the thing that restrains people from having a good time. Our concerts don't mean anything—they are an experience in letting your guts out.

Gene Simmons describing Kiss's appeal as a fantasy to their fans, "Kiss Is Rock's Rocky," *The New York Post,* April 23, 1977.

The real Kiss Army was lying in wait in Kansas City when Kiss arrived for a show in the brick-oven summer heat of July 1976. I'd only been on tour for a few weeks but the strange way of life I was living had started to seem normal. Life on tour revolved around making it to the next city and the next show; the next airplane and the next airport; the next hotel and the next hotel room; and whatever girls were available at the next backstage door or at the next hotel bar.

For the crew, life revolved around setting up and tearing down the *Destroyer* stage production, a cumbersome and clunky contraption that was more suited to a theater stage than a traveling rock show. Long drives from city to city kept them on unimaginably tight schedules, and often the show was only put together a few hours before the arena doors opened to the crowds of kids outside. I learned that Kiss was often impossible to deal with—"arrogant" and "bratty"—but unwavering in wanting to deliver a top-flight show.

Every week was divided into five or six cities and each day was sectioned into individual parts. Each day had a different wake-up time depending upon the flight schedule. Despite its chaotic and disorganized image, the rock 'n' roll business is really very structured and demands a degree of scheduling and order that rivals a military operation.

Kiss was encamped in Kansas City's newest and most luxurious hotel, the Crown Center Plaza. The hotel was integrated with a modern and sleekly built shopping plaza financed by Hallmark Cards. It was the location of my earliest conversation with Gene. In his suite, we talked the afternoon before the show. The room was cluttered with Fresca bottles and room service trays stacked on the floor looking like they'd been sitting there for days. The phone never seemed to stop ringing, and its red message light blinked constantly.

Gene asked me how I found Kansas City and I said it seemed okay, but I didn't know if they had any good restaurants, one measure by which I judged a city. Gene let out a loud laugh and told me he had quite a different way to evaluate cities. Gene said the single most important criterion was "the quality of the pussy." To Gene, my restaurant standard must have seemed hopelessly bourgeois. He told me my outlook would change as the tour progressed. The phone rang and Gene picked it up. Without even waiting to find out who was on the line, Gene barked into the receiver in mock seriousness, "Do you like pain and tire chains and Hostess Twinkies?" He then laughed, told the caller, "Room 520," and hung up. Moments later, there was a knock at the door. As I got up to leave, Gene opened the door and ushered in his visitor, a pudgy ash blonde with enormous breasts tucked into a Kiss T-shirt who looked to be in her late teens. Giggling and nervous, she could barely manage to say "Hi, Gene," without stammering. I made a quick exit as Gene pulled the girl toward him and turned to smile broadly at me. "See what I mean?" he said.

I quickly caught on that "shock rock" groups weren't welcomed with open arms by hotels. This was frequently a problem for Kiss; some hotel chains refused to rent rooms to them. Hotels felt that rock musicians and their entourage were at best Philistines and at worst barbarians who would plunder their properties and ravage their more respectable guests, sending them into a state of terror. Hordes of fans rampaging through the premises were a real threat. Kiss's penchant for returning to the hotel directly from the show once it ended, in their full regalia and makeup and stomping through the lobby in giant platform boots, was enough to send most hotel managers into a state of apoplexy. Their fears weren't unwarranted, as I found out after the first Kansas City show.

The Crown Center Plaza had a very large lobby area, full of leather couches, plush chairs, end tables, and custom-woven carpeting which tastefully displayed the logo of the hotel's name. At 11:30 that night, the lobby was virtually deserted. I could see a few bellhops in the distance, passing the front desk to deliver papers and small parcels and moving luggage from the adjacent lobby area to a back cloakroom. The only sound heard was the murmur of two middle-aged businessmen chatting on a corner couch and the trickling of an indoor waterfall.

But the Kiss Army had just arrived outside the front doors of the main entrance. Not Kiss themselves, who had returned from the concert that night and entered the hotel through an underground parking garage, then taken a freight elevator so they could make their way unobtrusively to their hotel rooms. And not the Official Kiss Army, a coast-to-coast fan club that spread Kiss news to loyal followers. But the *real* Kiss Army had arrived, the fans from the show which had ended only minutes earlier at the Municipal Auditorium, blocks away.

There were hundreds of them marching almost in lockstep up the circular driveway that fronted the Crown Center Plaza. Like an army of invading ants about to storm a hill, the Kiss Army strode fearlessly toward the hotel's main entrance, a long wall of glass doors hinged together, maybe 50 feet wide end to end. This human wave lunged toward the bank of doors and without skipping a beat swarmed into the lobby, overpowering the lone sentry posted outside, a doorman attired in a colorful Beefeater's uniform.

As they surged through the doors, they sounded like an invading army of foot soldiers, ready to commence their occupation of the lobby of Kiss's hotel. The huge mass of fans soon packed every inch of lobby space, standing practically on top of each other, sweating, smoking, screaming, grunting, drinking, belching, cheering, and dripping with perspiration.

Then the chanting began. "Fire-house, Fire-house, Fire-house," the name of one of Kiss's more well-known songs. "De-troit Rock City! De-troit Rock City! De-troit Rock City!," a Kiss song which had become something of an anthem to their fans in Detroit, a Kiss stronghold. The crowd then shifted gears and started a football-style cheer of the individual names of the Kiss members—"Gene, Paul, Peter, Ace! Gene, Paul, Peter, Ace!"

The fans continued to shout, and by this time, scores of horrified hotel guests and employees had materialized. A pack of maurauding Visigoths who had seemingly arrived out of thin air were violating their sanctuary. Guys with shoulder-length hair and dirty work jeans with T-shirts emblazoned with the cover from the Kiss *Destroyer* album. Girls in fearsome leather get-ups that stuck to their bodies like a second skin, reeking from the sweat that drenched them. Eyeliner melted down their cheeks like little black rivers, stopping at the corners of their mouths. Many of the girls' faces were flecked with paste-on silver sparkles, their lips smeared with gaudy lipstick moistened from the humidity. There were even a few Kiss impersonators in full costume, including a pint-sized version that looked barely out of grade school. It was a phantasmagoria come to life.

But the invaders made no moves to take captives or to stake claim to their newly won territory. They simply milled about the lobby, more stunned by the fact that they were all there together than motivated by any thoughts of damage and destruction. A few took up temporary residence outside the locked entrance to Trader Vic's which was off to the side near the bank of doors in front. They'd made it unmolested and undeterred to Kiss's hotel simply to meet Kiss and "party" with them, rock 'n' roll vernacular meaning getting drunk, doing drugs, having sex, or just hanging out.

According to one of the hotel managers, someone in Kiss allegedly announced on stage that night in front of 8,000 fans that the group was staying at the Crown Center Plaza and after the show, "everyone (should) come back and party with us!" It wasn't true; Kiss never announced that on stage. But there had been trouble at the show when Kiss took the stage and someone in the audience turned on a fire hose in the Municipal Auditorium, sending a wave of water shooting into the hallway floor outside the arena. Firecrackers had also been set off in the audience. More serious violence had occurred the week before, when *The Kansas City Star* reported bottle throwing and fighting at Arrowhead and Royal Stadiums.

This mob of fans had simply discovered where Kiss was staying, not the world's most tightly guarded secret, and banded together to conduct their assault and to "party" with Kiss. That was the how and why of their brief journey to the Crown Center Plaza.

With the lobby now resembling a giant staging area, packed with hundreds of troops from the Kiss Army awaiting command, the hotel prepared to marshal its own forces. A high-pitched security alarm was set off and within minutes, a detachment of Kansas City police cars sped up the driveway in front of the hotel's lobby. Policemen jumped out of the cars, sirens blaring and lights flashing, as the cars careened around the circular driveway. As the policemen rushed to enter the hotel, the Kiss Army froze in their places. More bewildered than bellicose, the intruders looked stunned and helpless. They'd come for a party, not to do battle.

One of the officers announced to the crowd that arrests would be made unless they surrendered and left the premises. The commotion that had rattled the place just minutes earlier had died down to a mild hubbub. The fans groaned their collective dissatisfaction and started to shuffle their way to the doors, past the blue column of police officers.

Three rough-looking fans with pock-marked faces and stringy hair, glassy-eyed and flushed, refused to budge, even after the police warning. They were obviously drunk or stoned and had plopped themselves in the middle of the floor of the lobby's seating area. One of them was carrying a small, black tape player and the scratchy sound of a Kiss song could be heard squawking out of the speaker. "We're here to see Kiss and we ain't leavin'," one of the intruders threatened. These were the hard-core fans, decked out in black Kiss T-shirts with Kiss Army cloth patches affixed to their jeans and wearing Kiss insignia pendants hanging from chains strung around their necks.

The police, who had been remarkably restrained up to this point, were in no mood for troublemakers. It was bad enough pulling night duty to police the Kiss concert, but having to bust up an unruly mob of fans at their hotel was worse. They weren't about to prolong the agony. The sooner they could clear the place and end the ruckus, the sooner they could go home.

Two burly policemen briskly marched toward the rebels, yanking them to their feet. As the rest of the army was making its way through the lobby doors, they unceremoniously carted the three rebels out. The point wasn't lost on the crowd. There were no more sit-down protests.

The Kiss Army had given up their territory and vanished. The lobby was intact, but it looked like the floor of the auditorium where Kiss had performed that night, covered with the remnants of a typical rock show: cigarette butts, beer cans, torn backstage passes, ticket stubs, food wrappers, chewing gum, paper cups, and assorted other garbage. A hotel clean-up crew emerged to remove the mess.

While all of this was happening, Kiss and its entourage remained isolated in their rooms. It wasn't unusual for a pack of frenzied fans to storm their hotel after a show. The hotel's assistant manager called me after the invaders had left the premises. There would be a huge bill to settle and the moment of reckoning would be early next morning. At 8:00 a.m., the damage bill, totaling thousands of dollars, was paid without protest. Furniture was chipped, tables were broken, carpets were ripped, and cigarette burns were found in many of the couches. All of the custom carpeting had to be foam shampooed to get rid of the smell of stale beer. We were told never to come back again, not exactly a surprising footnote to this incident.

On the way to the airport to make the flight to the next show in St. Louis, I rode in the limo with Paul and Ace. I thought they'd be shocked at how much the lobby damage was at the Crown Center. They just shrugged it off with a laugh. Damage bills at hotels were everyday occurrences and Kiss's fans were often so crazed and out of control, it was practically impossible to stop them. Even the concerts had damage bills, as I was learning, sometimes running into thousands of dollars a night. It was all part of the business of rock 'n' roll and was an unavoidable cost of touring. Without the fans, there wouldn't be any Kiss and without the craziness, it wouldn't be rock 'n' roll.

Right from the beginnning, I flew first class with Kiss on the commercial flights we took. Some of the Kiss staff, mainly the bodyguards and road managers, flew with us, usually in coach. The production crew had their own set of touring buses and trucks. Carl and Howard wanted the band to perceive me as being on an important business level, not as a roadie or one of the band's gofers, so they arranged for me to always travel "with the partners," which was how Carl referred to the Kiss members. They were equal partners in their business. It also provided me with an opportunity to get to know each of them better.

On one trip, I sat next to Gene. I looked admiringly at the cover of a fashion magazine from the on-board rack, probably *Vogue* or *Town & Country*, staring intently at a young, slim-hipped beauty with porcelain features. Nudging Gene, I remarked how attractive I found the girl on the cover. He quickly threw cold water on my opinion. "That's not what you want," he insisted. "She looks like a plastic flower. Too fragile. What you want is a real woman with a big ass that you can grab from the rear who's got tits that'll knock you in your face. Someone," he said, "you can wrap your loins around and swap spit with," an expression that Gene often used to describe what people do when they're in the throes of passion. He then whipped out a photo from the attache case he'd carried on board. "This is what you want," he insisted, tossing a picture in my face of a slutty-looking creature, mouth agape and eyes squinting, with thighs like piano legs and breasts sagging to her waist that would require a harness to support. "Look at those nipples! You could use them for coat hangers," Gene exclaimed. A sly grin came across his face, and he looked as if he were about to start drooling over the photo. I nodded that I got the message. Gene was an evangelist for wanton lust.

When we weren't in airplanes, we were in airports. Or traveling to and from airports. Or checking in and out of hotels. All of this traveling produced some strange scenes. Gene, Paul, and Ace sported huge aureoles of shoe-polish-black hair that bounced over their shoulders. Peter's was long and graying. Everyone wore sunglasses. Gene stood out in any crowd, even without his hair tied back in a knot as it was on stage. He often had chains draped across his chest and over his hips, and was covered in layers of leather and animal skins. His platform boots, which had big dollar signs painted on the sides, came all the way up to his knees and made loud clumping sounds when he walked. Gene felt it was important to maintain credibility with the fans by carrying his stage persona to the street, even if it meant wearing clothing that was excruciatingly uncomfortable. It was part of keeping Kiss's larger than life image intact. Ace had a very different persona. He would roll off the plane at the end of a trip, practically tripping over his own feet, and break into spasms of laughter while trading jibes and wisecracks with anyone crossing his path. By the time he reached the punch line, Ace was already in hysterics.

Paul was sometimes embarrassed by all the commotion Kiss created but he took it in stride. In the mid-'70s, he'd earned the nickname, The He-She. It had to do with the inordinate amount of time and attention he paid to fluffing his mane of wavy black hair and the frilly clothes he favored at the time, usually in mauve and fuchsia tones. He sometimes bought froufrou women's blouses at trendy boutiques to wear off stage. Behind his back, Ace and Peter would joke, "Is it a He or is it a She?" A surprise party was once organized for The He-She in Omaha. Paul entered a darkened hotel room and when the lights went on, several dozen guys including the three other band members and some of the roadies and staff were standing there to greet him, all wearing women's clothes, wigs, high heels, and makeup. It was a bizarre drag scene. Paul took it good-naturedly. As time passed, the nickname was forgotten.

It was a peculiar niche I fell into with this job. My two bosses, both seasoned businessmen who had become successful, self-made entrepreneurs, were more than twenty years my senior. They were both mentor types, strong-willed and eager to teach me the ropes. Our clients were more like my contemporaries, about my age, but with backgrounds that were worlds apart from mine. They grew up as city kids in the outer boroughs of New York, not in affluent suburbia. Only Gene had continued his education past high school. But they were street-smart and scrappy, clever in a way I hadn't really known before. Kiss had started something from nothing and had quickly become wildly successful and very rich, short-circuiting the more typical long and arduous climb to the top. It was odd but never uncomfortable for me to be sandwiched between these two different worlds.

I had my own image problem at first, apart from Kiss getting used to my being around. No one could figure out exactly what I did or why I was on tour. At various times, people that I came in contact with mistook me for a traveling efficiency expert, the band's lawyer, their personal accountant, a private detective, an undercover narc, and once, the band's private drug dealer. Walking into small-town banks with the proceeds from the previous night's Kiss concert to wire back to our bank in Cleveland also brought suspicious stares because of the huge wads of cash I carried in my briefcase. The bank people were always relieved when I told them the money was from the Kiss show and not from some nefarious activity. A few times I was asked to show my laminated Kiss ID pass for positive identification.

The promoters didn't exactly get it, either. At a stop in Charleston, West Virginia, I walked through the building early one morning to watch the crew set up the show. I was in my business manager's uniform of jacket and tie. Phil Lashinsky, a veteran promoter in that neck of the woods, came running over to me, smiling from ear to ear, gave me a firm and friendly handshake, and slapped me on the back. I was pleased to meet him but when he looked at me expectantly and asked, "Is everything okay?" I knew something was wrong. Phil thought I was a local fire marshal checking out the building for the show that night.

Early in the tour, Carl Glickman showed up in Baltimore for a meeting with Kiss after the show. We assembled in one of their suites around midnight. Carl brought along another traveler on the tour, Bob Brown, whom he wanted to introduce to Kiss that night. Bob was an experienced sports arena manager from Cleveland whom Carl hired as a consultant for the tour to make recommendations on how to streamline logistics. Ace stared at us, hardly knowing me and knowing even less about Bob. He asked Carl, "What's the difference between him and him?" pointing to each of us sitting around a coffee table. Carl simply said, "he's temporary," pointing to Bob, "and he's permanent," pointing to me. That was sure to clear up any confusion.

But as the relationship strengthened between the band and Glickman/Marks Management, my function became less amorphous. Kiss began to rely on our ability to follow through on business and financial matters. Money was always the major item with Kiss and as their fortunes rose, the role of business manager became more prominent. Howard and Carl had wanted someone around their clients at all times—"the presence," as one staffer referred to me—to make sure that the account was taken care of. It was a shrewd move. The four Kiss members were becoming increasingly intertwined with their financial custodians.

By the middle of September 1976, Kiss was off the road. They were about to start a new album, *Rock and Roll Over,* after being on tour nearly all year. Howard Marks was hosting his annual party in Little Italy. Everyone was required to show up in black tie at Puglia's, an old-fashioned storefront restaurant with a dilapidated charm all its own. Long tables cramped the room where everyone sat family-style for simple Neopolitan fare, heavy on red sauces, peppers, and garlic. Homemade wine, strong enough to choke a cow, was the featured beverage. By the time Gene, Paul , Ace, and Peter showed up—Peter and Ace in rented tuxes and Paul and Gene in black leather and frilly white silk shirts—Puglia's was packed with at least two hundred guests. Dozens of passersby looked in, some pressing their noses against the windows.

A trio of middle-aged Italian musicians played during most of the meal. By midnight, Kiss took over and started playing rock favorites from the '60s, songs from Led Zeppelin and Jimi Hendrix. It was wild and everyone loved the craziness of seeing Kiss play cover songs in a simple little restaurant in Little Italy. The husband of one of Howard's ad agency employees wasn't impressed. He told Howard they sounded awful and couldn't wait for them to stop playing. Howard turned to him, his face reddening, and let him have it. "Well, Ted," Howard said icily, "they're all millionaires and you're not. What does that tell you?"

A few weeks after the Puglia party, Kiss left for L.A. to do the *Paul Lynde Halloween Special* on ABC, and by the end of November, they were back on tour. Kiss's popularity was snowballing and the money was about to come rolling in.

3

Building the Perfect Hype

The Diplomat Hotel in New York City's Times Square was a seedy old rat trap where the ballroom could be rented out for private parties and dances. Paint peeled off the walls, and on the sidewalk in front, grizzled-looking barflies loitered all night. But the Diplomat was smack in the middle of midtown Manhattan and an easy commute for the denizens of rock clubs and the ballroom scene. Kiss began promoting themselves in grungy places like this by August 1973, not long after they first began playing together. The word spread, and a small clique of fans began to flock to their shows.

Paul and Gene had begun an earlier incarnation of Kiss known as Wicked Lester in 1970. They signed a deal with Epic Records, who put them in a recording studio to make an album. But the band fell apart, and by April 1972, Paul and Gene began playing with Peter to form the nucleus of a new band. For months, they rehearsed day and night in a loft on West 23rd Street, and by January 1973, Ace had joined as lead guitarist. They decided on *Kiss* as the name for their group. As Kiss began to take shape, they started doing shows in clubs outside of the city. Their repertoire was limited at first, often taking "requests" to play some of their more familiar songs two or three times during the set. It's hard slogging for any new act to build a following and Kiss played to as few as three people some nights. They did radio jingles at Electric Lady Studios in Greenwich Village to make pocket money, where they met record producer Eddie Kramer. He had worked on early recordings by Jimi Hendrix and Led Zeppelin and Kiss persuaded him to produce their first demo tape.

Kiss realized early in the game that they would need a manager. Someone would have to be their champion and develop the Kiss concept of a hard rock band with a shocking image and what they hoped would soon be a one-of-a-kind stage show. It was bound to be a tough sell. Everyone in Kiss was a relative neophyte to the music business, but they were regular viewers of the TV show, *Flipside,* a syndicated program about the record industry. In the pre-MTV days, it was one of the only shows on TV where recording artists could be seen. The director was Bill Aucoin and Kiss pestered him repeatedly to come down to see their show at the Diplomat. Kiss's idea was to try and find someone who had contacts in the music business and Bill obviously qualified. On each program, *Flipside* featured the head of a different record company introducing one of the label's top artists and showcasing a new artist as well.

Things clicked quickly with Bill and Kiss. Bill loved what he saw—the raw energy, the excitement of the fans, the visual potential of the Kiss concept, the promotional possibilities—and Kiss trusted Bill. His enthusiasm made a big impression on them, and they deluged him with homemade tickets to their shows. Bill was won over by their determination. He agreed to become Kiss's manager, but countered their condition that he had to get the group a record contract within two weeks by adding a stipulation of his own. Kiss would have to be dedicated to rehearsing and performing around the clock. It would take a monumental effort to develop the group, and unless they were committed to the task, he wasn't interested. Kiss and Bill agreed to each other's terms. The group gave Bill a handwritten scrap of paper outlining their deal which they signed. It was Bill's first management contract. On October 15, 1973, Kiss and Bill signed a formal agreement cementing their relationship.

He was the perfect choice for Kiss. Kiss was built around visual gimmicks; Bill had early success directing live TV shows. He'd gotten his start as a camera-man at the public TV station in Boston while still a student at Northeastern University and later worked at Teletape studios in New York. Kiss was a young act with a new and unusual angle to music and stage shows; Bill was new to the role of artist manager, but instantly recognized the importance of image to Kiss's career. Kiss needed an aspiring impresario like Bill who was a gale of energy and imagination and not shackled to old ways of doing things. A more seasoned music veteran might have tried to steer Kiss away from their harsh image and persuade them to tone down the extreme elements of their persona. But Bill wasn't freighted with the heavy baggage of experience that would compel him to compromise. It was an ideal match.

Bill became very close with the Kiss members. They took him in as an equal, like a fifth member of the group. Kiss adored Bill. He was like a big daddy in many ways, someone in whom they could confide and who would counsel them in every area of their lives. Bill was to be an integral part of Kiss. He would be both taskmaster and confidante. In an interview in the April 8, 1976, issue of *Circus,* Bill talked about his early interest in Kiss, saying "I was excited because they were showmen . . . because they not only wanted to play and play well but to really entertain the audience." Bill was also impressed by their spunk, putting up their own posters around New York and, as Peter described it, "playing every show like it was Madison Square Garden." He also knew that

Shep Gordon, Alice Cooper's manager, was planning a movie career for the shock-rock performer, taking him off the concert circuit. Kiss, in time, could fill the void left by Alice Cooper's departure.

Bill had his work cut out for him. Their early makeup was crudely applied and their stage costumes were patched-together homemade jobs. Leather jackets and satin pants, all black, were embellished with metal studs and silver accents. Gene's first cape looked to be shiny pieces of black vinyl stitched into a batlike design. As he spread his arms, the cape would flap open. Chokers were picked up at pet stores. Leather wrist bracelets, crosses, chains, and pendants finished off the look. Paul, quite a bit chunkier then, had his face disguised by a raccoon-like mask before switching to a single star over his eye. Ace's face above his nostrils was covered with silver paint in a jagged pattern, looking like an exploding sunburst. Peter brandished a dagger. It was an image sure to shock the uninitiated. Not surprisingly, early stage clothes were bought at the Pleasure Chest in Greenwich Village, a boutique catering to S&M tastes. At one of their first gigs in Amityville, Long Island, at The Daisy, a fully made-up Kiss pulled up to the club in a mail truck, and were nearly chased away by the bouncer, who could hardly be blamed for failing to identify them as that night's act.

Bill would have to glamorize all of this, smooth out the rough edges and give it some razzle-dazzle. Money was scraped together to design more elaborate costumes and refine the makeup. And Bill's eye as a director was put to use teaching Kiss how to strike exciting poses for photos and make the best use of props, lighting, and backgrounds for layouts. Over the years, Kiss would invest enormous sums to hire top photographers to define their image for the public. Bill also began videotaping their performances for later review. He fell comfortably into the role of image maker.

Kiss counted Alice Cooper and the New York Dolls as influences. Alice Cooper had already earned a vaunted reputation for a ghoulish image and a theatrical stage show while the Dolls had become known for garish makeup and an *outré* appearance. Among their idols were early Led Zeppelin, Jeff Beck, and lesser-known groups like the Move and Humble Pie, English bands popular with the rock cognoscenti. But Kiss always aspired to be something entirely new, the band that they would most want to see themselves. The Kiss mystique was to always appear in makeup and never allow themselves to be photographed without it. Each member became identified with a distinct character: Gene, the monster; Paul, the lover; Ace, the spaceman; and Peter, the cat. Their true identities would be hidden from the public. To avoid projecting an effeminate image, they always struck macho poses in photos. "Kiss" became their name because of its suggestiveness and its sexual connotations: the word meant something different to everybody. An earlier name for the group was Fuck, but this was rejected as commercially impractical. Kiss always took their image seriously, as did their fans. It was only a joke to their critics.

Originally, Bill had a partner in managing Kiss, Joyce Biawitz. They shared the office on East 55th Street that Howard Marks loaned them. After a few years, Joyce split with Bill. She'd become romantically involved with Neil Bogart, the head of newly formed Casablanca Records in Los Angeles, and Bill couldn't shake the feeling that while he was negotiating with Neil for Kiss's record contract, Joyce was in an awkward position, serving two masters.

Bill had met Neil through the *Flipside* show which Howard co-produced with Bill. As Bill began devoting more of his time to Kiss and less to commercials and TV work, he bought out Joyce's interest in his music production company, Rock Steady. Kiss signed with Casablanca in 1973 and in February 1974, released their first album, *Kiss*. Joyce married Neil and moved to L.A.

A showcase for record company executives was arranged for Kiss in L.A., shortly after they became one of Casablanca's first signings. The group wanted to make an unforgettable impression on their audience of record company honchos. Kiss never suffered any pangs of self-doubt about their image, but some at Casablanca, including Neil Bogart, were getting cold feet. Maybe it was a little too over the top, too harsh and too extreme.

Neil had expressed misgivings about Kiss's makeup and costume image before. While recording their first album at Bell Sound Studios in New York, he telephoned the band after seeing their first publicity photos. He told them that if it turned out to be just a fad, they'd be stuck with that image; he argued for them to drop the makeup. Kiss was convinced that he was wrong, and they went ahead with their made-up faces for the album cover.

But Bill stuck by the group's decision to keep Kiss as Kiss despite ridicule and predictions of failure by many record industry bigwigs. In September 1974, Casablanca severed its distribution ties to Warner Bros. Records and became fully independent.

Bill moved quickly to take Kiss out of the shadowy demimonde of clubs and ballrooms. He wanted them on tour playing around the country, opening for other, more well-known groups. A punishing grind of tours began with Kiss tearing across America in a station wagon, carrying all of their own equipment and costumes. Their first big show was at the Academy of Music in New York, opening for Blue Öyster Cult on New Year's Eve, 1974. Gene's hair caught fire during the performance. Kiss soon developed a reputation for blowing away, literally and figuratively, nearly all the bands they opened for with their high-energy showmanship and primitive pyrotechnics. From the start, Kiss wanted to be the ultimate spectacle. The show would enhance the music, but the band never lost sight of the fact that the reason there was an audience was because people expected more than music.

Gene's ambitions were characteristically more blunt. In an October 25, 1975, interview with *Melody Maker,* he said, "Well, I'm in it to make money. I'd like to make that perfectly clear." But the money was yet to come. Casablanca Vice President Larry Harris told *Cash Box* in a March 6, 1976, interview that in Kiss's early days, "We were spending more on advertising alone than the group was bringing in."

Kiss's disguises became a key element in the hype that was starting to build for the band. They went to fanatical lengths to conceal their identities from the public, even when they were virtual nobodies, and to prevent their faces from being photographed when they weren't made up. Contrary to popular myth, they didn't wear makeup off-stage when they weren't performing. But Gene did have a problem with his platform boots, which he wore regularly even when he wasn't on stage. A girl had won a dream date contest with Gene that a rock magazine had sponsored. Gene had trouble squeezing into her tiny Volkswagen beetle, and she had to ask him to remove his platform boots before she could close the car door.

A central figure in Kiss's early success was Sean Delaney, a friend of Bill's, who had worked in Off Broadway theater. He wrote songs with Kiss and helped them to perfect their stage show and choreography. He was also Kiss's first road manager, traversing the country with them in their station wagon. Alan Miller, who became Bill's right-hand man, was instrumental in creating many of Kiss's early promotions and publicity stunts, including the founding of the Kiss Army Fan Club.

Publicity was a constant struggle in the early days, and the media initially put up a wall of resistance to Kiss. Carol Ross-Durborow, who was in charge of Kiss's publicity while head of the music division at Rogers & Cowan in New York, and, later, with The Press Office, an Aucoin Management subsidiary, "heard laughter on the other end of the phone" when she first began pitching the band to the press. No one took them seriously, unless there was a negative angle to the story. About all the press would pick up on were possible links between Kiss and devil worship or Satanism, or the purported Nazi symbolism of the double-S lightning bolts in their logo.

On their first tours as an opening act, Kiss was quickly dismissed by the press as gimmicky in their reliance on visual effects like flash pots and open flames for shock value and lack of musicianship. But by early 1975, they were getting more attention than the bands they were opening for. Kiss was constantly having run-ins with the groups who were headlining—major acts including Steppenwolf, Black Oak Arkansas, ZZ Top, and Savoy Brown—when Kiss got a stronger audience response than they did. Soon, Kiss decided to headline on their own. At one of their first headline gigs, Kiss played the Sahara Hotel in Las Vegas for a two-show "Glitter Night" featuring Rush as the opening act on May

29, 1975. Kiss came close to selling out both the 8:00 p.m. and the 2:00 a.m. show. *Billboard* reviewed the show in its June 14, 1975, issue as having "unleashed controlled chaos in visual heavy metal" and with a sound that rivaled "nuclear detonations at nearby Yucca Flats."

The early Kiss records—*Kiss, Hotter Than Hell,* and *Dressed To Kill*—received little airplay and registered minimal sales. It wasn't until the *Alive!* double album was released in late 1975 that the group's overpowering live performance was captured on record. *Alive!,* produced by Eddie Kramer, sent Kiss to the top of the charts for the first time and sold millions of records. They could now headline shows at arenas. The national media became interested in Kiss, and they soon appeared on the top-rated TV program *The Mike Douglas Show.* Psychologist Dr. Joyce Brothers sat next to the group to explain the Kiss phenomenon to America. The knocks from the press had helped to bond Kiss with their fans, and the band's ascending popularity had made them too big to ignore. With Bill as the locomotive, Kiss was picking up steam at an ever-increasing pace.

Kiss may have hit it big with a chart-topping album and national TV appearances, but their *Alive!* road tour was plagued with mechanical breakdowns, malfunctions, and mishaps. The stage set was cheaply built and had to be nailed down each night to prevent it from breaking into pieces. Peter's drum riser was iffy, and on a given night no one could be sure if it would rise to its four-foot height or start getting jerky and collapse. Pyro shot off without warning, and near misses from flying shrapnel and toppling stage props became par for the course. The fans were certainly getting their money's worth, though; the show was authentically raw and rough. Much of what happened on stage was done by winging it from night to night.

One of Bill's earliest sermons to Kiss was to promote themselves at all times. Talk big, act big, project success—it'll pay dividends. Early in Kiss's career, not long after they started as headliners, the commercial flight they were supposed to take to their next show was suddenly canceled and they had to rent a private jet. Kiss had photos taken in makeup and costume, with the jet as the backdrop, and sent them to magazines and newspapers across the country. The message was that Kiss was so big, such a phenomenon, that they always flew to gigs in a private jet.

That was the whole point—not just making Kiss big, but making it seem bigger than it really was. With *Alive!* at the top of the charts, the strategy was paying off. The perception of Kiss created by the media was that of a supergroup in a league of their own. Other groups sold comparable amounts of records and tickets—Led Zeppelin even more—but Kiss was perceived to be bigger because it dominated the media through hype. And everything in Kiss was measured in millions—millions of dollars, millions of tickets, millions of records, millions in stage gear, and millions of fans.

An early publicist was startled to see one of the Kiss members jump out of a taxi in New York one afternoon. To her, it was unthinkable that anyone in Kiss would ever deign to use public transportation. The myths about Kiss's exalted status had convinced even their own publicists, proving how successfully the hype was working.

Bodyguards surrounded the Kiss members to prevent overzealous fans and photographers from snapping their picture while out in public without makeup. They also helped to foster the image of Kiss as something big and important. Unauthorized photos were purchased—thousands of rolls of film over the years—from fans and professionals who were quick enough to catch Kiss at an unguarded moment. On occasion, strong-arm tactics were employed by the bodyguards to retrieve film from the more recalcitrant picture-takers. The hype was self-perpetuating. The more Kiss's identities were shielded, the more interest there was in trying to photograph them. And still more publicity resulted when would-be Kiss photographers were kept at bay by the band's private security force.

Surprisingly, the news media usually cooperated in protecting Kiss's identity. It made good copy for the tabloids and rock magazines. As long as a gimmick captivated their readers, they went along. The press who helped to keep the band's faces under wraps were rewarded with exclusives about Kiss events and stories. And Kiss reciprocated by making themselves easily accessible to the media for exploitation. They would do anything to get attention. It was a perfect *quid pro quo*.

Security for Kiss became an integral part of their operation. "Big John" Harte, a tall, beefy fellow built like a linebacker, joined Kiss after *Alive!* was released and handled their security for years. In the world of Kiss, security meant more than protecting the band from photographers: shuttling the band members to and from gigs, coping with their personal problems, and running interference with fans and outsiders were all duties that fell to the security staff.

Despite the success of *Alive!* and their new status as superstar headliners, Kiss was in the hole with Casablanca for a fortune in unrecouped advances and tour support costs. They had been on the road since 1974. Neil Bogart claimed he'd pumped nearly $1 million into the group in their early days, according to an interview he gave to *The Los Angeles Times* on February 4, 1979. Worse, Casablanca was still hip-deep in returns of the ill-fated album, *Here's Johnny—Magic Moments from the Tonight Show*. And Bill was unsure how long he could continue to keep Kiss touring as headliners since monies were only then starting to trickle in. He was financing the tour's travel costs with his American Express card.

Kiss needed money and Bill was willing to consider just about anything. In early 1976, Carl Glickman, Howard Marks, and a third partner, a wealthy shopping center developer from Cleveland, reportedly agreed to pony up $100,000 for a stake in Bill's financial interest in Kiss. The money would be a bridge loan until royalties from Casablanca came in and Kiss's deficit was wiped out. The deal proved unnecessary. Within a few months, the cash crunch was cleared up and the royalties from *Alive!* and the escalating concert fees for Kiss as headliners took care of the problem. Bill could afford to go back to his investment consortium and ask them to void their $100,000 commitment in exchange for canceling the deal. By the spring of 1976, Glickman/Marks Management had signed on as the group's business managers.

There were two Kiss groups, as Howard Marks told me early on. According to him, the Gene-and-Paul group were the sane, straight, and level-headed members who avoided drinking and drugs of any kind. They were also the band's creative axis. The Ace-and-Peter group was the wild-and-crazy contingent, often causing problems and upsetting things. Gene and Paul tolerated their behavior to keep Kiss functioning. Strangely, Ace and Peter were the married ones. But Howard's analysis of the two Kiss groups proved to be telling. Paradoxically, it was this duality that had made Kiss so successful.

Gene was the only group member with a post-high school education, having graduated from Richmond College in Staten Island, New York. He had once worked as a boy Friday at *Vogue* before becoming a school teacher, an experience he recounted in an interview in the October 28, 1980, issue of *Circus* as "...pretty rotten; I wanted to kill those little pricks." His teaching career on the Upper West Side of Manhattan didn't last long. Eventually, he became a full-time musician and partnered with Paul. Rock 'n' roll and its easy access to girls and sex and the lure of big money were strong motivators for Gene.

Born August 25, 1949, he was a native Israeli. Gene had thick, curly hair and a swarthy complexion with deep crease lines that stretched from the sides of his nose to the corners of his mouth. Intense and focused, he often appeared to be brooding, looking born to play his chosen monster role. Gene was the most animated of the group, and his facial expressions ran the gamut from mildly leering to maniacal. His legendary tongue, nearly six inches in length, was enough "to make close friends with anyone," as he put it. At 6 feet 2 inches, Gene was also the tallest in Kiss.

He had come to this country with his mother, Florence, at age 9, while his father remained in Israel. Gene struggled through Yeshiva school in New York while his mother supported the two of them. Not long after Glickman/Marks Management became involved, he asked Carl Glickman to travel to Israel to buy a condominium apartment for his father, then working as a carpenter. Gene helped to support his father for years, but kept his distance from him. Phone calls and stacks of letter from his father poured into our office but went unanswered. Gene avoided any personal contact with him. He bought his mother and her second husband an attractive home in suburban Long Island, New York. Florence, a concentration camp survivor who had worked for years in a dress factory, could now afford to live a relatively affluent life.

Gene had a loving relationship with his mother, a sturdy, handsome Hungarian woman with a thick accent who called Gene "my darling sonny boy." In the early days of my involvement, she would come to our offices and receive cash disbursements Gene had authorized. Sitting at my desk, she would carefully and methodically count out each and every one of the $100 bills—which totaled $50,000 at one point. She was then known as Florence Lubowski.

Gene adopted the stage name Gene Simmons early in his career but never dropped his legal name, Gene Klein. He had come to this country as Chaim Witz. Despite the fact that for years he became indignant if anyone dared to mention the Klein name, he could never bring himself to discard it. As a result, it had to be used for passports and legal documents and became common knowledge.

Gene's ghoulish stage persona grew out of his passion for horror movies. He'd been a lifelong fan of Boris Karloff, Bela Lugosi, Lon Chaney, and other veteran horror stars of the '30s and '40s. He loved doing impersonations, particularly Lugosi with his chilling voice and Hungarian accent, and would happily rattle on for hours talking about his favorite movie monsters and how they influenced his Kiss character.

Gene liked to talk. He seemed to cruise on an oral jetstream through an endless sea of topics. Gene professed to know just about everything and was constantly dispensing advice, issuing *pronunciamentos,* and spewing opinions like an open fire hydrant. He could be pedantic to the point of condescension and would often infuriate people. Peter used to call him Professor Dope; he thought Gene lacked common sense.

But Gene was intelligent and widely read, especially in history, and he spoke or at least understood several languages including Hebrew, Hungarian, and Spanish. Outside of a handful of confidantes and intimates, though, Gene spared no effort to disguise his intellect and bury it beneath the sort of troglodytic exterior he felt was appropriate for rock stars. There seemed to be a very rigid and specific code of conduct for rock star behavior according to Gene, a kind of Robert's Rules of Order for Rock. A rock star couldn't be intelligent or articulate; he had to be boorish. A rock star couldn't be seen in any public place except where *habitués* of the rock scene are found, like rock clubs, rock shows, and parties for rock people. Once in Detroit, I invited him to dinner at the London Chop House, an elegant restaurant favored by the city's elite, similar to New York's 21 Club. When we arrived, the manager welcomed us, but insisted that Gene wear a tie which he was happy to provide. Gene complied, but looked mortified. He sat glumly in the dimly lit, wood-lined dining room for the entire evening, terrified that someone might recognize him and subject him to ridicule—a rock star capitulating to a restaurant's dress code. Considering the patrician crowd, that wasn't very likely.

There were more rules. A rock star could never be seen reading a book. Indeed, Gene amassed a large collection of comics over the years which he toted with him while on tour. Even at business meetings, he would sit and read comics. At interviews, if a reporter had the temerity to ask Gene about any subject apart from rock music, he sidestepped the question by claiming he didn't know anything except what he read in comics. And the most important rule was that a rock star had to be aggressive, even animalistic, about sex at all times, offering belligerent and offensive sexual innuendo, loudly and in public.

There was probably a kernel of truth in some of the rules. Young fans of rock stars have their own sixth sense about when their idols are straying from the path of rock rebels, dimming their appeal to them. But this set of rules was distorted and dogmatic and became a parody of itself. It certainly produced some bizarre extremes of behavior. The "Pictures" were Gene's *pièces de résistance,* an ever-expanding collection of Polaroid photos from the SX-70 that he took with him on tour. The Pictures were photos of hundreds, later thousands, of girls with whom he had sex on the road and who appeared in various poses and states of undress. The Pictures were Gene's pride and joy, and he would proudly display them to anyone expressing even the most tepid interest. They were confirmation of his status as a budding Casanova of the rock world.

The Pictures, though, had a grotesque and hideous quality to them. They were much more of a turn-off than a turn-on. Some of the photos looked like the type seen on posters on street corners where groups like Women Against Porn assemble to collect signatures for antipornography initiatives. Gene's pictures showed no signs of violence, but they were gross. Girls were shown spread-eagled across beds, tongues wagging, wearing high heels and Kiss T-shirts rolled up over their breasts. Girls were shown bent over, revealing every anatomical detail. There were plenty of girls posing on all fours, and there were shots of girls pulling apart their vaginas for a close-up. Some pictures depicted women who had contorted their bodies into pretzel-like formations. For the most part, The Pictures were about as erotically stimulating as a side of beef hanging from a hook. Gene took great delight in seeing people's reactions to his photos, especially from women he showed them to. When he was out of earshot, they frequently expressed revulsion.

Shocking people was important to Gene. He often walked through hotel lobbies after the show was over, spitting out the kerosene which he used for his stage fire-breathing. It was mixed with artificial stage blood, a gunky-looking red liquid. Gene wanted to be perceived as a strong macho type, and took pains to chastise underlings for unmanly behavior. New hires were often caught off guard when he told them to "act like a man" if they appeared indecisive or wishy-washy. To drive home the point, Gene would mimic what he felt was unacceptable male behavior by carrying on in a whining, simpering manner. Paul and I once played a joke on Gene about this neurosis of his. In a coffee shop, the three of us sat down at a table. Loudly and pointedly, Paul and I each asked Gene, making sure that everyone around us could hear, "So how was that truck driver you were with last night, Gene?" People turned to stare at Gene. He almost blew a gasket, hollering at Paul and me, practically throwing his food in our faces. Gene wasn't amused by this little joke of ours.

Paul, the band's front man on stage, was born Stanley Eisen on January 20, 1952. While not the spokesman for Kiss, he was the catalyst for the show and the emcee, a spark plug whose mastery of stage acrobatics and vocal bravura kept audiences fired up. He was a disciplined devotee of Led Zeppelin's lead singer, Robert Plant, who brought fans to their feet with his shrieking warble and kept them panting. Paul fashioned his stage persona around his role as the lover.

Tall and sinewy, with a muscular physique and thick, bushy eyebrows that stretched to the edge of his hairline, Paul had an angular face with pouting lips. In some of Kiss's promotional materials, he was described as having the type of body Romans and Greeks carved statues of and the kind of face Renaissance and Medieval artists tried to capture in their oil paintings. He also had what looked like a cauliflower ear that was always carefully covered by his huge mane of shoulder-length hair. Years later, he would undergo a series of complicated operations to have the deformity corrected.

Paul grew up in Queens and attended the New York City High School of Music and Art, later immortalized in the movie and TV series, *Fame*. His ambition was always to become a rock star, and he took odd jobs including driving a cab and working as a counterman at a Kosher food store to make ends meet while playing in bands. His wavy hair was a problem for him. When his attempts to iron it failed, he tried taming it with a product called Perma Straight.

Paul was the most artistically inclined in Kiss and had the temperament to match. His solid appearance to some extent belied his personality. He was the sensitive one. He told people he had an aura. He was the heartthrob of the group. He was also touchy, and had a thin skin. Anyone unlucky enough to offend Paul was likely to elicit a flash of anger and a caustic riposte. People felt they had to be deferential to Paul.

For years, Paul worshipped Gene. Gene was more glib, more forward, more approachable, and more uninhibited, and seemed to have the self-confidence and grasp of worldly things Paul lacked. And Gene was the center of attention on stage, a monstrous brute who became the symbol of Kiss and was the most frequently photographed. Paul was an unashamed acolyte of Gene.

There was a push-pull effect of the chemistry between Paul and Gene that led to changes. In later years, Paul's confidence increased, and he took pains to put himself much more in the spotlight than Gene. Paul became, in fact, well-spoken, more careful about what he said in public than Gene and more self-controlled. He tried to cultivate a central role for himself, particularly when Gene's ceaseless self-promotion turned to prattle and embarrassed the group. But for now, Paul was content to be in Gene's shadow. Like Gene, he bought a home for his parents in Long Island.

Ace Frehley, the rock 'n' roller from the Bronx, was born April 27, 1951. He grew up with a tough crowd and was a veteran of a few street gangs. Music eventually became more important and he taught himself to play guitar. Gangly and with hair that was long and lank, he was the group's spaceman on stage and off. He had developed his own cult of devoted fans who were electrified by his tremulous guitar solos and wobbling space walk while performing. The spaceman character fit Ace to a T. He seemed to exist most of the time in a trancelike state, halfway between somnolence and alertness. He would sit for hours in stony silence and then, unexpectedly and without provocation, blurt out a comment or observation, which was often surprisingly lucid and incisive. He would then lapse back into the trance. Despite the technical wizardry he possessed, Ace confessed to chronic laziness and was content to submerge his potentially keen intellect. His mind was seemingly clouded most of the time from drinking and pills.

Ace played in many bands in the New York area and to support himself during the day, he once had a part-time job as a liquor delivery man. It was a frequent source of jokes within the band, like putting a fox in charge of the chicken coop. He was the life of the party and a well-known jester who counted Rodney Dangerfield among his idols. Ace was popular with everyone he met and was the least pretentious of the group. As he put it, he was "a real character," whose deafening cackle was his personal trademark. Ace could be ornery at times, and he often acknowledged people trying to engage him in conversation by grunting or making a nasal "acck" sound. Often, he seemed barely able to complete a sentence.

Ace's face was puffy and pitted from acne, partly the result of the makeup his job required. Over the years, his face became increasingly crevassed, and he underwent dermabrasion to alleviate the problem. Ace was tall and slender, standing over 6 feet. Ace's real name was Paul, but two Pauls in one band was too confusing. Ace became his nickname. In Kiss's early days, they often called him Scraps as he had a habit of picking over whatever food was left over from their take-out meals.

Ace joined the band through an ad in the *Village Voice* which sought a "flashy rock guitarist with balls." He auditioned for Gene, Paul, and Peter and got the job as much for his musicianship as for his unusual personality. He was nervous and slightly drunk when he played, falling into the walls and having a hard time keeping his balance, but he seemed to fill the bill. Talking with Ace was to be on the receiving end of a sudden and high-pitched shriek of a laugh. He fit into the nascent Kiss concept of creating a personality group. Ace was later credited with designing the Kiss logo featuring two lightning bolts for the double "S" letters. He came up with his own makeup design of two silver stars splashed over his eyes.

Ace vacillated between reveling in the rock 'n' roll lifestyle of excess on the road and being lonely and isolated. His May 1976 wedding to Jeanette Trerotola, an Italian girl from suburban New York, was a huge affair at New York's Americana Hotel that attempted to link two sharply different worlds. Ace and his pals, many with long, scruffy hair and bizarre clothes, symbolized the rock world. Jeanette came from a large family. At the wedding, many relatives showed up, including her grandfather, Joe Trerotola, one of the highest-ranking officials in the Teamsters who was known as Joe T. Her father, Vinnie, was also a Teamsters official. At times, the two camps reportedly appeared to face off against each other, with each group congregating separately on opposite sides of the large hotel ballroom. One friend of the band, a gay musician who came dressed in a black leather motorcycle jacket and knee-high boots, supposedly came close to inciting a riot when he congratulated family members by giving them bear hugs and kisses on the lips.

On the road, Ace often seemed to fall into boredom and depression. His trademark became the ever-present Dom Pérignon champagne bottle, which he clutched while walking around backstage or at the hotels. As Kiss's financial status rose, so did the champagne guzzling. Ace tried to counter the boredom and depression by nonstop partying and by flying in his buddies from the Bronx and Westchester. A kindly and generous person, he was looking for companionship, but his friends took advantage of his generosity. They were only too glad to help themselves to the favors he provided and play the role of court jesters to Ace. But this antidote was only temporary. Before long, the friends would leave and the depression would return. As Ace put it, he was "bored with life."

Peter Criss was the "one who made it interesting," which was how he described the way he fit into the group. The oldest member of Kiss, Peter was born December 20, 1945. Lean and trim, he was shorter than the other three, and had long locks of gray and silver hair falling below his shoulders. Peter was a bit jowly and his chin seemed to disappear into his neck. The fleshy bags under his eyes aged him beyond his years. A few years were shaved off his official age for p.r. purposes.

Peter was the guy from the streets. He had grown up in a rough neighborhood of Canarsie in Brooklyn and he had the volatile temper and scars to prove it. Peter had been in a few rumbles in his youth running with local gangs. His idol was Gene Krupa, the jazz drummer, and as a teenager, he practiced hard to emulate Krupa's style. Peter dropped out of high school to play in New York nightclubs and girlie bars like the legendary Metropole Cafe and the Peppermint Lounge. He had cut his teeth playing with scores of R&B and rock bands. With one of them, a group called Chelsea, he had recorded an album. When Chelsea broke up, Peter was out of work, desperate to join a new band. He took out an ad for himself in *Rolling Stone,* saying that he was looking to "make it" and was willing to "do anything." It led to a phone call from Gene and an audition. Gene and Paul liked his spirit and his rock 'n' roll outfit of velvet jacket, pants, and scarves; Peter got the gig.

Once in Kiss, Peter dropped his given name of George Peter Criscuola (pronounced Cris-COLA). He had actually forgotten that his first name was George. Shortly after Kiss took off, Peter attempted to change his name legally. He filed court papers in New York affirming that his first and middle name was Peter George. The papers came back when they didn't match his birth records showing that his name was George Peter. He filed a second time, without a hitch, and legally changed his name to Peter Criss.

Peter was the most extreme in everything. He was desperate for attention, perhaps as the result of a childhood that he often spoke of as unhappy, and seemed to require affection and stroking in liberal doses. He was the most boastful and loved to exaggerate. He always had to have the biggest, the most, the best of everything. He also did drugs, a condition that appeared to become increasingly serious as time passed. What Peter thrived on was the challenge of making you deal with him and having you succumb to his irrational rantings and ravings. Having Peter on tour as a traveling companion could be an unnerving experience.

Peter scared people. The young girls working in the offices of Aucoin Management as well as many who traveled on the road seemed genuinely frightened by him. They never knew what to expect, or when he might become hostile. But Peter was, curiously, the most fun to be with if you knew how to handle him. Once you resisted his self-indulgent carryings-on and his play-acting, Peter calmed down. The facade was dropped and he accepted you. Peter could be charged up and pixieish, particularly when he mimicked Gene and Paul's foibles. Of course, most people never saw this side of him since he was often in a sour mood. As a result, he got the reputation as being the most interesting member of Kiss simply because he was the most unpredictable. He relished this role, to be sure.

Peter also had a sensitive and caring side. One of my first duties for Peter was to go to Woodlawn Cemetery in the Bronx with him to purchase a marble headstone for his grandmother's grave site now that he could afford it. His grandmother had been largely responsible for rearing him, and this was his way of paying his respects.

For a person with a very limited education, he had quite an appreciation of travel and history. He liked to think of himself as a *bon vivant*. When he wasn't having one of his mood swings, he could be charming and lively, particularly when he was away from the rest of the group and could unwind. But the mood swings appeared to be sudden and sharp. On tour in Europe in 1976, Peter reportedly demolished his hotel room, wrecking all of the furniture and making shards of every mirror and piece of glass. Supposedly, the entire contents of the room were pulverized, and Peter supposedly threatened to walk out onto the ledge of his window sill until a bodyguard grabbed him. When Peter grumbled about bolting the tour, the road manager reportedly seized his passport, making him a captive for the duration.

Peter had various ways of covering up his drug use. He suffered from insomnia. He couldn't sleep at night so he tried sleeping during the day. After awhile, he couldn't sleep during the day or night so he just stayed up all the time. Peter called himself a hypochondriac, and carried around a leather satchel full of pills and medications of all sorts to treat various ailments. Peter said that he got sick very often. He also claimed to have allergies. On more than one occasion he told me—with a completely straight face—that his allergies always acted up while he was in L.A. It was a safe bet that whenever we were in L.A., Peter would contract a severe sinus problem. He said it had something to do with the smog, despite the fact that while in L.A., Peter often holed up in his hotel suite, staying up days and nights and never going out of doors to inhale the smog. Peter would stretch the limits of his imagination to conjure up excuses to cloak his drug use.

The combustible mix of personalities in Kiss created an unusual dimension to their appeal, transcending what came across in their records. Building the hype for the band succeeded by exploiting this chemistry and connecting it to their visual image and the mystique of their live shows. Few bands had emerged whose image and wildly divergent personalities so perfectly symbolized the helter-skelter world of rock. Kiss's constant regimen of touring and seeing their fans in the flesh was crucial to the success of this image.

Sharpshooters, Leather Girls, Preachers, and Platform Shoes

It's almost like Hitler-rock, because that audience—because of their beat, they're mesmerized by the music. I mean they have that audience hypnotized. They could say "We're going out there and lifting up this building," and they'd just go lift it up. That's the kind of control they have. That's why their following is so strong and indestructible.

> Promoter Steve Glantz commenting on Kiss, quoted in "Kiss: Invasion of the Glitter Goths," *Circus* Magazine, April 8, 1976.

Promoting rock concerts isn't for the faint-hearted. It's a high-risk business appealing to gamblers who aren't distressed by that paralyzing feeling of fear when the ground is about to drop out from under you. But promoters don't dwell on the negatives; they like to roll the dice.

In the '50s and '60s, promoting rock shows was for the most part a small potatoes business. The promoters paid a flat fee for a recording act to show up at a hall, printed and sold tickets, paid a fee for the use of the building, and pocketed the profits, if any. The acts were often mismanaged by amateurs. Sometimes they would tour on weekends only, just to make extra money. It never dawned on most of them that they should get a percentage of the profits if the show did well. And the promoters weren't about to offer it, either.

The business took on a rough-and-tumble character, notorious for shady dealings and sharpshooters who promoted shows on a fly-by-night basis. Many acts handled their business on the road sloppily. Disappearing monies, phantom tickets, and box office settlements taking place at gunpoint weren't unheard of. It took a special breed of person to want to be a rock promoter, and consequently concert promotion remained a stepchild of the music industry for years.

But by the '70s, things had started to change. The success of the Beatles reinvigorated what had become a stagnant record industry. A slew of groups soon emerged as big record sellers who could also draw large crowds on the road—Led Zeppelin; the Eagles; Crosby, Stills, Nash & Young; the Allman Brothers; Grand Funk Railroad. As the record industry expanded and more artists were signed to labels, new configurations like eight-track and, later, cassette tapes, widened the market for music. Sales of recorded music in the United States doubled, from less than $2 billion in 1970 to $4 billion in 1978. And touring was becoming an important element of the record companies' marketing strategy to promote their acts.

Arenas were built in the late '60s and early '70s to house basketball and hockey teams as well as college sports. Multimillion-dollar bond issues were floated and local sales taxes were imposed, and tax incentives to private investors provided the funding for state-of-the-art facilities to replace aging auditoriums built in the '40s and '50s. Impressive new complexes like Market Square Arena in Indianapolis, the Summit in Houston, and McNichols Sports Arena in Denver could now compete for professional sports teams to locate in their cities.

All of this augured well for rock 'n' roll. Even championship teams and the biggest conventions don't fill an arena every day, and an empty arena means lost revenue. Local promoters were quick to fill the breach by bringing big-name talent into town to keep the building managers' calendars chock-a-block with concert dates. The building managers reciprocated in their own way. They granted exclusive or preferential treatment to those promoters who could bring in the most business, giving them good deals on the use of their facilities.

By the mid-'70s, a handful of promoters had emerged as the major players, or "A-list promoters," as they were often called by booking agents. Each had his own territory, jealously guarded from the others. Disputes over poaching could erupt into Hatfield and McCoy proportions. The A promoters were generally the first choice of the booking agents for their top acts; if an A-list promoter didn't want to book the show, a B-list promoter was found, usually someone less well-financed and frequently less reliable and experienced. The B promoters were often solicited to bid on concerts as a way to leverage the A promoters to pay more money for acts in a given market.

A tribelike structure started to evolve among the A promoters. Each key promoter in his territory was like a chief who was responsible for keeping peace with his rivals over territorial integrity. The country was carved up along geographic lines of demarcation. Major promoters maintained a sort of uneasy alliance with each other. Jules Belkin was the key promoter in Ohio and Michigan, which included the major cities of Detroit, Cleveland, and Cincinnati; Bill Graham controlled San Francisco and the smaller cities in the Bay area; Pace Concerts, a company run by Lou Messina, was the major force in Houston and Dallas and many smaller markets in the southwest; Ron Delsener was the key man in the New York metropolitan area; Cecil Corbett and Jack Boyle, partners for many years, dominated many lucrative markets in Florida, Virginia, the Carolinas, and Washington, D.C. Larry Magid prevailed in Philadelphia and Dave Lucas in Indianapolis and other midwestern cities. Frequently up for grabs was southern California, including L.A., with many promoters vying for business in a diverse and competitive market. Many of the major promoters backed smaller operators in nearby markets to expand their territorial influence.

Promoters "buy" shows from the artist's booking agent. They are responsible for guaranteeing a certain minimum fee for the act to perform plus a percentage of the gate or the show's profits if it does well. The promoter has to make all the organizational arrangements—local transportation, staffing, stagehands, production, catering, building rental, tickets—and to advertise and promote the show. If the promoter doesn't keep his costs under control or if the show stiffs, meaning it sells less tickets than he predicted, the promoter will lose money. Most shows are gambles. Promoters thrive on this gut level instinct where they sense an act will do well in a given market for the right price, whatever that is. And business judgments that put tens if not hundreds of thousands of dollars at risk are often made on nothing more than gut feeling.

Promoters know a good thing when they smell it, and early on they smelled money with Kiss. Even without much radio airplay, the size of Kiss's audience increased at a torrid pace. The groundswell was so strong they could headline at the biggest arenas, playing in front of as many as 15,000 fans each night in a different city. Kiss was in overdrive. Who would want to pay money just to see a band show up with a few amps and a spotlight when they could see an extravaganza like Kiss? A Kiss show had become an event, not just another concert. It was something to be at.

Platoons of fans would mob the box office at arenas once tickets were put on sale. Radio stations were besieged to play Kiss records and to give away concert tickets. Contests were organized where legions of Kiss look-alikes in full regalia would appear in public. Whenever Kiss came to town, a whirlwind was unleashed and every newspaper, radio, and TV station in every hamlet, burg, and metropolis eagerly jumped on the bandwagon, squeezing the publicity value of the event for every drop that they could wring from it. A reporter for *Creem,* Jaan Uhelszki, put on makeup and a stage outfit to appear with them at a concert in Johnstown, Pennsylvania. Her story, "I Dreamed I Was Onstage with Kiss in My Maidenform Bra," appeared in the August 1975 issue. As she put it that night, "...I am the only Kiss with tits."

An early promoter, Steve Glantz, first saw the group in Wyandotte, Michigan, at an ice skating rink, He later booked Kiss for three nights at Detroit's Cobo Arena in 1975. Detroit soon became Kiss's El Dorado, where a fanatical following guaranteed continuous sellouts.

In October of 1975, Cadillac, Michigan, provided Kiss with one of its most unusual promotions. The coach of a struggling high school football team had written to Bill Aucoin about how inspired his players had become after seeing Kiss at Cobo Arena. At practice sessions, he now played Kiss albums to fire up the team. Bill and Carol Ross-Durborow, Kiss's publicist, staged a media event in Cadillac—the Mayor declared a special "Kiss Day," streets were renamed in their honor, the football team wore Kiss makeup, and Kiss arrived with a squad of reporters and photographers in tow. It was a huge p.r. coup that made the national press.

The fervor of Kiss's fans made dollar signs glitter in the promoters' eyes. Kiss's appeal was magnetic, pulling the kids into the halls as if a cult ritual was being performed. In a way it was. At Varsity Stadium in Toronto, the commercial impact that Kiss was having wasn't being overlooked by the press, either. A reviewer for the *Toronto Star* caught the essence of the Kiss phenomenon in a September 7, 1976 review:

> ...Kiss is something more than a rock band. It's a cause, one only peripherally connected with the music it plays. You don't go to a Kiss show. You become a part of it, wearing make-up like the band, sporting a $5 Kiss T-shirt and $1 button or carrying a $4 poster. And you make sacrifices.

To the promoters, Kiss was a gift from the gods, an act custom-made for hard-sell and hype. They were in their glory. Promoters fought tooth and nail to book as many Kiss shows as they could crowd into the itinerary. By the mid-'70s, Kiss had overtaken Alice Cooper as theatrical rock's top draw. Kiss now symbolized a unique brand of glamorized decadence, striking a raw nerve with their rabid and youthful following. With fans camped out in sleeping bags outside arenas, waiting to buy tickets the next morning, Kiss was dynamite for the promoters.

Performing in out-of-the-way places was a key ingredient to Kiss's success. Kiss would appear anywhere and take with them their legendary stage show with all of its trappings—the full arsenal of explosions, fire, smoke, flash pots, flame shooters, bombs, props, lights, and sound. No town was too small for Kiss to appear at a local hall. To stay on tour for as long as Kiss did, as much as nine months a year, they had to play everywhere.

In the summer of 1977, Kiss did a major tour of Canada from east to west, performing in places like Moncton, Saskatoon, Lethbridge, Kitchener, London, Regina, and Sudbury in addition to the bigger cities of Calgary, Vancouver, and Winnipeg. But some of the more remote cities didn't have airports, except landing strips for private planes. So Kiss chartered its own plane, an aging twin-prop Convair looking something like the type of aircraft seen in Indiana Jones movies. It was big inside, with a bar lounge area, lots of overstuffed chairs, gold shag carpeting, a few small brown vinyl couches you sank into, and a galley. It wasn't plush, but it had a sort of homey, old-fashioned feel to it.

The Convair become the Kiss clubhouse in the sky. Girls would sometimes be picked up in one city, taken on board, find themselves on the couch, and wake up the next day in an unknown city. Approaching Sudbury early one morning, we saw below us sprawling chunks of crag and valley. Sudbury is ripped apart from strip mining, and the rugged terrain was used to test lunar landing vehicles for the Apollo space program. One girl on board our plane had been drinking all night. When she was suddenly wakened by the plane's vibration and looked outside, she became panic-stricken. She thought Kiss was landing on the moon.

Paul was then dating a girl whom he'd stolen away from a musician in one of the opening bands for Kiss. Their undulating bodies were often seen beneath a pile of wool blankets, rolling off the couch and onto the floor. By the time the plane landed, their clothes were strewn throughout the cabin. One of the bodyguards sleeping in a chair once woke to find a bra and Paul's boot in his lap. In even mildly bad weather, riding in the Kiss clubhouse was bumpy and nerve-wracking. As the plane pitched forward and banked into turns, we were tossed around the cabin like hamsters being shaken in a cage.

Dick, Chuck, and Judy helped to maintain the clubhouse atmosphere. Dick and Chuck were the pilots and Judy was the stewardess. Dick and Chuck were quick to allay any fears we might have about the plane and their expertise as pilots, no matter how bad things looked. Once when sparks started shooting out of the right engine, sending blinding flashes of light into the night sky and causing a violent trembling in the cabin, Dick came back to take a look and said, "Don't worry about it." When oil started to leak from under one of the wings, dripping like molasses out of an open jar, Chuck would come into the cabin, take a look, and say, "It's nothing." They were always unperturbed.

On the tail end of the Canadian tour, we were on approach to Seattle and could see Boeing Field below us, a private airstrip Boeing uses for its planes. As the landing gear was heard unlocking, Chuck and Dick started arguing in the cockpit, loud enough that all of us in the cabin could hear. "What are you doing? Are you crazy? We're landing at the wrong field! I told you not to land at Boeing!" And then Dick started yelling, "Don't give me that crap! You gave me landing coordinates for Boeing, not SeaTac [Seattle-Tacoma International, the major commercial airport]. How was I supposed to know you changed your mind? You're a fuckin' jerk." By this time, Gene looked like a ghost; he hated flying to begin with and often skipped plane trips altogether by riding with the truck drivers or on the bus with the crew. Chuck and Dick kept arguing. Suddenly, the plane jerked upward, climbing to a higher altitude as the speed increased, and the landing gear was brought back up. We were now on approach to Sea-Tac, having narrowly missed hitting a small Piper aircraft which had crossed our unscheduled flight path. The Piper veered off to the left and dropped altitude sharply as it rapidly descended. The Convair experience was the first and last time Kiss chartered a plane for a tour.

A huge windfall can be made by promoters in one night with the right act, and in the late '70s, Kiss was the right act. One promoter who made good money on Kiss was Cecil Corbett. Corbett was no stranger to Kiss. He had come to know them when they first started their career, playing in front of a hundred or so people at several of his clubs in the south. These were sweaty and grubby places, dark and gloomy inside, where cigarette smoke hung like a bluish gray cloud over the audience and the smell of cheap booze permeated every corner. Up-and-coming rock bands needed to play places like this to generate word-of-mouth and get a buzz started to develop a following. From there, record sales and radio airplay would hopefully pick up, and eventually the bands would move up the ladder and play in bigger halls, opening for bigger acts. Then, with a lot of luck, they might headline on their own. Clubs had been an incubator for Kiss, where they could grind out song after song in the stifling heat of a dank, grimy room on a stage that was hardly big enough to hold all of their gear. This is where the fans came to check out their new idols and revel in the excitement. Kiss was known for its raucous and raunchy show that sent fans into a frenzy. This was where the diehards went to get their red meat.

Kiss had made it to the big time of arena rock, and Cecil was the ringleader for a block of shows in his territory. Asheville, Fayetteville, and Charlotte, North Carolina, and Greenville and Columbia, South Carolina, were all stops on the schedule that continued through Christmas and into early 1977. As the Kiss show rolled into town, Cecil licked his chops, knowing full well that a killing was just around the corner. The shows were mostly sold out in advance and he was in promoter's heaven.

A voluble and husky man who looked to be in his forties, the excitable Cecil was straight out of central casting for the role of rock concert promoter. He had a rumpled look in his work jeans and baggy shirt, and was a bit thick around the middle. Cecil had a densely matted weave of gray hair, carefully coiffed in a style that hugged his head like a helmet. He was always in a state of perpetual motion—talking a mile a minute, barking orders at lackeys, and fielding scores of phone calls.

Backstage in Asheville on March 1, 1977, Cecil greeted me like a long-lost nephew and embraced me with a bear hug. He confessed instantly that he was the world's biggest Kiss fan and that he had been "with 'em from the start." He was boisterous and bubbling over with enthusiasm. A good promoter has to believe his own hype and Cecil was a very good promoter. He rattled on like a chatterbox in his lilting drawl and in minutes I learned that he hailed from Camden, South Carolina; that Kiss was the biggest act he'd promoted since he started in the business, booking bands in beach clubs; and that he'd recently been to a weight clinic and successfully completed their regimen.

"Hey, Chris, how d'ya like the hotel? Lemme tell you, it's unbelievable. They've got a championship golf course that'll knock your socks off. Hey, the restaurant—it's five stars! Even Bill Aucoin'd like it!" Bill wasn't around; he seldom showed up except for shows in the big cities. Cecil was a friendly and obliging Jed Clampett character, but I hardly had time to digest any of this before he came over to put his arm around my shoulder. Something important was about to take place. He was going to introduce me to Miss Judy.

A tall blonde woman strode toward us. Cecil saw her and waved excitedly for her to come over. Judy was around 30, slender and attractive, her long hair slightly streaked in sections. Judy had small features and long, narrow fingers, meticulously manicured with freshly painted nails in one of those vivid fashion colors that matched her silk piqué blouse. Her face was partially obstructed by an oversized pair of designer eyeglasses, the kind with a lot of gold trim. Expensive jewelry jangled from every limb—no baubles or gewgaws. Judy looked radiant, but it was a bit overwhelming for the backstage loading dock of an arena.

Cecil pulled Judy to his side and introduced me. She smiled broadly and we talked about the Kiss show and when the band would arrive. The long, laborious process of putting up the show had ended, having started at the crack of dawn with local stagehands working with Kiss's crew. Cecil had to get back to the hotel and so did I. I said goodbye to Miss Judy and left the building. As I would later find out, Miss Judy was a fixture at concerts in the south and remained so for years.

By 8:00 p.m., the show was sold out. The Civic Center in Asheville was only a few years old and could hold about 7,600. Streams of fans could be seen being turned away at the box office in front of the building. In a sleepy town like Asheville, Kiss was probably the entertainment event of the season.

Later, I rode to the Civic Center in a limo with the band. We entered the arena through a narrow gate on the side of the building where the trucks load. Fans had parked themselves at the loading dock for hours, knowing that sooner or later, Kiss would have to arrive through this entrance. The driver sped past the box office in front of the building and headed toward the loading dock next to the backstage door. A swarm of fans clogged the driveway, screaming, yelling, and pounding on our limo. Inside, we felt the tremor as fans kept beating on the doors and windows. They were all young, mostly guys, and looked to be delirious. A girl with wavy bleached blonde tresses flaying wildly over her face was screaming so loudly, I thought she'd burst a blood vessel. When Gene rolled down his window half-way to show his face—he wasn't yet in his monster disguise—all hell broke loose. It was as if the shroud of Turin had been unwrapped and the face of Christ was revealed. The crowd was awestruck.

But there was another crowd in front of the Civic Center on the opposite side of the building. This crowd was marching in unison, about a dozen strong, under the arena's marquee. These weren't Kiss fans. They were older, neatly dressed, and clean-shaven, and carried their own set of placards. These were a loosely-knit band of preachers, southern Baptists, Evangelicals, and believers in Biblical inerrancy. They saw Kiss as agents of Satan and the bane of civilization. To the preachers, Kiss was a plague, and they were carrying out an unceasing campaign to eradicate the plague from their community. To them, Kiss was a deadly serious matter.

We were in the Bible Belt, where a strong streak of fundamentalism prevailed. Promoters were frequently exhorted by fundamentalists like those in the group across the street to cancel Kiss shows. In some towns, their influence was so strong that ticket sales slowed down when they took to the local airwaves. Breathing fire and brimstone, they implored mothers and fathers to keep their children away from the Hades which awaited them at the Kiss concert. Many insisted that the band's name was an acronym for Knights In Satan's Service. The preachers and their following were a regular nuisance to deal with. Mostly, they were bothersome but harmless. Gene hated the south anyway. He thought everything below the Mason-Dixon line was an uncharted wasteland, full of Bubbas, Goobers, and peckerwoods where "y'all" was the national motto. The preachers just gave him one more reason to dislike the place.

The overhead gate clanged to close behind us as our limo screeched to a halt inside the arena. Kiss jumped out of the limos and headed for the dressing room. The opening act was already on stage and Kiss would have about an hour to get themselves in makeup and costume. Kiss went through a raft of opening acts during the late '70s, including AC/DC, Judas Priest, and Iron Maiden, many of whom used Kiss's coattails to become headliners on their own.

One of the roadies tipped me off earlier that the Leather Girls would be backstage at the show. It wasn't hard to find them. They were set up in a small room off the corridor where the dressing room and production offices were located. Two girls wore masks and were clad from head to toe in dominatrix-style leather bondage gear. Inside the room, they displayed their S&M accessories—dog collars, whips, chains, metal rings, ropes, and the like. The band didn't pay much attention to them; they seemed to be around more for the amusement of the crew. One roadie pulled me aside and cupped his hand over my ear, obviously about to share a secret with me. "These girls'd suck the chrome off a trailer hitch!" he declared, then started guffawing. I burst out laughing. On tour with Kiss, there was always something new and unusual.

I found my way to a large lounge area made into a makeshift press room where reporters and radio and TV people were congregating along with photographers. Once Kiss got into makeup and costume, there would be the inevitable photo sessions, interviews, and introductions to fans who had won contests to meet Kiss backstage. At every stop on tour, Kiss set aside time for local press at the halls, preening for pictures and joking among themselves. Kiss ended up on the front pages of the next day's local papers and as lead stories on the local TV news programs. Most small towns and cities are starved for interesting stories to cover; having Kiss in town was newsworthy.

Precisely fifteen minutes before Kiss was to take the stage, they came out from the dressing room in full battle dress. Standing nearly 7 feet tall in their gigantic platform boots which rose to their kneecaps, Kiss strode toward the contingent of press who were huddled in the lounge. The band was swathed in black spandex body garments from head to toe, set off with distinctive patterns of rhinestones, sequins, zippers, chains, and wrist bracelets, all in silver. Gene plodded down the corridor, weighed down by what looked to be the entire contents of a hardware store, thousands of metal pieces, studs, chain link across his chest, and breast armor. Ace was rolling and swaying while he walked, fidgeting with his silver foam V-shaped chest piece. Next to Ace was Peter, slipping on his black gloves. Paul was the last to leave the dressing room, still spraying his hair with enough Aqua Net so that every strand was as immobile as a starched collar. As the four of them walked by, a few security guards rolled their eyes and several backstage guests dropped their jaws and gasped.

Once inside the lounge, video cameras rolled, reporters stuck mikes in their faces, Instamatics clicked, cameras set off rapid-fire strobe flashes, and young fans with parents in tow swarmed to get close to Kiss. Bodyguards formed a ring around Kiss to prevent things from getting out of hand. Everyone seemed to be talking at once, and Kiss fielded questions shouted by reporters. They were seasoned pros at jousting with the press, trading jibes and deflecting barbs by cutting up and clowning. Kiss played the part of a bunch of wise guys from New York. Unlike many rock bands, they weren't morose sourpusses. Mugging for the cameras, Gene growled and struck menacing poses and exclaimed, "'What a way to make a living!' Ace, looking tipsy and toting a champagne bottle, had a battery of Rodney Dangerfield one-liners ready which he delivered in a matter of seconds, drowning out the punch line by exploding into gales of laughter before he finished the joke. Paul and Peter started up a repartee as Paul fluffed up his towering hairdo and Peter joked that he'd been spraying it since he arrived in Asheville. Peter made sure to tell the reporters that Kiss was "the most loudest" rock band in the world. The press lapped it up.

Kiss's self-effacing humor and moxie won over much of the media despite the hold-your-noses-and-plug-your-ears attitude that many of them had toward the music. Unlike many groups, Kiss courted the press. Any publicity was good publicity. Kiss had molded themselves as a personality group of four unique superstars. Gene once described Kiss as a being like "a band where there are four Neil Diamonds."

I was surprised to see a local promo man from Casablanca Records. Outside the major cities, you normally had to search far and wide to find a rep from the record company at a concert. Record companies were just beginning to appreciate the importance of touring. The senior execs at most labels seldom ventured from their lofty perches in New York and L.A. to see acts playing in the trenches of America's heartland. For them all that schlepping in and out of second-rate hotels and airports was a drag. But with Kiss, it was changing. Kiss owed their success as a record-selling act to being on the road and playing the Ashevilles and Fayettevilles and Dubuques and Pine Bluffs of America. Casablanca recognized that still more records could be sold by getting the local retailers and radio people excited about Kiss in these towns. And, as I discovered, it was in these remote backwaters that a lot of money was made in the concert business.

I caught up with Cecil at around 9:30 p.m. He wanted to see the start of the show and wish Kiss well before they went on: We watched from the left side of the stage. An announcer—in fact one of the traveling bodyguards named Eddie Balandas—delivered the intro in a stentorian voice, blasted through the band's sound system. "ALL RIGHT, ASHEVILLE! YOU WANTED THE BEST, YOU GOT THE BEST. THE HOTTEST BAND IN THE LAND . . . KISSSSSSSSS!"

The crowd exploded in a deafening roar. Jets of thick liquid fog and smoke from dry ice started spewing across the stage, enveloping the elaborate set-pieces and platforms, and a blinding, strobelike battery of high-intensity lights flashed in front of us. The four Kiss members suddenly appeared as the hazy mist from the fog began to lift, running down a set of walkways, instruments at their side, and tore into "Strutter." The entire audience was on their feet, cheering and waving wildly, rushing toward the stage. By this time, our ears had been assaulted by the repercussion of an explosive charge timed to go off once Kiss hit the stage. A Kiss show was so indescribably loud that hearing anything but the concert sounds was impossible. It was a convenient time for me and Cecil to leave and start our business. We adjourned to an inconspicuous office next to the box office window and cashier's drawer. We sat at a long conference table in a drab-looking room, surrounded by an open office area filled with rows of desks and chairs, each with adding machines on top.

Cecil gave me a box office statement to look over, showing how many tickets had been sold. Shuffling through some more papers, he handed me an accounting of the show's expenses and various documents and invoices. All of this gets pretty routine night after night. Settling shows is usually boring. But it's where the money is made in big-time rock for both the promoter and the act, especially in small towns.

By this time, my duties on the road had expanded. I was no longer just the undefined "presence" provided by Kiss's business managers to keep an eye on things. I took on the job of tour business manager, which meant handling the finances. I replaced a Kiss employee, Tom Butler, who had been with the group for about a year. Essentially, the job involved doing the tour accounting, negotiating the show settlements with the promoters, and coordinating the itinerary with the booking agency. I become known as The Wallet, a term coined by Gene. I never liked it much, but it was better than being called a bagman.

Asheville had just under 7,600 seats sold. At $7.50 per ticket, a typical price in the late '70s in a small market in the south, the gross after taxes was about $55,000. And then came the deductions for expenses—hall rental, stagehands, box office services, staffing, catering, limos, advertising, insurance, production supplies. This added up to around $17,000 since the hall was on a flat-fee rental and not a percentage of the gross and very little had to be spent on advertising. There would be a profit of $38,000 for the show. That left Kiss with $32,000 since their deal was 85 percent of the show's profits; Cecil would end up with $6,000 for his 15 percent. And this was just one show in Asheville, a relatively small venue. There were scores of places like this, hundreds all over the country, smaller cities with much lower costs for advertising, building rentals, labor, and local services, especially in the mid-'70s. A slightly larger building with a 10,000 capacity could easily bring in over $50,000 to Kiss for one show.

The economics were very simple. Five of these shows a week at an average of $40,000 could generate $200,000 in income to Kiss. There was a ton of money to be made from touring and by staying on the road for 20 weeks: $4 million in gross income was easily attainable, especially when monies from the sale of T-shirts and other merchandise at the halls was factored in. This wasn't just some piddling fee for a show in the boondocks but a down payment on a much larger treasure that steadily accumulated, night after night, over the course of many weeks. It added up to Big Business, and places like Asheville were important cogs in the machine.

The promoters didn't do too badly, either. The dynamics of the concert business had changed in the '70s and promoters could no longer rake off 40 or 50 percent of the profit. They also ceded much of the responsibility for production to the artists. The acts took control, providing their own sound and lighting systems on the road and a complement of technicians to run the show as an entirely self-contained operation. With these changes, promoters were cut down to a smaller profit percentage, often 15 or 20 percent for a headline act in a big hall. With an act like Kiss, a 15 percent overnight return was as good as money in the bank, at least most of the time. Getting a string of Kiss shows could be a windfall.

Promoters also knew how to widen their profit margins and fatten their coffers with a variety of tricks that usually fell just short of outright stealing. Most of the tricks were pretty obvious, like getting rebates from the halls after the act was charged the full rental fee according to the contract. This would take place after the show was settled with the act when the promoter and the building manager worked out a private arrangement. Building managers often did this to provide incentives to get promoters to steer concert business their way. Promoters could also get their local suppliers—stagehands, limos, caterers—to submit one set of bills on the night of the show to settle with the act and another set of bills, for a lower amount, to the promoter, who would pay the lower amount later.

For the real sharpshooters, advertising could be a gold mine. The promoter could do the media buying himself through a dummy company and collect the standard 15 percent commission on advertising buys. The advertising would be charged as a show cost to the act at the full price inclusive of the commission. Alternatively, promoters could make deals with local radio and TV stations to provide blanket coverage of spot ads in predesignated time slots for a fixed fee. The promoter would submit an invoice at the settlement for the rate card costs, a much higher amount.

And the most brazen promoters would fall back on an old favorite—unmanifested tickets. These would be sets of tickets not appearing on the official box office record which indicated the amount of tickets printed for the show. The unrecorded tickets would be sold "off the manifest," and the monies collected by ticket agents retained by the promoter wouldn't be included in the box office gross reported to the act. A variation of this scam was "roll tickets," a traditional stand-by. If a show was sold out, you could have people selling tickets off a roll, the type used at carnivals for rides, and let people in through a side door. In the case of most rock shows, particularly in the '70s, festival seating as opposed to reserved seating was the norm, meaning no actual seats but standing space only. A few hundred extra people in the building wouldn't even be noticed.

In the days before computerized ticket services, ticket outlets away from the building's box office could be a mother lode for a sharpshooting promoter. Who could really find out what the deals were with these ticket agents who distributed tickets in the neighboring towns? Most of these outlets were far from the box office, and the agent carried his ticket allotment and cash monies around in a shoebox.

Over the course of hundreds of shows, the list of possible peculations grew endless. But most of these practices were—and are—difficult if not impossible to prove, especially if they are sub rosa arrangements with local suppliers or buildings. An act comes to town, and it's unrealistic to expect to be able to conduct a full-scale audit in the space of the few hours set aside to settle the financial terms for the show. You take the best deal you can get based on what you have to work with and try and curb the most egregious violations. Touring is really one of the last vestiges of vaudeville in the way the business is handled.

Promoters complain that the nature of the business feeds this chicanery. The acts demand too high a guarantee, the deals are too tight, and most shows break even or lose money. As a result, the profit margins on winning shows wind up being too small. Some confess that if they don't cheat, they can't survive. It has kind of a Darwinian twist to it—the strong survive by preying on the weak. More sophisticated, computerized financial systems to monitor expenses have made inroads, but computers can be trained to cheat as well.

In Asheville that night, everything seemed in order. The show was sold out and the next day, the *Asheville Citizen* reported it as one of the largest crowds the building had ever had. The profit column showed a tidy number for Kiss. Cecil Corbett would pocket $6,000 for his troubles. With another four shows coming up on the tour, some in larger venues, he could expect to make at least $30,000, as all the shows were sure to sell out. And on a later leg of the Kiss tour, he would probably do a few more shows in his territory. Rock 'n' roll was a very good business.

Cecil and I walked out of the office, toward the arena. From the back of the arena floor, we watched the show, now under full throttle. Paul was doing his best Robert Plant-style warble, bending and twisting the notes up and down the scales, while waves of frenetic drumming from Peter resonated against the arena walls. Cecil started to chuckle, and then shouted in my ear how he had spotted Kiss as a winner "way back" when they were playing clubs and opening for other bands. I nodded my approval. He was now cashing in on a smart call he'd made years earlier, backing an unknown act that might have sent him over the edge of a cliff. But on the marathon Kiss tour in 1977, there weren't many bad calls by promoters. Business was booming and most of them made a killing. Kiss was on a roll.

5

Perpetual Motion Machine

They are 11, 12, and maybe 13, walking the streets of exurbia swinging their little red Panasonic eight-tracks and singing lurid songs—songs about hookers, boozing, a doctor who cures "sick" girls by allowing them to make love to him, a 93-year old man who falls in love with a 16-year old girl. The songs . . . are by a group called Kiss.

From "An Outrage Called Kiss," *The New York Times Magazine*, June 19, 1977

Thousands of fans swarmed the airport in Tokyo at 4:30 in the afternoon when Kiss's plane, a Pan Am Clipper Ship painted for the voyage with the Kiss logo on the fuselage, landed on March 19, 1977. (For years, Peter believed that the 747 was owned by Kiss because their logo was on it.) When Kiss, Bill Aucoin, and I walked down the jetway toward the terminal, an endless sea of faces with mops of black hair stretched behind the fences bordering the runway. We could hear the screaming and cheering over the din of planes taxiing nearby. Kiss was about to take Japan by storm, where every show was sold out months in advance and the press stood ready to chronicle Kiss's every move and utterance.

Bill was sure Kiss would be big in Japan. Kissmania had electrified the country; the tour was ideally timed to exploit Kiss's phenomenal success. Their kabuki-style makeup and glittery costumes would capture the imagination of the Japanese fans and set the public abuzz. The Kiss show, with all its flash and glitz, would galvanize audiences throughout the country and create a bonanza of publicity for Kiss's promoter, Mr. Udo. Photo opportunities abounded, from traditional Japanese gardens to ancient temples to the hurly-burly of the Ginza. Wherever Kiss went, mobs of people would follow.

But first Kiss had to get out of Haneda International Airport. Mr. Udo and Kiss's security chief, John Harte, had worked out a plan in advance for the group to deplane in makeup, allowing the press to take plenty of pictures of their airport arrival. Once we arrived in customs, officials would stamp their passports and waive the band through, dispensing with at least some of the usual formalities. That plan proved to be short-lived. Customs officials in Tokyo were notorious sticklers for regulations and backed away from the original plan. Kiss had to adjourn to a separate room, remove their makeup, have the inspectors check their real faces against the ones on their passports, and then put on the makeup again. What we had been told would be "no problem" turned into an unavoidable delay. Once outside the terminal, several thousand fans rushed our waiting limos and security had to push them away, fearful that they would smash the windows.

Kiss's arrival for a series of ten shows for their first Japan tour in March and April, along with the usual panoply of promotions, wouldn't be enough for Kiss, no matter how tumultuous the welcome. While the band was 10,000 miles from the United States, the campfires at home had to be kept burning. The American media had to be constantly barraged with hype since Kiss wasn't on the road there to stoke the fires. Kiss's popularity had accelerated so quickly in the last year that any pullback in press and promotion could deaden the enthusiasm of fans back home. Bill had a solution to the problem that was big and expensive, and he had the man to make it happen.

Al Ross had entered the picture recently as the publicity chief for Kiss. Al worked out of the offices of Aucoin Management in The Press Office, a subsidiary. Gregarious and personable, Al had a deft touch for wooing the press. He could've been a character in *The Front Page*. Somewhere in his forties, Al sprinkled his speech with more than a few "babys" and "how are yas." He was the prototype press agent and had been in the business for years, with acts like Grand Funk Railroad, the Osmonds, and Blood, Sweat & Tears.

Al and Bill hatched an ingenious solution to the press problem in the United States. We would take the press with us to Japan. The U.S. press contingent would come along, write stories while on tour with Kiss in Japan, take photos, review the shows, and feed the stories to the magazines and newspapers back home. There would be no lull in the domestic hype. And there would be plenty of stories left over to use for filler in later publications. It was simple, it was big, and it had never been done before by a rock group on this grand scale.

A dozen journalists were picked by Al for the press junket, mostly from rock and music publications and a few from the wire services. They would stay for the duration of the tour—about three weeks in five cities including Tokyo, Osaka, and Kyoto—and they would fly first class with Kiss, stay in their hotels, and have all expenses paid. This was no nickel-and-dime affair. It would cost a lot of money.

Kiss loved Japan. Fans showered them with affection, the record company lavished huge sums on staging promotions that were custom-made for a media-mad country, and the promoter made a bundle by bringing over an act that epitomized showbiz, American-style, a formula that seldom fails in Japan. Kiss performed for nearly 60,000 fans in Japan on their sold-out tour. There were hundreds of security men at every hall, and ushers assigned to each row of seats to keep the fans under control. Enthusiasm has very clearly defined limits in Japan, and overexuberant fans jumping out of their seats had a high-powered flashlight beamed into their eyes. *Variety*, in its April 6, 1977, issue, described the Kiss show as "Busby Berkeley-like," commenting that between the tour's estimated production cost and the traveling entourage including the press, it was "perhaps the most expensive rock 'n' roll out-of-continent tryout. . . ."

While on tour, the band spent their free time on shopping sprees, loading up on tons of camera gear and electronic gizmos. They'd only recently come into the big money, and for Ace, who never had much when he was growing up, it was a chance to go hog wild. Every kind of toy he ever craved was ripe for the taking in the Ginza's shopping arcades, hundreds of tiny stores spilling onto the sidewalks of narrow streets and alleyways, all chock full of video cameras, recorders, electric guitars, studio gadgets, and telescopes.

Mr. Udo introduced the Kiss entourage to one of the more sensuous experiences of the Orient, the traditional bathhouse. Passes resembling oversized supermarket coupons were carefully doled out—they were easily worth several hundred dollars each—to the band and their inner circle for complimentary admission. Inside the bathhouse, slim, petite girls in white shorts and tops perambulated through a Japanese rock garden that led to a corridor of private rooms where each suite was sealed by a sliding wooden door. The girls escorted us to a tiled bathing area and disrobed us before we immersed in the warm, sudsy water. Then it was into the suite for a rubdown with hot oils and a body massage which included an unusually intense and almost heart-stopping hand job.

Ace and Peter never made it to the bathhouse; they brought along their wives for the Japan trip. Gene wouldn't be caught dead in a commercialized pleasure palace where sex was for sale; he closeted himself in his suite at the Hotel Okura with a local playmate he had found. Paul supposedly made one visit and found the experience memorable. When one of the band later asked him what was so great about a hot oil massage and a hand job, he replied, "If you could do that to yourself, you'd never leave your room."

The price tag for the press junket and Kiss's enormous production was close to $250,000. It was a mindboggling sum for a promotion stunt, but it wasn't without results. Kiss's tour of Japan was widely reported in the U.S. press, filling the gap when Kiss was absent from home base. The Japan extravaganza with all of its hoopla—round-the-clock interviews in hotels, planes, and on the Bullet Train; photos of Kiss wearing kimonos with Buddhist shrines as backdrops;

press conferences in every city with TV coverage; Kiss dressed in centuries-old ornate Japanese silk robes—was a superb promotion. It was the Kiss hype in pure form, savvy, innovative, unusual, and unprecedented.

⁜

Touring with Kiss—in Japan or anywhere else—was like being sucked into a vortex. Every activity was compressed into small compartments of time and every minute had to be maximized on their tightly wound schedule. Kiss never seemed to stop touring. It was like being in a marathon without ever seeing the finish line. There was barely enough time in any one place to check the time zone you were in to set your watch. Almost daily, it was an enervating and dizzying succession of airports, hotels, limos, rent-a-cars, and arenas. Between connecting flights, layovers, and drives, entire days were consumed by traveling. But it was this formula that worked for Kiss. There were more than 200 shows from 1976 until early 1978, and in most cities, Kiss either sold out or came close.

We hurtled from city to city at a breakneck clip. And the cities were something else again. There aren't 200 New Yorks, L.A.s, San Franciscos, and Chicagos in America. But there is, as I found out, a vast universe of places like Muskegon, Bismarck, Huntsville, Butte, Salina, Waco, Rapid City, Dubuque, Bozeman, Fayetteville, Dothan, Port Huron, Lake Charles, Evansville, Johnstown, Erie, Peoria, Lafayette, Waterloo, Grand Forks, Sioux City, Sioux Falls, Fargo, Johnson City, Beaumont, and Hampton Rhoads. There seemed to be no end to the amount of completely unknown and unheard-of cities that could be booked for Kiss shows. Some were so isolated that the truck drivers carrying the stage show had trouble finding them on standard road maps. Kiss's grassroots following was built on playing secondary and tertiary markets which other acts avoided.

Tours melded into one another, segued between photo sessions, recording sessions, TV appearances, press interviews, and endless publicity stunts, like their promotion for Marvel Comics in February 1977. A sample of each band member's blood was taken to be mixed in with the ink that would print the first batch of a special edition Kiss comic book, which eventually sold 400,000 copies. I hardly noticed when the albums started, and then they were finished. Each album took only about three months to do, and making one was our only respite between tours.

Destroyer, released in 1976, reached #11 in *Billboard*. *Rock and Roll Over* came out at the end of 1976 and also hit #11. *Love Gun* reached #4 in the charts by the summer of 1977, and by the end of that year, *Alive II*, a follow-up double album to the immensely successful *Alive!* record, reached #7. A special reissue of the first three Kiss albums in one collection, entitled *Kiss—The Originals*, hit stores in midsummer 1976. In the spring of 1978, another double album was released, *Double Platinum,* a package of greatest hits. Kiss and Casablanca became known for the bonus items inserted in the albums including posters, tattoos, trading cards, stickers, and full-color booklets featuring photos of Kiss in concert, like a souvenir program. The repackaging of old material into both live records and greatest hits compilations mined the group's back catalogue of songs and previously recorded tracks for every nickel possible.

Kiss always made sure that they were in print. By the late '70s, *Creem, Circus,* and *Hit Parader* had nonstop coverage of Kiss, including cover stories, backstage photos, pinups, and foldouts. *16 Magazine* and *Super Teen* were now on board with their own Kiss coverage. A Kiss artwork contest allowed fans to submit Kiss inspired illustrations which would be judged by Kiss and exhibited in the rotunda of Madison Square Garden for their February 1977 show. Kiss and Casablanca took out huge amounts of advertising in these magazines as well as in trade papers including *Record World, Cash Box,* and *Billboard,* promoting the latest releases in full-page color ads. Thanks to the combination of publicity and paid advertising, Kiss was never out of sight.

Dominating the marketplace was a cornerstone of Bill Aucoin's strategy to keep the group in perpetual motion. It was certainly reaping its rewards. Albums like *Love Gun* and *Alive II* were produced for around $150,000 each while Kiss's income from record royalties and music publishing (the income generated from song copyrights) reached an astounding $17.7 million for the three-year period between 1976 and 1978. Casablanca, only a few years earlier a pipsqueak operation, had become the hottest label in the business, riding a wave of success from Kiss, Donna Summer, and the Village People.

Kiss's success in barnstorming the country, swelling their ranks of followers through live shows and interminable touring, changed a lot of thinking in the industry. Record companies began creating marketing plans for new album releases that would dovetail with concert tours. Casablanca was early to seize on this with Kiss, who had been producing as many as two albums per year in conjunction with touring. Hundreds of thousands of dollars were spent by Casablanca supporting Kiss on tour, intensifying local promotions in markets where Kiss was booked. Retailers were cajoled into putting up elaborate point-of-purchase displays and posters in stores; radio stations were persuaded to tie in the local appearance of Kiss with contests and increased airplay; and as more money became available, Casablanca bought blocks of spot TV commercials nationwide to cross-promote the concerts with the records being shipped to the stores. Howard Marks Advertising did most of this work.

What had been a haphazard, hit-or-miss arrangement, with artists touring on a scattershot basis without much involvement by record companies, was now evolving into a professionally managed marketing campaign. Executive

Vice President of Howard Marks Advertising Rosanne Shelnutt coordinated Kiss's album artwork and designs with tour promotion and merchandising, supplying concert promoters with ad mats, photos, and specially prepared radio and TV commercials. It was an early effort to make record selling and touring a unified effort. And the promoters became a key link in all of this; they were forced to keep up with the changes in the business that were thrust upon them.

Keeping Kiss on the road was the function of American Talent International, Kiss's booking agency in New York. They signed Kiss when they were still an opening act and ATI was a struggling new agency. As Kiss's fortunes rose, so did ATI's. They became specialists in rock bookings and handled a large roster of acts including ZZ Top, AC/DC, Bob Seger, Neil Young, Joni Mitchell, and Rod Stewart. Jeff Franklin, the principal owner of ATI, had started booking bands as a teenager in Ohio. By 1977, at age 33, Jeff was the head of the top rock agency. Gruff but agreeable, Jeff had a sharp business mind and saw himself as a deal maker *extraordinaire*. In *Billboard*'s December 10, 1977, story on ATI, Jeff was described as "rock 'n' roll's answer to Irving 'Swifty' Lazar." Jeff proved to be dedicated in promoting Kiss, particularly in the beginning when they were desperate for money and needed as many gigs as could be squeezed into the calendar. He had a close relationship with Casablanca's Neil Bogart, who had already made a sizable commitment to the group. Jeff was also loaning monies to keep Kiss working.

While Jeff ran the agency, the task of dealing with Kiss and booking the shows fell to Wally Meyrowitz, the senior agent at ATI and a part owner. About Jeff's age, Wally was high-strung, excitable, fast-talking, and crazed about his job. A short man with thinning, curly dark hair and beady eyes, he was the perfect choice for Kiss. Wally was unrelenting and wouldn't take no for an answer, going to the last mile to get what he wanted for Kiss. Breaking down the doors to get Kiss bookings in their early days wasn't easy—many promoters balked at the kind of production demands that Kiss required. But Wally pressed ahead, often booking tours that looked like they were done using a blindfold and a set of darts.

Wally was well liked by both Bill Aucoin and the Kiss members. He was not liked, I learned later, by Howard Marks or Carl Glickman. They found him too crazy, too disorganized, and too much of a rock 'n' roll type whose behavior swung wildly from one extreme to another. While in his office, I sometimes heard him scream like a hyena into the telephone or watched him pound on his desk and throw papers across the room. At other times, he could be a cutup, provoking spasms of laughter from the band. Whatever Wally's shortcomings, the ATI strategy worked for Kiss. Between 1976 and 1978, Kiss's income from personal appearances was $7.1 million, a virtually unheard-of sum at that time. ATI was the linchpin in keeping Kiss on tour. Promoters scrambled to get on the bandwagon and book more shows, earning ATI a 10 percent commission.

And promoters like Cecil Corbett who booked many ATI acts were rewarded with Kiss dates.

Some of the stops on the Kiss tours revealed a grim and unsettling world that is frequently masked by the superficial glitziness of rock shows.

The border town of El Paso, sitting on the Rio Grande, was a bastion of Kiss fans. Most of the year, El Paso is steaming hot with miles of flat, dusty terrain reaching to the reddish-brown mounds of desert hills miles from downtown. Weather-beaten and crumbling, the Coliseum was a huge barnlike structure built to house cattle and livestock shows. Banks of floodlights illuminated the front entrance, and chain-link fencing with what looked like ribbons of concertina wire circled the perimeter of the building. It looked like a prison camp, ominous and foreboding, but it had been built to hold over 11,000 people and Kiss could pack in even more. Gene always loved the news that a venue had oversold its official capacity and fans would be bursting out of the seams.

In August 1976, fans at the Coliseum streamed through the parking lot in cars, in pick-up trucks, and on foot. Empty bottles of Tecate, Thunderbird, and Wild Turkey were chucked along their path. Inside was a nasty and fearsome crowd. These cranked-up fans, with their clenched fists and scowling faces, were ready to do more than rock. The pungent aroma of marijuana masked the fetid stench of the hogs and steers that were often on display for livestock auctions in the building. Many in the crowd had bloodshot eyes; some were staggering, even keeling over. This was a rough-looking, seedy bunch. Some wore leather jackets and had heavy chains wrapped around their waists. Fist fights broke out constantly, and several young toughs pummeled people to the ground who got in their way. One group was punching out a path to get closer to the stage. The opening act, Bob Seger and the Silver Bullet Band, was whipping up the audience with their chugging guitar solos and wailing vocals.

It was dark inside the Coliseum, and there was no air-conditioning. Fans stood shoulder to shoulder in the heat. I felt like I would drown in my own perspiration. I stood behind the stage barricade and saw glass flasks and half-sized bottles of booze being passed around in the crowd.

Uniformed El Paso police were posted near the ticket takers in the outside lobby, but concert security in T-shirts were responsible for the main floor itself. This arrangement created a kind of safe haven for violence and drug dealings inside the hall in a few isolated areas. Toward the back of the hall behind the bleacher seats set up on either side huddled a small group, barely out of their teens, exchanging bags of marijuana and small vials of cocaine. Seconds later, they scattered into the crowd. Clouds of marijuana smoke could be seen throughout the hall.

First aid stations of the kind I had first encountered at Roosevelt Stadium were put to extensive use here. People routinely passed out or got sick, either from the heat or from fighting, and were carted off to a backstage facility with beds, medics, and stretchers. It resembled a mini-M.A.S.H. unit. Victims of drug overdoses and drinking, passed out and lying on cots, were found there.

I normally walked through the hall before and during the show to check out the crowd and inspect the ticket gates and turnstiles to see that things were going smoothly. But this crowd was frightening. At any moment, somebody could pull out a knife and start on a rampage. The fans were getting increasingly charged up while waiting for Kiss to start, and in the darkness of the Coliseum, everything could easily slip out of control.

When Kiss took the stage, the crowd ignited, shouting uncontrollably. Only the earth-shaking crunch of Kiss's wall of amps and speaker bins built like oversized air ducts could drown them out. I hustled toward the security of the dressing rooms backstage. That El Paso concert was a harrowing nightmare of the worst elements of a rock show. Years later, the Coliseum was extensively renovated and upgraded to become a more hospitable venue.

⁘

The kids who came to see Kiss ached to experience what Kiss symbolized with their decadent imagery, raw energy, and hedonistic sloganeering. And Kiss skillfully tapped into their adolescent yearnings for rebellion and sexual urgings, setting off powerful feelings that simmered inside them. Kiss was a vehicle for releasing those pent-up frustrations that throw teenagers' lives in turmoil and tug at their emotions. Bob Ezrin, who produced the *Destroyer* album, told *Rolling Stone* in their March 25, 1976, issue that Kiss was a "social phenomenon . . . a caricature of all the urges of youth." The kids were looking to make a connection and with Kiss, they did.

The Kiss message was that there was no message, no subtext, and no subtleties. Which is what the kids wanted to hear. You could read anything you wanted into Kiss—sex, partying, pleasure seeking, rebelling, aggression. Kiss's attitude sent out the signal to fans that it was okay to cut loose and let it all out for a few hours in a jam-packed arena, immersed in a frenzy of blinding lights, crushing sound, and ear-splitting explosions, before returning to the drudgery and dreariness of their lives.

And many of the fans led exactly that kind of life. Kiss developed a huge following in the midwest's Rust Belt in older industrial cities like Detroit, Cleveland, and Indianapolis and a slew of small factory towns. Guys showed up at the concerts who were barely out of high school, with grimy hands and in frayed work clothes—shift workers from GM, Ford, and food processing plants nearby. Girls came who were still in their teens, going to beauty school, working as hairdressers and manicurists, taking orders at the local Dunkin' Donuts, sales clerking at Woolworth's, or working the graveyard shift at factories and mills. Kiss gave them an escape from this bleak, dead-end world.

The fantasy world that Kiss created for their fans was critical to their success and is what enabled the band to connect with them. The liner notes in the first *Alive!* album were mock hand-written notes from Gene, Paul, Ace, and Peter designed to titillate their fans' developing libidos. Paul and Ace wrote about "getting off" and being aroused; Gene addressed his fans by calling them "victims" and told how he liked to do "painful things . . . to make you writhe and groan in ecstasy. . . ." Peter warned his fans about getting their "claws" into the record. On the full-color sleeve to *Love Gun,* rivulets of blood spilled onto a pavement, spelling out the word Kiss. The band had fashioned an image that would bond them with their fans' desires and dreams. Shrewdly crafting this image was the domain of Bill Aucoin and Howard Marks Advertising, whose copywriter, Peggy Tomarkin Greenawalt, wrote much of the copy for their album notes, tour programs, fan club newsletters, and commercials.

Not surprisingly, all of this synthetic imagery drove Kiss's critics up the wall. Early in Kiss's career, the media dismissed Kiss as knuckleheads or as a clown band that relied on charlatanism to attract a following. But as Kiss began to dominate the media, the critics were forced to take notice and give grudging recognition to the band's success. In his December 3, 1976, column in *The New York Times,* pop music critic John Rockwell described the impact that Kiss had on "the biggest subculture in the pop music world, teenagers." Kiss, he said, gave their fans the "illusion of anarchy."

The groupies were never far from the trail of the Kiss tour. They seemed to have built-in radar and knew the hotels, the venues, the flights, and the arrival times without ever seeing an itinerary. As Gene observed, they knew how to "do the research." Kiss attracted the more extreme types, which was logical considering that Kiss's image was so sharply defined on the outer limits of rock 'n' roll.

It wasn't difficult to figure out what compelled the groupies to be groupies. America is mostly a succession of one small town after another, many bland and humdrum, forming an unbroken line of drab Main Streets and cookie-cutter shopping malls. Driving through the midwest, the endless flatness becomes hypnotic and most of the towns and their buildings appear like neat little cubicles surrounded by miles of empty space. Life for teenagers is often uneventful and boring. Movies and TV are their window on a more exciting and daring world, and music supplies the emotional stimuli to connect them to something very different. When Kiss came to town, every teenage hormone became energized and every traditional more and ritual was shattered. At least for a few fleeting hours, the crashing boredom and paralyzing monotony would be broken.

The arrival of Kiss was like a UFO landing. But to the groupies, it had a much more personal significance. It was a chance to experience every pubescent fantasy of sex, drinking, drugs, and all of the sybaritic delights that they had heard of or read about. Sex and drugs were the frankincense of rock 'n' roll. And Kiss was purportedly the ultimate band to do both sex and drugs with. Their concerts invariably brought out some of the fringe elements of the local community, including casualties of broken homes, alcoholism, drug abuse, and emotional disorders. Some groupies were so desperate to meet Kiss that they would do anything for the privilege. A girl once pulled me aside near the backstage entrance at a show in Oklahoma City and asked, "Do you want to fuck me between my tits?" I passed.

So they came to see Kiss, camping out in front of the hotels, traipsing through the airports, and hovering near the backstage doors. Most of them were pretty pathetic, girls with makeup clinging like pancake batter to their faces, snapping gum and slurping beer and soft drinks. Some were festooned with rock 'n' roll trinkets and dressed in bizarre getups that made them look like extras in a low-budget science fiction movie. Others wore spandex and nipple-tight halter tops, with layers of hair so stiff from hairspray that it looked like lacquer. This bunch could easily be dispensed with. They might make it backstage, but nowhere near the band's dressing room, let alone their hotel. And if there were guys among their ranks, equally driven Kiss fans who hungered to meet their heroes, they were immediately banished. Kiss's bodyguards and road managers handled the selection process. It was okay for guys to buy records and tickets and get autographs, but who wanted to party with them?

The groupies were always among the first to get backstage passes from the road crew, frequently in exchange for sexual favors or drugs. During the day, the crew set up the show while the band traveled from the previous city. Groupies would be stationed near the stage door entrance once the crew had arrived. The more popular girls would be invited onto the crew touring buses, sometimes for hours, taking on all comers. A few on the crew had a profitable sideline peddling drugs to fellow workers and in some cases, to the Kiss members that did drugs.

But once the band arrived in late afternoon for a sound check, a sort of run-through for the show to check the sound levels, all of this activity ceased. The crew resigned their posts and the girls beautified themselves, touching up their makeup and teasing their hair, hoping to be claimed by one of the band. But sometimes they had competition. Often, the better-looking girls didn't show up until the evening or were already known to the band and waited at their hotels. They were the more seasoned groupies, dressed in sexy rock 'n' roll outfits with fringed suede jackets and leather miniskirts. These groupies knew the band would be expecting them, since they were well known on the rock circuit.

Unlike the ragtag bunch that had to curry favor with the crew, these groupies had a different tack. "I only fuck the band" was their attitude. Social rites in this environment were based on a sort of tribal hierarchy, with Kiss as the headmen.

Only certain types of groupies would make the cut. The band didn't have any particular profile except that they had to be female and fairly attractive—no fatties or Brünnhildes. Brains didn't count. There was so little time available, intelligence would be superfluous, like a wasted asset that couldn't be tapped. But they should be characters. This was always important to Kiss. They liked people who hung out with them to be a little offbeat. And they also realized that outside of big cities like L.A. and New York, they couldn't count on superstar groupies and model types beating a path to their shows.

Kim from Ohio surfaced somewhere in the Buckeye state at one of the many concerts Kiss did in Dayton, Cleveland, Toledo, Cincinnati, and Columbus. Kim started on one of the crew buses and worked her way up the ranks. She appealed to Kiss because of her looks—tall, willowy, and about 20, with long, straight light brown hair. And she didn't look at all like a groupie. She was more of a college coed type. In a kind of odd reversal, Kim eventually matriculated as an official groupie, traveling with the band. And then she became a colossal pain. A week before joining the band's entourage, Kim was sleeping in the back of a crew bus with whomever was available for the night. Now she had to have her bags carried, her luggage picked up, her airplane boarding passes handed to her, her limo on standby, and on and on.

She was also zonked out on every imaginable type of barbiturate and at times, was barely coherent, often stumbling when she tried to walk. Kim once dropped her purse in an airport waiting lounge and hundreds of pills and capsules in a rainbow of colors spilled out, tumbling to the floor and bouncing like jelly beans as they scattered in every direction. This led to her demise. Kim was unceremoniously dumped at the airport, still in Ohio.

Sweet Connie, a comely and pert brunette, was made a legend in a song by Grand Funk Railroad called "We're an American Band." She set records for the most amount of work that could be performed in one twenty-four-hour period from a kneeling position. Connie would have the entire road crew line themselves up inside an empty 45-foot trailer, drop their pants, and service them at an astonishing pace. And then she would go to the band's hotel. For many years, she sent Christmas cards with a set of nude pictures enclosed.

Helicopter Lady was one of the more unusual groupies in Miami. She was actually an attractive, robustly built girl who had earned her nickname as the result of an unfortunate accident that marred her good looks and left a series of striations on her face that looked as if they had been created by a helicopter's blades cutting into the flesh. Kiss didn't let her appearance bother them. One band member supposedly devised an ingenious way around the problem: "I just told her to put a bag over her head and then I fucked her."

Star was a major league attraction on the rock 'n' roll circuit in Chicago and also turned up in L.A. and Detroit. A Goldie Hawn type with long blonde hair, Star was the February 1977 Playmate of the Month, and Kiss appeared with her in one of the photos in the pictorial. In her *Playboy* interview, she described herself as a "one-band woman, but (I'm) not a groupie." Her band was Kiss and for a while, Gene was her man. She described Gene's music in concert as ". . . what sex would sound like if you could hear it." Star developed a kind of Velcro-like attachment to Gene. Eventually, she disappeared from the scene and we never heard from her again.

And then there were the Mommies, the young mothers of female Kiss fans. Mother and daughter would sometimes show up at concerts as a twosome, enjoy the show, and then return to the band's hotel. This is where the logistics could become a problem. If the daughters were too young, they were parked in the lobby and a bodyguard of Kiss's would act as babysitter while the girl fell asleep on the couch. Then mom would be free to go upstairs to the band's rooms. On one tour in Fort Worth, several of us were drinking in the lounge of the hotel bar with a Mommy and her underage daughter. While one of the bodyguards tried to occupy the girl's attention by plying her with Shirley Temples, Mommy had unfastened her bra and opened her blouse so that Paul could autograph her breasts. She assured us she didn't normally do this kind of thing.

One of the more bizarre stories involved Gene. A girl came to his room, turned off all the lights, and, lighting a set of votive candles that she had brought with her, arranged to perform a black magic ceremony. She went into some kind of trance and then they had sex. Afterward, she told Gene that he had to order her to perform any act of his choosing. According to the ritual, she had to obey. Gene told her to "go out and fuck everyone on the road crew." And she did.

It wasn't unusual for some girls to insist that Gene have sex with them while he was still in makeup and costume directly after the show, something he did obligingly. One girl told me that she was thrilled to have had sex with "a monster," no doubt a first. To Gene, they were all willing receptacles and being on tour provided him with an endless supply.

Girls were like furniture in this world; they were always around. Most of them hankered to be part of the Kiss scene, even those who weren't die-hard groupies. Hotel desk clerks, waitresses at the coffee shops, local reporters, airplane attendants, airport check-in agents, the girls at the Hertz counters—they were thrilled to meet anyone connected to Kiss and get a chance to go to the concert with a backstage pass.

It was strange to see them hours later backstage, not in their professional uniforms or work outfits but in flashy clothes like Capri pants, high heels, fishnet stockings, diaphanous blouses, and miniskirts, and laden with costume jewelry, ankle bracelets, and gold-plated earrings glinting in the brightly lit corridors. There was such a plenitude of girls at some shows that a long queue of them formed along the wall of the backstage area, like the receiving line of a debutante ball. They typically looked as if they had spent hours teasing and fluffing up their hair and heaping on lip gloss as thick as varnish.

It was even stranger to see many of these same girls the following morning at the hotel, leaving the Kiss members' rooms at 6:30 a.m., in time to make it back home and change for work. As Paul explained it to me, most of these girls probably had boyfriends in town who would have to devote months—maybe years—and spend hundreds of dollars on dates and gifts to get them to say yes to sex. With Kiss, it only took one night and a free concert ticket.

Gene was characteristically more blunt about it. He relished the nightly ritual of girls making their way up to his room where he lay sprawled out on his bed. The girls would be cooing and giggling in his presence—"awestruck" as he put it—and then their clothes would drop to the floor. Within seconds, they would be quivering on the bed, panting and moaning, offering themselves to him like sacrificial lambs, as he described it. To many girls, Gene had a God-like status. As he told me, it was essential to have at least one girl per night, preferably more, and "come twice to fall asleep." Filling this prescription was never a problem for Gene. "Everybody wants to fuck," he said.

It wasn't hard to understand all of this. To many of the girls, Kiss were superstars from another galaxy, far beyond the dismal life and torpid pace of Anonymous City, USA. Why would they want to pass up a once-in-a-lifetime chance to have sex with someone famous and create a memory that would linger forever, a kind of brush with immortality? It might not be ennobling, but it was a phenomenon so often repeated that one was tempted to call its lure universal.

The hard-core drug users had been put out to pasture by the time I joined the Kiss tour. The most notorious offenders had been purged. But drugs and drinking are almost always around the rock scene, particularly on a tour with a grueling schedule. Despite the efforts to get rid of all the more extreme cases, the scene could still be pretty seamy. One crew manager who was around for a few tours was constantly drunk, carrying a bottle in his hard shell briefcase to the halls each day. He was frequently found passed out in his hotel room or on the crew bus. Even on later tours, the problem persisted. A technician who was a whiz at fixing the stage gear turned a tidy profit selling drugs on the side to supplement his salary. He reportedly served a prison term in New York State. A couple of technicians were busted in Florida on one tour for drug possession and were never heard from again.

Local suppliers were often caught up in sordid and dangerous dealings, particularly the limo services. In Detroit, a popular driver was banned from working with Kiss after he repeatedly showed up at the hotel stinking of liquor. The band members said he'd been swerving the limo back and forth along the expressway coming in from the airport. In Alabama, a team of beefy drivers who looked like linebackers stuffed into sweat pants and zipper jackets made it clear they could get "anything you want," including cocaine and prostitutes. They ran a ring of local working girls and did drug deals when they weren't driving. In Texas, we once used a pair of drivers for shows in that region who looked like overgrown college seniors at a prom, gussied up in their uniforms of tuxes, ruffled shirts, and red satin bow ties. We called them Lummox Limo and hired them to come to California to drive for us for a swing of shows on a later tour. They were elated. We later found out why they wanted the job so badly. They were reportedly running a cocaine distribution operation, and one of the drivers had been jailed.

Kiss had to "keep on gigging," which was the way Peter described Bill Aucoin's desire to stay on tour for as long as possible. Road managers played a key role in this. Their official duties were to arrange the travel details to and from the hotels, airports, and venues, but they were also expected to perform as traveling comedians who could keep the Kiss members in stitches. Bill spared no effort to find road managers who were true *farceurs* whose routines were good enough to keep the band happy and make the long trips fun. Road managers had to cart around plenty of toys, novelties, party favors, practical jokes, and gizmos to entertain everyone while traveling. All of this filled a veritable Christmas trunk that was carried on board airplanes. The crew always referred to the road managers as "babysitters," but their job also required them to be mood elevators.

Frank Scinlaro, a jovial, barrel-chested veteran of rock tours who spoke in a distinct "New Yawk" accent and sported a full beard, was one of Kiss's more beloved road managers. A veteran of Alice Cooper and '60s groups like the Shangri-Las, Frankie came on board to "smooth things out" when the previous road manager became frazzled from the band's unending demands. His most memorable caper was in St. Louis when we were en route to the arena. Ace and Gene were in the backseat and I was squeezed in across from them on the limo's jumpseat. Frankie sat in front, next to the driver. We were stopped at a light, and next to us on the right was a car full of girls headed for the arena. The girls saw the limo and started screaming, "It's Kiss! It's Kiss!" Gene and Ace could see them but they kept their window rolled up. The girls started screaming louder to Frankie, who had his window rolled down. They wanted Kiss to roll down their window. The light changed, and both the limo and the car full of screaming girls accelerated. With the cars moving neck and neck, Frankie pushed the upper half of his body out the window, his head bobbing in the wind and his tongue making quick, darting motions back and forth. As the cars continued their breakneck pace, Frankie yelled at the girls, almost falling out the window, "Forget about Kiss, girls. I do everything!" Gene and Ace were hysterical, choking with laughter.

Some of the duties that fell to road managers were an extension of their personal involvement with the band members. In Washington State, a Kiss road manager was dispatched to visit an old flame of one of the band to talk her into getting an abortion. Since the last tour she'd supposedly become pregnant. A quip often tossed out in interviews by Kiss—"We like to go back to cities every nine months just to see what our children look like"—may not have been entirely a joke.

Peter delighted in pushing the road managers to their limits, having them on call around the clock. He felt this was the best way to test their capabilities. On one occasion, the test came perilously close to exceeding those limits. In East St. Louis, Illinois, a Kiss road manager had to fend off a gun-toting troublemaker at a grungy rock club in a bad part of town who had gotten into a shoving match with Peter and Ace and stolen Ace's leather jacket. The road manager had been ordered to get the jacket back. The next day I called Howard Marks to tell him about it, but Howard surprised me by saying that he had already heard the story. A tour staffer had called him very late the previous night, waking him with the news. "Don't worry, Howard, none of our guys was shot," was the way it was put to him.

Burnout caused the lifespan of road managers to be very short, usually lasting no more than a couple of tours. The constant craziness of dealing with both the rigors of the road and the quirks of four wildly divergent personalities became an unbearable burden. To travel with Kiss was to be a part of a wild bunch of marauding outlaws and misfits, busting loose in every town and shooting up the local landscape in a twenty-four-hour frenzy, then heading out for the next town. But this was how the perpetual motion machine worked that was making Kiss the biggest group in the country.

Glitter and Grit

It was to be a glittering week of sold-out shows at the Forum, celebrity bashes, and girls galore in Hollywood as Kissmania was sweeping the country. Kiss was booked into an unprecedented three-night stand at the Forum in L.A. on August 26, 27, and 28, 1977. The Forum can hold 17,000, and three nights meant a potential of over 50,000 fans, a major event that didn't go unnoticed by Casablanca Records. This was Kiss Week in L.A. and Casablanca had taken out a huge billboard on Sunset Strip to promote Kiss's Forum engagement and their current album, *Love Gun,* which had rocketed to the Top Ten of the *Billboard* charts. The band was shuttled around town in a convoy of stretch limos to visit radio stations like KMET where Kiss did on-the-air announcements to help promote the show. Press conferences were scheduled, interviews were lined up with phalanxes of reporters waiting their turn, and parties were in full swing every night. Casablanca's well-oiled hype machine was in high gear. Nothing could prevent Kiss's Forum stint from being an event of massive proportions. Or so it seemed.

A driving rain was pouring down at LAX when I came in earlier in the week on a night flight from Tucson, Arizona. The next day, the city was gleaming as the sun broke through the clouds and brought temperatures to the 80 degree mark. Rain in L.A. always left the city radiant, seeming to wash away much of the smog and haze. I was driving down Sunset Strip toward Casablanca's offices to meet with some of the staff. Much of the week's activity for the Kiss promotion was centered there.

The sun's glare drenched the offices of the Casablanca building in the heart of West Hollywood at the foot of the Sunset Hills. The indoor palm trees, wicker chairs, and ceiling fans had been deliberately placed to give the place a movie set feel, like Rick's Cafe in the Humphrey Bogart classic with the same name as the record company. I peered into Neil Bogart's office; he was talking on two phones at the same time. He waved to me and flashed a smile while pointing at the window behind him. He wanted to make sure I saw the Kiss billboard outside. Music was booming out of every office.

Neil was the archetypal record man, the epitome of success in the music business. Customarily dressed L.A. sharp—fancy shirts worn open-collared, gold chain around his neck, dressy suits with wide lapels, lizard shoes—he sported a fuzzy bouffant of brown hair. Neil was an intensely driven man who was widely acknowledged as the industry's oracle of hype in the '70s era. He had a habit of slapping people on the back and sometimes saying things like, "Workin' on a groovy thing, baby!"—his way of keeping the troops charged up. The Casablanca operation was one of hyperkinetic intensity.

Curiously, while both Kiss and Bill Aucoin respected Neil's promotional savvy at selling records, they kept their distance from him for the most part. Neil's boundless energy at promoting Kiss had been crucial to their success, but their relationship with him wasn't overly chummy. Bill envied Neil's success and the high profile he was getting in the press as a music mogul, a role which Bill craved for himself. And Kiss felt Neil was too much the hypester, always switched on to the point of overkill, eager to pounce on the next fad. Paul thought Neil's personality was like that of a game show host. The cover story of *New West*'s October 10, 1977, issue touted Neil as "The Ultimate Sultan of Sell."

I walked down the hall to talk with one of Neil's lieutenants about arrangements for the Kiss shows and the guest list for the big party Casablanca was throwing. It would be at Osko's, a space-age disco the size of several basketball courts. The guest list guaranteed that Osko's would be crawling with Playboy Bunnies, centerfolds, and models.

Our home for the upcoming week was L'Ermitage Hotel in Beverly Hills. Kiss had chosen this hotel since it was new—they hated anyplace old—and it had already earned a reputation for *ne plus ultra* standards of luxury. These were all critical considerations; cost was never a factor. The rooms were about $175 a night, triple the price of every other luxury hotel in town at that time. Kiss always insisted on checking into the top hotels wherever they were to maintain their superstar mystique.

Paul never liked the Beverly Wilshire anyway, saying it was "the kind of place my aunt would stay at." In other words, too stuffy. Gene despised The Beverly Hills Hotel. It was much too Hollywoody with all those "movie directors in berets running around and fat guys smoking stinky cigars." In any case, neither of these hotels would accommodate rock groups. L'Ermitage, with its canopied beds, wall-to-wall breakfronts with full bars and electronic entertainment centers, sunken living rooms, personal butlers, and Chippendale dining room chairs was the logical choice.

Ace appeared at my door around 11:00 the morning of the first Kiss show. It was unusual to see him awake at that early hour, but he wanted some spending money to go and hunt for vintage guitars while he was in town. He told me "a couple of grand" would be enough, and I went down to the lobby to get the cash out of my safety deposit box. Part of my job was always to have a lot of cash on hand for such things. When I got back to my room, Ace scribbled a receipt for the money and was out the door.

My phone rang a few minutes later. It was Bill Aucoin. He was in L.A. for the Forum shows and was also at L'Ermitage. He sounded like his usual chipper self, ribbing me about how many restaurants I planned to squeeze into the L.A. trip between orgies with groupies. But then his voice shifted gears a bit, becoming more low-key and serious. "Make sure you check the box office statements very carefully every night. The shows will do okay, but they won't all be sold out. The promoter's getting nervous, but it's nothing to get crazy over. Just make sure you tell him you don't have the authority to make any changes in the contract without my approval or the band's."

Of course, he was right. I didn't have that authority but it had never been an issue. For the most part, the promoters were bowled over with how well they had been doing with Kiss shows and were usually falling all over themselves to throw favors to the band. But this was a volatile business which could change in a heartbeat. Bill's call tipped me off to prepare for something I hadn't yet encountered. I didn't know it yet, but not only were the Kiss shows in deep trouble, the promoter was in even bigger trouble and Kiss was going to get stiffed.

To sell out the three shows at the Forum Kiss would have to draw 50,000 people in total—7,000 more than the 43,000 fans who had turned up on August 20, 1976, just one year earlier, when they headlined at nearby Anaheim Stadium. Fun Productions, an L.A. outfit which had produced the Anaheim success and was enjoying a reputation as a hot rock show promoter, was orchestrating the Kiss stint at the Forum. The impresario behind Fun was David Forest, a young promoter who had had a winning streak in recent years producing rock shows, including Cat Stevens, David Bowie, and ZZ Top. Bill Aucoin liked him and the two shared a penchant for extravagance.

David's flair for lavish excess had been in full bloom at the Anaheim show. A sprawling backstage hospitality area had been put up for the amusement of hundreds of invited guests. Under enormous circus tents and awnings could be found arcade games, pool tables, masseuses, champagne bar, dining tables, waiters and waitresses in uniform, buffet tables offering roast turkeys and steamship rounds of beef, a kaleidoscope of salads and fruits, and an ice cream stand. Outside the tents were a swimming pool, barbecue, and carnival rides. By comparison, the amenities at Roosevelt Stadium had been on a piker's scale. Guests overflowed into the Anaheim party, which started around noon on the day of the concert. By nightfall, after the supporting acts had finished and Kiss was set to end the show, hundreds had to be turned away because there was physically no room for them. I had to rescue a college friend and his date who were stranded in a parking lot; they had guest passes but were turned away at the backstage gate as the line snaked to the edges of the stadium grounds.

This Dionysian extravaganza was paid for largely by Kiss and had been exorbitantly expensive. But that didn't deter Bill Aucoin from calling upon David for yet another Kiss show the next year. But this time David would have to pay more money. The guarantee for the three Forum dates would be $60,000 a night, totaling $180,000, versus the $100,000 guarantee that Kiss had been paid at Anaheim, a record for Kiss at the time. David agreed to those terms.

Tickets for the shows were $7.50, $8.50, and $9.50. The economics of the deal for this series of shows dictated that unless close to 90 percent of the tickets for all three shows were sold, a difficult feat even for the biggest draws, the promoter would lose money. In short, the downside was huge and the upside was limited. David could make money only on the last few thousand tickets before the show was sold out. I asked Bill why a promoter would be willing to take such an enormous risk. Bill responded by saying that David was a *real* rock 'n' roll promoter," the type he liked, who wasn't afraid to take big chances and promote in a big way. He was perfect for Kiss.

The first show at the Forum was sold out and the second show was moving well, but when the third show went on sale, ticket sales started sputtering. The show was in trouble. For a three-night stand to be considered a success, both from the promoter's standpoint as well as the all-important perspective of the press, all the shows would have to sell out or come close to it. A third show with half a house would look terrible and create a disastrous media image for Kiss. In the world of show business, success is often measured by whether or not expectations are fulfilled. Doing three shows at the major venue in L.A., America's celebrity capital and a rock 'n' roll stronghold, without enough people in the audience to pack the place would make Kiss a laughingstock. The critics were always gunning for Kiss anyway, and this would just give them more ammunition.

It would also be a financial disaster for David Forest. Bill pressed David to drastically step up his advertising budget, but this can be dangerous for promoters anywhere and especially in a place like L.A., where ad costs are sky-high. The promoter may not be able to recoup the additional ad dollars by selling enough tickets to cover the outlay. Selling more tickets can, in effect, cost you too much money. But in the final week before the shows, Kiss and Casablanca kicked in money for a last-minute TV and radio blitz to boost ticket sales.

Backstage at the Forum during the late afternoon hours before the first show, Peter had reportedly become incapacitated, most likely from some form of tranquilizer. Groggy and fatigued, he was waiting in the dressing room with the group, who had just finished a sound check. A panicked Bill Aucoin was backstage. The solution cut right to the heart of the problem—get a sports doctor to come to the Forum right away and give Peter a shot to get him through the concert, hopefully without further complications. A doctor was rounded up quickly, apparently not a problem in L.A., and rushed backstage. He took care of Peter. The show would go on.

On the financial front, things were becoming more complicated. The audiences were big enough each of the three nights to make the shows look full. From the front of the house, it looked good. But as I was about to find out, it wasn't good enough for Kiss to get paid. The deal was that Kiss was supposed to get paid the balance of their guarantee on each of the first two nights of the engagement. On the third and final night, we were to get the last installment of the guarantee plus a payment for Kiss's share of the profits for the shows, if any. The Forum shows were an 85/15 split of the profits between Kiss and David Forest, and the shows were to be cross-collateralized. All of the costs for all three shows would be lumped together and treated as a single event.

I waited backstage on the last night for David Forest to come by the production office to start the show settlement. Promoters don't necessarily do their own settlements. They often send in a controller or an underling to do this work, reconciling the show's expenses with the box office income from ticket sales and paying the act. But for such an important engagement, where so much money had been risked, I expected David to appear. It was already after 10:00 p.m. and Kiss was in the middle of their show. I was sitting by myself in a swivel chair in a tiny cubbyhole of an office set aside for the production staff backstage. Most backstage areas resemble a sort of rock 'n' roll pigsty, and this one was no exception. I could hardly move my chair without bumping into some of the myriad litter—electrical cables, broken cases, busted amps, assorted tools, sprockets, wrenches, spools of heavy-duty black tape, and fragments of smashed guitars from the two previous shows' finales, not to mention the cigarette butts, fast-food containers, and empty beer cans.

After I had been waiting for an hour, I walked about 20 yards toward the side of the stage to watch the show's finale. The din of the audience had exploded into a roar. Ear-splitting explosions had been set off on stage. Paul was strutting to the staccato beat of "Love Gun," the title track from their current album. To my right was the stage, about 8 feet high above the floor, and in front of me was a huge barricade and set of gates designed to keep the fans contained and away from the stage. Two of the guys from Cheap Trick, the opening act, were next to me.

A thick white cloud of smoke engulfed the front of the arena. A rain of fireworks came shooting from the ceiling onto the stage, looking like Roman candles bursting in flashes of red, blue, white, and yellow. A hydraulic device lifted

Peter and his drum riser at least 20 feet into the air, revealing an enormous painted Chinese dragon with glowing eyes and a serpent's tongue. It unfolded from underneath the drum riser and rose high above the stage, nearly scraping the overhead lighting grid. Elevated platforms on opposite sides of the stage lifted Ace and Gene nearly 10 feet high as the platforms thrust forward. "Rock 'n' Roll All Nite," the show's climactic conclusion, was in full blast. Paul was swaggering and shimmying, waving his guitar and smashing it to the floor, splintering it into dozens of pieces. Some of the pieces flew out into the audience where fans fought for them like souvenir baseballs, jumping on top of one another to grab them. Streaks of what looked like the blue electricity from an electrical storm shot out from behind the drum riser as Peter's pounding meshed with Ace's droning guitar sustain.

Across the stage, Gene was high atop his own platform, motioning his bass in unison with Ace's guitar to the throbbing beats of the last song. Gene's chest armor was splattered with the stage blood that had gushed from his mouth during his earlier blood-spitting ritual in "God of Thunder." His hair had been singed when the flames from his fire-breathing stunt got caught in a downdraft from one of the large industrial fans placed on stage and shot upward. Ace was starting to totter from the occasional jerks of the lift platforms as he struggled to keep his balance. The clanging metal sound of the guitars droned on and a blizzard of confetti swept the stage, pelting the front rows of the Forum audience like rainbow-colored hail. A fiery explosion on stage triggered a white-hot flash of split second's duration. The final bomb exploded, making a cracking sound, like concrete being split into pieces with a steel hammer. The rumble was of stomach-wrenching intensity.

The four Kiss members came running down the staircase at the rear of the stage, bath towels draped over their shoulders and around their necks. They were soaking wet and their hair looked like they had just mopped the floor with it. A cadre of bodyguards and uniformed security was stationed in front of them and behind, clearing a path with flashlights in hand. Kiss hurtled toward a fleet of six stretch Lincoln Continentals, and as if on cue, girlfriends, wives, groupies, parents, bodyguards, and buddies all leapt like lemmings from predesignated spots into the waiting limos. It took only a few seconds and the limos sped out the Forum's back ramp.

I found Bill and David in the Forum Club, a dining area dominated by a large bar, huddled in a corner booth, immersed in deep conversation. Only a few other people were in the room. They were sitting beneath one of several murals which dotted the room, depicting players in action from various sports. Bill introduced me. This wasn't the first time I had met David, but I doubted that he remembered me. A dark-haired, engaging man, David, 29, looked drained, as if he hadn't slept in days. A brightly-hued floral print shirt hung limply on his frame. He greeted me nonchalantly, and after a bit of awkward banter, Bill motioned for me to get up from the table and have a private word with him.

"We're not going to get paid tonight," Bill told me. "David's refusing to pay the balance of the guarantee he owes Kiss. He says the show cost him a fortune to produce and he's looking at a huge loss—he says tens of thousands of dollars—which he can't afford. You're not going to be able to settle anything tonight. I've told the booking agency to handle the matter of collecting the monies for Kiss. They'll call us tomorrow." And that was it. Bill returned to the table to talk with David. I was basically excused for the night. It seemed so matter-of-fact, just another little business problem, to be dealt with "tomorrow." Neither David nor Bill seemed terribly upset, and there weren't any harsh words or histrionics. Everything was strangely serene. I was the last one in the place as the bartender started to lock up the cash register.

A day later I was summoned by Bill to come to a meeting at the offices of Bushkin, Kopelson, Gaims & Gaines, a prominent Beverly Hills law firm which represented many entertainment clients and whose senior partner, Henry Bushkin, was Johnny Carson's longtime attorney and business adviser. We met in a large, modern conference room around an oval-shaped table. The firm had been retained by Kiss's booking agency, ATI, and would also represent Kiss and Aucoin Management in the dispute with David Forest and Fun Productions. David was at the far end of the table, across from Bill. Marvin Mann, the controller for Aucoin Management, sat next to me, and across from us was a young man who had a similar position with Fun Productions.

Bill was not happy about being at this kind of meeting. He seemed to dislike meetings with lawyers, accountants, and business people where the subject was financial, something outside his natural milieu. He disliked even more the fact that there was a considerable degree of unpleasantness attached to this meeting. In blunt terms, Kiss had gotten stiffed, and he was, in a way, on the hook. He had chosen David as Kiss's promoter.

Bill was dressed in casual but expensive-looking L.A.-style clothes that suited his trim frame: a crisply pressed, tapered print shirt with two darts in the back, tan slacks with small pleats and knifelike creases, and a pair of brown slip-ons with a buttery, glove-leather look. David looked more laid back. A pale pastel cotton-knit tennis shirt with a polo collar fit snugly across his chest. He had on faded jeans with some obscure designer logo on the back pocket. He wore sneakers. David had a dour look, and he fidgeted with one of the freshly sharpened pencils that had been placed next to the pads of lined paper in front of everyone's seat at the conference table.

The meeting began with Bill making a speech about how he had picked David for the job because of the superb promotion he'd done for Kiss the previous year in Anaheim, the biggest single show of their career. Bill also stated that David had relentlessly pursued him to get the Kiss business for the Forum shows. Bill said David was completely confident that Kiss could sell out three consecutive nights.

It became clear that the mood had shifted considerably from what I had observed last night after the show. Money was the subject of this meeting, and in rock 'n' roll, nothing takes a backseat to money. There wasn't any of Bill's trademark lighthearted banter or witty asides. As for David, he had relished being in the center of attention, at least for this week, as L.A.'s biggest promoter of America's biggest rock act, basking in the media coverage which surrounded the event. Kiss, with all of its flash and glitter, was the type of act David loved to promote and Bill, a master of hype, was the type of manager he liked best. But all of this was now irrelevant. The shows were over, the festivities had concluded, and David was looking at a potentially ruinous financial disaster. This was now a Serious Business Matter and the mood was decidedly downbeat.

Bill went on to say that this campaign of David's, beseeching him to agree to the three shows, was so persuasive he ultimately succeeded in erasing any doubts that Bill had in his mind. Bill agreed to it, provided that David would be willing to guarantee the same amount of money for each of the three shows. In other words, the guarantee would have to be $60,000 for each show, a staggering sum in 1977. David had agreed to this and ATI had issued the contracts. Bill kept talking, agitatedly bouncing his leg under the table. I was impressed by the force and simplicity of Bill's version of events.

And then David began to speak. I was expecting the kind of long-winded and whining harangue that promoters are wont to make when they have bitten off more than they can chew, guaranteeing too much money to acts.

Promoters are gamblers playing for big stakes. Success serves to validate the seat-of-the-pants judgment they pride themselves on. When they lose, they grasp at anything that might cut their losses. They turn their gamesmanship to trying to get a giveback from the act, a reduction in the previously agreed-to guarantee. In other words, a guarantee isn't always a guarantee, especially if a promoter "gets hurt" and takes a big loss on a show. This is an integral part of the operational logic of the concert business. Promoters are always looking for givebacks from acts, through negotiations with the manager or the booking agency, to salvage what they can from the aftermath of bad business judgment.

David, surprisingly, seemed to be agreeing with every word Bill said. He didn't argue a single point. He didn't contradict any part of Bill's businesslike peroration. Then he switched gears. I braced myself for the truth about what his intentions were of settling the unpaid balance due Kiss.

"I was crazy to sign the contract in the first place. You must have known anybody would be out of his mind to agree to guarantee this kind of money.

Obviously, I was crazy and you should've known it. How could anyone sign something like this? I know I signed it, but I was crazy. And I would be even crazier to pay the money now since the shows cost me a fortune to promote and I'm looking at a gigantic loss even without paying the rest of Kiss's guarantee. I could go out of business if I paid Kiss any more money." David was breathing deeply and perspiration was trickling down the back of his neck.

Bill became furious. His face reddened, his neck vein started to bulge, and he jerked his chair as close to the conference table as it would take him.

"What kind of bullshit is that, David? You knew what you were getting into. It was your idea. What am I supposed to tell the band now? That you agreed to the money but changed your mind?"

The decibel level had risen sharply. Bill could not have relished the thought of having to tell Kiss that his hand-picked promoter had stiffed them. He seemed to try to avoid being associated with any kind of bad news and often relegated such unpleasant duty to subordinates. Everyone else in the room sat motionless. David retorted with more of the same, this time in a louder voice and a more animated style. His hands were flailing in all directions, and when the pitch of his voice reached a certain intensity level, it started to sound like a squeal. And then Bill started screaming. And David again. And then more Bill and more David, back and forth, like a ping-pong match, with occasional outbursts from Marvin Mann, our lawyer, and me. Everyone wanted to get into the act. "You're crazy." "I'm crazy." Back and forth between David and Bill, dragging on interminably. It became ludicrous. I looked at Marvin and his eyes rolled to the ceiling. This kind of a confrontation, where everyone communicates at the top of his lungs in a sort of verbal jujitsu, was new to me.

The meeting was spinning out of control. Our lawyer grumbled something about filing a lawsuit and attaching the receipts from the box office. I hastily added that this sounded like a good move, and then Bill rebuked me for talking out of turn. He was right.

It's possible to attach box office monies collected by the building from the sale of tickets that haven't yet been disbursed to the promoter. The process of attaching the box office receipts before they pass on to the promoter is costly and cumbersome and can take months, possibly a year, to resolve depending upon how hard each side wants to litigate. It's seldom done except as a very last resort.

David stormed out of the room, angry and upset. Only our side remained. Here was the essence of what the concert promotion business was all about, an unstable mix of unequal parts of money, gambling, instinct, and ego. When an unexpected turn of events results in a blunder of major proportions, the reaction can be like spontaneous combustion. Emotions were at fever pitch and logic had evaporated.

The law firm proposed that they attempt to work out a settlement with Fun Productions and avoid getting involved in litigation. Bill agreed to stay out of it rather than run the risk of another clash. Within a few weeks, a tentative settlement took shape; Kiss would get a small portion of the monies they were due. Papers were exchanged and signed. It was much less than what had been guaranteed, but Bill was led to believe that Fun Productions' financial condition was precarious and that David could close down the business at any moment and Kiss would end up with nothing. Bill agreed to the deal. David Forest wouldn't be the last promoter to fall victim to the lure of fast money and big hype that made Kiss so seductive.

❖

Arriving in San Antonio's Hilton Rio Grande for two shows in November 1977, I picked up a manila envelope marked "special delivery" at the front desk. It was from my office. I would have to get everyone in Kiss to sign papers for their investment in coal mines. We had already discussed the investment at an earlier meeting with Carl Glickman, Howard Marks, and the band's lawyers. Kiss would be able to shelter from taxes substantial sums of their income, now huge, by investing in natural resources, something the federal government was then encouraging. The papers had to be notarized, and I used the Yellow Pages to find a notary public in town who would come to the hotel to witness Kiss's signatures. A small sixtyish woman showed up, and I took her from room to room for the signings. She seemed dumbstruck by how much hair the four of them had. This particular transaction didn't seem very important at the time, just another business formality. A decade later, it would prove to be crucial.

A three-night stand at Madison Square Garden in New York climaxed Kiss's tour in December. The Garden showed its appreciation by putting up a giant photo of Kiss, featuring Ace and his smoking guitar, on the billboard display of sports stars and performers that was outside the main marquee on Seventh Avenue. A double show at the Capitol Centre in suburban Washington, D.C. quickly followed. I took the Eastern Shuttle back to New York the morning after the second show. Inside my Hartmann attache was $50,000 in cash, part of the show's proceeds, all freshly minted $100 bills in cellophane packets. The money was to be deposited in a New York bank. When I got to the office, a large package awaited me atop my desk, all done up in cheerful Christmas wrapping from Bloomingdale's. It was an Italian espresso and cappuccino machine, a gift from Gene.

That week, Kiss's gross income from concerts and merchandise topped $300,000. Right after the New Year, Kiss would do two-night stands at the

Olympia in Detroit and the Chicago Stadium, mammoth indoor hockey arenas which could hold crowds of 20,000. Promoters were clamoring for Kiss. The band was shattering attendance records throughout the country, gleefully announcing to the press that they had broken the record previously set by Elvis. Kiss was so hot, ATI could have booked them for another six months on the road. But Bill Aucoin believed that this would have been overkill; he had other plans afoot for Kiss that were bigger still.

1

Opening the Floodgates

"Everything here is won-n-n-derful!"

Neil Bogart talking about Casablanca Records,
The Los Angeles Times "Calendar," February 4, 1979.

By early 1978 Kiss was the 800-pound gorilla of the music industry. They could go anywhere they wanted; they were unstoppable. Kiss was one of the top-grossing concert acts. A second tour of Japan in March, this time doing five shows in Tokyo's famed Budokan, was another smash, eclipsing the Beatles' record. Kiss's success was reaching monumental heights. An NBC News Special with Edwin Newman, *The Land of Hype and Glory*, featured Kiss. They were on the cover of virtually every music magazine in America; Kiss T-shirts, toys, and paraphernalia were flying out of the stores; they had won The People's Choice Award for the single, "Beth"; they had been immortalized in a series of Marvel Comics; they were named America's Favorite Rock Group in a Gallup Poll of teens. They had released so many albums, including live records and greatest hits repackages, that they showed up in as many as four slots in the *Billboard* charts at one time. Their makeup designs were now officially registered with the government as commercial trademarks; they were profiled in a feature article in *The New York Times Magazine,* a rarity for a rock group; and they had just finished a coast-to-coast concert tour of sell-out shows. Their gross income for 1977 had been a breathtaking $10.2 million. Their popularity had reached mythic proportions. And it was all beginning to go straight to everyone's head.

Bill Aucoin now saw Kiss as something bigger than a rock group. Touring had been great up to now, but who needed it anymore? It had done the job. "Does Led Zeppelin tour every year?" was how Paul put it. They didn't, and Kiss now saw themselves in Led Zeppelin's league. The proliferation of toys, comic books, T-shirts, and the like had already begun to create an image of Kiss as fantasy characters and not merely rock musicians. Something on a much grander scale was needed, something that would elevate Kiss to still more rarefied heights. Another album coupled with another tour would be ho-hum at best. Kiss had to become Super Kiss.

Bill was percolating a plan for this. He was in his element. Having propelled Kiss to record-breaking success, he could now unleash his considerable creativity to make Kiss even bigger. Bill's idea was to expand upon Kiss's group image, turning them into four individual larger-than-life superstars who were far more than simply a rock band and a concert act. He wanted Kiss to record *four* individual solo albums, not a group album. And Kiss would appear in a two-hour TV movie special for NBC, the first time a rock group would star in their own network movie. There would be a double-barreled assault by Kiss on TV and on multiple albums.

Bill had no problem persuading the group. They were ecstatic. Bill was a savvy salesman who knew how to hit the right buttons with his artists. Tired of touring anyway, they were tantalized by the idea of doing their own thing in the studio and appearing in America's living rooms in a special movie all about Kiss. Bill and Kiss fed on each other this way, with Bill always coming up with bigger and grander ideas which would boost their egos and flatter them. And what better way to further exploit the cult following each had developed than by making them into individual superstars? This new, improved Super Kiss concept had a lot of selling points.

Bill's Olympian plan seemed to be everything that was best about Kiss—daring, bold, unprecedented, ambitious, exciting, original, innovative, and, of course, expensive. But it was also overreaching. The campaign would turn out to be too much Kiss in too many ways. One of the axioms Bill had successfully followed for years was to limit Kiss's exposure and control the supply. By doing so, he heeded a cardinal rule of show business—always give the public a little less than it wants. Now, the floodgates were opening and the public was to be deluged with Kiss. It proved to be a critical juncture, one of those corners you turn only to discover, years later, that it took you down the wrong road. But we were about to turn that corner and shift into overdrive. Kiss was hitting on all cylinders.

I flew into L.A. in early May 1978. We were back at the Kiss campground in Beverly Hills, L'Ermitage Hotel. A tall, hulking giant standing about 6 feet 4 known as Mr. Tiny greeted me at the registration desk. He was Kiss's current road manager and would make sure they made it to the movie set on time each day, a job of no small importance. Kiss liked Mr. Tiny's bulldozing presence. Mr. Tiny set up command central in his hotel room, often sitting on his bed in a Buddha-like position, dispatching his team of bodyguards to keep tabs on the group.

Hanna-Barbera, the creators of Yogi Bear, would produce the movie for NBC within a four-week schedule in and around L.A. By the time I arrived, Kiss was already rehearsing. A fleet of Cadillac Sevilles with drivers took Kiss to the studio every morning where rehearsals, run-throughs, and coaching provided everyone in the group with a Berlitz-style crash course in how to act. Predictably, the script was being rewritten daily. Bill assigned one of his new executives, Rick Grimaldi, the task of working with Kiss and the writers each day to punch up the dialogue.

The script was a stumbling block from the beginning. Before production started scripts were circulating back and forth between Bill's office in New York and Hanna-Barbera in L.A., and drafts and redrafts were picked apart. The creative objective was for the movie to make Kiss look bigger than anything—no mere rock group—and to make them more outlandish than ever. Kiss would be immortalized as fantasy superheroes who had leaped from the world of rock 'n' roll into a magical TV universe that had been created for them. Although Kiss would perform a few songs, music was not central to the movie. The role model was more the Fantastic Four than Led Zeppelin. Kiss would be the ultimate fantasy heroes and everything about their stage personas would be magnified, intensified, and aggrandized to the Nth degree.

Kiss Meets the Phantom of the Park was chosen as the title, and Gordon Hessler, an Englishman who had directed mystery movies and TV shows, was picked as the film's director. The storyline had to do with four Kiss superheroes doing battle with an evil scientist, played by Anthony Zerbe at his most unctuous, who lives in an amusement park and threatens to make clones of Kiss. A liberal dose of special visual effects was budgeted. Each of the Kiss members would have unique superpowers, like X-ray eyes, laser vision, flying, invisibility, and so on. Apparently, NBC's idea was to throw in enough special effects goodies to keep the kiddies from turning the prime-time dial.

Gene made sure everyone knew what direction Kiss was taking with the TV movie. In a May 1978 Hanna-Barbera press release, he said: "When I originally read the script, the first thought that came into my mind was comic books. I think that's the flavor of this film. There's a villain and we're the good guys. It's your basic American dream situation where you've got superpowers. . . ." Kiss was beginning their transformation from the threatening, hard-core, decadent image symbolized by the *Destroyer* look of 1976 to a kinder, gentler, and more benign appeal that would fit comfortably in the pages of a superhero comic book.

Shooting a movie was a rigorous ordeal for Kiss. Up early every morning, six days a week, and hanging around a set for hours waiting for something to happen wasn't the kind of fast-lane lifestyle they were used to on the road. Some of the movie crew cracked jokes about how long the glamour boys of rock would last or if they would even finish the movie at all. Teaching the four leads how to act on the job wasn't easy. Predictably, Gene and Paul were the most disciplined. With Ace and Peter, everyone was glad that they usually made it to the set each day. They often appeared to be half-asleep, eyes drooping and bundled up in terry cloth robes to ward off the early morning chill in the Hollywood Hills where exterior scenes around a swimming pool were shot. Other scenes were filmed at Magic Mountain, an amusement park about an hour from L.A., where a mock concert was staged for the movie's climax.

Peter was battling his own personal demons during the movie's filming. The shooting schedule was constantly being rejiggered to accommodate him. Toward the end of the filming, Peter exploded in anger in his suite at the L'Ermitage, smashing a guitar while in a fight with a girl he was seeing in L.A. At 4:00 a.m., he phoned Fritz Postlethwaite, Kiss's tour manager who was on location for the movie production, telling him to "call my lawyer—I just killed someone." Luckily, he hadn't. Peter's girlfriend eventually became his second wife despite her close call with a guitar.

Just before Halloween on the night of October 28, 1978, *Kiss Meets the Phantom of the Park* aired on NBC. Kiss was seen on national TV for two hours by tens of millions of people in their own movie, a first for a rock group. The ratings weren't record-breaking, but the movie did pull in the expected audience of teens and subteens in large numbers. A screening party was held for Kiss, their friends, and the people who worked for them at Aucoin Management, ATI, Glickman/Marks Management, and other companies. The mood was festive, and while the movie was airing, everyone cheered Kiss on, laughing at all the right moments and applauding feverishly at the end. When the house lights went up, smiles flashed and endless rounds of congratulations and accolades were heaped on Kiss. A fun time was had by all, except Kiss. Paul and Gene had a glazed look in their eyes and Peter was strangely subdued, almost withdrawn. His original dialogue had been so garbled that it was re-recorded with another actor's voice. Ace was busy telling jokes, unperturbed by what was on the screen, cackling from beginning to end.

In its October 28, 1978, review, *The Los Angeles Times* described *Kiss Meets the Phantom of the Park* as a "four star abomination . . . a five-minute idea for a cartoon disguised as a two-hour TV movie." There was little argument from Kiss; they hated the movie.

They didn't say so that night, but it became clear in the months that followed that they hated it. They thought the movie made them look like buffoons, putting them in ridiculous settings and playing the role of imitation comic book superheroes. "Well, we've just proven that none of us are actors," noted Paul, months later. They said they didn't look at all like a rock group. They were right about that, but wasn't that the point?

As time passed, their hatred of the film grew, and it became a real sore spot between them and Bill Aucoin. It was a major miscalculation which Bill took the heat for and which opened the first major fissure in the Kiss-Aucoin relationship. The movie played in theaters overseas under various titles and continues to show up on late-night TV. It's become something of a cult classic, a camp version of a rock 'n' roll fantasy of the '70s. But to Kiss, it was a huge mess and they felt they were pandering to kiddies. For years, no one within the Kiss organization was allowed even to mention the subject of *Kiss Meets the Phantom of the Park* in their presence. But the damage had been done and for better or worse, America had just seen two hours of nonstop Kiss cavorting as superheroes on network TV. The new Super Kiss image had been indelibly ingrained in the public mind and there was no turning back.

And the movie was only part of the new thrust. For the first time in the history of the record business, there would be four solo albums from one band all released *simultaneously* on the same day. The albums were slated for release in September, when kids would be going back to school and in time for the TV movie promotion. Each of the solos would be the consummate creative *oeuvre* of each band member, his statement to the world of rock and to the public that he had arrived and deserved to be taken seriously as an artist. That was the thrust of Bill's concept, to give them credibility as musicians. And Casablanca saw it as a jackpot for the record retailers, a quadruple Kiss release on one day. Neil Bogart was prepared to let loose a blaze of publicity.

The recording sessions were supposed to start once the movie's principal photography was completed. Four separate albums required four separate studios, four separate producers, four separate production staffs, four separate budgets, and on down the list. Gene, Paul, and Peter opted to stay in L.A. to record their albums, while Ace would go back to New York. I stayed in L.A. All of this was going to cost a lot of money, and it would all be happening at once. As always, Kiss refused to skimp on anything.

Studios were booked, then unbooked. Producers and engineers were hired and fired. The minions required to attend to Kiss's daily needs—drivers, bodyguards, cooks, maids, valets, secretaries, technicians, assistants—were employed and deployed. My job was to find them suitable mansions or penthouses where they could retreat to a comfortable repose when they weren't in the studio recording. When Beverly Hills real estate agents sniffed that Kiss was in town, the switchboard at my hotel lit up like a Christmas tree. And there had to be appropriate transportation, too. Mercedes, Rolls-Royces, Porsches, and Cadillacs formed the core of the Kiss fleet of luxury vehicles. Musicians, almost forgotten in this whirlwind, were also needed. Four sets for four albums and nothing but the best session musicians available. A ton of money was required for all this, and the bills kept pouring in.

Peter rented a baronial Tudor mansion in the posh Holmby Hills section in what's become known as the "golden triangle," midway between Bel Air and Beverly Hills. The home was once occupied by Vincent Price and, of course, came with a legend of its own. The mansion had too much of everything—an endless maze of bedrooms, living rooms, dens, a billiard room, screening room, wine cellar, secret hideaways, guest quarters, tennis courts, garages, and an Olympic-sized swimming pool. On weekends, Peter would throw parties for his friends and the staff in L.A., roaming grandly from room to room. The next day, Peter would get on the phone and tell everyone he could reach he'd just thrown the most lavish bash at his mansion and the guests included such luminaries as Cheryl Ladd, David Janssen, and Raquel Welch, along with a host of others. Peter had a very vivid imagination. Few, if any, celebrities ever came. After a few months in L.A., he came to like "this Hollywood Babylon bullshit."

At the time, Peter was recuperating from a car accident. On the last day of shooting for the Kiss movie, after his scenes were finished, Peter was in a rented Porsche that collided into a street lamp and skidded across a major intersection in Marina del Rey. Within minutes, the car had been engulfed by flames and it was quickly reduced to a charred rubble. Strips of burnt rubber tire tracks were practically embedded in the street. Peter wasn't seriously injured but Fritz Postlethwaite was badly burned in the crash. Two months of hospital treatment and extensive physical therapy were required to get him back into shape.

Vini Poncia, who had worked for years with Richard Perry, producer for the Pointer Sisters, took charge of Peter's album. The result was an album that was true to Peter's background and taste, softer than the others and with an R&B influence in many of the songs. It was the type of music that Peter had grown up with.

Paul rented a low-slung, ranch-style house buried in one of the canyons behind Beverly Hills and tooled around town in a white Rolls-Royce. When Paul showed up for the first day of recording at a studio in the Valley where we'd cut a deal, he decided by midafternoon that he didn't like the place. Switching studios cost us our $60,000 deposit, nearly half of the album's total budget. "It's cheaper than not doing an album," huffed Paul. His penchant for snippy remarks like that one was one reason that people were often uptight around him.

Paul also parted with the producer, Jeff Glixman, who had recently worked with Kansas, a chart-topping band in the mid-'70s. Paul and Jeff didn't hit it off; Paul wanted to be in control of the album and produce it himself. Jeff was gone after a short time, but under the terms of his contract, Paul had to pay him anyway and Jeff got producer's credit for nearly half of the songs. Paul's solo album was the most Kisslike, but more technically polished and not as head-pounding.

Gene always had a problem in L.A. because he didn't drive. He was carted around in a black Cadillac Coupe de Ville driven by his bodyguard, Eddie Balandas, who also doubled as the announcer for the Kiss shows. Eddie, a husky, athlete type with slicked-back blond hair, had become a virtual alter ego of Gene's and for years was his gatekeeper to the outside world. Gene found a penthouse on Wilshire Boulevard near Westwood Village which served as his base.

Gene had his own angle for promoting his solo album—he would assemble an all-star cast to play on it. Gene's "special guests," as they were credited, were flown in from all around the country and included Bob Seger, Cher, Helen Reddy, Janis Ian, Donna Summer, members of Cheap Trick and Aerosmith, veteran guitarist Jeff "Skunk" Baxter, and the Azusa Citrus College Choir. The album included a rendition of "When You Wish Upon A Star," from Walt Disney's *Pinocchio*. Gene's solo album was a very ambitious production calculated to show off as many musical influences as possible. Kiss collaborator Sean Delaney produced the record with Gene.

I didn't have much to do with Ace's album. He stayed at home in New York City and worked at studios in New York and Connecticut with producer Eddie Kramer. Ace and Eddie clicked. Ace's record turned out to be the heaviest and the murkiest of the four solos. Songs like "Ozone" and "Wiped-Out" rhapsodized about being wasted and hoping to find girls who'd want to be zombies, too. Ace's record was the most disciplined in one respect—it was the least expensive of the four to produce.

Kiss labored on, working on a tight recording schedule in order to complete the albums on time. They all had to be ready on the same date to allow for them to be pressed and shipped to the stores. Beautifully painted covers, each featuring a full-face painting of the respective Kiss member, had been commissioned by a top illustrator named Eraldo Carugati. Auras of red, green, blue, and purple radiated behind the individual Kiss faces, creating a three-dimensional effect.

A massive promotional and advertising campaign had been orchestrated by Casablanca, touted as the biggest in record business history—$2.5 million. The budget included $800,000 for TV ads, $400,000 for radio spots, $800,000 for newspapers and magazines, and $500,000 for various in-store promotional displays. The release of the four solos was planned to tie in with the air date of the TV movie on October 28. It would be a promotion-packed onslaught of Kiss at full blast.

Aucoin Management was bolstering Casablanca's efforts, churning out hype of its own. The albums would contain promotion gimmicks, each one featuring a fold-out poster of the individual Kiss member and a flier listing merchandise that could be ordered through the Kiss Army Fan Club. Kiss had successfully used album inserts in the past to promote their mail-order business and to give fans a freebie, like a cardboard gun with a Kiss logo on it for the *Love Gun* album.

Thousands of elaborate press kits, comparable to those put together by major Hollywood studios to promote movies, were sent to journalists around the country. The kits featured color reproductions of the Carugati paintings, cassette tapes of interviews with the individual Kiss members, color slides and prints of Kiss's latest publicity photos, and mountains of press releases. Full-color Kiss picture disks would also be pressed, then a record industry innovation. A special Kiss 4-Pack plastic bag was designed for retailers to promote the sale of all four solo albums as a single purchase. Even the overseas licensees of Casablanca got into the act. Pye Records in the U.K. would issue four singles from each of the solos, pressed in colored vinyl and packaged in picture bags containing a paper mask of the appropriate Kiss member. The Kiss promotion would be a public relations and media event of Klondike proportions.

95

In a final, unprecedented move, Casablanca announced that there would be a grand total of nearly *five million records* of the four Kiss solos shipped nationwide. This wasn't just unprecedented, it was unbelievable. Even the music industry, no stranger to hype, found it hard to swallow. Neil Bogart, the mastermind behind the idea, was never bashful about predicting success. He was riding the crest of a wave with Casablanca as sales for the independent label would hit $100 million by the end of 1978. Neil shipped over one million copies of each solo album so that each would individually be "shipped platinum" and automatically be certified as a million-seller by the Recording Industry Association of America. That designation would be announced in the press the same week the records were released, with full-page ads in *Billboard* and other industry publications. (Not long after the Kiss solo releases, the RIAA changed its rules for awarding platinum records, requiring audited sales of one million copies and not just shipments.) In an interview with *The Los Angeles Times* on October 3, 1978, Neil revealed that he expected his $2.5 million ad campaign to push eight million Kiss solo albums into the stores by Christmas. It was huge. It was incredible. It was Super Kiss.

Advance previews of the new albums were held in eleven cities, including one press party at New York's Electric Lady Studios, where Kiss recorded many of their albums. By the end of September, the four solos were in the stores.

Not one of the albums made a big splash in the charts. Only Ace had a hit single, "New York Groove," which reached #13 in *Billboard*. His album peaked at #26. Gene's album reached #22. Paul's managed a #40 spot, but Peter's didn't make the Top 40. Despite the mammoth campaign, each of the solos sold only from 600,000 to 700,000 copies. Although the solos were different from one another stylistically (they weren't generic Kiss music), none outsold the others by much. They ended up doing collectively what a new Kiss album, a single album, probably would have done at the time, about two to three million copies. It was way below the blockbuster results Bill and Kiss had been predicting.

But for Casablanca, the Kiss solos were a bomb that threw the company into chaos. By January 1979, Casablanca had returns of over two million Kiss solos. Collectively, the solos sold a lot of albums by anyone's standard, but the industry works on the basis of expectations. If you press five million records, you are expected to sell that many; otherwise you've failed. That was essentially the perception with the Kiss solos. It was seen as a promotional boondoggle.

The financial consequences were even more calamitous. The millions of returned Kiss records delivered a crippling blow to their operations. Compounded with other failures they were having at the time, the Kiss release was a disaster. By early 1980, the company was put up for sale. Kiss had spent over $1 million to record the solos and pay for all of the attendant costs, double their original budget. Kiss would barely eke out a profit by the time recording expenses, commissions, and record company deductions for all of the returned records had been accounted for.

Casablanca's decision to release four solo Kiss albums hadn't been applauded by everyone in the company. Neil Bogart's earlier calamity with the Johnny Carson album of snippets from the *Tonight* TV show gave some senior executives cause for concern about repeating the same mistake. But Neil's instincts prevailed. It had come down to a matter of "style," and in the record business, that's typically the deciding factor in promotions. Neil's instincts had erred. The Kiss solo album promotion was a case of ultimate overhype. It was too much Kiss at one time, even for a group that seemed to be at the summit of their success.

Kiss's media blitz from the TV movie and the solo album promotion raged until the end of 1978. Whatever the shortcomings of this double-barreled tour de force, it was only a prelude to what was building to make the following year still bigger. The Kiss hype had reached the saturation point and the market was flooded with Kiss albums, solo albums, merchandise, toys, and the fallout from the TV movie. There was only one direction for Kiss to go to crystallize the new Super Kiss image that they craved. And that was, unsurprisingly, more Kiss.

The "mother of all shows," the "ultimate concert," and the "show of shows" was how Kiss's return to the concert trail in 1979 was described as ideas and plans were bandied about. There would be a new Kiss album, too. And there would be another massive promotional build-up to trumpet the return of Kiss to America's arenas and stadiums and to burnish the Super Kiss image. Bill Aucoin believed that to keep the media's interest from waning, Kiss always had to top themselves—clearly a Promethean task.

The opening round in the new campaign was set for February in New Orleans. Ric Aliberte, a young Aucoin Management promotion executive, scored a public relations coup by having Kiss selected as kings of the Mardi Gras, leading the annual parade as Grand Marshals. The parade would be on national TV and Kiss would be high atop an elaborate, tiered float, loaded with rhinestones and sparkles and glimmering jewels with silver and gold streamers trailing behind them. Kiss would be ensconced in an ormolued gazebo structure 10 feet above the base of the float, with each member of the group on his own throne. Like a quartet of Louis Quatorzes, they would wave to their subjects lining the streets all around them, casting out plastic commemorative tokens minted to memorialize the reign of Kiss. It fit perfectly with the new Super Kiss image.

Kiss loved the idea. There would be parties galore and everyone was advised by Bill and Ric to bring not one but two tuxedos to the event. There would be such a crush of festivities a back-up tux would be necessary. A promoter made an offer for Kiss to play the Louisiana Super Dome, the largest indoor stadium in America with a capacity of over 70,000. And the hype would be the perfect bridge between last year's events and the forthcoming tour.

But Kiss never made it to the Mardi Gras. "[Parade] Captains Cancel Mardi Gras" was the headline of the *New Orleans Times-Picayune* on February 21, 1979. A police strike was creating havoc in the city, and the mayor's office told Kiss's representatives they couldn't guarantee the usual level of security. As a result, all the Mardi Gras parades were canceled. Ric said that he received death threats, allegedly from the local police who were locked in a bitter dispute with the city. The Mardi Gras cancellation proved to be a harbinger of things to come.

So it was back to business. Kiss began an endless series of meetings to plan a tour of tours that would begin in June and run to the end of 1979. This was to be no ordinary show. Their last U.S. tour appearances had been in February 1978, and in a year's time, they had scaled new heights of fame, notoriety, success, and hype. Kiss could no longer hope to satisfy their expanding army of fans with simply another stage show. Bill got everyone psyched up about how big an event a tour of this magnitude would be and how spectacular the effects and the production had to be. Kiss was told to let their imaginations run wild. And they did.

Kiss wanted to expand their role as icons of pop culture, like Disney characters. Bill and Kiss felt they should widen their audience, reaching out beyond the hard rock fans that had been the base of their past success. By creating an even more stylized and fantastic persona, they would appeal to a younger demographic and broaden their market. That was what the TV movie had been about. It may not have come out the way they wanted, but the image had been established and now they had to try and build on it. Kiss couldn't be an ordinary rock group, having invested so much capital in making themselves look extraordinary. The music would also have a more commercial sound—less hard rock—and pop producer Vini Poncia was brought in for the new Kiss album. A brief collaboration in the studio with Gene, Paul, and producer Giorgio Moroder, who had a string of hits with Donna Summer and the *Midnight Express* soundtrack, went nowhere.

Vini had gained Kiss's respect for being able to produce Peter's solo album, a feat which had required considerable perseverance and stamina. Bearded and with tufts of dark brown hair, Vini was somewhat laconic, but his background as a songwriter and musician and his work with Melissa Manchester and Ringo Starr gave him solid credentials as a commercially successful producer. He would be an integral part of the new formula to multiply Kiss's success. Bill was characteristically confident that he could nimbly maneuver Kiss into position to tap the kiddie market and still hang on to the hard-rockers in their teens and early twenties. The album would be titled *Dynasty*.

All the stops were pulled out to organize Kiss's 1979 tour around the expanded Super Kiss concept. It became like the Manhattan Project. The planning meetings ran continuously. A daily schedule was issued by one of the Aucoin Management secretaries posting the times and places of the meetings each morning, and by lunch time, it had been replaced by a revision. The meetings seemed to go on around the clock. For each of them, Bill's staff prepared notebooks and binders with detailed charts, diagrams, drawings, technical specs, and schedules. Minutes of each meeting were taken by a stenographer, transcribed, and distributed within twenty-four hours.

The broad brushstrokes of the show were becoming visible. The lighting system would be a hexagonal grid with moving pieces, an innovation at the time. And it would overwhelm any lighting system seen before, radiating 400,000 watts of brightness. The sound system would be monstrous, capable of reaching the threshold of pain and beyond, with countless cabinets and bins stacked to the ceiling on the wings of the stage as well as suspended above the stage. It would be of seismic power and dimension. The stage and the set would sweep from one end of the arena to the other, 80 feet in width, resembling the flight deck of an aircraft carrier. Runways would thrust out into the audience, and hydraulic lifts would be installed behind the wall of sound cabinets. From there, the Kiss members would be individually lifted by the hydraulic system high above the stage and emerge from behind glowing auras, like beings from outer space. The concept for the stage design came from Paul.

The pyro would be the most spectacular and state-of-the-art that could be designed, eclipsing anything Kiss had done before. Powerful explosives would wallop the fans. Each Kiss member would have his own personal special effect, too, that simulated the effects used in *Kiss Meets the Phantom of the Park*. Paul would shoot laser beams out of his eye utilizing a special eyepiece; Ace would turn his guitar into a space blaster and shoot down elevated speaker cabinets; Peter would have a drum riser that turned in all directions and moved backward and forward while being propelled to the ceiling; and Gene would become a flying monster, suspended by a huge rig and streaking across the stage and into the audience while in midair.

And the costumes would be *le dernier cri*. They would be stupendous, ravishing, outrageous, and overwhelming, on a par with Las Vegas and Liberace, but in a rock 'n' roll style. The predominant color of each costume would be keyed to the individual Kiss member's special "aura" shade—steel blue for Ace, emerald green for Peter, blood red for Gene, and deep violet for Paul. The glow of the auras symbolized their superhero powers. Ace's costume would be a stylized space suit, with silver boots and a pleated cape that fanned out; Peter would be wrapped in great shawls of green fur like a cat creature; Paul would have an Elizabethan look featuring a purple jacket with leg-of-mutton sleeves, tights, rhinestone-studded choker, wrist wraps, a star belt buckle, and platform boots; and Gene would be a living gargoyle, dressed in boots with claws and a flowing flame-red cape. To top it all off, there would be a laser show, something that had never before been attempted by any band on the scale Kiss had in mind. Kiss would burst through a cerulean blue laser curtain that filled the width of the stage with columns of light beaming from floor to ceiling. It would be impossible for anyone to confuse this incarnation of Kiss with a mere rock group. It would be a very bulked-up Kiss that would hit the road in the summer of '79 for a tour dubbed as the "Return of Kiss."

A regiment was enlisted to prepare the battle plan, and platoons of technicians set out to assemble the production. There were metalsmiths and metal workers; bootmakers and boot shops; electricians and electrical engineers; carpenters and architects; sound designers and sound engineers; lighting directors and lighting technicians; costume designers and costume fabricators. A Hollywood costume designer, Pete Menefee, was recruited to create the costumes for Kiss, and a choreographer, Kenny Ortega, signed on to teach Kiss some new stage moves. Ortega later did the choreography for *Dirty Dancing*.

And where would this show of shows be seen? Only in the biggest arenas in the country. A few stadiums were booked, too. A convoy of trucks, eight or more just for the indoor shows, would be needed, and far more for the outdoor shows being planned. Multiple engagements, two or more shows in one building in the same city on consecutive nights, were to be the keystone of the tour's strategy. The show was such a leviathan, it would be impossible to pack it up and do another show the next day in another city. It was the biggest rock tour ever attempted and the biggest indoor stage production ever conceived. It had become more like a mammoth military-industrial project than a road show.

After one of many meetings at the Aucoin Management offices, I lingered after the teams of technicians and production managers departed. They were still being peppered with questions from Paul, Peter, and Ace who left with them. It was already after 6:00 p.m. and many of the office staff had gone home. Gene stayed on the telephone for a while doing promotional call-ins to radio stations that were lining up with promoters to hype the tour. Gene was always the best at these call-ins. "Hi, this is Gene Simmons of Kiss and the most incredible show of all time, the show of shows, is coming to Indianapolis," he boomed. He had the gift of gab and the mellifluous voice to make the most mundane event sound enticing. Hype was his *métier*.

Gene and I were sitting in a dimly lit room at a round marble-topped conference table piled high with papers, blueprints, and reams of spec sheets. Cartons of files and press clippings lined the floor. Gene had finished his round of calls. It wasn't within the purview of my job to give creative advice, but I felt comfortable talking to Gene and, with a little hesitation, asked if he thought that maybe the extravaganza now taking shape, as impressive as it was, might not be a little too much of a good thing. Maybe it was a bit too much Kiss. He thought this was a "very interesting point," but without skipping a beat, he explained to me that "Kiss is no longer just a rock group. Only Paul thinks it's still a rock group." He ruminated about how Kiss was now something far bigger. Kiss could do anything, it was so enormous. Kiss was a concept. A big concept. And it was up to Kiss to shape and define that concept in whatever way they thought best. His words seemed logical in their own way. Gene was always comfortable with big ideas. I nodded my understanding, and we left the room.

According to Gene's *tour d'horizon,* Kiss had transcended the world of rock 'n' roll. We had now entered the era of an institutional Kiss where Kiss's influence would emanate like rays into every aspect of pop culture, media, and entertainment. Kiss could do everything and anything; they were omnipotent and omniscient. It was pretty heady stuff. This was no longer an ordinary job working for a rock group, if such a job ever was ordinary. I was connected to something on a cosmic scale. Gene's words imbued Kiss with an almost metaphysical significance. He sounded like a sage invested with a special set of powers. Everything about the show of shows now fell into place. This show would travel the countryside and bring Kiss in all their glory to their devoted followers. It would be a shrine that would be transported across the land, stopping along the way for committed believers to pay homage to Kiss and for Kiss to perform their ritual. And the followers would flock to this traveling shrine to bear witness at their own version of Lourdes. It was intoxicating.

With preparations for Kiss's production in full swing, Howard Marks called me into his office. By this time, Howard had moved Glickman/Marks Management and his advertising agency out of our modest abode on East 55th Street. Business was booming for Howard, too, and commissions from Kiss as well as his advertising accounts were piling up. Howard had rented a floor of offices in a luxury office building at 655 Madison Avenue on the block adjacent to Bill's offices. And Howard had spared no expense. The entire floor was gutted and refurbished and every office was configured according to a blueprint Howard had created himself. The short-pile wall-to-wall carpeting was charcoal gray. The walls throughout were white. Teakwood furniture and rosewood credenzas with marble tops were in all the executive offices. Color accents were done in touches of crimson and chrome. Lithographs by Warhol and Lichtenstein were scattered throughout the corridors and the reception area. It was very Madison Avenue.

I walked into Howard's office which, naturally, was the largest. On his wall were Calder prints, large geometric shapes in primary colors contained within a simple black frame. A wide and deep black leather couch sat underneath. Behind his mahogany desk was a bank of windows overlooking Madison Avenue. Across from his desk, about 10 feet away, was a floor-to-ceiling custom-made wet bar built into a large chest of Formica white cabinets. A high-tech assortment of expensive audio and video equipment and a large Sony TV monitor faced him. I sat on the couch. In front of me on a matching black lacquer table was an assortment of Steuben glass objects. This was, to be sure, a power office.

Howard looked the part of the potentate of this corporate fiefdom. He was wearing a navy serge Oxxford suit, with white shirt and Tiffany gold cufflinks shaped like shirt buttons. By this time, he had put on a few more pounds. I don't know what I was expecting to hear, but certainly not that the Kiss show "wasn't big enough." Howard started by saying that he'd been speaking to the band, in particular to Gene, about the tour. He had also spoken to Bill. The subject was the production of the show, not the economics of it. This was a little unusual for Howard. He tended to be more involved in the sales, marketing, and advertising of Kiss's records and not so much in the touring area. He left that to Bill and left the mechanics of the tour's finances and administration to me since I was on the road. But this seemed important. He said that it was of paramount importance to Kiss that whatever they did on tour and in any public appearance must be "big enough." Now that they were superstars, everything had to be maximized, taken to the farthest limits imaginable.

Gene was especially vocal about what was necessary, according to Howard. He was the spokesman for the group, followed by Paul. Ace and Peter were typically less involved. Gene thought that as ambitious and awe-inspiring as the show of shows was shaping up to be, it might not, in his words, be "big enough." Of course, it would be a spectacular show. Of course, it would please the fans and excite them to no end. Of course, the show would set new records of attendance as well new standards for production and staging. But something was still lacking. It wasn't yet Super Kiss. There was an element missing. Something to really put Kiss over the top. What was needed was Kiss World.

Howard went on. Kiss World was an idea that had been conceived by Gene to extend the concept of Kiss and take it a giant leap farther. Kiss World would be tied to the concerts and be an integral part of the tour, but it would exist separately. And what exactly was Kiss World? A traveling amusement park, themed to the world of Kiss and everything it stood for. It would travel with the tour and be erected next to the arenas where Kiss would play. Since Kiss expected to perform for several shows, Kiss World could continue for days, like a traveling Disneyland but built around the Kiss concept and characters.

And what a world it would be. Thrill rides and roller coasters, space mountains and space voyages, a 3-D movie dome with 360-degree movies of Kiss, a fantasy park of Kiss characters and sets from past tours and photo layouts, games and attractions all keyed to the Kiss characters and their exploits. And of course, there would be a Kiss museum to exhibit the artifacts and memorabilia of Kiss "through the ages." Kiss would come to life in a world built around their fantasy personas using Madame Tussaud-like figures—Gene in a dark grotto with stalactites dripping from the ceiling; Paul in the drawing room of a medieval castle surrounded by wenches; Ace cruising at warp-speed in a starship; and Peter in a jungle lair protected by a ring of lions and tigers. The possibilities were endless.

And there would be merchandising. Tons of it. You wouldn't be able to walk more than a foot without running into a stand where vendors would be hawking every type of Kiss paraphernalia ever dreamed of and fans could queue up to plunk down their money. What Gene had in mind for Kiss World was Kiss meets Ringling Bros. and Barnum & Bailey and Six Flags, with a Wal-Mart of merchandise thrown in.

Kiss World would be set up contiguous to the arenas or stadiums in one of the parking areas or an adjacent field. Kiss World would open in the morning, either the same day of the Kiss show or a day in advance, and run until the evening. Separate tickets would be sold. Merchandise would sell like hotcakes. Kiss World would be such a unique attraction that people would drive for miles just to see it. It would be a financial and promotional bonanza. It would be the ultimate in commercialism and hype. It would be the essence of Super Kiss.

It sounded great to Howard. Kiss World was big and Howard liked big things. "This is exactly what Kiss needs to make themselves into an event and the promoters will love it," he said. Howard always projected a feeling of certitude whenever he expressed an opinion. My job, of course, was to put Kiss World together and sell it to the promoters. I was a bit dazed by the idea at first but it certainly intrigued me and it was unquestionably a bold and innovative concept. Besides, I'd written my thesis in graduate school on the theme park business so I did know something about it. Plans for Kiss World would go forward. Some of the Kiss members might be a little unsure about it—Paul didn't think it was a very "rock 'n' roll" idea—but Howard felt that as the plans evolved, they would all come on board.

In early March, I flew to Sarasota, Florida, to meet with a pair of circus promoters I'd located, Jim Nordmark and Skip Doyle, who had a well-known circus operation there and liked the Kiss World idea. They had a good grasp of what we were trying to accomplish and how to logistically integrate the traveling amusement park with the Kiss tour. Since it was early spring, their business was slow and they were only too happy to find some new customers.

From our initial meeting at their offices in Sarasota we began a series of meetings at other locations around the country to inspect sites and evaluate equipment to be used. It soon became too big a project for one company alone. Jim and Skip, working together, would be the principal contractors, but they would use outside suppliers to provide Kiss World with everything it required. And it was looking to require a lot.

There would be rides, generators, motors, fencing, tents, power lifts, heaters, air conditioning units, vacuum pumps, scaffolding, tarpaulins, refreshment stands, power cables, air compressors, turnstiles, ticket gates, collapsible walkways, midways, trailers, lighting, banners, booths, film projection units, a movable domed theater, wax models, and a portable diorama. A convoy of trucks would be needed. A separate production team would have to be responsible for Kiss World to make sure it was completely self-contained and didn't interfere with the Kiss concert. We would need to book ringmasters, carnival barkers, acrobats, midgets, sword swallowers, fire-breathers, giants, bearded ladies, and magicians. In other words, something for everyone. There was some discussion about using circus animals like lions, tigers, giraffes, and gorillas, but this was vetoed as being too messy, not to mention dangerous. Not surprisingly, a lot of space was needed at each location, literally tens of thousands of square feet. Kiss World was starting to make the Kiss concert look like a low-budget side show.

We pressed on, mobilizing our forces to make Kiss World a reality. I started to get feedback from the promoters. Most of them were lukewarm about the idea even before I explained to them what it would entail. There were problems about how to advertise Kiss World so it wouldn't conflict with the concert. There were logistical problems having to do with the use of the parking areas.

Jules Belkin, our Cleveland promoter, had serious doubts that there would be enough space for both Kiss World and the cars for the concert. There were zoning and ordinance problems. An attraction like Kiss World might not be able to get permits to set up in every community. Other issues, like security, insurance, ticketing, gate control, cash collections, power, waste removal, fire protection, police, etc., began to surface. How we would split the costs and the income from Kiss World with the promoters was a problem.

We started to get signals that maybe the concept of Kiss World wasn't entirely clear, even to people within our own organization. When I was in L.A. on Kiss World business, I met briefly with Stuart Silfen, one of Kiss's attorneys from New York. I visited him at his hotel. "This is Chris Lendt," he said to his wife. "He has the best job in the whole Kiss organization. He's putting together a huge traveling carnival for the Kiss tour with tents full of dancing show girls." It was half true.

In the middle of Operation Kiss World we ran into a major setback. Jim and Skip had split up their business following a huge dispute about Jim owing Skip his share of a partnership interest from a recent circus tour. It had nothing to do with Kiss World, and I suspected there was other bad blood between them. They had been in the circus business most of their lives, a rough-and-tumble world where trouble and tempers can flare up at the drop of a hat. They had agreed to go their separate ways, but each one wanted to get the Kiss World business and do it on his own. That was out of the question. There was no way that either of them, acting alone, could handle the project, which was snowballing. Worse, if one got the business and the other didn't, the loser would automatically sue Kiss. It was a nightmare. Kiss World was now in jeopardy.

After days of wrangling with Skip and Jim over the telephone from New York, I finally gave them an ultimatum. Either work together on Kiss World as planned or Kiss would cancel the whole project and take it to somebody else. It worked. They were dragooned into service for the remainder of the project and agreed to a truce. It turned out to be a moot point. Kiss World's days were numbered. While in New York, I contacted promoter Ron Delsener about the project. He liked the idea and put his production manager, Keith Kevan, at my disposal to work out all the logistics. There were three shows at Madison Square Garden planned, and organizing a Kiss World in New York City would be a Herculean task. Keith walked with me to inspect the only site near the Garden that would be available for Kiss World, a sprawling parking lot at Eighth and Ninth Avenues between West 50th and 52nd Street. At the time, it was a huge parcel of undeveloped land, flat and wide open and exactly the right dimensions for Kiss World. We circled the lot and started making plans.

And things really started mushrooming. Hundred and hundreds of details, large and small, started swimming around inside my head. Kiss World had become a labyrinth of such complexity and with so many logistics, contingencies, and nettlesome details that it was overwhelming. It could end up burying everybody, including Kiss. It could also end up as a monumental folly, which is what I started to envision when staring at the harsh reality of the corner of Eighth Avenue and 50th Street. This was the cauldron of Hell's Kitchen, one of New York's roughest neighborhoods. This is where America's favorite rock group, Kiss, was going to stage a huge carnival. Inside would be rides, attractions, games, and circus tents; outside would be drug dealers, hookers, muggers, and street gangs. The dichotomy was absurd. It would be like Disneyland had been plopped down into the center of Dante's Inferno. We wouldn't just need fences and gates, we would need barricades with turrets and marksmen inside them. Sentries would have to be posted and outfitted with bandoleers. And a phalanx of police would have to patrol the streets.

At that point, walking around the lot, I broke out into hysterics. Keith had no idea why I was laughing uncontrollably and I didn't let him in on it, either. It had gotten too crazy, too complicated, and too over the top. I knew that Kiss World, as clever and ingenious an idea as it was, would never work. It was a chimera.

The next day I met with Howard. He seemed unperturbed. No doubt, there were problems and obstacles, but these were "just a few wrinkles that we'll have to iron out." Howard never liked details. He was a big picture person. Besides, he said, Gene loves the idea of Kiss World. Kiss needs something big like this. I then told him that in order to go ahead with the project in time for the start of the Kiss tour, we would have to sign a contract with Jim and Skip. Kiss would be obligated for an initial payment of $400,000 over a period of weeks to organize and operate Kiss World. There were a lot of extras that hadn't yet been budgeted which would be additional. We would be flying blind. Howard started to blanch, then modulated his enthusiasm. He would discuss it with Bill and the band. He asked me to prepare a summary of where we stood on the project. I told him that saying that there were "just a few wrinkles" in Kiss World was an understatement. It was more like something on the scale of making a landfill out of the Grand Canyon.

Within a week, Kiss World was dead. Jeff Franklin, the head of Kiss's booking agency, ATI, had intervened. He had spoken to Howard after talking about Kiss World to many of the promoters. They felt it would cost them too much money and be too much trouble. Besides, they were already concerned about how many Kiss tickets they could sell on the upcoming tour; sickly sales were being forecast for a number of acts planning summer tours. Kiss World looked like one big headache that they didn't need. Plans for Kiss World were put on hold indefinitely. It never surfaced again. I was both relieved and disappointed. Kiss World would have turned out to be the Titanic, though.

The task of pulling together the technical and production elements for the Kiss show was given to an Aucoin Management executive, Ken Anderson. Ken, then 41, came out of TV production where he'd been a lighting director and had worked with Bill long before he took on Kiss. Bill tapped him in 1976 to organize the Kiss touring productions. An indefatigable worker, Ken had to keep the Kiss members happy and design the show that they wanted and make it work every night. These were frequently mutually exclusive goals, and his was often a difficult and thankless job. Most of what Kiss wanted had never been done before in rock 'n' roll or anywhere else, for that matter. Bill relegated himself to a more creative and less hands-on role, charging Ken with making it happen. As the idea man, Bill would spend countless hours with the band, spiking them with bigger and grander ideas to attempt. Kiss had entered the '70s with a roar. Now at their zenith, they had to end the decade with the impact of *Götterdämmerung*.

In the final weeks of May, the show was assembled at Nassau Community College in Long Island, New York. Rehearsals would take place there. First, a week was scheduled, then it was stretched to two weeks. Two weeks would have to do, since the facility wasn't available any longer. In the college's huge gym, the show was built and rebuilt, constructed, torn apart, and reconstructed; lighting systems were modified, expanded, contracted, and reconfigured; sound systems were added to and intensified; special effects, lasers, and pyro were doubled and tripled and people to run these things were added almost daily. Technicians and stagehands had to be put on the payroll at a moment's notice, and a makeshift employment office was set up in one of the vacant classrooms next to the gym where the Kiss stage was erected. Endless loops of cables were unspooled all over the floor, along with water hoses which provided cooling for the lasers. And the set was tinkered with continuously. Months of work went into building the set even before it was delivered to Nassau Community College.

It cost a small fortune. Hundreds of thousands of dollars in start-up costs just to bring the show into Nassau Community College and hundreds of thousands of dollars more once we set up there. But money was never a concern of Kiss. They didn't want to hear what this was costing. Budgets were submitted at meetings, and they just laughed at the figures. It was a big joke. Money didn't matter, this was Kiss. That was boring stuff for "you guys to deal with." Kiss's job was to create the show. "Your job" was to make it work. And this was to be the show of shows. They were right about that, at least when it came to costs. Staging and set costs had reached the half-million dollar mark and now included a multi-tiered stage with five elevators, built-in fog machines, and Peter's motorized drum riser that levitated to the ceiling.

Finally, mercifully, we ran out of time in Long Island. Everything had to be trucked 1,136 miles to the first show in Lakeland, Florida. Of course, when the show was packed up it could no longer fit into eight trucks, and another two trucks had to be commandeered to get everything to Lakeland. Once there, we would have, of course, more rehearsals. And hundreds of thousands of dollars more would be spent.

Lakeland is a steamy little town near Orlando, flat as a board and with few distinguishing characteristics. Several highways run into and around the town with the usual fast-food chains dotting both sides. The sun beats down during the day, creating a harsh glare, which boosted sales of Kiss baseball caps and sunglasses while we were there. The Lakeland Civic Center is a squarish, modern facility that holds 10,000 and was new at the time. The periphery of the Civic Center grounds was rimmed by a dense thicket of foliage and forestation.

I flew to Orlando with Kiss on June 11 to begin full-scale production rehearsals. The crew had already been there for a week, and five days were scheduled for Kiss, including rehearsal and two shows in Lakeland that would kick off the tour on June 15. On the plane trip down to Florida, everyone in the band was upbeat and chipper. There was a lot of talk about what songs would be included in the show and how all the effects would work. It was Kiss's show, but sweating out the details and making it happen was up to the hundreds of workers now swarming around the stage like an army of worker ants. No one on the plane trip asked about ticket sales or things like that. It was silly. Of course, all the shows would sell out.

The band was tireless once they got to the Civic Center. Kiss rehearsed day and night. Cars shuttled them to and from the Hyatt near Kissimmee, a resort-style hotel. There was activity at all hours, and the crew appeared to be functioning on the brink of exhaustion. At about midpoint in the schedule, Bill Aucoin arrived in Lakeland. He came to see the final days of rehearsal and also had some unexpected news for Kiss. The band had just finished a run-through of the show. Bill and the group adjourned to a dressing room backstage for a private meeting. A local security guard in a T-shirt and shorts and looking like a tackle from the local college guarded the door. Twenty minutes later, everyone emerged from the meeting. The band returned to the stage and resumed rehearsing. Bill beckoned me into the dressing room, which was now empty. It was hot outside and Bill was wearing cut-off jeans and sneakers without socks.

Bill dropped a bombshell. "The second show in Lakeland is canceled. The first show will sell out, but the promoter will never be able to sell enough tickets to do a second show. And the second show in Savannah is canceled for the same reason," he added. Bill then pulled a rumpled piece of paper from the back pocket of his jeans and started ticking off several other cities that were falling out of the tour itinerary. In nearly every city where Kiss had expected to do multiple shows, there was only enough demand to do one. The stadium show in Pontiac, Michigan, was also shaky but would stay in the schedule. A second show at the Omni in Atlanta was scratched. Madison Square Garden would now be two instead of three shows; as recently as April, promoter Ron Delsener had put six days on hold at the Garden for Kiss. A total of seven Kiss concerts were lost. Bill wrapped up his talk, handed me the list, started to sigh, and then chuckled nervously. His face tightened and he told me to meet with the rest of the production staff and make sure they started working on changing the logistics. He walked out of the dressing room and headed to the stage to watch the rehearsal.

It took about thirty seconds to let all of this sink in. The tour was now going to be a huge financial disaster. The itinerary had been confirmed until Labor Day. The strategy of the tour was predicated on doing two or more shows in most cities. The idea was to do at least four shows per week in two or three cities at most and take advantage of the economies of scale. A second show in the same arena, once it's already set up and promoted, is far more profitable than having to promote and stage two separate shows in two different cities. But it wasn't going to happen as planned. Kiss wasn't big enough to do that kind of business.

Chinks in the armor were starting to show. I picked up my itinerary and used the information Bill had given me to project what the rest of the summer would look like. Now that shows were being dropped, there would be many weeks when Kiss would only perform two or three times. The economics were starting to unravel. The soft economy was partly to blame, crimping ticket sales for other tours as well. An article in the August 11, 1979, issue of *Billboard* reported that the Kiss show had start-up costs of $2.2 million. The show of shows was looking to become the disaster of disasters.

The single show in Lakeland did sell out. The audience was packed into the Civic Center, hardly able to move in their places on the floor. It was steaming inside. Even the most powerful air-conditioning system can be defeated by a mass of overheated and writhing bodies wedged together. There were the usual Kiss fans in bizarre getups, head-to-toe leather, and Kiss costumes and makeup. Some carried banners welcoming Kiss to Lakeland and others had signs saying "I Love Paul" and "Kiss Rocks Florida." A small clique of girls in their early twenties, blonde with beach-party good looks, were right up in front facing the stage. Jeans as tight as bandages hugged their hips, and the flimsy tank tops they had on didn't stand much of a chance of preventing their sloping breasts from spilling out the sides. These were south Florida girls, real hitters, who made it to all the rock shows. They were angling to get noticed by Kiss's security chief so they could be spirited out of the audience and into the backstage area.

A sizable contingent of junior Kiss fans were in the audience, a new development. Very young fans, some in grade school, who were hanging onto the arms of mothers and fathers were conspicuous at the show. Before, the fans were mostly hard core, hard rock, and heavy metal. Now, there were a lot more toddlers with parents, coming to a Kiss show in the same way as they would take a family trip to Disney World a few miles down the highway.

According to Bill, these young fans were evidence that Kiss had succeeded in widening their audience. This was the master motive behind Super Kiss and doing the four solo albums, the TV movie, and staging this spectacular stage show with a dizzying display of special effects, pyro, and lasers. Bill was always so convincing, you found it hard to doubt the logic of his arguments. He'd been such an unqualified success with Kiss, you hesitated to quibble. But teens are very self-conscious about their identity and their peers; how could they have the same rock band as their idol as a bunch of kiddies who had to drag their parents with them? Even being in the same place would make them feel weird. Things were changing with Kiss's audience and we first saw it in Lakeland.

At 9:40 p.m., the sound of Led Zeppelin's "Whole Lotta Love," which had been playing through the house p.a. system, was suddenly cut off. The house lights went down, screams and shrieks echoed inside the arena, and a thundering noise blared through the giant speakers on stage, sounding like an industrial elevator with hydraulic pumps being switched on. Strobe lights flashed like lightning across the darkened stage as four conelike auras appeared from behind the enormous speaker cabinets and platforms that lined the stage from one end to the other. Silhouetted by streaks of bright arc lamps that swiveled wildly, Kiss could be seen rising from beneath the stage as they were lifted to a point just underneath the massive lighting rig.

Kiss was illuminated in their aura colors—red, blue, violet, and green—as the four stood frozen in power poses with instruments at the ready. Clouds of smoke swirled over the front of the stage. As Kiss revealed themselves, the fans started a roaring ovation, loud enough to nearly drown out the hydraulic sound. The elevator noise then shut down, the intro to Kiss boomed through the speakers, and the band emerged from their auras and came to life, caught in a crossfire of high-intensity beams that cut through a curtain of fog and dry ice. Kiss burst into "King of the Night Time World" as the audience exploded.

The stage was spectacular. It looked like the aircraft carrier Nimitz had crashed through the back of the Civic Center into the front row of the audience. Hundreds upon hundreds of silver modules fitted into trestle-like arms jutted out from above the stage, soaking it in a kaleidoscope of colors. Plumes of smoke, fusillades of explosives, and a hail of fireworks shot out from all directions. The crowd was deafening, surging to the front of the stage. A steel barricade ringed the stage from end to end creating a moat between Kiss and the security guards who manned the barricade in front. Fans who tried to climb over the barricade were picked off by the guards and tossed back into the audience. The area in front of the stage at Kiss shows was always a madhouse.

Peter's drum riser dominated the stage, rolling forward and backward on cue, like a tank on treads. Ace's guitar sounded like metal being sheared off as it spewed clouds of smoke and sparks, speaker cabinets exploded by remote control, Gene flew across the stage and into the audience on his flying contraption, and Paul made impressive glissades from the slickly polished curving ramps that wound around the front of the set. The costumes were blinding with all of their glittering rhinestones and sequins. Paul's rakish-looking Ibanez guitar, its surface covered with jagged mirror pieces, refracted the beams from the spotlights into a thousand flickering rays. The Kiss electric sign was ablaze, flashing the individual Kiss letters in rapid-fire sequence.

The show had the force of a tidal wave, crushing you to the ground as it washed over you. This is what the fans came to see and feel, the bone-crunching power of Kiss. But what the fans didn't know was that a nasty electric shock had leveled Ace earlier in the show, badly burning his hand when he touched a metal railing on stage, nearly knocking him out. By 11:20 p.m., the show was in its final seconds. Tiny triangular sponges with the Kiss Army logo stamped on them were released from the ceiling of the arena and dropped to the floor, bouncing off the heads and shoulders of the crowd. Peter was now 26 feet high above the stage as his drum riser propelled him near the overhead lighting grid and rockets fired off beneath him. Paul came flouncing down the stage runway, yelling "Good night, Lakeland, we loooooooove yooooooooou!" in his mock southern drawl. Another ear-splitting blast rattled the building as tiles started shaking loose from the ceiling above the stage wings. The stage went dark and the show was over.

Dripping wet with their makeup sliding off their faces, Kiss ran down the rear ramp of the stage and into the dressing room where they huddled by themselves to unwind. They would critique the show together before heading back to the Hyatt. Following them inside was Bill. A few minutes later, Bill came out and called in some of the production staff and the crew for the laser system. About a half-hour later, they all left the dressing room except for Kiss. Bill called me over near the door where he was standing.

I knew what was going on. The lasers didn't work. They only functioned for an instant during the show. It looked like someone was holding a flashlight with a blue beam, focusing on a distant cloud of smoke. Bill was a bit prickly talking about the subject. He said something about filing a lawsuit since the system didn't work as he and Kiss expected. But the laser people were going home the next day with their equipment, not to mention the $250,000 it had cost to build. They planned to fix everything and then return.

It seemed like Murphy's Law was starting to operate. Costs had soared to the stratosphere, shows were dropping out of the itinerary, an expensive special effect was about to be junked, and the tour had only begun. I had the feeling this was more than just hitting a few rough patches. We hadn't even made it to the next city yet. Miami was in two days and there was barely enough time to get out of Lakeland and put up the show in Miami. There wasn't any time to sort out the problems just starting to dog this tour. Everything was happening fast and no one could think past the next show.

111

The return of Kiss, 1979. Standing on the band's stage set and under its hexagonal lighting truss in the Pontiac Silverdome, executive production manager Bill McManus with arms akimbo (front left) next to tour manager Fritz Postlethwaite. McManus Enterprises designed the lighting for Kiss and was general contractor for the band's tours from 1977 to 1980. Sound levels on stage were so intense that the audio technician had to be enclosed in a three-sided plexiglass booth. (Photo courtesy of McManus Enterprises.)

Kiss and entourage on tour, 1979. Ace (far left), Paul (center left), Gene (center right), and Peter (right front), plus security chief John Harte (far left, kneeling), production manager Steve Gansky (fourth from left, kneeling), tour manager Fritz Postlethwaite (next to Peter, kneeling), and the author (second row, left in business attire). Nearly 100 people worked 24-hour days to construct the Kiss show in each city. (Photo courtesy of McManus Enterprises)

Kiss on tour, 1977–78. Paul demolishing his guitar during the band's finale, "Rock'n' Roll All Nite" (Photo courtesy of McManus Enterprises.)

Kiss on tour, 1977–78. Gene and Ace, front and center, playing in unison. (Photo courtesy of McManus Enterprises)

Kiss on tour, 1977–78. Smoke engulfs Peter's drums as Paul opens the show with "I Stole Your Love." (Photo courtesy of McManus Enterprises.)

Kiss on tour, 1977-78. Gene belting out "God of Thunder" while atop his lift unit. (Photo courtesy of McManus Enterprises.)

Kiss on tour, 1977–78. Spinning fireworks illuminate the stage during the climactic "Black Diamond." (Photo courtesy of McManus Enterprises.)

Kiss on tour, 1979. Back of the hall shot of Kiss's frenzied and fired-up fans. The Kiss Army would camp out in front of the box office to make sure that they got tickets. (Photo courtesy of McManus Enterprises.)

Eric Carr unmasked.
Eric, Kiss's replacement
for Peter on drums
from 1980–91, in his
hotel room in Rio de
Janeiro, June 1983.

Ace Frehley in mufti.
Ace in Central Park,
New York, circa 1980.

Peter and Lydia Criss. Flying down to Bangkok and Singapore, March 1978.
Peter holding up a book on one of his most cherished idols, Frank Sinatra.

Debra Jensen, Playboy's Miss January
1978, getting a Coppertone tan in L.A.
that summer. The following year, Debra
would become Peter's second wife.
(Photo courtesy of Rosie Licata.)

The author and Kiss Manager Bill Aucoin. Chris and Bill clowning in Kiss costumes backstage at one of the band's stadium shows in Australia, November 1980. Kiss down under was one of the biggest promotions ever for a rock band. (Photo courtesy of Patrick Jones Studios.)

119

The author, Peter and Lydia Criss, and Rosie Licata. Chris, Peter, Lydia, and Rosie enjoying the exotic sights of Bangkok in 1978. Chris quickly became Kiss's travel expert.

The author and an unidentified partygoer. Chris working overtime at a Kiss party in Sydney, Australia in November 1980. (Photo courtesy of Patrick Jones Studios.)

The author and Gene Simmons. Chris and Gene outside the dressing room in Maracanã stadium, Rio de Janeiro, June 1983.

Rosie Licata and Ace Frehley. Former Kiss bodyguard Rosie Licata backstage with Ace in New Jersey, then touring clubs with his own band, in September 1995. Months later the Kiss Reunion Tour would be announced. (Photo courtesy of Rosie Licata.)

Peter Criss, Ace Frehley, and Fritz Postlethwaite. Peter and Ace dressed to kill in honor of tour manager Fritz's wedding in New York, November 1978. (Photo courtesy of F.R. Postlethwaite.)

Promoter Barry Mendelson, Paul Stanley, Gene Simmons, Vinnie Vincent, and Eric Carr. Barry mugging with Kiss at the Mardi Gras in New Orleans, February 1983. (Photo courtesy of Donn Young Photography.)

Producer Vini Poncia. Vini, producer of Dynasty and Unmasked and two solo albums by Peter, in Los Angeles, 1978. (Photo courtesy of Rosie Licata.)

Paul Stanley in Kiss video shoot. Paul surveys the set of "Let's Put the 'X' in Sex," 1988. Racy lyrics and romping with sexy models was an effort by Kiss to reignite the raunchiness that had been one of the band's earliest trademarks. (Photo courtesy of David "Romeo" Bonilla.)

Paul and video vamps. Video vamps on the set of "Let's Put the 'X' in Sex," 1988, awaiting a command from Paul. (Photo courtesy of David "Romeo" Bonilla.)

Paul Stanley and Gene Simmons unmasked in the mid-'80s. Despite an intensive regimen of touring and recording, the unmasked Kiss was never able to rekindle the excitement of the '70s era Kiss. (Photo courtesy of David "Romeo" Bonilla.)

Paul Stanley unmasked during the "Animalize" tour in 1984/85, churning out a rhythm attack onstage. Once the makeup came off, he developed a more central role in Kiss, especially with Gene living in L.A. and pursuing a movie career. (Photo courtesy of David "Romeo" Bonilla.)

Kiss onstage in Berkeley, California. Downsized for the '80s, the band performs at the Berkeley Community Theatre in February 1984. Rebuilding Kiss's career would prove to be an uncertain undertaking. (Photo courtesy of David "Romeo" Bonilla.)

Kiss onstage in Berkeley, California. Gene, Paul, and Vinnie Vincent (in the middle) at the Berkeley Community Theatre atop the tank turret used for several tours in the early '80s. (Photo courtesy of David "Romeo" Bonilla.)

Bruce Kulick, Gene Simmons, and Paul Stanley. Bruce, Gene, and Paul in suspended animation during the final moments of the show on their "Animalize" tour, 1984–85. Bruce was Kiss's third lead guitarist since Ace left in 1982. (Courtesy of David "Romeo" Bonilla.)

Eric Carr, Vinnie Vincent, Paul Stanley, and Gene Simmons flanked by bodyguards and staff in Rio de Janeiro. Kiss prepares to take the stage at Maracanã stadium in Rio in June 1983. It would be more than a decade before the band returned to makeup and costumes.

127

8

Cracks on the Surface

Swingos was one of the more intriguing curiosities of life on the rock 'n' roll circuit in the late '70s, a big city hotel that catered to rock bands. A squat, motel-style building in downtown Cleveland that was a stone's throw from the seediest part of the city, Swingos offered traveling bands all the amenities they craved—twenty-four-hour room service and a bar the size of a basketball court. Each of the rooms was done up in a special decor, from purple carpets, velvet chairs, oversized chandeliers, and upholstered walls in a palette of hues, which looked to me like Contemporary American Pimp, to Space Age Modern, where all the rooms had white shag carpets, stark white walls, white modular couches, and chrome-framed beds. After heading north from Florida, we planned to arrive in Cleveland by mid-July and have a few days off. The overdone atmosphere of Swingos was perfect.

Miami had turned into a debacle. Kiss played the Sportatorium, a concrete monolith that holds 16,000, located way out of town in Pember Pines. The only way in and out is a lonely two-lane highway that stretches for miles. At night the Sportatorium looked like a maximum security prison, isolated from any semblance of civilization, circled with barbed wire and police dogs patrolling the flood-lit grounds. We caught some people selling bogus tickets to fans. Those tickets weren't counted in the concert gross; the money collected went right into the pockets of ticket takers and their confederates. I ordered a drop count of how many stubs were collected and checked the number against the officially reported attendance. There was a discrepancy of around 700 tickets. After a stormy meeting a settlement was hammered out, and it wasn't until months later that Kiss was paid.

After a month on the road, it was obvious that Super Kiss required a staggering amount of manpower and materiel to keep it running. Nearly one hundred people were needed in each city for the shows, to set up and break down the show. There were double shifts of stagehands and double teams of truck loaders. Everything was constantly being redesigned and rebuilt. Change orders were issued daily. New equipment and machinery were shipped in as old equipment was hastily mothballed. The tour had become a sinkhole for money. Just getting from one city to the next was like trying to turn a supertanker. But Kiss was undeterred. The show had to be perfect. In front of the stage, the show looked spectacular. Behind the stage, it had become a lumbering dinosaur. We would have a meeting about all of this while in Cleveland. When money mixed with rock 'n' roll, there were always lots of meetings.

Carl Glickman phoned me at Swingos the day I arrived. He wanted to make sure that I had directions to his new house, where he was hosting a party in Kiss's honor. He told me to tell Kiss they could bring their bodyguards, road managers, girlfriends, wives, or whomever they wanted that night. No one had to get dressed up if they didn't feel like it. I thanked him for the call and told him we'd arrive by 7:00 p.m. Gene's initial reaction was that he didn't want to go. He thought there would be press people around and the party was just a way for Carl to show off. As Gene phrased it, "...he's so big, he can throw a party for Kiss and get them to come." But this was Gene's ego working overtime. Carl hated any kind of personal publicity and was probably the least likely person to want to throw a celebrity party for his own self-aggrandizement. I told Gene the party was simply Carl's way of being a gracious host to his clients, since they were in his town for two concerts at Richfield Coliseum. There wouldn't be any press at his house. Gene was mollified and decided to go.

Carl's mansion was a handsome English-style manor house on several acres of finely manicured lawn in the moneyed suburb of Shaker Heights. It was twilight as we rode up the private driveway to the mansion, shrouded by twisted elms and weeping willows. The neighborhood is a forest of Old World estates. Carl greeted us at the door and we saw Howard Marks sitting in the living room. Kiss and their entourage barged through the doorway, the band mostly dressed in fancy leather pants and cowboy boots from Tony Lama. The limo drivers parked themselves in the foyer and the bodyguards plopped into overstuffed chairs in the den.

Carl showed the Kiss members around his house and they were dutifully impressed, heads turning and each nudging the other approvingly. It looked like the home of an important person, tastefully and elegantly furnished with armchairs, antique armoires, Scalamandré silk curtains, and porcelain vases and lamps. A few Picassos were scattered throughout the mansion's many rooms and a Rolls-Royce was in the garage. The group ambled around the house, oohing and aaahing at the luxurious surroundings.

Kiss was pretty well behaved that night, not wanting to look foolish in front of Carl or play the part of rock stars. Now that they were earning enormous sums of money, their perspective had shifted. They could see what money could buy and how people who had it lived. While Carl came from a completely different world than they did, the common denominator of earning big bucks was important. They weren't struggling musicians anymore. They were millionaires.

The household staff served dinner French-style from silver platters. Bottles of Echézeaux were lined up on top of a long walnut cabinet in the dining room. Ace drank his dinner, bottle after bottle of Dom Pérignon which Carl had stocked up on in advance. By the end of the meal, Ace was on the floor clutching a champagne bottle, laughing himself senseless. Carl had a bemused look on his face while everyone else, including Howard, just smiled and shook their heads. This was vintage Ace, yukking it up and getting smashed on champagne. Ace was rolling around the floor, cackling loudly and cracking jokes that were completely incoherent. Lying on his back and kicking his feet, he started burbling, "Carl! Carl!" Ace pointed to me as he began to get up. I was sitting across the room. "Carl! You're his idol! He idolizes you! You're his hero!" He was referring to me. The whole room exploded in laughter while my face turned beet red. I cringed in my chair, wishing I could disappear under the table. I may have admired Carl, but idol worship it wasn't. But it was funny and Ace obviously enjoyed himself that night—at least until he passed out and a couple of the bodyguards had to carry him out of the dining room.

With the itinerary in shambles, shows falling out left and right, and the tour burning through cash like a forest fire raging out of control, we had to try and come to grips with reality. High-flying Kiss was vectoring toward a financial fiasco and everyone was getting edgy. At least, everyone except Kiss. Carl, Howard, and Bill Aucoin prevailed upon the band to meet on one of our days off in Cleveland. I would be there as well as Ken Anderson, the production director, and Bill McManus, the major supplier for the tour who provided nearly all of the tour equipment and production services.

The meeting was on July 19 in Carl's office in the Leader Building, which he owned. A soaring Gothic office tower on Superior Avenue, Cleveland's main downtown artery, the Leader Building is an imposing, meticulously preserved structure of vintage 1911, with hundreds of narrow rectangular windows in a neat gridlike pattern. I arrived with the Kiss members and the elevator we took to Carl's floor displayed burnished wood surfaces and polished brass fixtures. Although it was noon, Peter and Ace were still groggy and had puffy eyes. Gene was in a leather outfit from head to toe despite the torrid heat. Ace and Paul were dressed in jeans and T-shirts and Peter wore a green jogging suit with a large white stripe down the front. We sped past a receptionist into a conference room. Bill Aucoin, Howard Marks, Ken Anderson, and Bill McManus were already there as was our booking agent, Wally Meyrowitz. Fritz Postlethwaite, the tour manager who supervised the show's production on the road, was also present, now fully recovered from the previous year's auto accident with Peter. Slender and small-framed with straight blonde hair, Fritz had started with Kiss as an audio technician in 1975.

The conference room was large enough to hold a dozen or more and our group just filled it. We sat around a wide, rectangular mahogany table in dark brown leather arm chairs, making small talk. The room was very traditional in style, business-like and no-nonsense, like a corporate boardroom. Oak paneling gave it a masculine feel. Ace had taken to calling everyone "Curley" on this tour so there were quite a few "Hey, Curleys!" After a few minutes Carl walked into the room and the chatter died down. Carl was wearing a dark gray suit, ventless, with a chalk stripe in it, hand-tailored with four neatly cut buttonholes in each sleeve. A white broadcloth shirt and a sincere-looking deep maroon tie with an indistinct pattern reinforced his serious image. He was holding a black leather cigar case made of glove leather. Three of the tubular compartments were bulging with Montecristo No. 2 cigars from Havana, the kind shaped like torpedoes. I could tell this was going to be a three-cigar meeting.

Carl was respected and looked up to by the Kiss partners. Each of them held a 25 percent share of the Kiss business. It was an extension of the original concept behind Kiss—a personality group of four distinct but equal personas. Carl's involvement gave Kiss a certain big-business cachet. A graduate of the Harvard Institute of Financial Management, a kind of intensive training camp for senior financial executives, Carl was active in many businesses and civic affairs. He was also an art collector and kept photos of his Picassos in his wallet.

By now, the respective roles of Carl and Howard had been fleshed out. Carl would take charge of the financial oversight, the investments, and dealing with the accountants on tax matters. Howard's responsibilities were to deal directly with Kiss and work with Bill on the business side of their career in records and touring. Since Howard was based in New York, he would have a more hands-on role than Carl and be more involved in the daily lives of Kiss. This suited Carl fine since he had no patience in having to deal with four rock superstars with egos to match. Carl had previously run afoul of Peter when he tried to resolve a problem with Peter's landlord when the lease to Peter's apartment expired. Carl confessed to the landlord he was new to the music business and wasn't used to working with "prima donnas." Peter heard about it and went ballistic.

Carl was used to dealing with business types who were more concerned with the nuts and bolts of things than appearances. When I suggested at one point that the financial statements for Kiss should be printed on better-quality paper, not computer paper with perforations on the edges, and we should put everything in bound volumes with embossing, he scoffed at the idea. He thought this was an idiotic waste of money. "Financial statements should be printed on fish wrap," he said.

Carl spoke first. He began by saying the tour was losing "a lot of money" and ticket sales were soft in some markets. It was his job to give it to Kiss "straight," as he put it, and come up with solutions to the problem. Carl's bluntness had a bracing, medicinal quality to it, not at all showbiz-like. We would propose alternatives to the group and advise them of the financial ramifications. Kiss, of course, had the final say about what to do or not to do. Howard chimed in that all of the key people had been assembled as a sort of "braintrust" to advise Kiss on how to cut costs and save money on the tour. Howard always had a flair for the apt turn of phrase.

Carl was already well into the first Montecristo when Ken Anderson was asked to speak. Ken bore a striking resemblance to Kenny Rogers, minus the beard, and had a thick head of graying hair carefully combed and neatly cut. He started by reviewing the budget for the tour and talking about the balance of shows on the itinerary. As he spoke, he removed his jacket to be more comfortable, revealing a checked shirt with western-style stitching. He looked drained. Wally Meyrowitz handed him some papers with the latest routing information on the tour bookings. ATI had agreed to a reduced commission of 7 1/2 percent for this tour.

Ken's job was to turn Kiss's fantasies into realities. He started to talk about how much all of the special effects were costing on a weekly basis and how many people the show required to put up. The trucks were filled to the gills and were so tightly packed that loading and unloading each night were taking hours longer than projected. The Kiss members had changed the specs for the stage, the set pieces, and the props so many times that the carpenters couldn't figure out what they were supposed to be doing anymore.

Ken wearily continued. Promoters were complaining that backup generators were needed to handle the electrical service for the lighting, an unheard-of development for an indoor show. One promoter thought he must have had enough power to illuminate a small city. The costumes were so extravagant and with so many separate pieces that two wardrobe people weren't enough. The sound system was peaking almost nightly, the monitors were too intricately designed, the drum riser was so big it required a separate team to place it on stage, and, worst of all, Gene's flying contraption was a nightmare to make work.

Bill McManus jumped in. He was a large, dark-haired man with small features, wearing steel-rimmed glasses and a shapeless jacket. His voice had a slightly high-pitched ring to it. He added to what Ken had said and threw in a lot of technical jargon. On the previous Kiss tour, Bill McManus had suffered a bad fall during a rehearsal and broken his wrist. Bill Aucoin gritted his teeth while listening to the litany of production glitches, knowing this was a problem he'd have to quickly resolve. Kiss sat impassively, not displaying any reaction.

Ken summed up by proposing that Kiss consider modifying some of the show to do more concerts each week on the second half of the tour. As it stood now, with a show this enormous, many of the smaller cities and secondary markets would be impossible to perform in, limiting the number of cities available to Kiss. And multiple shows except in New York and L.A. were mostly out of the question. Howard interjected that we'd also reviewed the travel costs of airfares, personnel, hotels, limos, and other extras and he motioned for me to go over this.

I ran down the list—the cost of suites for the band members; the cost of bodyguards; the cost of round-the-clock limo service; the extra people on tour including a team of "observer roadies" who were learning their jobs as stage technicians in an on-the-job training program; the cost of Ace's champagne bill each week; the cost of room damages at the hotels; the cost of flying in high-priced consultants and office staff from New York, not to mention girlfriends and creative gurus; and on and on. The tour budget, if you could call it that, was larded with this kind of stuff.

Bill Aucoin, who seemed almost bored, suggested we get down to some specific solutions. Carl was puffing away, the aromatic fumes of his cigar wafting into a ventilation duct in the ceiling. Gene waved his hands wildly to divert the smoke from his drift. He was an inveterate antismoker.

Ken came to the point. He and Fritz had come up with a way to provide Kiss with an "A show" and a "B show." Basically, the A show would have everything, but only be erected in the major cities where there was sufficient time and manpower. The B show would be a scaled-down version of the full array of effects, staging, and production. It would be the same show with most of the same production, but it would be more compactly presented and designed to get in and out of more cities and venues. In short, Ken explained, it would make the tour more economical and deliver a top-flight Kiss show in more places. Fritz had previously developed a B show approach when it became apparent that ticket sales were slowing and smaller venues were likely to be booked by ATI to fill in the holes in the itinerary. But the band had howled over the idea. Ken was now giving it a shot, glancing at spec sheets in front of him as he spoke.

Drawings were passed around along with a memo spelling out what the two shows would consist of. Then Carl asked me to circulate a series of budgets showing what the financial results would be if this concept was implemented. Stacks of papers flew back and forth, covering the conference table. Bill and Kiss started firing away with questions. At first, they asked mostly technical questions, prodding for details. The pros of this, the cons of that. How high would this be, how much of that would there be, how big, how little? How much pyro, how much sound, how many lights, what about the stage ramps? It droned on and Fritz, Ken, and Bill McManus fielded all questions.

Paul and Gene did most of the talking for Kiss, following up questions and answers with more questions. Ace was squinting a lot of the time and didn't say much. He did make a persuasive pitch about the importance of his smoking guitar effect and how this had become a focal point of the show, but then lapsed back into a half-sleep. Peter was mostly silent. He usually let Gene do the talking on these matters. He grumbled once about how his levitating drum riser and drum kit, which had proliferated to a triple-sized set, was "the most important part of the show," and then stopped talking. Everyone listened politely to what he had to say, nodded, and then moved on.

And then the posturing started. Bill Aucoin thought all of these proposals were pragmatic, but if some of the effects and production values of the show were deleted, even if only in smaller cities, "it wouldn't be the same Kiss show." More specifically, it wouldn't be Super Kiss. Bill was fearful about diluting the Kiss concept and tampering with a carefully concocted formula. He then started off on a long soliloquy about how important it was for "Kiss to be Kiss" (translated, to be "overwhelming" and "excessive") and that we were jeopardizing his creative strategy of building Kiss into something bigger, more powerful, more awesome, more of an event, with every show. And this was the show of shows. How could we now start to diminish it? The drumbeating had begun.

Gene and Paul wasted no time falling into line. They sprung into action, defending every element of the show and how important all of it was. The thought of eliminating Gene's flying rig, even for only a portion of the tour, was unthinkable. This was the essence of Kiss. No matter what, that had to stay. Paul refused to compromise about the lights. We had to have the most and the biggest or it wouldn't be Kiss. The fans would be outraged and feel cheated otherwise. The sound couldn't be touched; if anything, it should be louder and with more cabinets. The pyro wasn't to be discussed at all; there could be no Kiss without pyro and Kiss had to have the most. They were also concerned about safety. Their former pyro man, Moose, had part of his hand blown off when an ill-timed bomb sent shrapnel flying in all directions. Working for Kiss could be a hazardous occupation. Whatever the amount of production crew needed, however many trucks and buses were required, that was Ken's problem to sort out. Just do it. A collective "so what?" greeted every problem mentioned. Bill and Kiss were unmovable.

Howard spoke up. The B show concept would mean many extra dates on the tour, bringing in much needed revenue to offset the extraordinary expenses. Paul and Gene were quick to bury the B show idea. They were adamant. The idea of a B show was heresy. It was an insulting idea that an act as big as Kiss, let alone Super Kiss, should play anywhere without the full Kiss production conceived for this event. It was tacky, anyway. Kiss was much too big to play those small towns out in the boondocks; they had outgrown those kinds of places.

That stuff was okay in the past but now it wasn't nearly big enough. Playing Podunk was beneath Kiss. Podunk would have to travel to see Kiss at the big cities where their shrine to the fans would be situated, in all of its splendor.

By now, Carl was well into his second cigar and Howard could be heard sighing. It was clear what was happening. Egos were pumped up like balloons and everyone was trying to outdo the other. Bill Aucoin had gone out in front, and Gene and Paul led the charge from behind. Ace and Peter nodded their assent at various intervals and provided moral support. It had become strictly an emotional issue. Facts and figures were irrelevant. They had dug in their heels. Kiss had to be Kiss, period. Bill and Kiss were trying to hang on to their grand illusion at any cost. They didn't want to face the glaring reality of sluggish ticket sales and canceled concerts.

Carl said that if changes weren't made the way the tour was organized, Kiss would lose "at least a million dollars," based on the projections. Paul responded tartly, "Well, it's cheaper than not touring." The room fell silent momentarily. A kind of awkward feeling gripped everybody. We had committed the mortal sin of suggesting to Kiss that they be a little less Kiss. Dismantling even a minute portion of their traveling colossus was unthinkable. They were intractable. It was if we were reactionaries, against all progress. We were Luddites.

The meeting started to fall apart. Everybody kept repeating themselves. Howard and Carl made one last stab at trying to get them to at least cut down on some of the extras—the suites, the limos, the unnecessary people, the liquor bills. I went over the list again. Kiss felt Ace's champagne bill for a weekly supply of Dom Pérignon, charged to the tour at roughly $1000 per week, should be paid by him personally. Ace had his own custom-made steel traveling case to carry a supply of Dom Pérignon at all times. The case was loaded onto one of the eight 45-foot trucks to get to the next city, then off-loaded and put in a van to be driven to the local hotel. Ace agreed, he would pay for this personally. Peter, for his part, agreed not to charge his Dunhill cigarettes to the tour. I cleared my throat and looked at the next item on my list.

We moved on. Suites? There had to be suites for the band at all times, otherwise they would be no better off than the roadies. Do you want us to share rooms next? Limos? Kiss had to have round-the-clock service, as many as four cars in each city, sometimes for days on end, running into thousands of dollars per day. Do you expect us to take cabs? There had to be cars on duty at all times because no one knew when the moment would strike that they needed to get somewhere. And the extra crew? The show had to be perfect regardless of how many people it took. How else can people learn their jobs unless we bring new people on the road to be trained? Kiss was too complicated, not like any other band.

Finally, they agreed to one elimination. We would fire the advance man. His job was to travel ahead to each city and collect the keys from the hotels to hand to the Kiss members upon their arrival at the airport. He also set up the suites at the hotels with a preordained assortment of fruit trays, tropical juices, beer, Pepsis, Tabs, liquor, hors d'oeuvres, and cheese plates. He did bed checks as well, which meant checking that only king or queen beds were provided in the rooms, and he inspected each suite to make sure all were comparable in size, location, decor, and amenities. There was a complexity to all of this that rivaled diplomatic corps protocols. We would be able to get by, hopefully and prayerfully, without an advance man. In reality, Kiss's concessions were just sops. These few items would save a few thousand dollars a week, not even a drop in the bucket on this tour. Carl and Howard both looked exasperated.

Everyone was now getting fidgety. Paul had already gotten testy, a bad sign. Ace, Gene, and Peter were restless. It was time to call it a day. The bean counters had done their job and pleaded their case and Kiss had disposed of the matter. We had done our duty but we were still bean counters, well-intentioned but myopic. And what did we know about rock 'n' roll anyway? Kiss would now go back to the business of being Kiss and this little interlude would soon be forgotten. The meeting was over and everyone filed out of the conference room. It was late afternoon. Carl went back to his office and talked privately with Howard. I walked out with Ken. We were moving inexorably toward a day of reckoning somewhere down the line and all of us bean counters knew it.

As the summer 1979 tour staggered on, another casualty was The Cruiser. When the tour was planned, Kiss decided to augment its normal complement of a security chief and four individual bodyguards with a professionally trained police officer. Kiss had expected hordes of people at every airport, hotel, and arena. A bonded police pro would work with the local police to control the multitudes. A firm in Boston specializing in industrial espionage, counterterrorism, and high-risk security assignments was retained. A retired police officer came on board, a Joe Friday type and who had handled security details around the world for VIPs. He would handle the Kiss operation and, where necessary, coordinate with the FBI. This kind of protection doesn't come cheap; his company received about $2000 a week, plus expenses. The Cruiser earned his nickname because in every city he would head straight for the local police station to meet with the proverbial "Sgt. McNamara" and press a patrolman and police cruiser into service to escort Kiss's motorcade from the arena back to the hotel and the end of the show. This became his only duty; there weren't any bomb threats, terrorists attacks, rioting crowds, or spies to ward off. After a month or so, even Kiss saw the folly of this and let The Cruiser go.

Unfortunately, the idea that Kiss needed a level of security on the scale of a traveling head of state was symptomatic of the kind of thinking that prevailed.

If this was Super Kiss, then super security was needed, too. That attitude filtered through the organization. At a stop in Greensboro, North Carolina, the road manager for Kiss, George Sewitt, a recent hire, proudly announced upon checking in at the hotel that he'd rented two full floors for Kiss, their entourage, and the security detail, about forty rooms. When I told him that we really didn't need quite that many rooms, he looked crestfallen. "When I signed up for this job, I was told it was bigger than Elvis," he said.

Partying reached new heights during this tour. Ace was the self-appointed host of hosts, the partyer without peer. Almost nightly, his suite was brimming with guests, and at times what looked like a conga line would snake out the door and into the hallway. Booze, of course, flowed like water. Room service waiters practically tripped over each other in the hallway making deliveries. Ace was often sprawled out on a sofa or on the floor, cracking jokes while guzzling champagne. The music and general hullabaloo kept up until the wee hours. The next day, the room looked like a cyclone hit it. Some of the partygoers hopped from city to city, showing up in Ace's suite on successive nights as the tour progressed. To some, it was like a traveling social club. Regulars had colorful nicknames like Big Red, Swamp Rat, and Sweat Hog. Despite the boozing, Ace wasn't so much self-destructive as bored and unhappy. His high octane diet made life on tour bearable for him.

The party rooms were hot, drunken, druggy, and messy—a mass of humanity crowbarred into suites that were too small for the number of bodies packed into them. At times you almost fell over people walking through the rooms. Typical partygoers were people working for the promoter, radio station staff, desk clerks and hotel waitresses who sneaked in, and swarms of girls who drifted in from the show. Ace gulped Dom Pérignon and traded jokes with the guests. As things loosened up and some of the guys got woozy, they'd start pawing at the girls in the room. Paul sometimes showed up briefly, trotting out his girl for the night while checking to make sure that there wasn't anything better available in the party room. Peter was often around, Ace's frequent party mate. The din from the TV set mixing with the stereo and the clatter from so many people talking and laughing could be heard all over the floor of the hotel.

Coke and pot were in plentiful supply and from time to time, poppers were passed around, small glass ampules that when broken, released a dose of amyl nitrate. Inhaling amyl nitrate sends a powerful rush to the heart and it's used for angina attacks or as a sexual stimulant. I got coaxed into trying one by Ace and Peter. In a couple of seconds, I felt a jolt surge through me like I'd been plugged into a wall socket. I started to hyperventilate and then conked out briefly. When I had revived, Ace and Peter were howling with laughter.

By late night, plastic baggies of pot were easy to find, along with small glass vials in the bathroom and on the floor. The bodyguards were responsible for policing the rooms before check-out to get rid of any incriminating detritus. But the rooms were nearly always a wreck, empty champagne and beer bottles and half-eaten room service meals littering the floor, bed linens stained with booze, furniture trashed, and carpets burned with cigarette butts. A smelly, stale odor from all the smoke trapped inside made the rooms reek.

Backstage, girls were asked if they wanted to "party" with Kiss after the show. This could mean sex, getting high, or both. The girls had antennae of their own and knew if they said yes and went back to the hotel with Gene and Paul, it would mean sex only. They were never involved in any drinking or drugs. Those that weren't shunted to Gene and Paul would wind up with Ace and Peter, where anything was possible. Once in a while, girls would be invited to the dressing room for a quickie, usually in a cramped bathroom stall. Girls on the road had a sixth sense about drugs. The more drugs believed to be available with a band, the more girls that showed up backstage and at the hotels.

Many of the girls hanging out didn't need much of a push to get raunchy at the after-show parties. If someone in Kiss was around, they'd pull him into a corner, tongue-kiss and stroke his crotch while unzipping his pants. One girl pulled down her pants to reveal a Kiss tattoo on her rump, then asked the band to autograph it. A few of the girls were single-minded in their obsession, offering to "do anything I have to so I can fuck Gene Simmons." They usually ended up in a room for a few hours with various partygoers, each of whom claimed to be Gene's personal bodyguard and road manager.

Whenever Casablanca executives showed up on tour, the parties got extra wild. Ostensibly, these people came to keep tabs on the local record retailers, hype the disc jockeys and radio programmers, and check on the promotional campaigns for Kiss records. Some were on the Artist Relations staff, a largely p.r. function of glad-handing the artists and massaging their egos, watching the show, and schmoozing with them in the dressing room and back at the hotel. Gene and Paul didn't like many of these record company emissaries and stayed away from them for the most part. Ace was a different matter. Gene and Paul were always afraid that Ace wouldn't make it to the next show after an all-night bash where loads of booze and drugs coincidentally turned up following a record company road visit. They had similar worries about Peter.

Gambling was Ace's Achilles heel. Before this tour, I had been on one of his junkets to Atlantic City when he rented a Learjet for a night at the tables at Resorts International along with some of his buddies. This time we were headed for Las Vegas. Ace's idea for the trip had been for us, along with his bodyguard, to dress up in cowboy outfits and walk into the casino at Caesars Palace. We were in Oklahoma City so I shopped at a western clothing store for a red gingham checked shirt, orange kerchief, and brown jeans cut like jodhpurs. When I put on the outfit and Ace saw how ridiculous I looked, he canceled the plan. We flew to Vegas in street clothes.

I had about $20,000 in cash with me when we pulled into Caesars and got our room keys. We immediately hit the tables. Even without his makeup, Ace was recognized right away in the casino as the guitarist for Kiss. Not that he made any attempt to hide the fact. In fact, he basked in the attention he was getting. His cackle could be heard from one end to the other of the giant casino, bustling with customers at midday. Ace rode a winning streak for hours, then hit a dry spell, playing mostly blackjack. We went back and forth between Caesars and the MGM Grand across the street and by late night, we ended up back at Caesars.

The main event at Caesars, like any casino catering to high rollers, is the baccarat table. While Ace and his bodyguard sauntered over to a blackjack table with a small sign in front that said "$500 Minimum Bet," I hung around the baccarat table to watch the action. The table is set up in a corner of the casino floor and cordoned off from the crowds. By now, Caesars was packed and the loud, jangling noises from slot machines and the shouts and screams of charged-up gamblers echoed through the room. The best-looking women are usually at baccarat. Many of them are shills, given money by the house to play with and make themselves conspicuous. It's a form of p.r. to help draw in customers.

The bodyguard found me since Ace needed money. I left the baccarat table to link up with them at the roulette table. He collected about $3000 from a couple of winning picks and was overjoyed, like a kid at the World Series. A cluster of curiosity seekers hovered around the table to watch Ace. A mound of colored chips piled up in front of him as a crowd gathered from behind. He handed out $100 chips like Lifesavers to the croupiers and waitresses who came by with drinks. As a gesture of good-heartedness, he even handed one to me. "Go buy yourself a girl," he said, as I made a beeline for the bar. Vegas was then much more of a wide-open city and less concerned about catering to families and conventioneers. Girls beckoned at every bar in every hotel and Caesars was like a mecca. By the time we left Vegas, Ace's luck had turned. He dropped around $30,000, more than I had with me, and he had to get credit from the casino. The next day I had my office send a check to Caesars to pay off his markers.

Peter seemed to require a coterie of people around him at all times. The bodyguards who traveled with Kiss were more like companions and valets anyway, but for Peter, one was never enough. The security chief, John Harte, was originally conscripted. A gentle giant, he helped to calm Peter. And when it became apparent that John couldn't do the job alone, Peter's drum technician was brought in from the crew and put up in the hotel room next to Peter's. They made sure that Peter's every amusement was provided for and that he wouldn't get too depressed and destroy his room or leave the tour. Downing bottles of Remy Martin helped to ameliorate his anxieties.

Peter's rantings and ravings about hating the road were a chronic irritation that everyone had to deal with. It was hard to tell if he was trying to call some imaginary bluff or if he really was going to split from the tour. And he was unpredictable. He explained his long bouts of sleeplessness and staying up for days on end by calling it "insomnia." After blacking out his hotel windows, sometimes with newspapers, Peter would collapse into a deep sleep for 15 hours or so, usually awakening the following afternoon. He would then order breakfast. This was manageable if we weren't traveling that day but when we were, it became obvious why so many people were necessary to attend to Peter. He was sometimes wrapped in blankets and pillows and helped into a limo to get to the airport, boarding the plane with people propping him up. With his face sagging and his eyes sunken, he sometimes sneered at passers-by while spewing a torrent of profanity. Peter earned the nickname Ayatollah Criss. His mummified appearance wasn't easily forgotten.

Damage control was a function of the squad that looked after Peter. Sometimes it took an unusual twist. In Atlanta, I knocked on his hotel room door and he emerged looking like Rambo. He was bare-chested, wearing a utility belt hoisted around his waist, a bandanna around his head, and camouflage pants. He invited me in after first looking furtively to the left and right, checking to see if anyone was lurking on the hotel floor. He told me he was target practicing with a BB gun by aiming at trucks which passed outside his window in the distance. His room was on a high floor of the Peachtree Plaza, overlooking a serpentine loop of highways. It was often unclear whether Peter was pulling a prank just to get attention or was serious.

We also had to cope with the Vesuvius-like eruptions sometimes heard in Peter's room at night. Furniture crashing, TV sets collapsing, and what sounded like yelling, with Sinatra music often playing in the background. Suddenly, the sounds would end. There would be a lull in the storm and then, minutes later, it would start up again. The next day things were back to normal—except of course for the damage to the room—and nobody even mentioned what they had heard.

I was personally fond of Peter despite his self-destructive behavior. But I had learned to be wary of him. In the fall of 1978, I traveled to Paris with him and we stayed at the Inter-Continental Hotel. Peter told me someone from Vogue Records, the Casablanca licensee at the time, would be coming to the hotel to drop off a package. Peter said it would be left in my box at the front desk under my name since he wanted to remain incognito. Later, I picked up the package and delivered it to Peter's room. According to Peter, he'd asked the record company to put together a set of press clippings about Kiss from newspapers and magazines in France. When Peter greeted me at the door, he grabbed the package, tore it open, and a small plastic bag of white powder fell out. I didn't notice any press clippings.

Guns were a big item in Peter's life. Before the '79 tour started, Peter had given me a leather pouch to safeguard for him since he was in the midst of a divorce and was changing residences. He told me the pouch contained some of his "private papers." When I brought the pouch home, I opened it. Inside was a .38 revolver. You could never take any chances with Peter since you never knew what to expect.

One of the tour staffers once took it upon himself to try and regulate Peter's intake of drugs. He felt that if he knew exactly which drugs Peter was doing at any given time, he could predict and control Peter's behavior. He would be Peter's pharmacist. It didn't work. Peter could outsmart anyone in this department. He was also quite knowledgeable about the effects of drugs, both through talking with the many doctors who prescribed the pills and from the *Physician's Desk Reference* on pharmaceuticals he kept at home.

Peter's estimation of me had risen considerably the previous year, when I organized a trip to Bangkok and Singapore. Right after the Japan tour in the spring of 1978, Peter and his wife Lydia joined me for a vacation. I knew that Peter liked traveling to exotic places and thought this would be an unusual experience for all of us. To be on the safe side, Peter's bodyguard, Ross "Rosie" Licata, came along. Rosie was something of a spectacle himself, with every inch of his arms and chest covered with tattoos, but he was a faithful companion to Peter.

Arriving at the airport in Bangkok, Peter was unprepared for the steaming jungle heat and the primitive conditions. He said it looked like we had just landed in Vietnam, and while riding into the city in our hired car, the Doors' song, "Break On Through," came on the radio. It was the perfect backdrop; Peter always referred to the Doors and other '60s groups as "Vietnam music."

In Bangkok, a connection was made through an enterprising taxi driver named Thongchai, who arrived at Peter's suite at the Siam Inter-Continental with enough morphine and local marijuana, known in the States as Thai sticks, to wipe out a small army. The whole thing cost about $50. We started on the Thai sticks, the effect of which was very potent and hallucinogenic after only a couple of hits. I kept seeing strange images, like Humpty Dumpty, on the ceiling. We then moved on to the morphine. I had trepidations at first, but was sufficiently loosened up by this time to snort a small amount. A rush began flowing through me, warm and soothing and filling every corner of my body. I was floating on a billowy cumulus cloud moving slowly across the sky. It was a strange, uneasy experience, very relaxing but scary at the same time. We were all nodding like junkies, babbling incoherently.

I lost control over every muscle and my limbs began to feel rubbery. After a while, I fell into a dreamy stupor, not knowing where I was. Peter became queasy and headed for the bathroom to vomit. I just passed out. I don't remember for how long; time simply melted away. It was an emptying sort of experience that deadened the senses and drained you of any energy to move or speak. I never repeated it.

Peter was eternally grateful to me for bringing him to Bangkok. He may have thought I was crazy at first, but the experience turned out to be something he'd never dreamed of. It was a first for him. In his eyes, I was now the Kiss travel expert.

Gene and Paul were positively straitlaced compared to Ace and Peter. Gene would cloister himself in his suite with girls running in and out in droves, like commuters at a train station. By this time, the Polaroid SX-70 had been supplemented with video cameras and VCRs to tape the action. The bodyguards had to set up the equipment at every hotel on tour. Gene was very egalitarian about who came into the room for these encounters. They were young and old, mothers and daughters, short and tall, fat and thin, beasts and beauties. All were welcome. It was more of a mechanical, assembly-line operation than a hedonistic oasis. In conversations with Gene, he told me that his biggest regret in life was "not having two dicks."

Gene often received Polaroids in the mail of girls posing nude, with their address and phone number scribbled on the back. Girls would write to Kiss and send nude photos of themselves in the hope that when the group played their neck of the woods, they'd get a call to come over to Kiss's hotel. As Gene and Paul put it in an interview in *Circus* in the January 20, 1976, issue, "There's nothing like knowing you're helping the youth of America undress."

Paul was the most reserved. Like Gene, he was a teetotaler, except for an occasional glass of wine. Both were very abstemious and did not smoke, drink, or use drugs of any kind. Paul was also very disciplined about eating and made a big effort to maintain a svelte appearance. But Paul was much more picky about women than Gene. Only the best would do. They had to be beauties, or as close as you could reasonably expect to find on a Kiss tour.

As a rule, the girls who gravitated to Kiss shows were much too extreme-looking and bizarre for Paul's tastes, especially the stage-door groupies. When there wasn't a full-blown party in one of the suites, we often had a Chicken Coop, a hotel room rented to accommodate the overflow of girls from the show. But the girls from the Coop were much too downscale for Paul. Most of them milled around like the cast from *Night of the Living Dead,* waiting to meet a band member. Paul felt that carousing with these weirdos was much too *declassé* for him so girls would have to be flown in from L.A., New York, Denver, Chicago, and other sophisticated cities. The girls would stay on tour until he got bored with them, which was about three days maximum, and then they would be discharged from service, always flown first class and with limos at both ends. At one point he was pondering whether he should use private jets for some of the girls. Paul always felt he had to make a big impression with girls, even if it meant going overboard. He had to lay on all the rock star trappings to make himself look important and that usually meant spending a lot of money on frills. In this respect, he was the opposite of Gene.

Paul also had another pastime. He often talked on the phone with his psychiatrist. Dr. Jesse Hilsen, who practiced in New York, had been Paul's shrink since the early '70s. It seemed to me that Dr. Hilsen had become a vital part of Paul's life. Paul never discussed with me the nature of his long-running therapy, but he did say that Dr. Hilsen was someone with whom he talked about every aspect of his life. This therapy could not have been inexpensive.

But Paul and Gene were in complete agreement about one thing. Ace and Peter's craziness had to be controlled and they had to be kept a safe distance from it. Controlling Ace and Peter was the responsibility of the tour staff. Whatever had to be done, just do it. Gene and Paul didn't want to know about it. Whatever the cost of keeping Ace and Peter placated so they made it to the next city was worth the price to keep Kiss alive and kicking. Paul often snickered about it, referring to them as "the smart people" when they were hobbling on board a plane or spread out on the couch of an airport lounge, out of earshot. Despite the sarcasm, he and Gene were dead serious. Too much was at stake to let it fall apart.

There was one important proviso. Gene and Paul insisted that Ace and Peter's personal expenses be accounted for separately and come out of their pockets. They didn't want to be contaminated by any of Ace and Peter's craziness by paying for it. By the time of the current tour these expenses had swelled from a few thousand dollars a month to as much as tens of thousands of dollars some months.

Cash had to be in plentiful supply at all times on the tour, especially for the Super Kiss tour. This was my department. I had to make sure that there was always enough on hand to cover any contingencies. Credit cards weren't much use for daily concerns like cashing payroll checks or buying production supplies from local vendors. And they were certainly of little value in paying for Ace and Peter's expensive habits.

My two bosses had given me strict instructions to make sure that whoever in the band wanted cash had to sign a receipt and take the money personally. They wanted to make sure that none of the craziness—drugs, booze, gambling, room damages—was charged to the tour as a business expense. That was the limit of my involvement. Ace and Peter had their own network of deal makers. But I never knew when I'd get called for a cash advance. I was always on standby except when they were on stage. As long as Ace and Peter were coddled and contained, America's supergroup could continue their march from city to city.

The tour hit a memorable moment when we arrived in Detroit for the show at the Pontiac Silverdome. We were staying in nearby Troy, Michigan. Limos pulled up in front of the hotel and everyone except Gene exited and headed inside. Gene remained in his car with the door closed. A few fans had conducted a vigil at the hotel waiting for Kiss to arrive. When the other three Kiss members rushed from the limos to the hotel and left them in the dust, the fans circled the area in front of Gene's car. They waited for the door to open to get a chance to see a member of Kiss close up, without makeup. The door swung back and there was Gene, slouching in the center of the backseat with his legs spread apart and a girl in front of him kneeling on the floor, giving him a blow job. It was one of Kiss's oldest and dearest fans, a tall, lanky girl with a great mass of fuzzy brown hair. She kept bobbing her head with a determined rhythm. She was oblivious to the crowd and Gene was grinning like a Cheshire cat. When she finished, she broke into a big smile. No one cared or had any qualms about it. It was a measure of how far out things had gotten on this tour.

Despite the fact that the tour was losing money hand over fist, *Dynasty*, the recently released Kiss album, was a big hit, reaching #9 in *Billboard*. A single from the album, "I Was Made for Lovin' You," was tearing up the charts. Kiss had shrewdly calculated that a song with a disco beat—1979 was the year the disco craze peaked—would be their ticket to getting airplay and moving up the charts. It would also help ticket sales. At the very least, *Dynasty* helped cushion the blow from a tour that had become unhinged, and helped to keep the group's spirits up. In August, Kiss received another boost when they were featured in a profile on the ABC News program *20/20*. The focus was on the big business impact of Kiss—expecting to do gross retail business of $100 million that year. Inflated sales figures were always a key element of the Kiss hype.

The *Dynasty* album set what must have been a record for the most amount of money ever spent on an album cover. Francesco Scavullo, the top fashion photographer who frequently shoots covers for *Cosmopolitan*, was hired to shoot Kiss for the album. The photo was a simple concept, a single tight shot of Kiss's faces with a very sharp focus. Hundreds of photos were taken but Kiss refused to approve any of them. The solution was to section each group shot into individual shots of facial parts—eyes, hair, mouths, lips, ears, etc.—like individual pieces of a jig-saw puzzle. This would produce thousands of permutations. The final approved "photo" of the four of them would be a composite of the best parts of all the photos. The laborious job of assembling this photographic pastiche fell to Dennis Woloch, the art director at Howard Marks Advertising in New York. Woloch was the regular designer for the Kiss album covers, the person who bore the brunt of the responsibility for turning Kiss's visual inspirations into finished products. Extensive retouching, air brushing, and transposing was required to make a perfect composite. The photo session was almost aborted when Peter and Ace got into an argument in the dressing room and nearly came to blows. Peter threw his fist into the makeup mirror on the wall. After being rushed to a hospital emergency room for treatment, he returned to Scavullo's East Side studio hours later with his arm wrapped in bandages. The album cover ended up costing nearly $40,000.

The *Dynasty* photo shoot also produced a set of photos of Kiss in makeup but without their usual costumes. They wore straitjackets. Scavullo had a tough time giving the band direction, unlike the pliant and docile models he was used to working with. Peter kept calling him "Frankie" instead of Francesco. One of the band asked him how he liked working with "crazy people" who don't take orders well. At that point, someone suggested that straitjackets might make Kiss easier to deal with. Fritz, the tour manager, was dispatched when Peter gave the order to get some. Getting four straitjackets in the middle of a Saturday afternoon was no easy task, but a couple of the road crew helped Fritz round them up from medical supply houses near Bellevue Hospital.

Kiss was still drawing big crowds in the summer of '79, but they weren't the sure-fire sellout of two years earlier. Many shows didn't break even for the promoters. Guarantees were high, most averaging in the $40,000 to $50,000 range, based on the record-setting attendance of the last tour. Some promoters bit off more than they could chew. Jack Orbin, a San Antonio promoter who booked a string of Kiss dates in Texas, took a huge loss when ticket sales soured in several cities.

Turnouts at most shows on the tour were in the 10,000 to 15,000 range, robust by any measure, but often not enough for the promoters to recoup the big guarantees they'd anted up before the tour had begun. And for Kiss, the big guarantees weren't enough to offset the holes in the itinerary from the canceled shows.

The Super Kiss show was way beyond flamboyant and had a certain Vegas-style gaudiness to it. The lavish costumes were gorgeous. The special effects, even without the lasers, were startling. But all the exaggerated opulence was pushing the Kiss concept into uncharted territory, more like a *Star Wars* extravaganza featuring comic book superheroes on stage. The kiddie contingent seen at Lakeland wasn't an anomaly; there were plenty of them at every stop who had undoubtedly been turned on by the Kiss movie, the Kiss toys, the Kiss comics, the Kiss dolls, and the Kiss everything. Backstage, there was a nightly parade of kiddies dressed up in official Kiss costumes and makeup, some lifted onto the shoulders of parents and others escorted by older brothers and sisters. A schoolteacher from Atlanta presented a petition from her grade-school class, saluting Kiss as their heroes of the year. The presence of all these kiddies at Kiss shows was telegraphing a message, but neither Kiss nor Bill Aucoin was picking it up.

Solo performances were a feature attraction of the show. Each Kiss member took center stage while the other three disappeared off to the sides. Gene would swing wildly from one end of the stage to the other on his Peter Pan flying rig while spitting blood and pounding a death rattling bass solo. A few times, the flying rig got twisted up and Gene ended up hanging like a limp towel on a clothesline suspended high above the stage. It got a lot of laughs from the rest of the group and the crew backstage. Paul would grind out a churning rhythm attack and Ace would create all sorts of otherworldly harmonics on his guitar that sounded like the eerie electronic tones heard in *Close Encounters of the Third Kind.*

Peter's drum solo was designed to be a high point. His enormous mobile drum riser thrust in all directions, like a Sherman tank. Peter himself, sitting behind a mountainous set of drums, would nearly vanish from sight. Peter often played the drums wildly and chaotically, seemingly out of control, punctuating each drum riff with the banging of a huge Chinese gong that sat behind him. The stage was so big that special dressing rooms for touching up the makeup and tuning the guitars were built underneath like a mini-bunker, and Ace and Paul usually listened to the solo from under the stage. They sometimes couldn't help laughing, hearing Peter's fevered beating and wild gyrations. "What's he doin' up there?" they screamed at each other. But it didn't matter to the fans. The audience was cheering with every beat that Peter struck, yelling for more. The mania the Kiss show created overwhelmed any concern for musicianship.

Tragically, there was an unintended side effect from one of the Kiss show's trademarks, Gene's fire-breathing trick. He'd learned it from a veteran circus performer, known as Amaze-O, early in his career. Some young fans tried to imitate his stage routine and suffered horrible consequences, burning themselves severely. *The New York Times* ran a story on November 12, 1978, about a boy in Baltimore who was critically injured when he attempted to imitate Gene's stunt. There were other incidents around the country. Gene took great pains in interviews and on radio and TV to warn Kiss fans not to even think about trying this trick.

Kiss's stint at Madison Square Garden in late July received a rare review and accompanying photo in *Rolling Stone*, a publication that gave Kiss limited coverage for most of their career. While sidestepping the music, their review in the September 20, 1979, issue lauds the Kiss stage show: "[It] has so many neat special effects that your pubic hair retracts and you become twelve years old again and the music doesn't matter." *Rolling Stone* also mentioned the many empty seats behind the stage. The audiences for the second shows still left on the schedule were noticeably thinner.

By September, another major upheaval was looming and this one had nothing to do with the tour. Bill Aucoin's management contract with the group was up for renewal and they planned a big showdown with him. Paul and Gene were prepared, if necessary, to drop him; Ace and Peter were undecided. The showdown was planned for Fort Wayne, Indiana, a bleak industrial city in northeast Indiana, home to tire and rubber manufacturers. Kiss had selected this city since there would be no diversions or distractions. More importantly, a number of people would be flying in for the meeting—Bill Aucoin; Paul Marshall, their attorney; Howard Marks; and Carl Glickman—and Kiss didn't like the idea of this group coming to one of the glamour metropolises. They should come to a boring, dreary, inconveniently located town with a second-rate hotel, and suffer along with them.

Bill didn't travel on tour with Kiss very often. He felt it was largely unnecessary since Kiss had a full complement of people to handle the tour duties. Besides, he was heavily involved in managing a slew of other new bands which he couldn't do by being on the road constantly with Kiss. Managers do this at their own peril. If they leave their mainstay artists on tour by themselves, little problems frequently turn into much bigger ones, like sores which fester into gaping wounds. It had started to happen with Kiss. This was a bone of contention with them—the amount of attention he was devoting to handling new acts at their expense—and it had accelerated the timetable for the showdown.

A conference room was booked at the Holiday Inn for the all-day affair. I wasn't invited to the meeting, probably because it had a more personal dimension, involving as it did Bill's relationship with the group. Rumors were flying. Bill would be fired. Bill would resign. Bill would give up managing his other bands. There would no longer be a manager but a board of directors to advise Kiss. Bill would be paid a salary instead of a commission. The most preposterous of the rumors was that some kind of management tribunal would be formed replacing Bill, and Paul Marshall would preside as the chief justice. I never put much stock in that one.

By early evening, the meeting had concluded. You could hear laughter, and the room became very noisy. I found out later that a food fight had been in progress. Everyone emerged looking relieved if not exuberant. Carl, Howard, and Paul Marshall rushed to catch the last commuter flight out of Fort Wayne. I didn't have a chance to find out exactly what the outcome had been but it appeared to be positive at least as far as Bill was concerned.

That evening, Bill invited the band and some of the tour staff to join him for dinner. Peter was the only one in the group who took him up on the offer, and I and a few staff members also accepted. Having already earned a reputation as the tour's traveling gourmet, I booked the restaurant for the celebratory dinner. Cafe Johnell was a jewel of a restaurant that from the outside looked like a run-down warehouse but inside was very elegant and formal, with deep red velvet draperies and fabric-covered walls that gave it a classic continental ambiance. Small Greco-Roman statuettes dotted the corners of the main dining room, nestled in alcoves. Our group sat around a spacious banquette in the corner of the room underneath a faded print of an Italian landscape.

Bill appeared relieved. He looked like someone who'd just survived a terrible ordeal. From the few bits and pieces of information I'd been able to gather, he had had a dark cloud lifted from his life. We chatted a bit and he said the meeting went well and the outcome was satisfactory for him, but he didn't seem anxious to go into any detail. Peter was full of brio that night, boasting of how he'd "saved Bill's job." Thanks to him, Bill was staying on as manager. I praised him for this apparently selfless act and then we changed the subject. The dinner was splendid: shrimp de Jonghe, cannelloni Florentine, tenderloin of beef with sauce Béarnaise, potatoes soufflé, and a flaming baked Alaska for dessert. Bill also chose the wine, Château Haut-Brion, his favorite, and as a special treat for all after dinner, ordered a $500 bottle of Napoleon cognac. We had a very pleasant evening.

The next day, I phoned Howard in New York to find out exactly what went on at the meeting. He said the band had agreed to extend Bill's contract for another two years but at a reduced commission. His commission had been 20 percent of Kiss's income and would now be cut to 18 1/2 percent. There were also some adjustments on how commissions would be calculated, mostly technical changes which the attorneys would enjoy spending untold hours drafting into contract language, reshuffling some papers and replacing old documents with new ones. The biggest shocker was that Bill would no longer be allowed to earn commissions on tour income following the end of the current U.S. tour. Those are the guarantees and percentage monies that Kiss earns from doing concerts. Bill would only share in the tour income if there was a profit, otherwise he'd get nothing. But any staff employed by him to work on Kiss's tours would be reimbursed by Kiss. As it turned out, the commission cut was nothing more than a phantom savings. And the reimbursement arrangement was a loophole. By the following year, Bill's tour-related staff and their overhead expense would be a $250,000 annual cost to Kiss.

That was the gist of it. It was abundantly clear that the tour and its tremendous financial cost had taken its toll. Kiss was trying to stop the hemorrhaging. The commission reduction of 1 1/2 percent wasn't overly significant. It was more a face-saving ploy so it looked like Kiss had gotten something back from Bill, making the showdown a moral as well as a financial victory for them. When artists renegotiate their management contracts, particularly when the artist is a money-maker in the driver's seat, that kind of chipping away is typical of the jostling which takes place. But for an act like Kiss, which earned so much of their income from touring, it was a big setback for Bill. It was more evidence that the Super Kiss strategy was breaking down.

By October, we were in Texas for half a dozen shows. I was having dinner at the Palm in Houston with a couple of staffers and some Aucoin Management people. Our table was close to collapsing from the weight of the giant-sized lobsters we were served, with platters of fried onions that rose like teepees and bottles of Puligny-Montrachet. I finally managed to pull myself away from the table and make it to the bar. I started to chat up a raven-haired doe-eyed looker in her twenties named Candy whose tanned complexion made it seem like she'd been brushed with a touch of olive oil. Candy had overheard our boisterous dinner party and I noticed her glancing over when it became clear we were connected to Kiss. Candy was dying to go to the Kiss concert at the Houston Summit. She was also dying to meet Gene Simmons, an encounter I could surely arrange. Candy came back to the hotel with me in my car.

From the lobby of Stouffer's where we were staying, I phoned Gene's room. Everyone in Kiss had a code name or alias they registered under in the hotels. At the time, Gene's was Dr. Van Helsing (Dracula's nemesis), though he later switched to Dr. Doom. I told Gene I had a girl who wanted to meet him and he was only too happy to have me send her up. I gave Candy his room number and then walked back to my room. I never expected to see her again.

At 2:00 am, I was fast asleep until pounding on my door shook me out of bed. It was Candy. She asked to come in and said Gene had told her to come to my room. It seemed strange for Gene to offer his playmates to me—he was never particularly magnanimous in that way—but I wasn't about to psychoanalyze the situation. Candy came in and I offered her a drink. After about 5 or 10 minutes of casual conversation, Candy started taking off her rib-knit black sweater and jeans. She stripped down to her black bikini briefs before turning off the lights and getting into bed.

I woke up covered in blood the next morning. The bed sheets were dripping wet. Candy woke up and could see that my eyes looked as if they were about to fall out. "God, it looks like someone got shot here," she murmured. "I'm really sorry. I forgot to tell you. I was having my period." I told her not to be concerned about it. I would tear the sheets off and dispose of them. Now I knew why Candy was my guest for the night and not Gene's. Gene became uneasy at the sight of real blood in any form. The stage act was simply a role where he played the part of a blood-sucking monster. He even ordered his steaks "cremated" to make sure no red juices appeared on the plate.

After leaving Houston, word filtered back on Candy. There's always a story behind everyone you meet on the road and with the girls who typically hang out to meet rock groups, the stories often have a dark side. Candy was reportedly busted for selling drugs. When she was arrested, the police found bags filled with thousands of barbiturates in her trunk.

Kiss stormed through the south as the tour wound down into the final stretch of shows. It was like a battle-weary army ready to stand down, its armor dented and bruised and its machinery creaking. The Kiss army was tired and cranky and we were all looking forward to the Christmas holidays and saying our goodbyes after 6 months on the road. Touring quickly becomes an insular, almost claustrophobic existence. Every little incident is magnified to an exaggerated degree and everyone's idiosyncrasies take on an absurd significance. The novelty of rock 'n' roll wears off after a few weeks and the monotony sets in. You feel the sameness going from town to town where the only thing that changes is the name of the arena.

We came into Shreveport, Louisiana, an old-fashioned Delta city, for a routine show in December at Hirsch Coliseum. Kiss had recently finished a run of shows with newcomer John Cougar Mellencamp opening for them. Shreveport turned out to be the event of the tour in entirely the wrong way, a major turning point in the fortunes of Kiss. We'd all been operating on automatic pilot in those last weeks before Christmas and were going through the paces by rote.

Kiss was about an hour into their usual 90-minute set. Paul was spinning around on stage left and Gene was baiting the crowd on stage right. Ace was off to the far edge of the stage wrapped up in his solo and spewing clouds of smoke from his guitar. But Peter had unexpectedly shifted from his normally intense staccato beat. The song then started to slow down. Everyone in Kiss seemed confused, glowering at Peter. He just kept beating the drums, slower and slower.

Peter finally stopped playing entirely. Paul screamed to the audience, "Good night, Shreveport! We love you! Rock 'n' rolllllllll!" and confetti guns burst into the crowd, spraying them with the usual blizzard of multicolored paper shreds. As the house lights went up, Kiss rushed off the stage and ran into the dressing room, slamming the door after ordering everyone to leave the immediate area. The fracas in the dressing room lasted nearly an hour but the sounds inside were indecipherable.

Later that night at the hotel bar, I heard what had supposedly happened: Peter had been deeply offended by something Gene or Paul did or said and he was angry. He'd been severely slighted. To make matters worse, he'd just been through a bitter divorce with his wife, Lydia, and was planning to get married again at the end of December. The tour's pressures and the stress of his personal situation made him particularly vulnerable. He also announced that he was planning to leave the band after the tour, but needed time to talk to his lawyer and his psychiatrist.

It wasn't the first time that the rest of the band and the crew had to compensate for Peter's unpredictability. Fritz, who did play drums, frequently filled in for Peter when he didn't show up for sound checks. Earlier during the *Dynasty* tour, during one of Peter's bad spells, Fritz devised an emergency remedy. He had suited up in an old Kiss costume and waited in the wings to substitute for Peter if necessary. At the last minute, the plan was scratched when it seemed that Peter would be able to get through the show.

Paul, Gene, and Ace were in a rage. To stop playing and cut the show short in front of 10,000 fans wasn't something easily excused. And Peter's dictum that he would have no further discussions on the subject until he consulted his advisers didn't sit well with them, either. *The Shreveport Times* in their December 15 review of the show mentioned that there was no encore from Kiss, something of a surprise. Peter agreed to finish the tour, but his future with Kiss was a subject that would be held in abeyance until after the tour and Peter's wedding was over. Nothing more was said for the remaining week we were on tour.

A Learjet was flown in from New York to take Kiss home directly after the last show in Toledo, Ohio, on December 16. At an isolated airstrip at the Municipal Airport, a sleek, white jet with steel blue markings and pinstriping was positioned on the runway with the cabin lights on. It was nearly midnight. The airstrip trailed off onto an inky black field, barely lit by two rows of blinking aircraft lights on either side of the airstrip. Kiss's fleet of limos could be seen barreling down a single-lane approach highway coming toward the plane. The cars pulled within a few feet of the aircraft, halted, and disposed of their passengers. We climbed the small staircase to enter the plane. Minutes later, the cabin door sealed shut with a heavy thud. The jet engines started to whine and a powerful whirring sound increased to a high-pitched scream. The jet taxied into the distance and climbed sharply above the airstrip, vanishing into the night sky. The tour was over. It was the end of 6 months on the road and 78 shows. It would be the end of Super Kiss in America. But it wouldn't be the end of Super Kiss. Yet.

9

The M-G-M of Rock 'n' Roll

With Kiss a phenomenal success by the late 1970s, Bill Aucoin was on his way to becoming the top music manager in America. Pursuing his dream of an "M-G-M of rock 'n' roll" was the way that he could establish himself in the firmament previously reserved for the titans of the old Hollywood studio system. Bill articulated his philosophy in a press release for his company circulated in 1978:

> My basic philosophy concerning management stems from an admiration of the early film industry. I believe that an artist needs a total organization—a complete environment—around him. With that in his favor, the artist can create and grow without any fears, and it's the manager's responsibility to provide that atmosphere for the artist.

Bill would emulate the role of Louis B. Mayer, adapting it to the rock world and creating a studio-style organization. All of the artists would be under contract to him and he would provide a full range of services for all of their creative works. A big organization would be required. There would be subsidiary companies, divisions, branch offices, and key staff to perform every function. Many artists would need to be signed up to justify the expense. But it would all be worth it because by controlling the artists and every element of their career, the manager would be able to plan everything. The artist's image was too critical and too fragile to allow outsiders to monkey with. Even the record company would be kept at a safe distance so they couldn't bollix up the works. Control was crucial to success.

Bill had only been in the music business for a few years but he already had a well-developed philosophy of the role of artist manager. Managers are often street-smart types who get a lucky break with an act and try to hang on as long as possible, squirreling away the commissions for the rainy days sure to come. Life expectancy for music managers is short and when they run their course with an act, their career often fades out. Bill had very different ideas about the business.

The music industry was changing from the fly-by-the-seat-of-the-pants business it had been in the '50s and '60s to a more dynamic and multifaceted industry in the '70s. Bill's concept was of a professionally managed business, with structures in place to develop the artist's potential and maximize the money that groups like Kiss could earn in a short time.

Artist and manager would be closely linked. They would interact together with the record company. Publicists would play a key role as old-fashioned press agentry was being supplanted by modern public relations campaigns and media events. Merchandising was taking off, and the market for T-shirts, posters, and rock paraphernalia would become a gold mine. Touring in the United States was on an upswing as arenas sprouted up in towns across America. Film and TV would be critical as the music business became more visually oriented. Advertising techniques used in consumer marketing would now be used to sell records and concert tickets. Overseas markets were expanding, and international sales of records were increasingly important. Bill saw the artist and manager as inseparable in seizing those opportunities.

Commissions were piling up when Bill moved into his luxuriously appointed offices at 645 Madison Avenue in the spring of 1976. As Kiss prospered, Aucoin Management expanded by leaps and bounds. The hirings started quickly and people began filling the offices. Linda West, Bill's executive assistant, had been trained at Boeing as a systems manager for the Apollo program; she became the company's crack administrator. Alan Miller was an early associate of Bill's and was Vice President for promotion. Al Ross was the publicity chief who ran The Press Office, an Aucoin-owned p.r. firm. His wife Carol later took over this job when Al was promoted to Executive Vice President. Ken Anderson became Director of Production for touring. Other key staff later followed: Ric Aliberte, Director of Promotion for records; Jack Tessler, Director of International Promotion for records overseas. Alan Cohen, a CPA who was Bill's accountant, was in charge of business affairs. He had helped to finance Kiss and Bill in their early days on tour; when Bill's American Express card was canceled, they got Alan to loan them his card.

As Kiss raked in more money, Bill kept expanding. He ran out of space on the 15th floor of 645 Madison Avenue and took over the 14th floor. The new offices were soon filled. A financial department was set up under Marvin Mann, now Vice President-Finance; he had previously been with International Creative Management, a talent agency. Key executives for movie and TV development were brought in. Bill named Sean Delaney as Vice President—Artist Development; Delaney, who had worn many hats during his years with Kiss, would now be responsible for scouting talent and developing new artists. A merchandising subsidiary was started that would control all of the tour merchandising and licensing for Aucoin artists, including Kiss. Lee Friedman was named to head that company.

Film and TV soon became buzzwords at Aucoin Management. Years before MTV got off the ground, Bill told *Billboard* in a September 10, 1977, interview,

"You have to think of your acts visually as well as audibly. . . .TV or movie cameras are brutal. And if you're going to be able to bring your acts through to that medium, you really had better start thinking about it now."

Bill's experience as a director provided added impetus to his plans to expand into movies and TV. In 1972, he directed a video version of *Oh! Calcutta!*, an Off Broadway musical revue that caused a stir in the '60s because of its scenes simulating sex and a cast that appeared nude.

Kiss's TV movie, *Kiss Meets the Phantom of the Park,* had been "my ballgame," Bill recalled, as an initial thrust into the TV market. Plans were under way to try and expand into a Saturday morning cartoon show, based on Kiss, and possibly a feature film. Bill's operation would develop these and other music-related TV projects, including a Rock 'n' Roll Sports Classic that featured rock stars in the role of jocks.

Kiss became one of America's biggest-earning rock groups. In 1978, a year when Pete Rose made the front pages by announcing his *four*-year $3.2 million pact with the Philadelphia Phillies, the biggest contract in baseball history, Kiss took in $12 million. Bill was earning huge sums from their success and his next step was to open offices in L.A. Aucoin Management/West would be a large suite of offices on nearly half a floor of a high-rise luxury building in Westwood. Executives for record production, music publishing, business affairs, and record promotion were added. Aucoin Management/West had a music room outfitted with a piano and recording equipment. Throngs of aspiring singers and song-writers queued up to audition, a chore which largely fell to production executives Nick Smerigan and Eddie Wenrick. By the end of 1978, Bill's far-flung operation had close to forty people on the payroll. Bill believed that to develop Kiss's potential in all areas of entertainment, he needed this extraordinary setup. New projects would be taken on by the new executives to build the organization, yet Kiss remained his only income-producing client. Bill was unfazed.

He was always full of big ideas. He confided to me once when we were driving to the L.A. airport together that he wanted to have his company so successful that he could pay his top people $600,000 a year salaries. I was flabbergasted. It sounded unbelievable but somehow with Bill, you always wanted to believe. He was talking about expanding the company into the disco boom, franchising Studio 54s around the world, something that could have made a fortune for the promoters. I never mentioned Bill's blue-sky plans to Carl Glickman but I did ask him how Bill could afford to spend so much on overhead and personnel. "He can't," was Carl's blunt response.

Bill's personal lifestyle moved into an expansive phase as his business empire thrived on both coasts. Bill was wedded to the idea that showing success was as important as earning it and in a business not known for modesty, he spared no effort to create a personal monument to match his success in the music world. He chose Olympic Tower, a newly constructed building owned by the Onassis interests, which was fast becoming one of New York's most prestigious addresses, especially for *arrivistes*.

Rising like a black obelisk more than forty stories high, Olympic Tower overlooked St. Patrick's Cathedral on the opposite block. Bill's seven-room apartment on the 35th floor was an elegant cocoon walled in by floor-to-ceiling smoked glass. Marble from Italy, brushed stainless steel panels, hand-built burlwood cabinets and chests, sofas wrapped in colored pigskin, hand-carved bedroom furniture, wall and ceiling coverings of textured fabrics, gold-plated bathroom fixtures, mirrored dressing areas, and a media room chock full of video equipment and built-in speakers filled the apartment. Everything was done in an ultramodern style in contrasting tones of beige and black. Works by contemporary artists like Robert Motherwell and David Smith lined the walls, and pre-Columbian sculptures were scattered in the living and dining areas.

It was a stunning effect high atop a Manhattan tower and one of the top interior designers in the country, Jay Spectre, was responsible for it. Bill gave him carte blanche to do the job. The apartment was featured in the January/February 1979 issue of *Architectural Digest*. About the only thing it didn't have was a swimming pool, like one of Bill's Olympic Tower neighbors, arms broker Adnan Khashoggi, who occupied two full floors in the building. Bill's apartment was an eyeful. Every square inch of space was accounted for according to a detailed plan. I was never sure whether this wondrous creation actually reflected Bill's personal taste or was the kind of grand luxe environment that he felt was expected of him. The Olympic Tower apartment was certainly a show-stopper, though.

A houseman was soon hired for the apartment to coordinate Bill's increasingly busy social calendar, and a limo was leased to round out his pasha-like existence. The limo had license plates reading "GUI" (pronounced GEE as in geezer), which was short for Guillaume, Bill's original first name of French-Canadian origin. To celebrate his first Christmas in the apartment, he hired famed illustrator Milton Glaser in 1978 to design a customized Christmas card for a $10,000 fee. The card was a series of four graphic designs that fit together like the pieces of a puzzle. Each one represented a component of the "Aucoin Organization"—Aucoin Management, which managed artists; Boutwell, the merchandising unit; The Press Office, a publicity outfit; and Rock Steady, the music production and publishing arm.

The fact that Bill didn't own the apartment, but rented it on a short-term lease, never put a crimp in his interior design plans. It was vital for Bill to have a prestige address on Fifth or Park Avenue, but it was unlikely he would've been approved as an owner in a building in that upper-crust neighborhood. Being young, single, and in the music business—let alone connected to a wild rock group like Kiss—would have been automatic grounds for rejection by any co-op's board of directors. So Bill rented an apartment and spent a ton of money to make it look spectacular. Bill's financial advisers told him it was crazy to spend so much on a rented apartment. "He never worried about those things," one former colleague recalled.

The apartment soon developed a reputation for parties on a Bacchanalian scale. There were frequent bashes and soirees. Roederer Cristal champagne flowed like tap water. An exclusive society caterer provided the *recherché* cuisine. People came up and down in the building's high-speed elevators at all hours of the night. It was a very swinging place.

As a music impresario, Bill attracted a wide variety of guests. Some of the other tenants were reportedly distressed by those they saw waiting in the lobby for the elevator. Punk rock, heavy metal, heavy leather, biker types. Mohawks and crew cuts, Euro-chic and glitter rock—they all mixed it up together. There were also older, more mature guests including Henry Dormann, a wealthy magazine publisher who had been chairman of the *National Enquirer* and president of *Holiday Magazine*. Henry provided financial advice to Bill from time to time. He was well connected in the political and business world and had earned a reputation as a globe-trotter whose personal friends included many world leaders and Fortune 500 chiefs. Henry could be counted on to put in a well-placed phone call if Bill needed something. Bill saw Henry as a door opener and the two became friends; Bill's unusual lifestyle was quite a departure from Henry's more establishment background.

Bill's sudden elevation into the world of the rich and famous energized him. But he had to maintain a delicate balance between the elegant way of life symbolized by Olympic Tower and posh parties where he could rub shoulders with society's movers and shakers, and the world of the streets, which is what rock 'n' roll represents. Bill always wanted to have one foot in each world; now that would become more difficult.

When Aucoin Management went west, Bill leased a home in Beverly Hills, off Sunset Strip. Apartments were rented at the Beekman Towers on Park Avenue as corporate housing for all the execs flying between L.A. and New York. Travelers bound for L.A. would simply check into a plush hotel and rent a Mercedes. People were flitting back and forth between the two coasts on a regular basis. Things were in fast-forward.

During this period, Bill was busy signing new acts. He was passionate about developing new artists from scratch. To him, that was the most enjoyable part of the creative process. Once Kiss was a hit, he seemed to reduce his hands-on creative role. He felt some fine-tuning and tinkering to adjust things would be required, but he could devote more of his energies to developing new artists, his forte. Working with established artists was less appealing since their careers already had a distinctive stamp, one that he might not be able to change. Discovering new artists is largely based on instinct and gut feeling and Bill had certainly hit the jackpot when he bet on Kiss.

With the infrastructure in place, Bill believed he was now ideally positioned to put in motion his "M-G-M of rock 'n' roll." Artists would want managers who were clearly big-time, experienced professionals like Bill. Nightclub operators, disc jockeys, record promoters, and road managers—who often became managers simply by being in the right place at the right time—would fade from the scene. They were now obsolete. Artists would demand professional advice in all the key areas—record production, music and songs, costumes and wardrobe, promotion and p.r., merchandising, touring, stage production, business affairs. And with Bill's studio-style organization, he would get the cream of the crop.

Bill signed a raft of new acts—Starz, Piper, Virgin, New England, Toby Beau, Amanda Blue, Spider, and even the actress Yvonne DeCarlo. Groups flocked to Bill like bees to honey. His offices were constantly jammed with new bands looking to get Bill, the number one rock 'n' roll manager, to back them. One group that approached Bill was Styx, who went on to sell millions of records in the late '70s, but they never became clients.

Record companies loved signing Bill's acts. By cultivating a relationship with him, they felt they had a shot at signing Kiss when their contract was up with Casablanca. And Bill was ready to whip out his checkbook to subsidize his artists. In the music industry, record companies have to sign and develop scores of new acts in hopes that a handful will make it. Most acts never earn back the money the record company spends on them. Like any business, research and development is costly and chancy. But if a record company hits with one new act, typically signed for a low royalty and a modest advance, they'll make up for all the clunkers, just as movie studios need occasional blockbusters to cover all the bombs they've released. Although even the most successful manager can't match a record label's deep corporate pockets, Bill often chose to co-opt the label in financing new artists to get the control he wanted. But it was an expensive proposition. He had expected every label to make the kind of commitment he'd gotten from Neil Bogart and Casablanca, but that proved to be a false hope.

Managing all of these acts—most were bands with four or five members—became a juggling act. Each one had a record company, booking agent, and its own little network of relationships, personal and professional. A big part of the manager's job is to develop a personal relationship with the artist and their support system. Bill began having a hard time keeping track of all these people and kept adding layers of staff to deal with them, at one point putting on an assistant to keep track of artist's birthdays, anniversaries, and other personal matters.

Having such a large supporting cast at his disposal allowed Bill to adopt a hands-off style. He believed he could be a King Midas since his first artist, Kiss, had turned into gold. Why shouldn't the same thing happen with other acts? Neil's tremendous success inspired Bill to try to create a comparable success with his own company.

Even the rock press became suspicious about Bill's assembly-line operation. Michael Lee Smith, the lead singer of an up-and-coming band that Bill had signed, Starz, griped about the company's reputation as "..a kind of Louis B. Mayer kind of thing [where] Aucoin runs the whole thing and we're like his Judy Garlands...." (*Creem*, January 1977). He bristled at the notion that his band was being manipulated. When asked about how much control Bill exerted over his acts, Michael replied, "The only thing that's happened so far is that we have this song called 'Piss Party,' which is about pissing in other people's mouths and stuff like that. Bill did say 'You might want to change those lyrics.'"

The Aucoin Management approach was often formulaic. As Paul once put it caustically, "Give all the bands logos and teach them how to move around on stage and you've got a hit group." Bill gave his artists everything—carefully crafted images, slick logos, elaborately designed album covers, expensive photo shoots, subsidies for living costs and touring, coaching on how to dance and play in unison, heaps of press releases—but none of the bands ever made much money except Kiss. And Kiss was beginning to express resentment over how much time Bill was spending on other acts. He'd spread himself thin, signing one group after the next, resulting in less time devoted to Kiss. Bill recalled that at the time, Kiss would have liked him to work for them exclusively and not take on other acts.

Kiss, who knew they were the only act bringing home the bacon, complained that they were getting short shrift while Bill was busy building his "M-G-M of rock 'n' roll." The Kiss members let everyone know how angry they were about it, sometimes in meetings at our office with Howard Marks and at other times in off-handed remarks to the staff. Before Bill had taken on this music magnate status, the group held him in high esteem. They hung on his every word. His track record had been exemplary. They loved him. Now, the personal dynamics were changing.

Bill became difficult to reach, sometimes incommunicado. He was often on the road with his new acts, or in L.A. His staff covered for him and did much of the hands-on work that Kiss had gotten used to Bill performing. Just prior to a screening of *Kiss Meets the Phantom of the Park* in 1978, Bill asked Fritz Postleth-waite, the tour manager for Kiss, to drive to Peter's house and break the news to him that nearly all of his dialogue in the movie had to be edited out and re-recorded by another actor. His underlings did their best to dodge phone calls from irate promoters since they often brought bad news, like shows with diffi-cult production problems or low ticket sales. These calls were passed on to Wally Meyrowitz at ATI or to one of Bill's staff or sometimes to me. The nitty-gritty of the music business, especially the craziness of concert promotion, was typically handled by others.

Some of Bill's other artists had similar concerns. A former member of one of his most promising new acts recalled that Bill was seemingly "overwhelmed" by Kiss. While Bill was thought of as a "great manager" at the beginning of their relationship, by the end he felt that Bill had become "preoccupied with his social life" and was hard to reach. Bill was hoping to break their career with a few "big moves" rather than the many small but important steps he had taken to carefully build Kiss's success.

The personal management business is personal. Artists will seldom if ever accept a "chairman of the board" type. Managing artists is tremendously time-consuming and requires meticulous attention to detail. Linda West, Bill's executive assistant, described the Aucoin Management operation as a "whirlwind" at the time. She recalled that Bill was "bombarded with offers and proposals," the result of the company's success. But Bill quickly became "scattered" as he took on "too many creative projects and too many acts," she said.

Much to Bill's displeasure, Glickman/Marks Management began playing a bigger role in Kiss's affairs, performing duties considerably wider in scope than those of most business managers. It was an unwelcome change for Bill, who took umbrage whenever it seemed we were encroaching on his turf. At a meeting in his office with me, Wally, and our company's controller, Bill hit the ceiling when Wally said he was holding off on booking some tour dates because "the business managers told me they had to do a budget first." Bill's face turned crimson and he blasted Wally to make his point perfectly clear. "Glickman/Marks Management isn't the manager—I am. They're strictly the band's financial advisers." We all got the message.

But Bill's authority was slipping away. He continued to be in charge of Kiss's creative side, but we had to fill the organizational gaps and handle most of the business-related dealings. Having Howard Marks increasingly involved in managing Kiss didn't always sit well with Bill, but his inattention to their affairs left him no choice. Howard was happy to do the work, but it was costing him money for additional staff and overhead. We met with Bill and Kiss to ask the band if they wanted Glickman/Marks Management to continue our expanded administrative functions. If so, we would charge a $15,000 monthly client services fee beyond our business manager's commission of 5 percent. Kiss asked us to continue. Rather than deduct the extra cost from Bill's management commission—the work we were doing was really a part of what most managers do for their artists—Kiss agreed to absorb the fee. Bill felt that whenever his situation with Kiss was in some jeopardy, as it was with the client services duties, Howard would step in to rescue him. It was a way for Howard to keep in good stead with both Kiss and Bill.

Other tensions were rising to the surface. Surrounding himself with a coterie of aides, assistants, and factotums didn't endear Bill to Kiss, who had become accustomed to a much closer relationship. And Bill's flamboyant jet-set lifestyle also bothered Kiss. Bill became flushed with success. The Olympic Tower pad and the constant partying began to attract unwanted notoriety. People with the most tenuous connection to the music business would ask me if he still had "wild parties with all that champagne and glitz." Kiss had become embarrassed by all of this, especially Gene and Paul, who had never been comfortable with his partying. They would typically communicate their displeasure to Howard, and at times, I would also hear about it. Gene and Paul felt that Bill's behavior was taking its toll on how their careers were being handled, especially with all of his new projects. It wasn't that a manager had to be fogeyish, but Bill had become too extravagant. Bill states that Kiss never confronted him directly on this.

Ultimately, everything came to a head over merchandising. Merchandising was a prime target since Bill was in control of it. Bill saw merchandising as a major growth business for the music industry. And Kiss was the ideal artist to capitalize on this trend. He was dead right on both counts. Kiss was on its way to becoming one of the highest-grossing artists in the merchandising business through concert sales and retail licensing of T-shirts, programs, posters, and toys.

Traditionally, merchandising was an unsophisticated business run in a slipshod way. There didn't seem to be much money in it for acts on the road. A few people would go into a hall or an arena, set up tables, and sell some printed T-shirts with the group's picture or artwork on them. The halls often let the group's merchandisers sell their wares at the stands for a flat fee, as little as a few hundred dollars for the night. Bill initially hired Ron Boutwell to handle merchandising for Kiss's tours. A tall fellow with long blond hair who always wore sunglasses and a Panama hat, Ron became a pioneer in concert merchandising. He had started Boutwell Enterprises at home in 1970, and eventually handled the merchandising for Kiss, Barry Manilow, and Elton John.

As Kiss's popularity skyrocketed, the merchandising went through the roof. Buttons, badges, T-shirts, programs, posters, belt buckles, pendants, baseball caps, and all sorts of stuff emblazoned with the Kiss logo were hot items at Kiss concerts. The merchandise's graphics and photos were keyed to the album covers. By the late '70s, sales of merchandise reached $2.00 per person at the concerts, then a record. Tickets for shows were normally in the $8.00 range, except for the major cities where they would be a bit higher. Kiss T-shirts were a "gotta have" throughout high schools across the country. Having a Kiss T-shirt and going to a Kiss concert had become a fad, even if you never bought a record. The Kiss Army Fan Club expanded to stimulate merchandise sales through mail order, and the bags of mail came to their headquarters in Southern California in truckloads.

Before long, Bill realized he didn't need Ron Boutwell to do this and bought Ron's company. Now, Bill could control the merchandising on tour for Kiss, already going gangbusters, and the retail licensing, where companies were beating down the doors to license Kiss products. The royalties that could be earned from licensing manufacturers of toys, dolls, clothing, games, and related items to be sold in retail stores would make Bill and the group as rich as Croesus. Bill would not only have the control he desired, he would, in effect, own a license to print money, which is what the rights to Kiss merchandising amounted to in the late '70s.

Bill had a rich management contract with Kiss. He received a 20 percent commission on income from records, concerts, and merchandising. That's fairly standard for the industry (originally, he received 25 percent but when Glickman/ Marks Management was brought in, we took 5 percent and his commission was reduced to 20 percent). On some of the early song copyrights, though, he was the owner or publisher. Bill's original agreement called for him to receive 40 percent of Kiss's publishing income from songs. Songs generate copyright income every time a record is sold. A federal statute spells out exactly how many pennies per song a record company must pay to the owner of the song for every sale they report, either as an album cut or as a single. Music publishing and songwriting income are separate from the royalty paid to the artist for the recording itself. Later, Kiss renegotiated the copyright aspects of the contract, and ownership of the early Kiss songs eventually reverted to the band.

Bill had an equally lucrative deal on Kiss's merchandising. By purchasing Boutwell Enterprises, he would own the merchandising rights to Kiss, and the profits derived from exploiting those rights were split. Initially, the split was 50-50, but the formula was later modified to 60-40 in Kiss's favor. It turned out to be a bonanza for Bill as he was allowed to be paid twice on the merchandising income. First, he collected all the income and charged his merchandising-related costs against those monies, splitting the remaining profits with Kiss based on the formula. Second, he took a management commission on Kiss's share at his customary 20 percent rate. The arrangement remained in place during Kiss's peak merchandising years.

There was nothing sneaky about the merchandising deal. Bill's integrity wasn't the issue. Kiss was fully aware of the lopsided nature of the arrangement and that he owned the merchandising company. Even though it was openly discussed at business meetings, they were resigned to accepting it. They didn't want to rock the boat with Bill. He continued to have a Svengali-like influence over Kiss and they willingly acquiesced to the double commissions.

When Kiss exploded in the late '70s, so did the retail licensing. Bill now owned the merchandising company outright, renaming it Boutwell/Niocua (Aucoin spelled backward). The company became the conduit for all licensing and merchandising monies, and scores of licenses were negotiated by Boutwell/Niocua for Kiss products and paraphernalia in every product line that could be exploited—colorforms, radios, dolls, board games, model vans, makeup kits, lunch boxes, notebooks, Halloween costumes, garbage cans, shoelaces, belt buckles, children's clothes, record players, jackets, sweatshirts, jewelry, thermoses, kiddie guitars, jigsaw puzzles, watches. If a license could be had, Bill jumped on it, and manufacturers like Monsanto, Mego Toys, and Milton Bradley were eagerly courted. It was a key ingredient of the hard-sell formula Bill used to make Kiss a household name. Even a Bally pinball machine was created for Kiss, another first. It soon became a collector's item.

Licensing monies poured into Boutwell/Niocua. Between 1977 and 1979, Kiss's peak years, worldwide retail sales for merchandise sold in stores and on tour grossed an estimated $100 million. It was an unheard-of sum for a rock group. "Take the money and run" became Kiss's attitude, something that would come back to haunt them. Lee Friedman, a former entrepreneur in women's casual clothing in Manhattan, took over the operation in 1977. Bill chose him based largely on his background in apparel and wanted him to move quickly to expand the merchandising unit on a big scale by signing other acts.

Lee soon added Donna Summer, Cheap Trick, Queen, and The Cars to the roster. More people were added to the payroll. The operation had grown too large for the offices they had in the San Fernando Valley, and they moved into Aucoin Management's Westwood suite. Costs began to spiral "out of control," Lee recalled, as success came quickly to the merchandising company, then on a lucky streak. Describing the business as being "run like a playroom," Lee believed that one of the root problems was drug use in some quarters of the organization. The operation went from boom to bust in only a few years despite their ground-breaking success in licensing Kiss and signing new artists. Not having adequate financial controls in place to "balance" the company's rapid expansion turned out to be a major shortcoming, according to Bill.

Merchandising records were shattered throughout the 1979 Kiss tour. But many at Boutwell/Niocua had no experience in this kind of merchandising—selling at arenas every night to mobs of fans who hovered around tables of T-shirts and souvenirs, packed in like sardines. It was more like a carnival than anything else and the logistics of printing, ordering, trucking, setting up, checking inventories, and collecting cash were worlds away from the garment district and the retail licensing business.

When the Super Kiss tour had ended, Kiss was on the warpath. Their take from the merchandising was pathetic. They would earn well under $300,000 for 78 shows in 1979 after it passed through the Boutwell/Niocua operation. After paying commissions, it was reduced to a pitifully small sum. The huge advances received for licenses to retail manufacturers also collected by

Boutwell/Niocua were largely chewed up in overhead costs. Kiss blamed Bill for the less than stellar results. An audit revealed missing monies and bloated expenses, including multiple trips on the Concorde and lavish entertainment in London and L.A. Kiss's peak licensing years were over. Like most fads in the toy business, it had run its course, and because of the deal they had with Bill, relatively little money earned from Kiss merchandise made its way back to their pockets. The fact that the tour had begun with Boutwell/Niocua owing Kiss very substantial sums for licensing earnings only added salt to the wound.

Bill was called on the carpet. He was sharply criticized by the group since he'd been in charge of everything and had chosen the people to run the operation. Bill had been hoisted by his own petard. He had been adamant about being in control of Kiss's merchandising, fearful that anyone else would ruin their image. But in the end, much of the money went down the drain and Kiss's logo had been slapped on so many products that the market was swamped, disfiguring their image.

Kiss was distraught over the mess. We were asked by the group and their lawyer, Paul Marshall, to come up with a way to fix it. In early 1980, we came up with a plan. The retail licensing would be handled by Twentieth Century Fox Licensing, a company in business year-round and not just in business for Kiss. Through Steve Roberts, a Fox executive whose wife, Karen, had worked for Bill, we made a deal for them to take over Kiss's licensing. Coming off a record-breaking success, the merchandising of *Star Wars,* they were keen on developing new entertainment properties. The Kiss Army Fan Club, 100,000 strong at its peak in 1978, would also be run by an outside company, one that specialized in the mail-order business, Don Jagoda Associates. Kiss was in danger of being sued by attorneys general in dozens of states when customers' orders were never filled. Thousands of order forms filled with cash and checks had reportedly piled up in a West Coast warehouse. There weren't enough people to fulfill the orders and process the checks.

And Kiss's tour merchandising had to be revamped. It made no sense for them to be in the T-shirt and souvenir business, shackled with all the overhead of manufacturing and printing facilities, just to do a tour every year or so. Companies like Winterland and Great Southern Merchandising were emerging as specialists in this area, with the marketing and manufacturing muscle to do it right since they handled many touring acts. They also paid advances. Kiss could get big up-front money for their merchandising rights before the tours started.

Everybody bought the plan. Naturally, Bill was unhappy since it meant a diminution of his authority. Despite having so much control over Kiss, he was swept away by his dream of creating a rock 'n' roll studio, and he was too distracted to deal with the details of running it. But there was no alternative to the new plan and Bill knew it. By the end of 1979, Lee Friedman left to join Hanna-

Barbera and was replaced with an expert from the printing business, Dick Davison. But Dick was involved with the new merchandising operation only for a short transition period.

No one really knows exactly how much money was lost running Kiss's merchandising from the late '70s until 1980. Millions coursed through the pipeline but after so much was siphoned off to pay for the operation, and with costs escalating out of sight, very little flowed back to Kiss. Kiss's total take from tour merchandising and retail licensing for three of their biggest years, 1977 through 1979, came to less than $2 million.

Once the merchandising debacle had come to light, Bill had to stanch the bleeding his attempt at empire building had caused. Few of the acts he'd signed and invested untold sums to promote had registered more than a blip on the sales chart and not much more than a trickle of income had been seen from any of them. Toby Beau did have a hit single with "My Angel Baby," but soon broke up. Piper's lead singer, Billy Squier, left the band to pursue a solo career and had some top-selling albums in the '80s. Paul produced New England, which briefly toured with Kiss, and Gene produced Virgin, whose album was never released. Starz recorded four albums for Capitol before disbanding in 1979.

Midas was turning things into stone, not gold. Bad luck also played a part. Some of the groups were plagued by personal problems and internal conflicts which led to their breaking up. And one group's record label shut down operations when its corporate owner decided to pull the plug. Kiss was still Bill's only cash cow and his relationship with them had started to rupture.

The first round of belt-tightening had already begun in 1979. Marvin Mann confronted Bill with the reality that the company was losing money hand over fist and that he had been turned down for a bank loan of $1 million. Bill was shaken by the news that the rent couldn't be paid and firings were imminent; Marvin told Bill that thirty-five people had to be let go. Linda West was then working on a company reorganization.

The L.A. offices of Aucoin Management/West were shut down and the Beverly Hills house was vacated. Bill gave up one of the two floors of his New York offices and the limo with "GUI" license plates soon disappeared. By the following year, the company had slimmed down to a handful of key staffers and the merchandising operation was closed. Most of the firings were carried out by subordinates. Cutbacks and economizing were now unavoidable. Daily floral arrangements, breakfasts served on silver trays, and office visits by masseuses and manicurists were quickly eliminated.

But Bill's cash crunch was too severe to be fixed by simply doing without flowers and manicures. He now had to worry about the survival of his company. Jeff Franklin, ATI's head, arranged some interim financing to help Bill.

Jeff recalls that Bill was "extremely talented and bright," but overexpanded when he set out to become a "mega-mogul." Carl Glickman helped to put Bill on a budget. The year looked promising for Kiss, and Bill would be able to pull through now that his operation was downsized. He would have to spend most of his time looking after Kiss to keep himself in their good graces and hold onto his job. But he would be able to keep the Olympic Tower apartment.

Aucoin Management was more of a free-for-all than an M-G-M of rock. We had just entered the '80s and Bill, always ahead of his time in so many ways, had now crash-landed. For him, the excesses of the '70s were over. So was the money. The multimillions in commissions that Bill had earned from Kiss between 1975 and 1979 were mostly spent. The incredible rise of the Aucoin empire had rested on, and fallen with, a shaky foundation—the idea that by spending enough to create the perfect environment, artists could be molded, manufactured, and merchandised to the public with predictable success. Bill thought that with the right formula—and enough hype—it would just be a matter of cranking out the product and pushing it out the door. Bill's far-reaching and remarkably prescient vision about the music business proved to be accurate in many ways. But like many things connected to Kiss, it became a case of reaching too far too soon.

10 Hitting the Jackpot

In typical Kiss fashion, Peter Criss wouldn't have one wedding, but two. They would both take place during the week before Christmas, 1979. It was Peter's favorite time of the year since his birthday was just a few days before Christmas and the holiday season always made him sentimental.

The engraved invitations from Cartier were already in the mail before the Super Kiss tour wrapped up. First, in New York, there would be a prewedding party for Peter's family and friends, most of whom lived there, as well as his many business acquaintances. It would be held at Regine's on Park Avenue, a stylish jet-set disco and haunt of the rich and famous. A few days following the Regine's party, the actual wedding ceremony and reception would take place in L.A. where Peter's new bride lived as did most of her family and friends. Both would be glittering, gala affairs.

The bride-to-be was Debra Svensk, a statuesque Southern California beauty Peter told me that he had met in L.A. about a year and a half earlier at a party for Rod Stewart. Perky and blonde with a cheerful disposition, Debbie also possessed a very important pedigree: she had been *Playboy*'s Miss January in 1978. She had also been the model for Coppertone suntan lotion. Debbie was just twenty when she first met Peter (then using her professional name of Debra Jensen), and they hit it off right away. Whatever physical infatuation Peter had for Debbie and whatever Peter's rock star status meant to her, each seemed to strike a deep chord in the other. The relationship was tempestuous at times—Debbie was the girl in Peter's hotel suite in L.A. the prior year who supposedly had been knocked out during the smashed guitar dustup—but Peter seemed to have calmed down since then. There was only one problem—Peter's wife Lydia.

Peter and Lydia married in 1970 when he was a struggling drummer living in Brooklyn. An attractive, dark-haired Italian girl, Lydia worked as a bookkeeper and kept Peter together in every way possible. Without Lydia's support, it's doubtful Peter would have continued the difficult life of an unknown musician playing in bands and taking jobs like clerking at Brooks Brothers. But as Peter's success grew, Lydia's role seemed to shrink. Peter didn't seem to need anyone to take care of him and organize his life anymore. Success allowed Peter to indulge the more expansive side of his personality.

Peter and Lydia's domestic life sometimes broke out into open hostilities. On one occasion, Peter became enraged and drove his car into the wall of their apartment garage, demolishing the car's hood and front bumper. Peter ended up in the hospital. Lydia had loved the role of the rock star wife but Peter now had something different in mind. He wanted someone younger, more flamboyant, more glamorous, more in keeping with the new Super Kiss image. That someone was Debbie. Lydia retained Marvin Mitchelson, the Hollywood celebrity divorce attorney, to represent her once Peter filed divorce papers. An acrimonious proceeding followed and by mid-1979, it was over. Lydia got their Greenwich home, the Mercedes, a cash payment, and alimony.

I had gotten caught in the crossfire of Peter's divorce from Lydia. Since they had been Connecticut residents, the action took place there. Peter's counsel was a bulldog litigator from Stamford, Richard Silver. He had represented Linda Blair, who had starred in two of the three *Exorcist* films, in a recent case. Rick also handled matrimonial matters. I was deposed to provide details about Peter's financial status and his projected income from Kiss since this would determine Lydia's alimony. In an unusual legal maneuver, Peter's attorney obtained a ruling from the local judge allowing me to sit with him during Lydia's pretrial examination as sort of *de facto* co-counsel. Lydia's attorney objected—in fact, I wasn't even an attorney—but was overruled. The divorce was finally granted. Lydia recalled that life with Peter as Kiss prospered was "very exciting," but "didn't last long enough."

About 200 people came to Regine's on a cold, blustery December evening for the New York party. The event was flawlessly arranged, down to the engraved seating cards and the array of glasses in varying shapes for the wines and champagnes. Peter wanted to make the right impression. Black tie was mandatory; this was not to be a rowdy, rock 'n' roll party. Tiny Christmas lights twinkled, champagne flutes clinked, and a small orchestra played tunes from the '40s. It went off without a hitch.

I was to be an usher in the wedding ceremony, and flew to L.A. shortly after the party at Regine's. We offered to throw Peter a traditional bachelor party but he begged off. He wanted a private dinner with his best male friends at Chasen's, a classic Hollywood restaurant favored by the old guard of the movie elite including Ronald Reagan and Jimmy Stewart. Bill Aucoin, Howard Marks, Peter's father, his brother, and several Kiss staffers including Fritz Postlethwaite, gathered the night before the wedding in a paneled dining room at Chasen's, just off to the side of the main dining area. Unobtrusive oil paintings lined the walls of our room, where a long rectangular table had been set for us.

It was standing room only in Chasen's main room by 8:00 p.m. The crowd at Chasen's is older, more reserved, and sedate. It's a very clubby place, expensive and traditional, where being a regular can guarantee you a table at one of the crescent-shaped banquettes. Waiters in crisp white jackets and maitre d's in black tie slip inconspicuously between tables taking orders for the restaurant's world-famous chili and dishes like Hobo steak and cracked crab claws on ice.

Our party was well under way when it became painfully obvious that Peter and a few family members had been drinking too much. They got into a rip-roaring argument about who "had the biggest dick." As the argument raged, someone had the bright idea of tossing a pair of lamb chops around the table, maybe to distract the disputants. People from nearby tables who heard the racket and peered into our room were aghast, seeing a food fight in progress and hearing a cascade of scatological language. Peter was ranting, his tie and jacket thrown on a chair, his shirt unbuttoned to the waist, his eyes bloodshot, and beads of perspiration dripping down his forehead. A tall, slender blonde in the main dining room, laden with expensive jewelry, heard the commotion and walked toward us, glaring at Peter. The woman was not amused. She looked like she was going to have a seizure and stormed out of the room with her escort. Peter was out of control. Bill and Howard thought this might be an opportune moment to ask for the check and get Peter out of the restaurant before we got arrested or someone decked Peter. It was a blessing that we hadn't planned a more exotic bachelor party that night.

Two hundred guests had been invited to the ceremony and the reception, which were both to be held at L'Orangerie, one of West Hollywood's most prestigious French restaurants whose archways and gardens were patterned after Les Jardins Tuileries in Paris. The interior of L'Orangerie was classic if not palatial, with marble floors of alternating black and white squares and tall marbled columns in the corners of the room. There were several sets of French doors. Small, lattice-like window treatments allowed light to flood the room, and a sweeping, Impressionist-style mural of the French countryside during the *ancien régime* circled the main dining room. Bouquets of lilies, roses, and poinsettias were scattered throughout, filling the cream-colored room with bursts of color. Veuve Clicquot Carte Or, Château Beychevelle, and Meursault were being poured liberally for the wedding party. And then the guests began to arrive.

As splendid as the setting for this august event was, the guests seemed to cast a pall over the proceedings. The mother of the bride made it clear to anyone within earshot that she didn't approve of Peter and she thought her daughter could have done better. Gene, Paul, and Ace were there, but they were irritated about the whole affair, as if it were an imposition to attend. And Peter's recent fiasco in Shreveport had not exactly been conducive to an atmosphere of comraderie. Many of the guests complained about the timing, that it was just a few days before Christmas and had thrown a monkey wrench into their holiday plans. Peter's parents came, got into a tiff about not being seated at the head table, and bolted out the door during the salad course. There was a great deal of traffic into and out of the bathrooms. The atmosphere was closer to glacial formality than gaiety. By the time the wedding cake was presented, a traditional French croquembouche with tiers of tiny rounds of meringue and carmelized spun sugar soaring to the ceiling like a pyramid, most of the guests had left.

Fortunately, Peter and Debbie did not let the morose mood of some of their guests spoil the day. It had been a beautifully arranged, picture-perfect affair, but as often happens at weddings, the chemistry and the timing were off. The next day, they were off to Rio de Janeiro for their honeymoon.

The two weddings of Peter Criss were a fitting anticlimax to a climactic year. There were many changes looming, most of which were unknown at the time. Soon, a series of shock waves would permanently alter the landscape of the unreal world of Kiss.

The record industry entered 1980 with a thud. The disco craze of the late '70s had peaked in 1978 with the *Saturday Night Fever* soundtrack, which had sold tens of millions of copies worldwide. Kiss had caught the cusp of this craze with their "I Was Made For Lovin' You" single, their biggest since "Beth." But disco was now sounding a death rattle. A glut of disco-inspired albums recorded by an ever-expanding roster of formula artists the record companies had signed were now collecting dust in the record store racks. In 1979, record sales for the industry plunged by $400 million and the industry went into a tailspin that lasted for four years. For Kiss, though, things couldn't be better.

Casablanca Records, which practically invented the disco craze with the tremendous success of Donna Summer, the Village People, Parliament/Funkadelic, and scores of other artists, was in deep trouble. Under the aegis of Neil Bogart, the tireless promoter who had helped propel Kiss to early success, the company was now being crushed to death by millions of returns, unsold records sent back by the retailers for credit. Shortly after beginning his involvement with Kiss, Carl Glickman made what turned out to be a prescient observation. He wasn't an expert in the record industry, but he found it hard to fathom how any business could survive by allowing retailers to return 100 percent of the goods which they bought from the manufacturer. Unsold albums ordered by retailers could be shipped back to the record company for full credit. Stores were up to their eyeballs in stock, having overordered everything based on the unlimited returns policy. The returns policy was intended to stimulate retailers to buy new product. In fact, it had the reverse effect; what stuck in retailers' minds was how many records they had to return, a very big number with the Kiss solo albums. In the '80s, the returns policy would be changed, but in 1979, Casablanca was already a victim. Disco had died. And Neil was about to make a deal to cash out.

Since 1977, the company had been half owned by PolyGram Corporation, a Netherlands-based company with a strong international distribution arm. Jeff Franklin, ATI's chief, brought the Casablanca deal to PolyGram's New York headquarters; he was a key player in the negotiations. It was a propitious time for Neil Bogart to sell the label, especially since PolyGram was planning a concerted effort to capture the North American market, the largest in the world. Casablanca was then one of the most prominent companies; they could be folded into the already-existing distribution network that PolyGram was putting together, including the Mercury, Polydor, and London labels and some smaller ones as well.

In early 1980, PolyGram completed their buyout. Despite Casablanca's sales success, it wasn't a profitable operation, but PolyGram needed a well-known label with a top artist roster. Its reputation for enormous promotions and extravagance was hardly an industry secret. Neil would leave the company and start a new label of his own. An era of major acquisitions of U.S. record companies by foreign corporations had begun.

On the surface, it seemed like nothing more than the usual corporate musical chairs where company ownership changes hands but the business itself pretty much remains the same. New executives come and old ones go. Behind-the-scenes machinations of corporate managers and owners are seldom of interest to artists. But Kiss had a very keen interest in all of this. Their contract with Casablanca had a key man clause with Neil Bogart, a provision extended to only a handful of top artists, who have to bargain hard to get it. Kiss could terminate their contract if the key man left. And the key man had left.

Kiss was in the catbird seat. They had just released a worldwide hit album, *Dynasty,* which reached the Top Ten in the United States, France, and Germany, on the strength of "I Was Made for Lovin' You," a single which hit #1 in Holland. Kiss had just finished a marathon U.S. tour which generated millions of dollars of TV, radio, and press coverage. And PolyGram, an international company with a worldwide distribution system, recognized that Kiss was emerging as a top group in many European countries as well as in Japan and Australia. Whatever the financial shortfall of the tour with all of its craziness and waste, Kiss was now able to write their own ticket. On February 14, 1980, Kiss sent a letter to Casablanca in L.A. notifying them that they were leaving the label. Within months, there was a new deal.

"You've just made these four boys rich," was how Kiss's attorney, Paul Marshall, described their new contract to Howard Marks in a meeting at our offices just prior to the formal signing. Kiss would sign a long-term deal with Phonogram International, the record company subsidary of PolyGram, in April 1980.

The band was exultant. Kiss would be one of the highest-paid recording groups in the world. The contract gave them everything they wanted and more.* Howard had been instrumental in negotiating the megadeal and was showered with praise for his success at the bargaining table. He'd taken a particularly active and central role in the negotiations along with Kiss's attorneys Paul Marshall and Stuart Silfen, and Bill Aucoin. (Bruce Bird, previously Casablanca's senior promotion executive, had just been installed as the company's new president.) Howard was never one to flinch from asking for big bucks, which is what he did for Kiss.

Howard had gotten $15 million in guarantees for Kiss from the record company, then a mind-boggling sum. He saw an opening for Kiss which would never come their way again. They were at the crest of their popularity and Casablanca, now part of a much larger multinational company, desperately needed to keep top rock acts on their label to keep the distribution pipeline flowing with new products. The company didn't have that many top acts to begin with. And these Europeans had the money to make Kiss set for life. This particular game of corporate musical chairs gave Kiss the chance of a lifetime to hit the jackpot.

Artists customarily receive cash advances to pay for the recording of the album and as a prepayment against royalties to be earned once the record is released. Phonogram originally proposed a $1 million advance against royalties worldwide but Howard asked for $2 million for each new album, divided between North America and the rest of the world. If Kiss was doing so well overseas, they should get a separate deal for that. Phonogram consented. Donna Summer had filed a lawsuit in February to terminate her contract with Casablanca, and the new owners were unusually tractable. Another superstar defection from the label could cripple them.

There would be six guaranteed studio albums under the agreement plus provisions for greatest hits compilations and live albums. There would also be a fund of $350,000 to $500,000 per album for paid advertising and media to promote the records. This fund would be paid to Kiss and wouldn't be recoupable or deductible from royalties due them, something which record companies like to do with just about any promotional or advertising expense. Whatever they can charge back to the artist, the more money they keep.

Kiss would get paid a flat royalty of $1.20 per album based on a retail list price of $8.98.** Compact discs hadn't been introduced yet and a separate royalty would later be negotiated. And there would be no deductions from the

---

*Court records. *Gene Klein, Paul Stanley, Peter Criss, and Paul Frehley v. Phonogram International, B.V.* (1982), 82 Civ. 1150, U.S. District Court, Southern District of New York.

**Retail list prices today for top artists are typically $10.98 for cassettes and $16.98 for compact discs; albums have vanished from the scene.

$1.20 royalty rate, which would increase if the list prices were raised. This meant no packaging deduction or container charges for the cost of the album jackets and cassette cases, no "free goods" deduction for records shipped to radio stations or given away for promotions, and no deductions for any marketing costs the record company might incur to promote the album. Royalty rates are often a source of bragging rights among managers, business managers, and attorneys. But if the record company is allowed to deduct or charge back everything but the kitchen sink against the artist's royalty account, usually a percentage of the retail list price, the rate becomes meaningless. Kiss would get $1.20 per $8.98 album with incremental increases at sales thresholds above one million units.

There were other kickers. The contracts couldn't be cross-collateralized, another industry favorite. In Kiss's case, this meant they would get royalty accountings separately for both domestic and international sales. The sales reported on one side couldn't be combined or offset against the other for recouping the advances (each royalty account, domestic and international, stood on its own). And the catalogue of Kiss albums that had been recorded prior to 1980 on Casablanca would continue to be accounted for separately. These albums couldn't be cross-collateralized against the post-1980 albums. Tour support was also agreed to for a European tour.

Kiss's new deal had nearly $15 million in guarantees. The group had the right to deliver a new album to Phonogram every nine months, so they could collect advances on a regular basis if they wanted to. Casablanca/Phonogram needed product and Kiss had a track record of cutting albums at a rapid clip. It was an unprecedented contract. Perhaps a handful of superstars had record deals that even came close to what Kiss was getting. Whatever drubbings and cheap shots Kiss had endured from the press and from their musical peers, they were so rich now they could laugh in the faces of their detractors. And it was time to show the world. Awash with cash, they were ready to crash into the '80s.

Kiss didn't waste any time embarking upon their mission to expand their personal lifestyles on a par with what they had established for themselves in the business world. They had just finished a tour where they presented the show of shows in unequaled Super Kiss style. They had just signed a supercontract befitting their newly won status as a supergroup. A Super Kiss off-stage persona now had to be carefully conceived and implemented.

Ace had a head start. He'd moved to Wilton, Connecticut, a tranquil, upscale suburban community about 40 miles north of New York. Wilton was a sylvan setting of rolling hills, farms, horses, and streams that gently flowed through wide swaths of verdant farmland and open fields. Many parts of Wilton were isolated enough so that in winter, the hilly roads and craggy drives made access in anything but a four-wheel vehicle treacherous. But Ace loved the isolation and the privacy it afforded, far from the rigors of city living. Privacy was a priority with him. He bought a contemporary split-level home and retreated to the splendor of four beautiful acres overlooking a forest on one side and a farm just across the front lawn. Ace's wife, Jeanette, a cute and petite blonde with an appealing Gracie Allen-type personality, was somewhat less enthusiastic about Wilton. Most of Jeanette's family and friends lived closer to New York, a long and inconvenient trip from Wilton. This was Ace's dream, though, and she did her best to make the most of it.

The house itself was never really the dream. Ace's dream was to have a recording studio in his home, where he could escape at any time, day or night, and record his own music. It was not an unreasonable aspiration for a successful musician. Artists should be artists; that's how they make the money. The problem with this idea started after Ace came up with his plan for the studio. It was to have eight-track capability, suitable for doing professional demo tapes. It was to be built in a basement recreation room with baffling and acoustical tiles. And it was to cost about $60,000. Carl Glickman thought Ace's proposal made sense and $60,000 was a realistic sum for him to spend. Within weeks, Ace's vision had escalated. The original idea was way too modest in size and scope. It had all the earmarks of a dinky little basement studio with a few tape decks and reels and a couple of mikes lying around, something more suitable for a garage band. He was in Kiss. His studio had to be something much more grand, something state-of-the-art, the latest, the most modern, the most high-tech, the most sophisticated, the most advanced, the most professional, the most everything. It had to be on a par with Super Kiss. And he had to have it now.

It was then full speed ahead. Renowned studio designer John Storyk was retained. Engineers and consultants were brought in. Contractors were lined up. Plans were drawn for a completely subterranean studio to be constructed underneath Ace's property that would be all but invisible from the distance. It would be an underground bunker, some 20 feet below the ground, a fortress of solitude for Ace. It would have a recessed entryway and a sunken driveway with a separate loading area and be connected to the main dwelling through a passageway built into a tunnel. There would be twenty-four-track professional studio equipment purchased from MCI. An arsenal of tape machines, power units, generators, video monitors, harmonizers, equalizers, and electronic samplers would be needed, along with an immense console. The control room being designed would resemble the cockpit of a spaceship. Electrical lines, plumbing, access roads, water mains, sewage and septic tanks, telephone cables—all would have to be rerouted and redirected. Gates, landscaping, fencing, driveways, stone walls, new entrances would have to be installed. The requirements list seemed impossibly long, but Ace ordered everyone to press on.

I told Ace we didn't have a budget yet. Constant meetings with John Storyk at his Union Square office in lower Manhattan produced endless blueprints as the project mushroomed. Ace would phone John almost daily with change orders, creating a domino effect. One minor change could throw off the existing plans and technical specs and everything would have to be redrafted. It became impossible to get a handle on where costs were headed, and I had to retain a lawyer in nearby Greenwich to research whether Ace's home was zoned for commercial use. It wasn't, which meant Ace could only use the studio for himself and not rent it out to others, otherwise he'd be in violation of local zoning laws.

Never mind, Ace told me, he just wanted to use the studio for himself anyway. And as far as doing a budget, he knew it was "the smart thing to do," but he couldn't wait. "My head won't take it" was his response. Waiting around to make sure that all the I's were dotted, the T's crossed, and the numbers added up correctly was unacceptable to Ace. We had to forget about spending the time to do a budget. "One hit song will pay for the whole thing," no matter what the cost. "Just start building—now," were my orders. Ace's "head," as he put it, was unfortunately an excuse for a lot of impulsive, extravagant behavior. My two bosses as well as Bill Aucoin and the others in the band thought the whole thing was crazy. But Ace insisted. "Start digging" was the order. And dig we did.

Within days after the appearance of the first cranes, the primary contractor moved in. He knew a good thing when he saw one. Excavation began. Earth-moving equipment, power shovels, bulldozers, concrete mixers, steam shovels, air compressors, backhoes, sand blasters, dump trucks, flatbeds, pile drivers—all moved into position. Earsplitting blasts of TNT blew the earth apart. A huge crater ripped the ground open. Concrete shells formed rings around the crater. Cinder blocks fell into place. Steel rods and girders were lowered into the cavity. Rock crushers tore through stone to make way for trusses and piers. There were leakage problems, landslides, air-conditioning malfunctions, waterproofing defects, drainage and water runoff problems, and plumbing backups. A bathroom was added as a last-minute change order; the one already in the lower portion of the house would require a 20-second walk, a major inconvenience. Equipment was installed and ripped out. Walls were erected and torn down. Flooring was laid down and torn up. And everything was done over again.

Wilton had never seen anything like this before. It was as if the Taj Mahal was being constructed on someone's lot. It soon became the talk of the town. Rubberneckers in cars slowed down to stare at the gaping hole. The constant noise attracted neighbors, who stood outside the property and gawked. Ace soon installed an elaborate security system with video cameras, heat sensors, electrically operated gates, concrete walls and pillars, and a double-height chain-link fence around the property's perimeters. A Maginot Line would be drawn to seal off the studio and the house from the outside world. I asked Ace at one point if maybe the whole thing might not be getting out of hand. He looked at me like I was an idiot. Whenever the subject was brought up about how much the studio was costing, Ace went on the defensive. "How much money do I have?" or "Aren't I a millionaire?" were his regular retorts. He would brook no interference.

In late 1980, almost a year after construction had begun, the studio was finished. According to Ace, he'd come close to having several nervous breakdowns. But it was now ready. The dream had been realized. The studio was completed. Ace had his monument.

Ace's $60,000 home recording studio turned into a crushingly expensive white elephant. By the time he had finished, the cost of building the studio was double what the house had cost. As impressive as the studio was, it was little used. Kiss recorded a few songs there in 1981. None of them were hits. Within a couple of years, the house was put up for sale. Sotheby International Realty, which was retained to try and unload the property, circulated a color brochure to their clients. We could hardly get anyone to even look at the house or studio. Eventually, the recording equipment was gutted and sold for a fraction of the original cost. The house remained on the market for years until one of the neighbors bought it. Supposedly, they used the studio as a recreation room.

Paul's hunt for the ideal Manhattan apartment was a bit like the search for the lost city of Atlantis. What he was looking for might not even exist, let alone be on the market for sale. Paul could never quite make up his mind about what he wanted. His ideas changed each week. Park Avenue or Fifth Avenue. East Side, then West Side. High-rise, then low-rise. Townhouse or brownstone. Old building or new building. River view or city view. Uptown or downtown. Private street or prestige avenue. Floor-through or half-floor. Duplex or triplex. Penthouse or wrap-around terrace. Three bedrooms or four bedrooms. The permutations seemed infinite.

And he had an additional problem. Most of these places were co-ops, which meant a board of directors had to approve any new owners before they would be allowed to purchase the apartment. Boards are often made up of older apartment owners who are the building busybodies. Their idea of an ideal tenant is a married, professional person, a corporate executive, or a wealthy dowager, not a rock star bachelor in his late twenties with shoulder-length hair. The likelihood that he'd be blackballed by most boards cut down the choice of apartment buildings considerably.

After more than a year of looking, Paul found an enormous duplex on East 80th Street near Madison Avenue, not far from the Metropolitan Museum of Art, in a modern high-rise building that rose nearly thirty stories. Paul's apartment was near the top, far above the hoi polloi, with a double set of balconies and city views of upper Madison Avenue and the East Side. Through a fluke connection, we somehow got Paul's application approved by the board. It also helped that he wore a short-hair wig to the formal interview.

Now that Paul had his castle in the sky, he had to make it look like one and he had to act like royalty. Paul had always been status-conscious, and he had now entered his Studio 54 period. Almost nightly, he gallivanted around the disco scene, spending long hours in places like Studio 54, a beacon of revelry and exciting nightlife. Paul rejoiced at the thought of seeing and being seen there, since it was a beehive for celebrity connections and he could nuzzle with gorgeous cover girls in the upstairs VIP room. He loved staying out all night and returning home each morning with a knockout model draped on each arm. Gene thought it unseemly that Paul was running around New York like any celebrity seeker with disco fever, hopping from one in spot to the next.

But Paul had more than one image to live up to—not only was he front man in Kiss, he was late-night merry-maker par excellence and consort to supermodels and starlets. Although he was no longer dating Georganne LaPiere, Cher's sister, a former costar on the TV soap opera *General Hospital,* the list of his paramours with genuine celebrity status would continue to grow over the coming years. East 80th Street would have to be the right kind of place to bring his famous companions, a palace for Paul, in his and their honor.

Paul initially hired a young decorator he admired to do the work in his new apartment, but Bill Aucoin scotched that idea immediately. Paul needed a famous decorator, someone with a big name. It was much too big a job for anyone except a super-decorator. Paul's apartment had to look regal and posh, and only a top name would be suitable for someone in Super Kiss. Bill was an excellent tutor, who had taught Kiss early on that they had to be lavish and extravagant in everything they did and that being a success meant showing it, flaunting it, to the world. Bill recommended Jay Spectre, who had done a stunning job designing Bill's apartment in Olympic Tower. Once Bill put the bug in Paul's ear that anyone of a lesser stature might not be important enough to do the job, warning bells went off in Paul's head. It was too big a chance to take. Jay got the job. And he did spectacular work. After months of almost round-the-clock work, the apartment was magnificent. Custom-made burlwood cabinets, curved sectional couches, deep-pile Belgian wool carpeting, plush wall fabrics, Japanese silkscreens, state-of-the-art kitchen, rheostatic lighting, electronically controlled vertical blinds, and a media room built around a sunken couch with a bank of audio and video equipment filled the first floor. A winding spiral staircase led to the second floor master bedroom, featuring an oversized king bed adjacent to a double-sized bathing area with marble floors and a jacuzzi. There was a music room upstairs, displaying a glass-framed showcase of specially designed guitars, and the room was equipped as a mini-recording studio. Thickly upholstered rugs and Tiffany lamps abounded. It was very striking, very elegant, and very expensive-looking. Paul would not be outdone by anyone.

Yet the apartment had a certain coldness to it, a museum-like perfection. It was as if people didn't live there, and the rooms were simply used as backdrops for beautiful photos in interior design magazines. Cabinets were filled with shelves of Rosenthal china, Baccarat crystal, and Lalique vases because Paul felt it was important to possess these things. But they were seldom touched, and groaned from the weight. There were no books anywhere and no personal touches like photos or mementos. Everything was always in precise order. The kitchen was pristine, hardly used except for an electric juice maker, and the cupboards remained empty. And there were a lot of mirrors everywhere.

Paul had kept a sharp eye on what Gene had done to elevate himself in the world by dating celebrities and he wasn't about to be a second banana. (In fact, at one point he showed some interest in Cher, but the timing was off and it never got off the ground.) By 1982, he was dating Donna Dixon, the costar of TV's *Bosom Buddies* series. Blond and voluptuous with a sultry Marilyn Monroe voice, Donna was a smoldering beauty who could set off sparks just by walking into a room. Paul fell head over heels for her and made no effort to conceal the fact that they were an item. The more publicity the better. Paul would salivate waiting for her to show up at his posh bachelor pad so he could parade her around town like a prized trophy. When in L.A., Sundays were for Spago, the trendy Hollywood celebrity restaurant always packed with movie people. A friend of Paul's remarked that when they weren't out on display, they must've spent their time staring in the mirror, arguing over who would get the blow-dryer first.

Donna never failed to impress, even in the most unusual ways. One afternoon Paul popped into the Glickman/Marks Management offices with Donna to introduce her to Howard Marks. After about half an hour, Paul's hysterical shriek could be heard through the door of Howard's office. He burst out of the room, his eyes glistening from tears of laughter. I asked him what was so funny. He blurted out, almost unintelligibly, still choking with laughter, that Howard had just dropped his trousers. Howard had recently begun a crash diet to lose the extra pounds that had been creeping up on him. He hadn't yet altered the waistband of his trousers, which were now several inches too wide. When he stood up to say goodbye, Paul told me, the trousers had dropped down to his ankles, revealing his boxer shorts. It wasn't a sight easily forgotten.

Paul's relationship with Donna took a more serious turn when he gave her a diamond engagement ring. He had been dating her for nearly two years, and had even flown down to meet her family in suburban Virginia. He assumed, naturally, that he was the only one in her life. But in April 1983, Paul heard some very bad news; Donna, then 25, had just married Dan Aykroyd, the actor who had starred in *The Blues Brothers* with John Belushi. Dan had worked with Donna in the movie *Doctor Detroit.*Paul was devastated. He had no idea that Donna had been seeing Dan Aykroyd during the time they were involved. He did get the ring back, though. Paul asked Howard to intervene and negotiate with Donna.

Paul eventually sold the apartment. It had been a costly undertaking. But once Donna got married, the apartment lost some of its appeal. He had intended to live there with her but when that dream died, the memories soured and the place was an unpleasant reminder. Howard had ribbed Paul about spending so much time and money on building and decorating the apartment, saying it looked like he was planning for it to be his "final resting place." At the very least, Paul had hoped the apartment would be his palace for Donna. It didn't work out to be either.

Peter had been the first in the group to buy a house in 1977, just as Kiss was coming into big money. One of his happiest moments was when we told him at a meeting early that year that he and each of the Kiss members were now millionaires. He'd heard that there was a book on Wall Street that all newly declared millionaires could sign, sort of an official registrar for the rich, and asked me to check into this. I couldn't find any books on Wall Street for him to sign, but I would help him look for a new house.

Peter's choice was a Normandy Tudor-style home in Greenwich in a wooded area, very bucolic and private with a pond full of ducks nearby. Despite the tranquil setting, Peter could never quite remove himself from the antics he'd become used to on tour. Peter was fascinated by guns and had a small armory in the house. And the collection wasn't just for decorative purposes. One Christmas, as a way of bringing in some holiday cheer to liven things up, Peter supposedly shot up the Christmas tree. According to the oft-told tale, his wife Lydia had committed the unpardonable offense of not letting Peter put the star on top of the tree, an honor he reserved for himself. Lydia recalled something less dramatic as setting Peter off. Once Peter finally cooled down, his holiday rituals could resume. When the Greenwich house went to Lydia in the divorce, Peter had to start all over again.

For an interim period, Peter and his then-fiancee Debbie lived in an apartment on West 66th Street which Gene had sublet. Gene was in L.A. at the time. While watching TV on one of those large wall-sized projection systems, Peter apparently got angry when he saw an old boyfriend of Debbie's, an actor, on the screen. Peter, I was told, pulled out his gun and fired at the screen, blasting a hole into the wall behind it. Plaster and wallboard crumbled, leaving a gaping bullet hole in the living room. Our office quickly arranged for a plasterer to repair the damage. Gene had let me use the apartment for a few months until Peter and Debbie arrived. When he finally returned, I made sure to tell him that the damages weren't my doing. Fortunately for Gene, Peter and Debbie soon found other accommodations.

After marrying Debbie, Peter moved to another Connecticut suburb, Darien. In 1980, he purchased an eighteenth-century colonial home on three acres of prime property in one of Darien's best sections. Peter considered himself a homebody at heart. It had always been his wish to have a big, comfortable house in the country, something which he could only dream about as a child. And now he had been able to afford two dream houses in America's most exclusive neighborhoods. He was the country squire.

But the atmosphere of country gentility didn't dampen Peter's zest for living. Once, he greeted me at the door with a holster strapped around his waist and a revolver tucked inside. He told me that he sometimes walked around the house with a gun to scare Debbie. He may have been joking, but it certainly scared me. Living with Peter was enough to make anyone's nerves brittle, and it couldn't have been easy on the neighbors, either. One July Peter held a big outdoor party at the house and invited many of his family. As is often the case with summer parties in hot weather, it ran late and everyone drank too much. The next morning, one of Peter's relatives was reportedly found fast asleep on the front lawn, fully clothed, spread out in full view of the main street in front of his house.

After a few years of Darien living, Peter got bored. Upper-crust suburbia can be stodgy, and Peter missed the action of the city. He'd been used to hanging out at nightspots like Ashley's near Greenwich Village where rock stars and people from the record business mingled until the wee hours. And Debbie, in her early twenties, may have felt a little out of place in a neighborhood where most of the residents were much older and most of the men were corporate executives and professionals. Darien wasn't at all like the Southern California communities where Debbie grew up. As Peter's situation with Kiss changed, they eventually decided to leave Darien and sold the house.

❖

Super Kiss was now a reality, in both their professional world and in their personal lives. The megadeal with Phonogram guaranteeing Kiss millions for years to come was locked up. Paul, Peter, and Ace each had a fabulous residence for himself and a sumptuous lifestyle to match. Millions had been spent with blinding speed to create images compatible with their newly elevated status in the world. And Gene was chafing at the bit, ready to charge out of the starting gate and create his own larger than life world. His public romance with two of America's most glamorous celebrities would change his life and Kiss's image as well. Gene would stir up a whirlwind of attention and put him and the group in the glare of a different spotlight. In every way, Super Kiss was peaking.

Cher's Shrine and the Coming and Going of Diana Ross

I thought it would be the death knell of Kiss. From a publicity angle, this is not the most popular thing we could do. The fans who buy records think it's horrible. They're very jealous and possessive, but that's tough. I'm crazy about Cher. She's my first love.

> Gene Simmons talking about Cher, quoted in "She Still Shakes—Not Knits—Booties, But Cher's Approaching Domesticity with Gene Simmons." *People,* October 22, 1979.

I was warned to be prepared for anything because Cher was going to be on the set of the Kiss movie when shooting started in May 1978. Her blooming romance with Gene wasn't news any longer. Cher had met Gene earlier that year at a fund-raiser for California's then-Governor Jerry Brown. The next night, they went on a date which led to a hot-and-heavy long distance telephone relationship; Kiss was in Japan at the time. By spring, Gene and Cher were living together in L.A. Cher was trying to resuscitate a career that was in the doldrums, no longer a TV staple and not making hit records, either. She'd recently done a TV special for ABC with Dolly Parton and Rod Stewart. Her movie career was a long way off. Cher, 32, was then known as a comedienne and singer on the Vegas circuit.

Cher had become something of a real estate baroness in Beverly Hills, buying and selling homes as the market started to sizzle, flipping over properties for big profits. Cher, Gene, her kids, and the nanny and the cook commuted between a house in Bel-Air and a beachfront home in Malibu Beach Colony, a ritzy refuge for the showbiz elite. Her Malibu neighbors included Barbra Streisand, music mogul David Geffen, and Larry Hagman, *Dallas's* J.R. Cher's dream house, a 14,000-square-foot Egyptian palace with ten fireplaces, a moat, and a living room the size of a Pharaonic tomb, was under construction in Benedict Canyon. The price tag was a reported $5 million by the time it was finished four years later.

By the time Kiss started shooting *Kiss Meets the Phantom of the Park* in L.A., Gene felt it was time for *tout* Hollywood to know that he and Cher "knew each other in the Biblical sense," as he put it to the press many times. His success with Kiss had emboldened him to make his romance public. Gene decided to throw Cher a surprise party at Le Dôme, a fashionable watering hole on Sunset Strip that had become a magnet for music and record business people. The party was really more of a coming-out party for Gene than anything else, and an A-list was drawn up of important Hollywood types, most of whom were Cher's friends.

Gene didn't have a lot of experience throwing parties or performing the social rites of Hollywood. But he basked in the new-found attention he was getting from dating a real superstar who was known to the public as a top TV personality and not just to young rock fans. Being seen with Cher and tailed by the paparazzi gave Gene a notoriety he would never have had as a rock star. As the press hungered for more tidbits about Gene and Cher, Gene began to realize all this attention could end up being a millstone around his neck. It might make Kiss look "too Hollywood," like he was selling out. But he had already plunged into the Cher experience with characteristic zeal.

Ironically, Gene detested Hollywood and everything it represented—that is, until he met Cher. He hated L.A. and never liked spending time there, even on trips with Kiss. He thought it was full of phonies—bimbos, bozos, and cigar-chomping fatsos—all living in a way-out world where "Santa Claus lived under a palm tree." Gene was more at home on the road with the rock fans and groupies whom he saw as the salt of the earth. Movie and TV people were flash in the pans, disconnected from reality. Anyone touting L.A.'s merits would be pounced on by Gene who would go into a tirade about what a miserable place it was, inhabited by dimwits with gold medallions dangling from their necks.

Cher turned Gene's thinking around, opening up a whole new world for him. Dazzling parties, VIP treatment, palatial homes, press coverage to the saturation point in newspapers and magazines and not just rock rags, private screenings, movie premieres, access to elite private clubs like Pips, and all the perks of celebrity status. Gene had the envy of millions of American men who saw Cher as a sexy and bewitching superstar. He started schmoozing with all those movie and TV people he had previously disdained but was now starting to like very much. Grabbing the headlines and shameless self-promotion were virtues he had always sworn by. Celebrity dating created a whole new world of opportunity for Gene, and on the sidelines, studying every move, was Paul.

The party at Le Dôme would give his affair with Cher the patina of official recognition. Gene was in a quandary, wanting to make a big splash but not be too Hollywoody. His original idea, renting a tank and clanking down Sunset Strip, was rejected as a little too rock 'n' roll for Cher's crowd. It might make Gene look ridiculous. A late-night cocktail party would be more subdued and less risky. Besides, many of Cher's friends thought she was crazy for dating Gene, having recently ended a roller-coaster marriage with Gregg Allman, a troubled musician who had reportedly been in institutions for drug rehabilitation. And Gene was in Kiss, the weirdest of all rock groups. A party at Le Dôme would allow Gene to display himself in the proper light.

On the big night, the turnout was sparse. Hardly anyone showed from the party's A-list. The curving bar and glass-enclosed dining area off to the side were filled with the usual crowd of staffers, hangers-on, friends, and posers. In the back of Le Dôme, a buffet had been set up in the dimly lit rear dining room, furnished with plush green velvet chairs and brass ornaments and accents throughout. But there were no celebrities to be seen. Valerie and Deirdre made it, two scrumptious rock 'n' rollers just out of high school I'd last seen at the Kiss show in Baltimore. Some fans just refused to recognize geographic limitations. They were in leotard outfits that looked as if they'd been spray-painted on their drum-tight rear ends and wore little white bolero jackets that showed off their *décolletage*.

It was getting late and we were still waiting for Cher. Gene's face lit up whenever there was some hubbub at the front door, hoping it was Cher, and when it wasn't, his face tightened. He was starting to get a little anxious, working the crowd like a politician on the hustings, shaking hands and backslapping. He abandoned his usual off-stage Kiss look for the evening, showing up in a double-breasted striped jacket with an ivory silk shirt, opened at the chest with a furry mat of hair sticking out, and wearing black leather pants with a reptile belt. Custom-made cowboy boots with western curlicue stitching replaced the knee-high platform boots with dollar signs.

Finally, as the bar was closing, Cher arrived. She came in through a side entrance with a gaggle of friends in tow. Gene was elated, beaming like a schoolboy who'd just brought home a report card with all As. The wait had been worth it. Cher and Gene embraced and stood near the corner of the rear dining room with the buffet and an audience of remaining guests gathered to pay their respects. Cher didn't look at all like her radiant TV self. She was very simply dressed without any makeup, her long tresses limply hanging down her back. There was no gown or fancy jewelry or wild hairdo or skin-tight leather or transparent bodysuit. She was plain Cher, wearing a loose-fitting black sweater and jeans, and looking a bit wan. I was disappointed. I'd been anticipating the high-gloss version of Cher I was used to from TV.

Gene was giddy as he floated through Le Dôme with Cher on his arm. She appeared to be touched by the effort Gene made to throw a party for her and greeted all his friends cheerfully. The party soon wrapped up. A waiter yanked a glass of wine out of my hand and I knew it was time to leave. Gene and Cher disappeared out the side entrance and into a limo, snuggling in the back seat. The evening was over.

Gene's party for Cher was a turning point. Gene learned that in Hollywood, just throwing a party doesn't mean that people will come. There's always a party going on in Hollywood. You need a lot of candlepower to be noticed in Hollywood, and Gene discovered after the Le Dôme party that if you're going to play in the big leagues, you have to go all out. And it has to be no holds barred.

In the pre-Cher days, Gene had parsimony down to a science. Women were playthings who came with the turf of being in a rock band. They were available for free. Gene always referred to his girls on the road as "sluts," although not to their faces. On tour, I often asked him what he was doing on one of our days off. The answer was always the same—"I'm having a slut come up to my room." Getting Gene to spring for a taxi for one of his many visitors was like squeezing blood out of a stone. The idea offended him. He bragged that he never spent a dime on women and his idea of a date was a room service meal and a girl undressing in front of him. Cher changed all that.

After the Kiss movie and the solo album promotion, the spending started in a big way. Gene jumped in with gusto, feet first and raring to go. Parties, dinners, jewelry, trips to London on the Concorde for Cher, her children, and the nanny, clothes from the most exclusive shops on Rodeo Drive, and gifts of all sizes and shapes. The Kiss members were flabbergasted to see Gene, the macho man who could never fall in love and who hated Hollywood, going gaga for Cher and reading about his roller-skating parties and romantic exploits in the tabloids.

Gene let his imagination run wild and arranged a special birthday surprise for Cher that would be an extravaganza of its own. A tank driven by two midgets would greet Cher at her Malibu home on her birthday and behind the tank would be a high school marching band and a hand truck piled with gifts. A skywriter would fly overhead, creating a customized birthday greeting for Cher in the clouds. It was Gene's way of mixing love with a hefty dose of P.T. Barnum.

The crazy birthday stunts that surprised Cher at her doorstep were fun but more of a joke than anything else. They were really penny ante stuff by Hollywood standards. Gene was in Kiss. He had to do things in a big way. He was important enough to have Cher as his girlfriend, one of America's biggest celebrities. She had to be honored in a manner suited for royalty. Gene would have to build her a shrine.

By 1980, the site for the shrine had been chosen. Gene's first choice was The Dakota, a landmark Gothic building on the Upper West Side of Manhattan. The apartment's board of directors vetoed the application of Gene and Cher as co-occupants. Presumably, one rock star couple, John and Yoko Lennon, was enough. A new site was found. The Heart Foundation on East 64th Street near Fifth Avenue had decided to convert their stately building to a co-op apartment and move their offices elsewhere. The building didn't yet have a board of directors since it was still in the conversion process. There wouldn't be any approval problem for Gene. He grabbed it. Gene would have a penthouse. It would be a newly constructed apartment on what was now the top floor of the building, five stories high and overlooking the Central Park Zoo. The building was brick and mortar construction in a neoclassical Fifth Avenue style. Extensive renovations were under way when Gene signed his contract. He loved the traditional look of the building and the idea of being on the roof with wrap-around terraces.

The penthouse would look exactly the way Cher wanted it since she could oversee the construction of it from scratch. Only a shell existed when Gene bought the apartment. Gene had bought the two top floor units, and Cher could divide up the space to suit her needs. Every detail, from the configuration of the rooms to the furnishings and the decoration, would be handled by Cher's decorator, Ron Wilson, a celebrity designer from L.A. His clients included Johnny Carson, Kenny Rogers, and Don Rickles, and Gene would fly him in to take charge of the project. He had done all of Cher's homes in California. Nothing would be left to chance, and no expense would be spared. The shrine would be perfect.

All of this was a remarkable metamorphosis for Gene. Three years earlier, he was sharing a small apartment with a roommate on Riverside Drive. Now, he was building a shrine on Fifth Avenue. And for Cher, no less. Gene's lawyer even drafted a magna carta for them to co-sign which spelled out each other's rights and responsibilities while they were together and to avoid any palimony claims later on.

Cher had turned Gene's life upside down. With Gregg Allman and Sonny Bono out of the picture, the respective fathers of Elijah Blue and Chastity, Gene filled an important role for Cher's kids. He may not have been a surrogate father, but he was a doting and conscientious uncle, showering the kids with gifts and taking them on outings. This was a major turnaround for Gene. He confessed to hating kids before he met Cher. He developed a relationship that had an emotional side to it with a woman who was rich and famous in her own right. Like Gene, Cher was a risk taker who had struggled to make it, coming up the hard way. She was nothing like the subservient pushovers Gene was used to. Cher was never shy about letting Gene have it when he started to act bossy or play the big shot role, telling him "Simmons, you're an asshole." In their lighter moments, she called him Genie.

Gene came to love life in L.A. He developed a perpetual tan from his regular stays there, a kind of George Hamilton-style bronzeness. And he began carefully cultivating a network of contacts in the movie and TV world through his relationship with Cher. Gene now had ideas for himself that went beyond his role in Kiss. Cher was a good springboard for Gene's ideas. Her glitzy style wasn't unlike Kiss's and her sharp-tongued humor and moxie were a good match for Gene. He wanted to be a part of this bigger world of Cher's, and by building a shrine for her in New York, Gene hoped to ingratiate himself in a permanent way.

The New York penthouse was under construction for months. It was an overwhelming job to produce something as exotic as Cher had in mind. With several sets of contractors and designers working overtime, and Ron Wilson flying in periodically from L.A. to supervise, the penthouse began to take shape. Ron had supposedly asked that the local tradesmen he used in New York be given limo service "to save time," but Howard Marks balked at this when Gene told him about it. They would have to get by with cabs. Every inch of space, every nook and cranny, and every wall, floor, surface, and ceiling was custom-designed to conform to the grand plan Cher had created. Gene eagerly awaited settling comfortably into his rock throne with Cher next to him.

Mesopotamia in Manhattan would now overlook Fifth Avenue. It was dramatically different than any other New York apartment and unabashedly opulent. The foyer was what you would expect to find in early Pompeii: marble flooring with huge Doric columns, pillars, bronzed mirrors, and pedestals. The living area, with its earth tones mixed with raw fabrics in ash and straw colors, was a cross between Cher's Malibu beach house and a safari lodge. Faux stone surfaces gave parts of the room a prehistoric look, accentuated by carved cobra heads and replicas of desert serpents scattered about. There were also a few kitschy *objets de Disney* mixed in with the snakes.

A communal bathing area was created near the master bedroom. A Roman bath with sunken tub and a jacuzzi was surrounded by a large expanse of travertine marble. There were lots of gold fixtures and copper vessels for carrying water. To get to the master bedroom, you had to pass through the Roman bath area, an unusual if not inconvenient design feature. And in that lair, the sanctuary where the rituals of the shrine would be performed, the walls were covered with black, pinstriped wool. Bolts of men's suit material were picked for this. It was a handsome effect but very dark and the bed dominated the room like an altar. You felt like you were in the Batcave.

The apartment had a Cecil B. DeMille feel to it, overdone and dramatic. Everything looked like a prop a director had specifically chosen for a visual effect, from the ebony chests to the marble and granite to the snakes cast in bronze. Gene had poured well over a million dollars into the place, an enormous sum at that time. But Gene was delighted with it and Cher was thrilled. This odd, unusual apartment, with its Queen of Sheba grandiosity, had been meticulously rendered. This would be Cher's New York home, and how many women can say that a man has built a shrine to honor them? All the pieces were now in place for Gene and Cher to have a sparkling bicoastal life together.

There was just one problem. By the summer of 1980, Gene and Cher were no longer involved. In a world where relationships are measured in months, not years, the Gene-and-Cher romance had run its course. Gene's busy career with Kiss and their constant touring made life together difficult if not impossible. And Cher's career coupled with the problems of rearing two children stymied a more lasting involvement. Gene's concept of an open relationship which allowed him to bed down his usual assortment of groupies on the road also got in the way. Despite his hemming and hawing, he could never bring himself to give up trying to get into the pants of every girl that crossed his path. Gene's love life was very confusing to others, even within the Kiss circle.

Cher spent very little time in her shrine. With Gene continually on the prowl, she soon found a new boyfriend, musician Les Dudek. Gene lived in the New York apartment when he wasn't out of town with Kiss. He liked the place with all of its oddball charms, and its reputation as a monument to Cher was a source of pride. Besides, he now had a new steady girlfriend. But she wasn't about to live in a shrine built for Cher.

"There's something I want to tell you so you'll hear it from me first and not read it in the press," Gene said to a small group of us at Bill Aucoin's Olympic Tower apartment. You could hear a pin drop. "I'm seeing Diana Ross," he said sheepishly. A look of slackjawed astonishment came across Bill's face and I felt I'd just been hit with a stun gun. Several sets of eyes rolled to the ceiling. It was like a shock wave had whipped through the apartment, sending a tremor which caught everyone off balance. It didn't take long for the mood to shift. Dead silence was replaced by the sound of a chuckles and then hysterical laughter swept through the room. It was an almost unbelievable revelation.

It was early summer, 1980, and we were at Bill's apartment to make plans for the tour of Europe that was to begin at the end of August. Paul was there, too. We were sitting on an oversized pigskin couch in Bill's living room, staring out at the spire of St. Patrick's Cathedral, when Gene dropped his latest romantic bombshell. Gene was always the trailblazer for Kiss, but now he was really shifting into high gear. He was dating the reigning diva of R&B, a living legend of the Motown era and a superstar known around the world. The Hollywood period for Gene was going full-blast, first with Cher and now Diana Ross, two icons of the showbiz world. It was stunning news and Paul jumped on the irony of it instantly. "The next thing you know, you'll be dating guys," he said as howls of laughter filled the room. Paul loved to skewer Gene. When the laughter subsided, Gene's crimson face returned to its normal flesh tone and the meeting broke up.

Gene had met Diana through Cher. They were close friends. Both lived at least part of the year in L.A. and had homes there. The romance kicked off when Gene invited Diana to stay with him for an open-ended rendezvous to get acquainted at L'Ermitage in Beverly Hills. Gene rented two adjoining duplex suites, each with its own grand piano, carrying on a honeymoon of sorts for days until Diana had to leave for Lake Tahoe to perform. Now Gene's romance with Diana was on the front burner. As Cher had changed Gene, so did Diana. While Diana admired Gene's success in the rock world, that wasn't her world. And she also had children to take care of. Diana expected Gene to adapt himself to her social and family life and observe a more traditional decorum. Diana, like Cher, was several years older than Gene. But Gene's spell on Diana was obvious. When the two were together, Diana would be giggly and playful, holding hands and kissing and teasing Gene about "what a nice Jewish boy I've got." Diana confided in private when her guard was down that Gene was "incredibly sexy" and a terrific lover. She was put off by Gene's checkered past full of untold numbers of one-night stands, but she was apparently able to overlook this, hoping that he would turn over a new leaf now that they were involved and stay monogamous. Diana also began relying on Gene's business advice, seeing him as a brilliant businessman based on the success he'd had with Kiss. He became her mentor.

187

Gene had already begun to shed the symbols of rock stardom when he was dating Cher. Now that he was stepping out with a glamorous international superstar like Diana who hobnobbed with fashion designers like Oscar de la Renta, the old Kiss off-stage image of eye-popping kookiness had to go. Gene quickly junked the clunky platform boots with giant dollar signs painted on the sides along with his beloved skull rings, skull necklaces, and belt buckles displaying tarantulas in lucite. The primal look of animal skins and furs was replaced by Armani double-breasted jackets in muted patterns and silk shirts from Mr. Guy, a tony men's haberdashery on Rodeo Drive. He kept his hair, but that was now being carefully coiffed by a Madison Avenue salon at $100 a clip. Gene's debonair new image may have pleased Diana but Paul found it hilarious, referring to him as "the father of the band."

It didn't end there. Gene's little black book of concubines and the photo album were put in the closet to gather dust, at least for a while. I once asked Gene how he could remember all the girls he knew from being on the road and how he kept track of them. "Simple, "he said. "They're all filed under 'G' for girls with their first names and phone numbers listed next to their cities." His penchant for making shocking remarks, like walking through a crowded room and bellowing, "Kill all living things!" was also toned down. And the comic books were gone from the scene. Gene was assimilating into his new environment and the trademark Simmonsisms were history.

Gene's budding romance with Diana turned out to be a boon for Glickman/Marks Management. Diana didn't have an artist manager and didn't think she needed one. She'd been in show business since the early '60s, when she was still in her teens, eventually becoming one of the Supremes. The legendary Motown group went on to record a nearly unbroken succession of hits and by the '70s, Diana had gone solo. Movies soon followed, and Diana starred in *Lady Sings the Blues* (for which she received an Academy Award nomination), *Mahogany,* and *The Wiz.* The most successful album of her career, *diana* (she was spelling her name in lowercase letters then), was released in 1980 and sold millions throughout the world.

Diana, 36, didn't have a business manager, either. She wasn't interested in an artist manager since she wanted to be in full control of the creative direction of her career, but she did see a need for a strong business presence. The *diana* album was her last for Motown Records, the company that launched her career. Intensive business negotiations would be necessary before she could hammer out a new recording agreement, either with Motown or another label, and it seemed like a smart idea to have someone fill a business management role. And there would be tours, concerts, and other activities which would bring in big money as well.

Walking into my office in the last week of December 1980, Howard Marks greeted me with the news. "We have a new client, Diana Ross. There's a ton of work for you to do and I don't ever want to see you screwing around for months at a stretch on another road tour." I was delighted that we had landed a big catch like Diana. But the road tours hadn't been so bad.

Thanks to Gene, Glickman/Marks Management came highly recommended for the job of business manager for Diana. The pace-setting agreement Howard had negotiated with Phonogram for Kiss gave us considerable clout and we were becoming known as top-flight business managers in the music industry. It also didn't hurt that Gene was whispering sweet nothings into Diana's ear. Our deal was a standard business manager's commission of 5 percent. Things were looking up for me as well. I was promoted to vice president. My responsibilities expanded, and I became more involved with the day-to-day business dealings with the record companies and the clients' attorneys in addition to dealing with agents and promoters.

Howard was on top of the world. He had just signed one of the most prestigious artists in the entertainment industry, a superstar of movies and music. He was the business manager for Kiss, now one of the world's best-paid rock bands. And he was set to really rake in the dough. Two superstar artists can generate tens of millions of dollars in income in just a couple of years. As Howard put it, he was now a "super business manager." The lure of big money, big commissions, and the glamour of showbiz mesmerized him. Once Diana came on board, he gradually lost interest in his advertising agency and devoted most of his time to her and Kiss. Opening an office in Beverly Hills, Howard became a regular guest at The Beverly Hills Hotel, mingling with celebrities and bigwigs.

Carl Glickman was equally pleased. The company would have a much stronger financial base and not be dependent on one client alone. Things were going well for him, too. He was a partner in Bear, Stearns & Company, a power-house Wall Street investment firm, and would become a member of its board of directors once the company went public. The '80s were revving up.

Diana didn't need Gene to build her a shrine. She had several homes of her own including an apartment in the Sherry-Netherland Hotel, designed by Angelo Donghia, located a block from our offices on Fifth Avenue. Diana's main residence was a magnificent Greenwich estate overlooking the Long Island Sound on a peninsular property. She also had a home in Beverly Hills which was up for sale. Although Diana had many valuable properties, her income was limited. Her long-term deal with Motown paid her relatively little. It was the legacy of the Motown era when artists were signed, financed, and promoted to the hilt but were paid piddling royalties for the records they produced. Supposedly, even her Rolls-Royce had originally been registered under the Motown name. Diana's financial situation was further complicated by the fact that for years, she was one of three members of the Supremes, which diluted her share of past record royalties. And since Diana didn't write her own songs, there was no opportunity for her to earn song-writing royalties. Much of her income was generated through personal appearances in Las Vegas, Lake Tahoe, and Atlantic City, and small-scale concert tours.

Diana was aware that her fealty to Motown and Berry Gordy, Jr., its owner, had been costly. Even before Glickman/Marks Management got involved, she had commissioned an audit to review two decades' worth of her financial records and royalty accounts with Motown. After years of work, the auditing firm produced an encyclopedia-sized set of volumes detailing nearly every financial transaction between Diana and Motown. Audit claims were eventually settled for a very substantial sum, but no cash monies were due Diana. She had been overadvanced during those years, not a difficult feat since her royalty was so small. Motown had essentially functioned as a bank that provided revolving credit.

Howard didn't waste any time getting the record contract negotiations started. We were to work with John Frankenheimer, Diana's attorney, a partner in the L.A. law firm Loeb & Loeb. John's role became clearer as time passed. He was officially her lawyer, but like many music business attorneys, he also advised her on a wide range of business and personal matters and was a key player in her career.

Motown desperately wanted to keep Diana on the label. She had been one of their star performers since the early days and had just released the hottest album of her career. And Berry Gordy had for many years been romantically linked

189

with Diana, adding a powerful emotional element to the negotiations. More recently, Diana had married and divorced Robert Silberstein, an artist manager and former public relations agent. Diana's relations with Berry had been stormy at times but he had unquestionably been crucial in launching her career.

There was no shortage of contenders for the role of Diana's record company. PolyGram threw their hat into the ring. Capitol and Warner Bros. made offers. Virtually any company that knew Diana's Motown contract was about to expire was eager to make a bid. But Howard had a trump card up his sleeve. He wanted to find a record company that really needed Diana on their label, not just a company that would be happy to have her, which included most labels. Howard's idea was to sign Diana to a label that didn't already have a superstar female pop singer, so Diana would instantly vault to the top as their most prominent artist. And this hoped-for label would jump at the chance to sign Diana for big bucks. If nothing else, Howard could use that as a bargaining chip with Motown to up their ante. The perfect choice was RCA Records.

Since Elvis's death in 1977, RCA, once the world's leading record company, had struggled unsuccessfully to break new artists. They had no female superstars on their label and, in fact, had a shortage of any kind of star. Although they were mining a fortune from Elvis's back catalogue (a mother lode that became even more lucrative when the hits were released on CDs a few years down the road), a major record company can't sustain itself on repackaging old material by dead artists. They were hurting for a big star. They were well on the way toward becoming a rest home for aging artists in the music business. John Denver had been a superstar in the '70s, but he was now running out of steam.

Signing a superstar can boost a company's morale and be a potent stimulant in promoting sales and getting airplay for other artists on the label. The record business is a business of generating enthusiasm, both inside and outside the company. The superstar can fill the vital role of standard bearer for the label. For years, Elvis defined RCA Records to the public and the music industry in the same way the Beatles did for Capitol Records and Bob Dylan did for Columbia Records. Having a mega-seller like Diana Ross would give RCA the clout to sell more records to retailers, including newer artists it was trying to break, and get radio stations to play more RCA releases. Diana would create a ripple effect throughout RCA and the record industry since she was a superstar whose next release was sure to bring droves of customers into record stores.

Signing Diana was a shot in the arm that RCA needed. Barry Manilow and Kenny Rogers would soon be lured to the label with fat contracts. The RCA strategy that was evolving with Diana's negotiations was to sign big names with millions of dollars in guarantees in the hope of buying market share. By the mid-eighties, the strategy would backfire, and most of the high-priced talent would turn into Rip Van Winkles under the RCA umbrella. But Diana was on her way to landing a fabulous deal with the company.

Howard had learned that splitting the contract in two, domestic and foreign, wasn't a bad idea. It could double the artist's money. Diana was a strong seller overseas and Capitol/EMI Records, then the dominant international record company, was keen on signing her for the world outside of the United States and Canada. Now, Howard had two sizable offers to take to Motown, RCA for domestic and Capitol/EMI for international. This two-pronged strategy hadn't been his original plan. Boardwalk Records, Neil Bogart's new company which he started when Casablanca was sold to PolyGram, had made a serious bid for Diana. The negotiations broke down when Neil insisted on collecting 10 percent of the international earnings for his oversight function on marketing the records overseas, despite the fact that overseas sales would be handled by a separate distribution company.

Motown couldn't or wouldn't match the combined RCA and Capitol/EMI offers. They claimed it was too rich a deal for them. Motown offered a much improved contract over what Diana had before, but fell short of what the other two giants could guarantee. It was up to Diana to decide whether she should stick with Motown or sign with her two well-heeled suitors. She deliberated for quite a while since there was clearly an emotional side to the decision as well as a financial one. Motown had been her home for twenty years and she was friendly with many of the artists who had come up through their ranks, including Smokey Robinson, Stevie Wonder, and Michael Jackson. Diana finally phoned Howard. She would sign with RCA and Capitol/EMI.

In May 1981, the agreements were signed. Her initial advance from RCA was seven figures and Howard had a photo of the check enlarged to the size of a wall mural to present to Diana at our offices. She was thrilled to see a check of that size. Her Capitol/EMI contract dovetailed into the RCA agreement and provided her with an advance for the international sales of her first record. The first album with the new labels, *Why Do Fools Fall in Love,* was already being recorded for release later in the year. Diana was delighted. After a long career in the music business where she had been paid a meager royalty, she was now in the big time. Diana was getting top dollar and had earned the respect she yearned for from her record companies. She hugged Howard repeatedly, treating him like a long lost father. She looked at Howard as a kind of savior and naturally Howard was exuberant. Egos were overflowing and both Diana and Howard were aglow from their success.

Diana was on a roll and Howard kept up the pace. Not long after the record contract triumph in late spring of 1981, Howard renegotiated her deal with Caesars Palace in Las Vegas for a record-setting amount of hundreds of thousands a week. Diana had few rivals in that league, only Dolly Parton and a select handful of other superstar acts. We also geared up for a Diana Ross concert tour of the biggest arenas in the country, a type of tour that could now generate tremendous ticket sales. Phones were ringing off the hook with a barrage of calls from promoters willing to pay just about anything to book Diana for a show. She didn't use a booking agency so we had to oversee that function for her. Her relations with The William Morris Agency, her last agent, had become strained. We tried to get her to meet Jeff Franklin, ATI's chief, to handle the concert bookings, but she refused. Diana said Jeff was "part of that Neil Bogart crowd" and she wanted to stay away. She never made clear what her reservations were about him.

Diana was such a widely known celebrity that she attracted interest from all quarters. She was inundated with requests from charities and benefits to appear; the Joffrey Ballet in New York got her to perform with their dancers at a gala attended by President and Mrs. Reagan. Proposals for business ventures and investments, many involving minorities, came pouring into our offices. Many corporations made offers for her to perform at company parties and conventions for their employees, paying six figure sums for her to appear at these private gatherings and flying her in on a private jet.

Everyone was a fan of Diana it seemed. People of all ages idolized her, and many wrote tear-jerking letters describing personal hardships and misfortunes which had been overcome thanks to the inspiration they received from Diana. Even Peter Criss turned out to be one of her biggest fans. Peter always loved the Motown sound and patterned his singing style in the tradition of the full-throated, soulful style of the R&B greats. When he finally met Diana for the first time at our offices one afternoon, she quipped, "You're that white guy that sings black." Not missing a beat, Peter replied, "And you're that black girl that sings white." It was one of Peter's best bon mots.

Norby Walters was one of the first promoters we met who was itching to do business with Diana. A sharp talker with silver hair and a steely gaze, Norby, 51, was a self-described "agent of the stars," who had become successful as a top booking agent for black performers including Patti LaBelle, Luther Vandross, Miles Davis, and Kool and the Gang. He began his career as a nightclub owner in Brooklyn and later, Manhattan, before starting his own agency.

Norby strutted into our office and made some flattering remarks about the decor. Trim and draped in an Italianate suit, Norby oozed coolness. He was happy to be sitting in Howard Marks's office to talk about what he could do for Diana. And he loved the idea of putting Diana on the road in big arenas. Norby would be the perfect person to pull it off, he assured us. He would be both agent and promoter for Diana. Norby was sitting across from Howard's massive oval-shaped desk and I was sitting next to him. He told us he understood how to sell black artists to local promoters, who would partner with him on the dates, and how to get the best deals. And he emphasized what a cutthroat business promoting shows with black artists can be. There was a lot of truth to what Norby was saying. For years, the concert promotion business operated on a two-track system. The major promoters in most markets handled primarily white artists, rock groups like Kiss and the mainstream pop acts, while a separate group of lesser-known promoters handled black artists. Every booking agent had a list of promoters he could go to for rock and pop acts, almost always white, and another list for the R&B and soul acts, mostly black. Rarely would a promoter be on both lists.

I came right to the point and told Norby we wanted an 85–15 deal for Diana's shows like all top acts got at the time. Diana would get 85 percent of the profits and Norby would get the remaining 15 percent. Norby, not about to be outnegotiated in the first round, looked at me with a bemused expression, his eyebrows coming together and his brow wrinkling. He feigned not to understand what I was talking about. He then took out his scalpel and started slicing up my proposal. "You mean first we take the 15 percent off the top for my share and then we split the rest 85–15, don't you?" Norby said. I told him that's not the formula I had in mind—his way effectively doubled his take at Diana's expense—and we moved on. Norby wasn't out of the game yet. He looked Howard straight in the eye and told him pointedly that whatever it took to get Diana on tour, he was ready, willing, and able to do. Howard seemed a bit startled, then moved quickly to adjourn our meeting. We thanked Norby for his generosity and told him we would discuss it with Diana. We did, but she didn't think Norby was her kind of agent or promoter. We never met with Norby again.

Our offices were bustling with activity throughout 1981, thanks in large part to Diana. Howard's advertising agency picked up her business designing the album covers and supervising the marketing plans. Diana had become friendly with Rosanne Shelnutt, who ran the ad agency, and most of the work of supervising Diana's photo sessions and planning the media campaigns fell on her shoulders. Gene's influence showed up on the cover of Diana's *Why Do Fools Fall in Love* album. It was a glossy photo layout of Diana at her sexiest, wearing a skimpy zebra-striped bathing suit and lying seductively on a billowy satin sheet. "Sex sells" was Gene's philosophy. It apparently worked; the album went platinum and hit #15 in *Billboard*.

The Isley Brothers, one of the longest-running acts in the music business, also became clients around this time. The Isleys rose to fame in 1959 with "Shout," a single that eventually became a rock classic. A string of gospel-inspired R&B funk hit records followed in the '60s and '70s. Jeff Franklin asked us to take on the job of business manager for the group. He acted as their personal manager and directed their career. Having Glickman/Marks Management handle their money would relieve him of an unwanted burden. Jeff had known O'Kelly Isley for years; he had met him while Neil Bogart was general manager of Buddah Records, which then distributed the Isleys' label, T-Neck Records.

Jeff had done well for the Isleys in recent years, negotiating their T-Neck Records deal for distribution through CBS and keeping them booked through his ATI agency. The Isleys were then selling around 700,000 albums at a crack and could turn out a new record in six weeks' time at minimal cost. They wrote and produced their own material. Since the early '70s, they had released a new album every year, often reaching the Top Ten. Jeff had expanded his ATI base by setting up a separate company, ATI Equities, to manage artists and negotiate deals for them. The Isleys were then Rudolph, Marvin, O'Kelly, Ernest, Ronald, and brother-in-law Christopher Jasper.

Having another money-making client like the Isleys looked great on paper, but they had a pile of money problems. They had gone through years of unbridled spending and high living, purchasing huge estates and great quantities of jewelry and furs. Their record company had turned off the spigot and there wasn't going to be any money coming from them in the foreseeable future. The Isleys had already been advanced large sums which would take years to recoup. We cobbled together a plan to extricate the group from their predicament. A key element was for Rudolph, one of the older brothers, to sell his sprawling estate in New Jersey which was easily worth several million dollars. Rudolph's on-stage role in the group had become somewhat limited of late. He often pranced back and forth, pointing with his silver-tipped cane. At a meeting with the Isleys, Carl Glickman kept referring to Rudolph as "Rudy." Rudolph became irritated, repeatedly telling Carl, "Call me Rudolph." It was a hint as to where our plan for him to sell his mansion was headed.

During the Isleys' banner years, they had taken in a lot of money and each of the brothers had helped Rudolph to buy the mansion. His seniority entitled him to buy an impressive estate. With the Isleys, everything was one for all and all for one. Our idea was that Rudolph could now help out his younger brothers who, we were told, had originally chipped in to help him buy the house. He could move to a home in suburban New Jersey, comfortable and spacious, though not on the opulent scale of his estate. Of course, Rudolph's mansion wasn't the Isleys' only real estate problem. *The Record* of Hackensack, N.J., reported a long history of the brothers' tax troubles in its May 8, 1985, edition. Ronald had broken ground in 1976 on a huge ten-bedroom, thirteen-bathroom house on two acres of prime suburban New Jersey property. The house was assessed at nearly $2 million. In 1979, the IRS had seized several properties owned by the Isleys, including Ronald's house, for failure to pay $660,000 in back taxes. Ronald later regained control of the house, then lost it when the IRS seized it again. He reportedly got it back later. Several of the other brothers also had run into troubles with foreclosures, tax sales, and liens on their homes and run afoul of local tax authorities on their properties.

Our idea for Rudolph to sell his estate went over like a lead balloon. The brothers wouldn't think of dislodging Rudolph and he wasn't going to budge anyway. The Isleys' cash shortage was so severe that the lights on his estate were reportedly shut off when the bill wasn't paid. We were told that Rudolph had to walk around in the dark. The house sale was no deal. We had to come up with another solution.

Jeff Franklin put them back on tour. After a month's worth of shows, they had exhausted the number of markets they could play since they didn't have a hit single. We auctioned a health club they owned in Westchester County, but that brought a pitiful sum. Old barbells and locker room equipment aren't exactly a treasure trove of riches. The Isleys' money problems worsened and debtors seemed to come out of the woodwork. Our general manager, Martin Cornbluth, became friendly with the group and his reward was an unending stream of phone calls from bill collectors. The monies owed state and federal tax authorities were the straw that broke the camel's back. The Isleys had owed taxes for years. Money went out as fast as it came in. They owed hefty sums dating back to the '70s. And the Isleys had no way to pay the tax bills, or even to settle, since they claimed that they didn't have any cash to offer. Their only assets were their homes, and their principal source of income was their record contract, which had essentially dried up for the near term. The Isleys wanted to plead poverty and get the tax collectors off their backs.

The Isleys were a likable and amiable group who had survived many managers, agents, business managers, and accountants. But apparently they had closets full of fur coats, minks, diamond rings, custom-made jewelry, and gold and platinum bracelets. And they seemed to like to flaunt it, showing up in our offices decked out in full-length mink coats with jewelry hanging from every limb. The problem with this sartorial display was that it didn't jibe with their claim that they were hard-pressed for cash. The elaborate and lavishly furnished homes, the furs, and the blinding array of precious stones and jewels gave us—and no doubt the IRS as well—the sneaking suspicion that there was more somewhere.

We resigned as their business managers. It was too dicey relying on their claim of being cash-strapped. We couldn't be sure we were getting the straight story, and if we represented them before the IRS and other authorities and they disproved the Isleys' claim, we might get dragged down with them.

✥

I went out to L.A. at the end of January 1981 to straighten out a hornet's nest of knotty problems which arose from Diana's CBS television special, being taped on the West Coast. Diana was to do a big concert at the Forum for a paying audience that would also be taped for the TV special and aired a few months later. The production was a complex and confusing affair since a live concert had to be promoted and produced that would attract a crowd of over 17,000 and at the same time satisfy the TV people. The Forum's management was promoting the show, and Steve Binder, a well-known TV director of special events and music productions, was in charge of the TV side.

Little cracks had started to open in our relationship with Diana, even this early in the game. Things had been going swimmingly for the most part. We'd just begun reorganizing her career and restructuring her financial underpinnings. The record contract negotiations were then under way. But I soon discovered that Diana was capable of expressing anger, intensely and abruptly. I was about to find out why.

During the Forum stint, Diana was staying at The Beverly Hills Hotel, then a sandy pink stucco structure in a Mediterranean style that dates back to the 1930s. The hotel was a large compound of low-rise buildings and villas that sat on an imposing rise of meticulously tended gardens on Sunset Boulevard. The hotel's ambiance was like a chichi country club. Diana had rented a bungalow. The bungalows were like small villas with terra cotta roofs; each bungalow had several bedrooms and a dining and living room, and rental could run into thousands of dollars per day. Tidy rows of fresh-cut flowers lined the winding pathway to the front door of Diana's bungalow.

I had been keeping close tabs with the Forum on the ticket counts for the show. The show hadn't sold out but everyone was satisfied with the momentum. One of my jobs was to keep Diana updated about the show, the production, how things were working out between the Forum and the TV people, and anything else she should know about. Sometimes I would meet with her, other times I would talk with her on the phone. On this occasion, I rang Diana's bungalow from my room in the hotel. When Diana picked up the phone, I told her ticket sales were going well and the Forum's management felt the show would come close to selling out by the night of the concert. They were sure Diana would have a strong surge at the box office on the night of the show because black shows usually do a big walk-up business with last-minute ticket buyers. (The promoters presumed Diana's audience was predominantly black.) It all seemed very matter-of-fact and businesslike to me.

Diana became very angry. She screamed into the phone, "THAT'S NOT MY AUDIENCE! Who are these promoters, anyway?" My voice dropped to a barely audible level as my leg started shaking nervously. I started to mumble something in response to her question but I could barely get it out. I felt like I had just taken a roundhouse punch in the stomach. I began stammering into the phone and Diana cut me off, landing the final left hook. She was boiling mad. "YOU GO BACK AND TELL THEM WHAT I JUST SAID! THAT'S NOT MY AUDIENCE!" She slammed down the phone. It sounded to my ringing ears as if she had just shattered her receiver.

I had just suffered the heart-stopping wrath of Diana Ross for the first time. She had a short fuse and when she got mad, she really knew how to lay it on. I never got a chance to get a word in edgewise. But I had learned an important lesson. Diana Ross does not want to be thought of as a black act. I certainly had had no intention of offending her. Diana's view of her audience was radically different than the promoters, and she made that emphatically clear to me in the space of a few seconds. I never made the mistake of hitting that hot button again.

The concert at the Forum was sold out on the night of the show, February 5, 1981. To spruce up the show for TV, Michael Jackson, Muhammad Ali, and Quincy Jones came on stage for brief walk-ons. At the insistence of CBS, Larry Hagman was also included to dispel the impression that Diana's special was an all-black affair. Michael Jackson came on stage twice for a few seconds of dance steps while Larry Hagman and Muhammad Ali sang from the audience. A review in *The Los Angeles Times* on March 2, 1981, described the *diana* TV show as "pedestrian . . . tossed together for no other reason than to have Ross race through a medley of her hits."

I told Howard Marks, who had come out to L.A. and was also at The Beverly Hills, the story about Diana and her reaction to how the promoters categorized her. He covered his face with his hands and shook his head. It was a real doozy of a mistake for me to have said such a thing to Diana. Howard didn't get angry but he did remind me of how important a client she was to our company. We had to do whatever was necessary to keep in good stead with her.

A few days later I ran into Howard in the lobby. His face was lit up and he was eager to tell me a funny story. He'd been sitting in the famed Polo Lounge the previous night and "three floozies with at least an eighth-grade education" came over to his private booth to join him for a drink. Howard was a regular there, handing out $20 tips every night to the maitre d' to make sure he got a choice booth that faced the bar. He said the girls asked him what he did and he told them he was the business manager for Kiss and Diana Ross, to which one of the girls responded, "Oh, you must work for Mr. Lendt." I burst out laughing.

On the strength of the release of *Why Do Fools Fall in Love* Diana prepared to hit the road for a concert tour in the United States. The album came out in the fall of 1981. A promoter from New Orleans, Barry Mendelson, made the trip to New York to pitch Howard about getting Diana's business for a string of shows in Dallas, Houston, and Baton Rouge. He brought a cashier's check with him and guaranteed Diana several hundred thousand dollars for the tour. We were excited about the idea since Diana would play for big crowds in arenas. Diana liked it, too, and we made a deal. The shows would be booked for early 1982. It was a big coup for Barry Mendelson, who was willing to put his money on the table and make a sizable commitment to Diana to bolster his expanding promotion business. Barry, a snappy dresser, was a transplanted New Yorker who bore a slight resemblance to a more polished Woody Allen.

But first, Diana was to do the Super Bowl. On January 24, 1982, she would sing the national anthem at Super Bowl XVI at the Pontiac Silverdome in Michigan, outside of Detroit. It would be a homecoming for Diana. She was a native Detroiter, and appearing at the Super Bowl to sing the national anthem on TV for a worldwide audience in the hundreds of millions was a prized spot. We also arranged for her to do a concert the night before the game. This would be a kickoff before doing the concerts in the south. It was shaping up as a very big event. Howard Marks, Rosanne Shelnutt, John Frankenheimer, and Robert Summer, then president of RCA Records, were all flying in for the weekend. An added inducement, certainly for me, was that our hotel, the Pontchartrain, was in close proximity to the London Chop House. Despite my somewhat awkward visit with Gene a few years earlier, I had fond memories of their fist-sized veal chops and the twinkly lights strung from the coffered ceiling.

Diana's concert was booked at the new Joe Louis Arena in the middle of downtown Detroit, a 19,000-seat facility. The bone-chilling winter weather had no effect on ticket sales; the show had sold out quickly. Detroit was hot for Diana. We wanted to add a second show, but there weren't any open days in the schedule which would work, either for Diana or the arena. Howard and the arena's manager, Bruce Lahti, came up with the ideal solution. There would be a second show at midnight, right after her first concert. Diana okayed the idea—she was used to doing two shows a night at the casino theaters—and tickets were put on sale immediately.

"Miss Ross wants to see the check before she goes on stage," was how Diana's majordomo greeted me as he emerged from her dressing room backstage on the night of the concerts. I was taken by complete surprise. Obviously, I knew she expected to get paid for these shows but no one had told me she wanted to see the money before going on stage. But she was the client, and if that's what she expected, it wasn't for me to say no. However, I didn't have much time. She was supposed to take the stage in less than ten minutes. Racing down a long backstage corridor through a labyrinthine maze of tunnels and doorways, I made it to the manager's office. Nervous and out of breath, I explained my dilemma to Bruce Lahti, a short, stocky man in his thirties with a neat, blow-dried look. He smiled, rolled his eyes, and let out a hearty chuckle, putting his arm over my shoulder like an old friend. He had one of the accountants on duty that night prepare a check with a Paymaster stamping machine, payable to "Miss Diana Ross," then signed it

I grabbed the check and scurried back through the corridors to find Diana. By this time, she was in her stage costume, a white lamé dress bedecked in glittering sequins, and her hair was teased out and fluffy. She had obviously been waiting for me. I presented her with the check outside her dressing room door. She scrutinized the check, and having dispensed with that ritual, walked toward the stage as the sound of the orchestra swelled and the audience began clapping feverishly. I later discovered that the presentation of the check was an indispensible ceremony at Diana's concerts. It was her way of being reassured that she wasn't being cheated, another vestige of her earlier days. She certainly wasn't cheated in Detroit. It turned out to be one of the biggest paydays of her career to that point.

On stage, Diana was poised and graceful. She was a veteran performer whose presence commanded the attention of her audience and kindled an instant rapport with her fans. Sparrow-thin with head erect, she glided effortlessly across the stage, shifting tempos and alternating between intricate dance steps and interpretations of her most well-known ballads, like the theme from her movie *Mahogany*, "Do You Know Where You're Going To?" Most of her shows mixed newer material with a medley of Motown hits that were perfunctorily performed.

Despite pans from the critics, Diana's maudlin rendition of "Reach Out and Touch" was her signature song. Diana would walk through the audience and descend upon startled fans, sticking a mike in their faces and asking them to sing along with her as she hugged them. This touchy-feely routine dragged on interminably and seemed to make some of her audience restless. The show always sagged at this point, but Diana loved it, smiling radiantly from ear to ear.

Diana exited the stage a few times during her shows for quick costume changes. The sequined gowns and short, beaded dresses were replaced by creamy ruffles and shiny silk wraps that swaddled her body like a blanket. Diana was a maestro at working a crowd, energizing everyone and then lulling them into a warm bath of cozy sentimentalism. But her schmaltziness could become boring and repetitive. Diana never stopped telling the audience how much she loved them, how wonderful love is, and wouldn't it be nice if everybody loved each other. It was like overdosing on sugar and going into a diabetic coma. Diana's show usually lasted about an hour and much of it was devoted to the "Reach Out and Touch" routine.

Diana could dominate her closest professional advisers. Once we met with Diana at our offices and were joined by two of her attorneys. Diana burst into the conference room, in a marvelous mood, with a court reporter trailing behind her. She announced that the court reporter would take a verbatim record of the meeting, which we had called to discuss tax and financial matters. Diana said she liked having written records of meetings so she could review everything late at night while in bed. It isn't customary for clients to bring court reporters to business meetings to record the session word for word, since the information discussed is often personal business, private and confidential.

If the transcripts got into the hands of a reporter, they could be embarrassing or even damaging to Diana. Carl Glickman was furious. He asked to speak privately with the attorneys, and the three stepped outside of the conference room. Apparently, her attorneys weren't aware of the plan to have a court reporter sit in on the meeting. They agreed with Carl, it wasn't a good idea. If everyone present had to worry about the transcript possibly being leaked, they were unlikely to have a frank and open discussion. Returning to the conference room, Diana reiterated why she wanted a court reporter present. Now, the attorneys agreed with her. They told her it was a fine idea. The two attorneys had shifted gears. But Carl, not one to back down on a point of principle, said he would cancel the meeting or it could take place without him. The court reporter was dismissed.

Diana had two sides. She could be warm, charming, and gracious, inviting her staff and associates into her home or hotel suite and sharing stories about her life. Diana was a devoted and caring mother who went to great lengths to give her children the maximum amount of her time and attention. Talking about her kids, Rhonda, Tracee, and Chudney, and all the problems that mothers go through, was something that Diana relished. The three girls always took top priority in her life. But Diana's imperious persona was completely different. She dispatched orders to a retinue of aides and assistants who seemed to trail three paces behind her. Nearly everyone in our organization including me was instructed to call her "Miss Ross" at all times and those who breached that etiquette were sharply rebuked. A kind of caste system developed based on who could address her as "Diana," a privilege extended to a handful of executives and longtime musicians, and those who had to call her "Miss Ross," nearly everyone else. The "Miss Ross this" and "Miss Ross that" routine seemed pompous and self-important, especially on those occasions when Diana referred to herself in the third person, sternly warning her underlings, "You tell them that's what Miss Ross wants!"

After we began working with her, Diana opened an office of her own. It would prove to be a portent of things to come. She bought an impressive townhouse on the East Side, not far from our offices. Diana had set up a company called RTC Management (RTC being the first initials of her children), originally housed in a rented office on East 57th Street. Her idea was to have her own office and company to eventually manage other artists; her ex-husband Robert Silberstein, later known as Robert Ellis, would run the company. They had been divorced in 1977. Another of her ideas was to have a fan club and service organization called Rainbow Colors of My Life which would disseminate inspirational material to her fans. Neither project ever showed much success. By the end of 1981, Diana began limiting her visits to Glickman/Marks Management, preferring to spend most of her business time at the RTC offices.

At times, Diana would become flustered from the pressures and anxieties of her professional career. She would suddenly start gushing about having to bear the double burden of being both a performer and a single mother to her three daughters. Tears welling up in her eyes, Diana would vent many of the frustrations she usually kept a tight lid on: there was always too much on her shoulders, there were too many demands, too many obligations, and too many obstacles keeping her from balancing everything in her life. It wasn't so much self-pity as it was self-absorption. Diana's difficulties stemmed from her trying to do everything herself and rarely delegating to others even the minutia of her business. She even insisted on approving the color of the luggage tags used by her entourage during the time I traveled with her on tour.

201

Starting new business ventures for Diana was to be a big part of our company's role in her career. She became excited thinking about all the possibilities that were opening up for her in concert merchandising, fashion, cosmetics, and retail licensing. Diana was very keen on having her own line of Diana Ross fashion clothing in a popular price range for young women and a brand of cosmetics and fragrances that would bear her imprimatur. (Cosmetics and fashion deals with superstars like Elizabeth Taylor and Cheryl Tiegs can earn millions, and continue for years.) In L.A., I met with Linda Wachner, then head of Max Factor and now one of the fashion industry's most successful executives. Linda was very enthusiastic about getting Diana to link up with Max Factor and ultimately start a Diana Ross line of cosmetics and fragrances. She asked to meet Diana in Las Vegas, which was arranged. Diana was initially very excited, then inexplicably cooled to the idea. We were never able to get past the first step.

Playing Josephine Baker in a movie was the project dearest to Diana's heart. Diana had worshipped the legendary chanteuse for years. Baker, a black American singer who became a sensation in Paris in the 1930s, had been Diana's idol. Paramount Pictures had been negotiating with Diana's attorneys for her to star in a Josephine Baker movie and had made substantial offers. But the negotiations always collapsed supposedly because Diana insisted on having control over everything. None of the efforts to revive the project ever panned out. In 1991, Home Box Office produced their own Josephine Baker movie—without Diana—and it was one of the season's biggest hits.

We'd just gotten our stride working with Diana when storm clouds started moving in our direction. Diana had started to blow hot and cold with Howard Marks by the end of 1981. Her new riches from RCA and Capitol/EMI and her enhanced marquee value as a performer had begun to lose a bit of their sheen. Her accolades to Howard diminished in frequency. Although he and Carl were permitted to call her Diana—everyone else in our organization was ordered in a company memo to call her "Miss Ross" lest they be banished from the account—she began to be resentful of Howard's increasing dominance in her affairs. Diana had wanted a business manager, but not one with such a strong, dominating personality. Howard was anything but a yes-man. He insisted on the role of overlord, making decisions and telling people what to do. And Diana was equally determined to be the boss and in control over everything. It was a case of the immovable object colliding with the irresistible force. Diana's unhappy experience during her Motown years, when the record company controlled much of her life, led her to swing in the opposite direction. The volatile chemistry between Diana and Howard produced some powerful explosions.

The clash of the titans would be fought in Howard's office when Diana walked in, closed the door, and the meeting began. Hours would pass by. The tumult inside would be relieved at times by a silent, calm period. When the meeting ended, Diana often charged out of his office, bolting down the long corridor toward the reception area, her face tightened with anger. It became hard to predict what would happen when she came to our office to meet with Howard. Sometimes she would walk in mad and walk out madder. Other times she would walk in without any visible emotion or expression and emerge beaming and bubbly. It was jarring.

Howard's often overbearing personality was the catalyst for many of these episodes. Diana began to distance herself from him. The inevitable finally happened in February 1982, less than a year and a half after we started representing her. We'd just booked her first tour of Europe since 1977, set to begin in June, for big guarantees in every major venue on the continent and the U.K. And then we were fired. "Dearest Howard" was the way Diana's letter to Howard began. She had written it by hand and had someone deliver it personally on her behalf. Howard was sitting in Rosanne Shelnutt's office and called me in to deliver the news. He handed me the letter to read. It was flowery and vague, a kind of sugar-coated poison pill. She said she didn't want anyone in her life anymore who had a controlling influence. Diana now wanted to be completely free and in charge of everything herself. She alone would control every aspect of her career, including the business and financial side. With Diana, there was only room for one boss.

We were told to pack up and turn over all her files and papers to her lawyers. Everyone at our company was stunned by the news and how suddenly everything had happened. Our initial attempt to work out a settlement with Diana to compensate Glickman/Marks Management for the many deals we'd negotiated went nowhere. Diana claimed that since she hadn't yet signed a formal agreement with our company—a final draft had been submitted to her for signature—she should be free from any future obligations to us despite the fact that many of our deals would benefit her financially for years to come. Our lawyer, John Eastman, a prominent music business attorney whose clients included brother-in-law Paul McCartney, David Bowie, and, later, Billy Joel, recommended that we bring in a top litigator, Leonard Marks. Len had successfully represented Bruce Springsteen's former manager in a nasty dispute when Bruce fired him. Len also represented the Beatles in their long battle with Capitol Records over royalty payments.

We eventually settled with Diana for a relatively modest sum. It was bitter medicine to have to swallow. We had been successful in turning her career around financially and getting the money which she deserved from the record companies, concert promoters, and casinos. I don't think it was ever in the cards for us to last beyond a transition period in Diana's career. Once we had done the work, we became an unnecessary appendage that could easily be severed.

Diana pressed ahead with her career. Her European concert tour reportedly got off to a rocky start in London's Wembley Arena. In front of a capacity crowd of 9,000, Diana upbraided her sound crew for technical malfunctions, kicking over a monitor. The London press scathingly denounced her, creating a public furor. In the June 21, 1982, issue of *Jet,* music critic Peter Holt of the *London Standard* was quoted as saying, "It was the shoddiest outburst of show business tantrums I have ever seen." Days later, Diana apologized at a press conference for being "uptight." Diana continued to record for RCA until her contract expired in the late 1980s. Her albums following *Why Do Fools Fall in Love,* a million-seller, were less successful. She had not become the standard bearer that RCA had been hoping for. In 1989, Diana went back to Motown, no longer owned by Berry Gordy. She was given an equity stake in the company.

The romance between Gene and Diana continued past the end of our company's relationship with her. Gene's affair with Diana was less showy and flamboyant than his fling with Cher. In part, he was looking to avoid the flak he had taken from Paul about his romance with Cher, which was extensively chronicled in the tabloids. Paul was incensed about Gene's exploits, chasing after famous women to keep him in the public eye. He thought it made Kiss look ridiculous and detracted from the group's appeal to young fans, at least until Paul started dating his own celebrities.

Diana saw in Gene a strong and sexy earthiness which enticed her. She was captivated by Gene's animal magnetism and the way young rock fans were turned on by his outrageous stage antics and overpowering image. Gene was enamored of Diana's status as a superstar in an even bigger galaxy, a real personage of the entertainment world. Each provided something the other wanted. But conflicts inevitably arose between Gene and Diana. Diana's life was centered around her home in Greenwich where she spent most of her time with the children. Professional commitments like concerts and recording were scheduled to fit in with those priorities. Gene loved being center stage at all times. He was also rough around the edges. He once introduced Diana to a Kiss staffer whose girlfriend was black by saying, "I'd like you to meet my friend who dates black girls, too." The small group of people who heard this remark were taken aback. Diana was fuming.

Gene's reputation as a philanderer with his portfolio of girls and his voluminous little black book was a real sore point with Diana. She never knew what to expect from him or what he was doing when they weren't together. She wanted an anchor in her life, not a lothario. By 1983, the relationship fizzled. They continued to be friends but each went in a different direction with their personal life.

Gene began to spend much of his time in Hollywood and rented the shrine for Cher to a variety of tenants including Allan Carr, the flamboyant movie producer of *Grease*. The apartment was put up for sale and languished on the market for years. There weren't many buyers for something that offbeat and exotic in midtown Manhattan. As Gene put it, "I need to find a nut to buy my place." He eventually did find a buyer. When the New York apartment market heated up in the mid-1980s and prices skyrocketed, he made out very well.

Gene's years with Cher and Diana put him on the map as a rock 'n' roll celebrity of the first magnitude. Countless photographs were taken of Gene with Cher or Diana on one arm and the other arm coyly covering his face with a handkerchief in hand. The romances did a lot to put Gene in the limelight. But they didn't help Kiss's image as a rock band. The seeds of discontent were being planted for a backlash from Kiss's fans. Paul joked about one day turning on the TV and seeing Gene as a panelist on *Hollywood Squares*, waving at the camera and sitting next to Zsa Zsa Gabor and Charles Nelson Reilly. It was an improbable vision, but there was a grain of truth to it. Talking about Christmas plans to write 400 cards together and buy 200 gifts for friends, as Gene and Diana did in the December 21, 1981, issue of *People*, didn't enhance Gene's standing as a rock star. The celebrity-nourished notoriety eventually became an albatross the group would have a tough time getting rid of.

12 The International Beat

Wally Meyrowitz at ATI was hysterical when he called me in April 1980. He'd just heard the news that Kiss was canceling the big tour of England and Europe he'd booked for them. Wally thought Bill Aucoin was crazy for blowing off the tour, the group's first jaunt to the continent in more than four years, when a much scruffier and far less known Kiss played there. Wally was yelping in agony. All of his work would now be a worthless heap of shredded contracts and deal memos. I muffled the earpiece of my telephone as Wally bemoaned the sorry state of affairs, but his problems weren't the only ones we had to deal with. That morning, an ocean freighter was on the docks at New York's West Side terminal, ready to ship out with Kiss's equipment to a port near London. It would now have to be off-loaded and put in storage.

Everything had been ticking like a Swiss clock until a monkey wrench got thrown in. Kiss's negotiations with Phonogram were under way at the beginning of 1980 and the group was in the studio recording a new album for spring release. Vini Poncia was signed up as producer to reprise his *Dynasty* success, a worldwide hit. There would be a major tour of England and Europe, supported by the new Kiss release and the momentum from *Dynasty* and the "I Was Made for Lovin' You" single which had carried over from the previous year. Promoters abroad were excited about having Kiss come over. And Phonogram was especially anxious to see Kiss on the continent since they were about to commit to another six Kiss albums to the tune of $15 million.

But there was just one hitch to this carefully choreographed strategy. Peter was leaving the group. Or the group was asking Peter to leave. Both were correct. Peter's problems with Kiss had finally come to a head and they wanted to end the disruption. It was mutually agreed that Peter was out. A final meeting took place at a rehearsal studio in New York. Bill, along with Gene, Paul, and Ace, asked Peter to come and rehearse together to give it one last chance. They wanted to determine if they could continue playing with him in the band. After Shreveport, they had real doubts about Peter's reliability. Peter's increasingly dissolute lifestyle had become a major problem. On one occasion, I sat with Peter in Howard Marks's office for a business meeting. When Howard left for the day,

Peter slipped into his oversized leather chair and started clowning around, playing the part of "the boss." Peter often referred to Howard as "Happy Days" because of his resemblance to Tom Bosley. At one point, I got up to use the private bathroom in Howard's office. When I returned, neatly drawn lines of white powder had appeared on top of Howard's polished mahogany desk. Howard would have had a heart attack if he knew what his desk was being used for.

It wasn't Peter's difficult nature that ultimately put his future with the group in jeopardy, though. Howard had talked with the others, who told him they would put up with "ten times the amount of bullshit Peter put them through" if he was a great drummer. A superstar drummer in a heavy metal group can be the indispensable link between churning guitar riffs and pounding bass rhythms. Peter was no longer a great drummer. For many years, he had been a fine musician, but he had lost interest in playing with Kiss. It was unanimously decided that Peter would leave, voluntarily.

Peter's voluntary departure from Kiss was largely motivated by his being tired of playing in the group. He felt Gene and Paul were too bossy, too dominating, and not interested enough in allowing him to develop his own music for Kiss to record. His songs were much mellower and less hard-edged than the standard Kiss sound; "Beth" was Peter's style and became the group's biggest hit. He was unhappy in Kiss. Peter had just been divorced and remarried. He wanted to do his own thing and not be stuck in the background as Kiss's drummer playing a strict regimen of hard rock. Peter's unhappiness had been simmering for several years. At Magic Mountain in Southern California, where Kiss was shooting the final scenes for *Kiss Meets the Phantom of the Park,* Peter confided to me that he was sick of being cast in a "stupid Batman and Robin" cartoon-style movie. He wanted to be an actor in his own right. Playing Robert de Niro roles was more his style. He coveted a solo career as a singer—Frank Sinatra was his idol—and having his own private jet with a crest painted on the fuselage with the initials "P.C." in the center, like a monogram. The Super Kiss thinking had infused Peter's psyche. He wanted to take a shot at being "bigger than Kiss," as he put it.

Once this wholesale drama had ended and Peter agreed to leave, the most delicate maneuvering took place with Phonogram. Amazingly, they went along with the plan to retire Peter from the group and replace him with another drummer who would be developed into a new Kiss character. Kiss would be the three remaining members of the group.

The album then being recorded would have Peter's face on the cover, though, and Phonogram agreed to give Peter his own deal to do a solo album. It was an ideal situation. Phonogram wanted to keep Kiss and Peter in the family at any price. Kiss's new album, *Unmasked,* was released in May 1980 featuring a session drummer, Anton Fig, in Peter's place. Anton later played with many other groups before joining David Letterman's band.

The Kiss tour of England and Europe had already been booked and tickets were on sale in many cities. The shows were being promoted as the usual four-some with the close-up cover photo of their faces from last year's *Dynasty* album. Many of the tickets were printed in full color on double-sized ticket stock with the Kiss photo and the headline, "American Supergroup Kiss," in bold type. Box offices in Germany, Sweden, and England were swamped with hordes of fans standing in line three abreast to buy tickets. But there was a big problem with this promotion. Kiss was now a threesome. The obvious solution was to announce that Peter was sick but that the tour would go on as sched-uled. There's plenty of precedent for that. A replacement drummer, without makeup and costume, could fill Peter's place and the show would go on. It was Gene, Paul, and Ace who were in front of the stage and the most visible part of the Kiss show. But Bill and Kiss would have none of this. "Kiss has to be Kiss," they insisted, and until a new character to replace Peter was created and all of the p.r. ballyhoo unfurled, which could take months, Kiss would have to stay home. The same diatribe heard a year ago at the July 1979 Cleveland meeting was replayed and the group was once again parroting the party line—Kiss was too big to do that, it would tamper with the formula, the fans would reject them, they were too important for such shenanigans, and on and on. Bill and the band were once again marching in lockstep.

The tour was canceled, and on April 17, 1980, a press release was issued. Wally would start rebooking the tour to begin in Rome at the end of August, not the most opportune time of the year to start a European tour when summer vacations leave the major cities half empty. But we were stumped for alterna-tives; Kiss had to play Europe that year and a tour of Australia was already in the works for late fall. And now the bills would come in for cancellation charges from the promoters, most of whom had begun their advertising and promotion and sold tickets. This was now a sunk cost and in a few months, they would have to start all over again. Refunds would have to be arranged until an entirely new set of dates and places could be locked up. By the time all the reimbursements had been made, Kiss had laid out a small fortune for the cancellation.

❖

Mexico City is one huge population explosion, a sprawling mass of buildings, parched earth, ramshackle houses, hovels, and highways stretching in every direction. A thick, noxious, grayish haze is perpetually suspended over the city like an ominous cloud of soot. Cars and buses choke the streets and clog the traffic arteries, belching a trail of dirty exhaust fumes behind them. The Pan Am flight from New York had just landed and as the plane door unlocked and I ambled down the stairway, the heat and dust whipped across my face. There were over ten million people here and it would be no problem filling stadiums and bullrings with Kiss fans, our Mexican friends assured us. Wally and I had come to Mexico City to pave the way for Kiss. We threw some greenbacks at a burly looking trio of baggage handlers who rescued our suitcases from a rickety baggage cart headed for god knows where and flagged a taxi to take us to the Sheraton downtown. It was night, but the sticky heat made it uncomfortably humid.

Somewhere in the middle of the morass with Peter and the scuttling of the European tour, the Mexicans entered the picture. They wanted to bring Kiss to Mexico. It would be a first for an American rock group on the scale of Kiss. They would play stadiums or bullrings that could hold over 100,000 people in Mexico City or Guadalajara. And the Mexican promoters would pay big money, a ton of money. One million *dollares* for no more than four shows. Kiss had hit the jackpot again, snatching victory from the jaws of defeat.

It soon became clear that what sounded like the deal of the decade wasn't the type of tour we were used to staging. There were nonstop telephone calls and telexes between the Mexicans and our office. The itinerary was changed, modified, redone, and turned upside down and inside out. Dates were confirmed, then canceled. Cities were agreed to, then changed. Stadiums were booked, then switched. Government permits, a critical factor, were obtained, then revoked. We had to tell the promoters unless they came up with their nonrefundable deposit of $100,000, we couldn't spend any more of our time and money organizing this gigantic undertaking. Finally, they sent a wire transfer to ATI for the deposit.

Days later, three lumpy-looking middle-aged men in dated and ill-fitting business suits showed up at the Glickman/Marks Management offices. No one knew they were coming. They called me around 11:00 that morning and told me they were in New York to have a meeting. I wanted to be accommodating so I rushed all the key people to our offices from ATI and Aucoin Management. As I learned, this type of relaxed attitude seems to be a normal modus operandi for Latin American businessmen; they often just show up and take you by surprise.

Kiss's Mexican promoters were small-business types, not impresarios. They spoke no English and brought a young Latino girl who lived in New York to translate for them. I had carved out the international area as my specialty so I would be involved in negotiating this deal. Our promoters explained that they were the backers of a promotional venture put together to bring Kiss to Mexico. This was their way of getting into show business, bringing Kiss and the biggest rock show on earth to the Third World. They had hired a local impresario to handle all the technical and production details to make the tour work. They presented us with a sheaf of documents, and the meeting went on for a few hours. We talked about finances and then invited our Mexican guests to dinner at the Four Seasons. They were suitably impressed, sitting in the restaurant's elegant Pool Room and gazing at the stylishly coiffed ladies sauntering by in strapless crêpe de Chine evening dresses.

Everything seemed to be under control and the Mexicans assured us there was "no problem" with anything. I started to hear those words a lot. But within days of their leaving to go back to Mexico City, the whole itinerary had been changed around. Once again, cities were in, cities were out. Venues were booked, then canceled. Everything was in a constant state of flux. I was getting the feeling that this tour was a comedy unfolding. I could envision Kiss's trucks, all twenty of them for this monster of a tour, finally crossing the border and heading for the designated stadium, only to be diverted at the last minute to another stadium, possibly in another city. Mexico was looking more and more like a disaster waiting to happen. Sitting in New York, we had no way of knowing if these people had any idea what they were doing. I hadn't expected this tour to be a cakewalk, but there were tremendously complicated problems involving border crossings, permits, visas, security, insurance bonds, power generators, staging, labor, auxiliary sound and lights, and so forth that our promoters simply swept under the rug. It was now July and the trucks would have to leave by early August to make the trek to Mexico.

I called Wally at ATI. I told him we should fly down there to make an advance trip and confirm for ourselves that the promoters had the wherewithal to handle the tour and, just as important, had the necessary permissions from the government to bring Kiss into the country. This had always been a sticking point in the past in trying to pull off rock shows in Mexico. There were too many people saying "no problem" when the whole deal looked like one big problem. Wally agreed and we flew to Mexico City a few days later. The morning after we arrived we took a taxi to meet our promoters at their offices. It was a long drive from the Sheraton, and the sun was beating down on our un-air-conditioned Chevy. We were miles away from the central part of the city, which could be seen through a pale haze of smog. Our driver kept circling the block where the office was supposed to be, past a dilapidated strip of walk-up buildings and stucco houses sitting in yards choked with weeds. We were in a deserted section of town and the roads, what there were of them, were badly rutted. I kept telling the driver and Wally, "This can't be the place," but we continued to circle the block like a merry-go-round, always ending up at the same spot. I finally told the driver to stop, got out of the taxi, and inspected a small plaque that was posted outside a ratty old office building. A man was sleeping on the sidewalk in front of the building. The number and street matched my instructions and I signaled Wally to leave the taxi. We walked up a narrow staircase with old newspapers strewn across the steps. A few people from outside the building were staring at us. In our fancy linen shirts and cotton twill pants, we gringos were prime targets for a mugging.

At the top of the staircase, we opened a small door, one of those old-fashioned types with translucent glass and a brown wooden frame that was slightly bent. We walked in, shaking the dust from our shoes. The room was shabby and the chipped paint gave the walls a faded look. A few calendars and photos hung crookedly. Stacks of paper spilled to the floor. It was stifling and Wally and I were dripping wet. Our three Mexican friends were sitting like ducks in a row, grinning and cheerful, and a small electric fan was spinning on an adjacent table. They were drinking Cokes from greenish glass bottles and proferred a couple to us. The blades of the fan made an annoying, buzzing sound. Wally and I came right to the point. It was too hot and uncomfortable to dawdle. We wanted to see the stadiums, the official permits, and the contracts for use of the stadiums, and we wanted to meet the actual promoter who was arranging this extravaganza. They smiled without interruption and said in English, "no problem." A woman seated near them, who spoke in halting English, helped translate. Several file folders bulging with papers concerning the tour were piled up next to a twisted gooseneck lamp on the desk in front of her. She would make copies of all these papers and deliver them to our hotel.

In the meantime, our Mexican friends would take us on a tour of the facilities. Unfortunately, the actual promoter was in Guadalajara or Monterey—on business for the Kiss shows, of course. We left the office, climbed into a big sedan with a blistered finish and threadbare seat covers, and headed for the superhighway to see the Olympic Stadium. When we arrived outside the gate, we couldn't get in. The stadium was closed. There was no one around and every entry around the huge facility was locked. Of course, this was "no problem" because they had another stadium to show us which was better, anyhow. We tore across the city to another, smaller stadium. The rest of the day was a dizzying blur. Wheezing from the heat and the polluted air, Wally and I looked at one stadium after another and a few bullrings, too.

But what they call stadiums in most Latin American countries are simply enormous concrete shells with tiers of concrete slabs for people to sit on. There aren't any seats, and the facilities backstage, if there are any, are more suited to cattle than people. The stink of manure from the animal stalls was nauseating. I doubt there was enough electrical power in any of those places to run a toaster let alone 400,000 watts of sound and lights. They're built to house huge crowds of 100,000 to 200,000 to watch soccer matches or bullfights, not high-tech stage productions. Kiss's Mexican tour was looking like a wild fantasy.

By nighttime, we found ourselves in the basement of the Mexico City police headquarters, a cavernous subterranean structure next to the city jail. Walking through the catacombs, I could hear the sound of men clanging against the metal bars and wailing in Spanish. We were asked to wait in a large lobby area outside of the administrative offices. Dank and dimly lit, the room was like a dungeon and a musty odor from the lack of ventilation hung in the air. We had come to this uninviting place because our Mexican hosts were supposedly inside one of the offices dickering with a deputy police chief to secure permits for the Kiss shows. In Mexico City, the Federales wield considerable power over any public event taking place within the city district. Apparently it was routine to hold these types of negotiations at 10:00 at night in the basement of the police headquarters.

Finally, I started to laugh hysterically. The Mexican tour had gone from light comedy to complete farce. It was like starring in a Mel Brooks movie and being led around the city by the Three Latin Stooges masquerading as big-time international rock promoters. Bringing Kiss here wouldn't just be a disaster, it would be a catastrophe. Wally was laughing so hard he looked as if he was about to keel over. Eventually the Mexicans emerged from the meeting. Behind them was a plumpish man in a khaki uniform with a wide leather belt strapped around his waist, but he quickly disappeared. The Mexicans announced they hadn't quite gotten the "principal permit" but this would come "tomorrow" and would be, of course, "no problem." Wally and I hurried out of the building and found our way back to the Sheraton. We stayed in Mexico City another day, but never heard from the promoters. Several days later, they called me in New York. They wanted to stage another tour and have their $100,000 deposit applied to the new tour. I told them to come up with a contract for the stadiums and all the supporting documents and permits and we would discuss it. I never heard from them again. The deposit monies had been used up in rehearsing and preparing for the tour, and now there would be no million dollar payday.

Mexico was off but Europe was on. Another mass meeting took place at the Glickman/Marks Management offices to discuss the cost of the tour. Even with Phonogram kicking in a hefty subsidy, the tour was still budgeted to lose money. Kiss wanted to duplicate their U.S. Super Kiss tour of 1979 in Europe— no easy or inexpensive feat since something on this scale hadn't been done before. Gargantuan amounts of pyro had to be drop-shipped from country to country and Gene's flying rig alone took up two trucks. Astronomical amounts of equipment, staging, and personnel were also needed. Most venues in Europe weren't very modern then and to create Super Kiss in a less than super facility would be costly. Within weeks of finishing Europe, a tour of Australia was slated that was looking to be even bigger.

Canceling the tour in the spring and then starting it in late summer was another stone in our shoes. Wally had warned us that canceling a major tour in Europe leaves fans feeling cheated. Rescheduling it months later during the vacation season, when many kids are away from home, could create more problems. The effect all this would have on ticket sales was impossible to quantify or predict. But Wally's advice fell on deaf ears. We sat with Kiss around the large conference table in our offices on July 3 to discuss the upcoming tour of Europe. It was another instant replay of Cleveland in 1979—suites for the band, limos everywhere, extra security, extra bodyguards, more staging, more sound, more pyro, more lights, more trucks, more people, and everything big, big, big. Kiss had to be bigger than any group ever seen on the continent no matter what it cost. They wouldn't budge on anything where it was a question of "Kiss being Kiss." By now, I had heard this refrain so often it had become like a devout repetition of the rosary.

With Peter gone, it was more important than ever to maintain the Super Kiss illusion. A 30-year-old Brooklyn musician, Paul Caravello, who would be an employee of Kiss, not a partner, was to replace Peter. Immediately, he was renamed Eric Carr and assigned the character of a fox, with a costume and makeup design to match. The p.r. onslaught of press releases and photos of Eric as the new Kiss character was already in motion. Eric's character had been changed repeatedly before everyone agreed on the fox; one of his earlier designs looked more like a chicken costume with feathers sticking out. It was quickly modified.

With Bill once again leading the charge, Kiss decided that Kiss had to be Kiss and the end justified the means. Carl Glickman harrumphed that by the time the tour finished, the Phonogram subsidy "wouldn't come close" to covering the loss. Howard Marks asked Gene, Paul, and Ace to consider making one of their rehearsals in New York an actual show so that tickets could be sold to offset some of the soaring tour costs. They agreed.

Kiss's major business decisions were made at these meetings, since they could speak to all of their principal advisers at the same time. Peter used to refer to them as "board of directors meetings, like General Motors." He no longer attended every meeting, although he still had a financial interest in Kiss.

In the late '70s, the only expense that the Kiss members regularly groused about were the off-the-top commissions they paid. But now, the bills for Kiss's spending binge over the last two years were starting to come due. There were substantial outlays for promotion and publicity in addition to the cancellation costs for Europe. And Kiss's personal living expenses were headed out of sight. Paying for Gene and Paul's stupendous New York apartments and Ace and Peter's Connecticut homes plus Ace's studio required heaps of cash. Investments had to be liquidated, including a portfolio of stocks and bonds. Some of their investments had turned a sizable profit, but the proceeds had gone toward financing the ongoing business of Kiss. Others, like the coal mining investment, weren't easily converted into cash. The long-term impact of big spending coupled with asset sell-offs was often brought up at the meetings but no one in Kiss paid much attention.

Gene prided himself as the group's businessman. He grasped the economics of things, but his Super Kiss thinking seemed to overwhelm all else. With Gene, hype had no limits and was like a magic elixir that could solve any problem in the business of rock. He rationalized the excessive costs of "Kiss being Kiss" as essential to promote the group's public image. Gene believed whatever the cost of the hype, it would ultimately reap the reward of keeping Kiss's image intact. He was often described as being smart about business, "for a rocker."

Paul frequently had a pained expression on his face when the subject turned to finances. He was always kind of aloof, breezily dismissing the idea that Kiss should be managed in the same way as a more mundane enterprise. Like Gene, he seemed to feel that a special set of economic rules applied to rock groups. Paul projected an attitude that rock stars shouldn't have to occupy themselves with these concerns or be confronted with making choices that required creative compromise. Ace and Peter seldom had much to say on business and financial matters. They usually went along with the dictates of Gene and Paul, sometimes by default. They found sitting at meetings for hours a burdensome chore and became grouchy. Gene and Paul dominated the agenda.

The most bizarre idea for saving money came from Ace. Ace had heard about a way to eliminate paying taxes by converting a business to a church. The Universal Life Church was a well-known outfit at the time and for around a thousand dollars, a certificate could be obtained by mail that would ordain anyone as a minister. Income would now be tax-exempt since it was earned by a nonprofit religious organization. Ace thought this was a good idea for Kiss. We were finally able to dissuade him when *The Wall Street Journal* ran an article about the scam. The idea was dropped.

Ace was always glad to volunteer the services of his in-laws whenever Kiss ran into a business problem where a little muscle might help. Kiss was once embroiled in a dispute with Casablanca and Ace proposed that he put in a call to his family connections—his wife's father and grandfather in the Teamsters—to see about slowing down Casablanca's truck deliveries of records and wreaking havoc on their retail distribution. Hopefully, there wouldn't be any Kiss records on those trucks. No one ever took Ace up on his offers, though.

Important business was decided at these meetings, but a lot of what took place was posturing. The goal was keeping Kiss's spirits up and painting as rosy a picture as possible about what they could earn if they kept working. Motivating the group wasn't difficult through the late '70s, when they took in over $30 million in a three-year period. Their popularity was growing exponentially, their income was on an upward trajectory, and no expense was too extravagant. Kiss was on the road to unimagined riches and everyone wanted to keep the golden goose laying eggs.

Howard saw his role as the cheerleader who would provide the stimulus for positive thinking and hard work. He had come to see himself as Kiss's business leader, if not their manager. But Howard's presence became like an octopus, with tentacles reaching into every corner of Kiss's career. Howard negotiated the record contract, Glickman/Marks Management handled their money, and his advertising agency did the album covers, media campaigns, and merchandising design work. Bill had originally agreed to bring in Howard and Carl as business mentors to provide the financial acumen he lacked. Now, Howard was everywhere, although Bill was still officially the manager.

Bill, of course, had made mistakes of his own—some through inexperience and some as a result of his grandiose schemes about creating a rock 'n' roll studio. By 1980, he'd spent most of what he had earned with Kiss and had little to show from all of the other groups he backed. This didn't enhance his standing with Kiss. Despite the fact that Howard had originally been Bill's biggest booster, he now expressed the opinion, self-servingly to be sure, that Kiss had become "leaderless" under Bill.

Not long after Kiss signed their new record deal in 1980, an undercurrent of money problems became noticeable at the meetings. Dick Weidenbaum prepared volumes of financial reports for each band member. His firm did all the tax and accounting work for Kiss and worked with Glickman/Marks Management on financial matters. An engaging and even-tempered man in his forties, Dick became involved with Kiss at the behest of Howard Marks, a longtime client. Dick, a lawyer and CPA, proved to be a popular choice.

Gene complained constantly that "you guys talk a different language," claiming that the group never understood "all those numbers." But the band would get summaries written in plain English which they gave only a cursory glance to and immediately put out of their minds. Howard would exhort the accountants to make sure that Kiss's financial statements were prepared promptly but he hardly looked at them. Howard preferred to extemporize on most topics and present the big picture in a way that Kiss could easily grasp. Carl, a quick study, often had a hard time communicating financial details to Kiss. He always tried to find a bottom line number that would cut through to the heart of the matter. But it wasn't always that clear-cut. Sometimes any kind of financial shorthand is lost on people who aren't financially sophisticated.

As spending mounted, the cash shortfalls were more frequent. Kiss's investments were being sold, and the group started borrowing monies from banks as well. When a new record was delivered and the balance of the advance received, the loans would be paid off. Peter was always puzzled by this process.

He couldn't fathom why, if he and everyone in Kiss was a millionaire, the group had to borrow money. He had a point. The problem was that while each of the Kiss members had substantial personal assets like homes and property, their business was beginning to run deficits from the spending on all fronts. The last tour in 1979 had shown a big loss; the four solo albums went way over budget and sales fell below expectations; marketing and promotional costs had skyrocketed; commissions took a huge piece off the top; legal fees were ballooning; they had sizable tax liabilities because of their big incomes; and their personal living expenses soaked up the remaining cash. Kiss had to split what was left four ways. And now another tour was about to start which was sure to lose money—only how much money was in question—while more investments would be liquidated. As increasingly large sums were drained from Kiss's coffers, the Phonogram windfall would prove to be only a palliative, not a cure for the real disease.

Unmasked, the new Kiss album, had stalled in the charts by August. There were no hit singles and it was clear that at least in the United States, it wouldn't do nearly as well as *Dynasty. Unmasked* had an even more pop, commercial sound. The cover featured a cutesy sequence of cartoon illustrations with the group pretending to take off their makeup and unmask themselves. Everyone in the cartoons is talking with balloons above their heads. In the last panel, Kiss is seen on stage in their usual costumes and makeup and a "creepy reporter" resembling a cross between Pee-wee Herman and Gilbert Gottfried is seen smirking in front. He shouts, "I still say they STINK!" The Super Kiss image of four superhero cartoon fantasy characters was further solidified with the *Unmasked* cover. About the same time, Peter released his solo album,*Out of Control,* which proved far less successful than Kiss's albums.

Diana Ross and Gene were going strong when Kiss rented the Palladium in lower Manhattan and began rehearsing for Europe. Originally built as an ornate, art deco theater with a proscenium stage the Palladium has more recently been converted to a glitzy, high-tech club with multilevels of dance floors. The place was one huge steam bath, since the air-conditioning system broke down repeatedly. It was the end of July and we were all constantly drenched from the rain forest-like humidity inside. Diana had come to the rehearsals, her three kids tagging along and her Rolls idling in a back alley. Gene was like a kindly uncle, mugging for the kids in his ghoulish stage costume and makeup as he pranced around the stage wings. The kids were entranced. It was an odd sight since Gene had for years looked upon children as "little monsters" and would chase them away by shouting "scram!" On planes, he often joked that "screaming babies should be fed rat poison," while ordering the flight attendants to keep them under control. With Diana, he was now singing from a different hymn book.

Gene assumed the personality of the macabre character that he portrayed whenever he donned his costume and makeup. He became bellicose and demanding, storming across the stage during the Palladium rehearsals and ordering the sound company to "double everything." It was already loud enough to annihilate an arena-sized audience, let alone the people who could fit in a theater the size of the Palladium, which was designed to seat around 3,000. Major financial outlays were often decided on the basis of these emotional outbursts. On the '79 *Dynasty* tour, Paul had done the same, kicking up a fuss about the costumes. Costume after costume was tossed out because none of them fit right. As the rehearsal droned on, production expenses started climbing. Ken Anderson, the production head, was always in the center of this storm and at times he seemed ready to collapse.

On July 25, just before packing the equipment off to Europe, a show was put on for the public. Kiss would introduce Eric Carr, the new drummer, at the Palladium in their only U.S. appearance in 1980. Eric would appear in his fox stage persona and makeup. Originally, several shows were planned, but only one was put on sale. Ticket sales were sluggish. The show sold out but a second show would have been chancy. Demand wasn't strong enough for Ron Delsener, the promoter, to risk it. It was an omen of things to come, but everyone looked the other way, rationalizing that weak ticket sales were the result of minimal advertising for the show. Just one year earlier, Kiss had played two nights at Madison Square Garden.

Kiss kept the audience on their feet during the show at the Palladium, with fans cheering and waving clenched fists for nearly two hours. The reaction proved the group hadn't lost their touch. Eric was a dynamo on the drums, filling out the Kiss sound with a depth it hadn't had in recent years. Seeing Kiss in a theater and not an arena was a first for me. Everything seemed much more concentrated and contained and the overall effect was especially intense. Within a few weeks Kiss would leave for Europe and start their tour in Italy at the end of August.

Kiss had never played in Italy and the show in Milan's aging Velodromo Vigorelli stadium turned into a disaster. The group left the Hilton downtown for the stadium in their limos during the late afternoon but I decided to go a few hours later on my own by taxi. It was an almost fatal mistake. I didn't speak any Italian, the driver didn't understand a word of English, and he hadn't the slightest idea what a backstage entrance was. He let me off in front of the main gate where an unruly mob was pressing through the Velodromo's entry gates. I was carrying a locked Hartmann attache case which contained a bank pouch with maybe $5,000 in cash—dollars and lira. The pouch, displaying a Saks Fifth Avenue logo, was another gift from Gene. Swarms of people were rushing past me as I tried to find a guard or a stadium employee who could help get me inside, but it was hopeless. The beret-clad Carabinieri, Italian paramilitary police carrying machine guns, weren't overly friendly, either. They stood guard at all public events as an antiterrorist deterrent. I fumbled around to find my Kiss I.D. to flash, but no one was paying attention.

My only chance to get inside the building was to charge through the gates. That's what everyone else was doing. Hardly anyone seemed to have a ticket; they just leaped over the barricades or climbed over the turnstiles. I would end up being crushed by the crowd if I didn't make a move fast. I put my head down and pushed my way through, knocking a few junior Kiss fans to the ground, and ran along the inside corridor of the Velodromo. I was now inside the stadium. To get to the ground level where the stage was, you had to first walk up a set of stairs to the top of the bleachers which surrounded the oval stadium. I huffed my way to the top of the bleachers. Below me was an ocean of people filling all corners of the stadium grounds. I could see the stage way off in the distance in the twilight, hundreds of feet away. Now I had to make it to the ground level. Shoving everyone in my path like a raging bull, I used my attache case as a battering ram to get through the crowded aisles. I was knocking people down like tenpins. They must've thought I was on PCP but I made it to the ground level.

I jumped the barricade that hemmed in the bleachers from the stadium grounds, a bumpy grass field full of gravel and sand. Now that I was on the grounds of the stadium, I knew I could get to the stage and have someone take me to the backstage area. The group's sound and lighting personnel were set up on a platform in the center of the grounds, about 6 feet above the field. They were in the center of the stadium's grounds in a roped off area. It would be far less treacherous to get to where they were than to hazard another run into an even bigger crowd in front of the stage. I made a mad dash to the platform, waving and screaming wildly, until one of the crew finally spotted me and had a guard drag me up to their platform. I was winded but safe. But that was only the first act of this hair-raising adventure.

Night had fallen and Kiss took the stage. A thunderous boom from the wall of amps and stacks of bass bins and speakers washed over the audience. Kids streamed from the bleachers and the fans on the ground rushed the stage. When Kiss broke into their disco hit, "I Was Made for Lovin' You," a smash in Italy, the crowd went berserk. About an hour into the show, a group of left-wing militants known as the Red Brigade jumped the stage after hurdling the barricade in front which separated the fans on the stadium grounds from the 8-foot-high stage. "Kiss Fascista! Kiss Fascista!" they screamed, as a contingent of about two dozen seized control of the stage. Kiss stopped dead in their tracks. The music shut down in front of a crowd of 30,000 as Kiss bolted from their places while the militants kept shouting, "Kiss Fascista! Kiss Fascista!"

Kiss ran off the stage and tore furiously into the stadium's tunnel leading backstage. I was just below the stage behind the barricade watching the show. As Kiss left the stage, the Carabinieri rushed forward to grab the militants. Meanwhile, someone was getting bludgeoned on stage, either a militant or a fan, and was carted away on a stretcher. Bodies slammed into each other amid the sound of fists cracking. Kiss's intrepid road manager, George Sewitt, decked a couple of toughs who were closing in on the band. Sound gear started malfunctioning when mikes were knocked over and cables pulled apart, and an ear-piercing squelching noise kept pouring out of the speakers.

As Kiss raced through the tunnel in a panic, I chased after them. My heart was pumping so hard I thought my chest would burst open. Trailing behind us were a bunch of crazed militants waving red flags and screeching antifascist slogans in Italian. I wasn't sure where Kiss was headed as I sprinted to catch up with them, but chances are it would be a lot safer than standing near the stage and battling it out with the militants, dodging the Molotov cocktails they were lobbing at the stage. Sheer terror is a powerful propellant.

We hurtled down another long tunnel, knocking people aside as we barged our way toward the dressing room. Bodyguards were in front of us clearing a path and a few skinheads flanked us on either side, local tough guys with bald pates, tattoos, and motorcycle jackets. They were helping us out by keeping the crowd at bay. We were running so fast that Gene had thrown off his boots and was now galloping in his bare feet. Ace fell twice, losing his cape, and was nearly trampled. Paul was the speedster, dodging ahead of everyone, and bringing Eric, who looked petrified, along with him. The cacophony inside the tunnel from all of this commotion—the militants screaming, people running at breakneck speed, bodies falling to the ground, costumes being ripped apart, boots flying through the air and hitting the walls—was deafening.

A huge metal door swung open in front of the dressing room as we dove through the opening. Bodyguards scrambled to get inside and slammed the door shut. Once we had made it inside, our black belt bodyguard, a karate coach named Chuck Merriman, threw himself against the door to secure the lock. People were pounding madly on the door from outside in the corridor of the tunnel, making all kinds of menacing sounds. Inside, there was dead silence. We were sitting in a large athletic team locker room on benches. We were all in a state of terror, breathing heavily, not knowing what would happen next. Gene's face was frozen in fear. When I looked in the cracked mirror across from where we were sitting, I saw that my face was as white as a sheet. Paul told me I looked like a ghost with a bad case of the jitters.

The frenzy died down after about half an hour. An intermediary was let in who told us the militants had been ejected from the stadium. Kiss had to decide if they wanted to finish the show or leave now. Most of the fans were still in the stadium, waiting for the show to go on. Rather than risk a full-scale riot, Kiss decided to finish the show, with a phalanx of Carabinieri to protect the stage. We exited the dressing room where the promoter, a skinny young man with a tangled mop of long, wavy brown hair named Francesco Sanavio, was waiting for us. His girlfriend was hanging onto him. She was dressed in a wild outfit of leopard spotted tights and was crowned with jet black hair that resembled a diadem of horny spikes. We told Francesco we were going back on stage. He was his usual nonchalant self. I got the impression he'd been through scenes like this before.

We left Milan early the next morning. Watching Kiss on stage the night before, tearing through songs like "Christine Sixteen" with several dozen para-military troops circling in front, armed with Uzis and handguns, was a bizarre experience. I've learned since that what happened to Kiss is commonplace for visiting rock groups. It's part of the local color and excitement of the Italian pop music scene.

In London, we set another Kiss record—our hotel and limo bill for the week was nearly $70,000 and I had to keep three safety deposit boxes filled with hundred pound banknotes. Kiss's spending had become an open spigot. I had brought with me ten letters of credit from American Express, each worth $10,000. They were like bearer bonds and could be redeemed for local currency at any of their offices. The problem was that none of the London offices could cash more than one per day and I had to hire a taxi to take me on a tour of American Express offices throughout greater London to cash the letters, one by one.

We were set to play two shows in early September at Wembley Arena and more shows in the north country in Stafford and Chester. Our base for the British shows was the fashionable Hilton on Park Lane, across from Hyde Park. The late summer of 1980 was also the height of the Arab invasion of London and the Hilton was a veritable mecca for Arab visitors. The lobby overflowed with men in billowy white robes and brown cloaks with large kerchiefs covering their heads, held in place by thick, twisted cords. Wally Meyrowitz flew over for the London shows. He assessed the situation in his typically succinct way saying, "You know there are a lot of Arabs in this place because the elevator is dripping with oil when you get out." You also knew because every night, the hotel was teeming with gorgeous British and European call girls, stunning women loaded down with bracelets and necklaces that made their flesh sag and wearing couture ensembles from the top fashion houses.

Diana Ross made it to London and watched one of the Wembley shows, surreptitiously stationed in the stage wings out of sight from the audience. Gene gave one of his more energetic performances. The flying rig brought cries of delight from the fans as Gene ordered up columns of flames to shoot into the air and then flew across the width of the stage. Ace's levitating Les Paul guitar exploded in midair when he fired on it with his other guitar, this one equipped as a rocket launcher. A spectacular array of pyro arranged by a top-flight movie special effects company lit up the stage with blinding flashes and a cascade of multicolored rockets, flares, and sparkles.

The Super Kiss philosophy was broadcast loud and clear to the continent when Gene was interviewed by *Melody Maker* in the September 6, 1980, issue in an article titled "See Me, Hear Me, *Buy Me!*" A photo of Gene thrusting his trademarked Axe bass guitar, then being marketed in the states by Kramer Guitars, appeared prominently. According to Gene, Kiss had only scratched the surface with their merchandising onslaught:

> I want a Gene Simmons piggybank that'll stick out its tongue so that you can put a quarter on it and watch the coin pop back in its mouth—I don't want Mickey Mouse to have a corner on that market. There's nothing that Superman, King Kong, or Mickey Mouse have got that we haven't or can't have. I want a Kiss car and that's being worked on at the moment by Chrysler in the states. I want Kiss World, a traveling amusement park, and that's also being planned, and I'm totally serious about all of these things.

At Kiss's London press conference at Picadilly's Princess Anne Theatre, there were lots of queries about Diana Ross, much to the annoyance of Paul. She was, and is, a superstar in England. Gene dodged the questions—he only wanted to talk about Kiss, not his love life—and then went into his usual animated spiel about how big Kiss was. Kiss was super in every way—the most money, the biggest shows, the most records sold, the biggest mansions, the richest deals, and so on. Kiss also made sure everyone knew their tour of Europe and England was going to lose a fortune, but they loved putting on these extravaganzas. Kiss's attitude was they could now afford to thumb their noses at the critics who never took them seriously to begin with, but Gene so overstated everything that he often came across as a bit of a gasbag.

One of his more preposterous statements was that the "K" in the Chrysler K-Car, a prototype fuel-efficient auto being developed in the United States, actually stood for Kiss. Kiss would soon have their own car in America. It wasn't true, but Gene's hyperbolic declarations were certainly in keeping with the Super Kiss image. None of this made any difference to the British press, though. They lapped up whatever codswallop Gene dished out and were only too happy to print it.

Journalists, record company execs, and promoters were always amazed at the number of people who traveled with Kiss on tour. The production itself required a contingent that resembled a Roman army, with all the operations stratified by function and rank. The Kiss members were enveloped by road managers, bodyguards, personal assistants, and, at times, Bill Aucoin and executives from his organization. Sitting one night in Trader Vic's, downstairs in the London Hilton, Ace, Wally Meyrowitz, and I shared a few rounds of Mai Tais served in glasses the size of fishbowls. Ace was planning to go out to a rock club. The logistics involved for this seemingly simple excursion unfolded as we were drinking. Our security chief, John Harte, was on his way down from his room. He would handle Ace and also bring a second bodyguard as his relief. The road manager would coordinate with the local record company representative as to which club was the best choice. They would make the necessary arrangements and the road manager would work out the details and join us shortly. He would then give instructions to Ace's bodyguard who would go upstairs to advise the limo driver of the destination and the approximate departure time. Daimler limos were standing by in front of the Hilton for around-the-clock use by Kiss. Once at the club, security there would augment the Kiss contingent. Ace left when the bodyguards and the road manager showed up. Wally asked me why Kiss needed so many people hovering over them all the time. I told him that traveling with a full complement of aides was something they couldn't be talked out of; they insisted on all the cosseting.

Kiss had a special problem in Germany. The Kiss logo couldn't be used. The stylized rendering of the double "S" in Kiss's logo is a dead ringer for the double "S" design of the Nazi storm troopers known as the SS. In Germany, the display of Nazi symbols is punishable by imprisonment, something neither Phonogran nor Kiss wanted to risk. So a squarish double "S" replaced the lightning bolts for Kiss on all their German records, posters, and advertising.

Germany wasn't a huge success. Munich and Stuttgart did well, but an open-air show in Frankfurt near the U.S. military base had a poor turnout when rain and high winds swept the region. Our promoters there, Marcel Avram and Marek Lieberberg, said the spring cancellation was the major reason for the so-so attendance. In Germany, fans are disappointed when shows are canceled and plans change. It goes against the grain of the German mentality for order and organization. The second time around, fans are often hesitant to buy tickets. They're not sure if the artist is serious about coming at all. And promoters have a tough time building the momentum again for another promotion.

Marek, a former journalist who had promoted shows for years, offered a trenchant analysis as to how the Kiss audience stacked up against those of other rock groups. "Most of the fans who are coming to rock shows are complete idiots who behave like animals. But at least with Kiss, it is excusable. They are too young to know any better," he observed.

Tony Joannou, the promoters' tour manager, was a genial and accommodating host in Germany. We struck up an immediate friendship. In Hamburg, he sent me to Club Amphore, one of the more infamous private sex clubs for a night that seemed to get weirder every minute. In the bar, a tiny stage was wedged in front of several rings of tables, where small lamps provided the only light inside. On stage were strippers who invited guests to have sex with them in front of the audience. There was no charge if you did. Behind the stage was a maze of private rooms and whirlpool baths where zaftig girls circulated in the costume of your choice—nuns' habits, leather and chains, G-strings, school girls' uniforms—and offered bottles of German *sekt,* a sweet sparkling wine, at lofty prices. When I saw the girls presenting bills for $500 to their besotted customers, I knew it was time to call it a night as I grabbed a towel to dry off.

Scandinavia was always big for Kiss, and Oslo and Stockholm drew huge crowds in their biggest ice arenas. Thomas Johansson, the major promoter in Sweden, had brought Kiss over in '76 when they were just starting to build a following. On that tour, Ace had reportedly gotten roaring drunk after the show and fallen into a large pool filled with model boats at a Tivoli Gardens restaurant while hundreds of diners looked on in panic.

France wasn't Kiss country, particularly in the provinces. Except for Paris, where every major act played in a tent structure since there weren't any arenas then, the shows did poorly and one was canceled. But there was a consolation prize that made the trip memorable, arranged by promoter Albert Koski. The little village of Collonges au Mont d'Or, near Lyon, is the home of one of France's most hallowed shrines, the restaurant of Paul Bocuse. I made the pilgrimage with Bill Aucoin and one of his executives, Jack Tessler, who was traveling with us. We had floored it in our tinny rental car from Avignon, about 130 miles away, where Kiss had played the previous night. It was a harrowing trip along narrow roads and hairpin turns. We pulled up in front of the restaurant in mid-afternoon as most of the luncheon guests were leaving. Monsieur Bocuse greeted us and we were escorted through the country provincial house to a dining room filled with rich tapestries and arrangements of wild flowers picked from the gardens next door. The meal was easily worth the aggravation—soupe aux truffes noires, loup en croûte with sauce Choron, volaille de Bresse with sauce Fleurette, and a cornucopia of desserts which included Île Flottante and gaufres de la Grand-Mère Bocuse. A couple of bottles of Krug Grande Cuvée helped us wash down the repast. I paid for the lunch with a sack full of French francs from the show the night before, carried into the restaurant in a plastic shopping bag. Three hours later, we left to join Kiss in Lyon who were snacking on soup and sandwiches in the hotel cafe.

The Sofitel in Lyon tried to prevent us from checking out two days later. We'd vacated our rooms and were about to jump into the three limos parked in front of the hotel to make it to the airport when the hotel manager ran after us, yelling something in French about one of the rooms being wrecked. I'd just paid the hotel bill and no one had mentioned anything about damages, so I ignored his cursing and histrionics. But he was unrelenting, chasing after me with a bill in his hand and looking frazzled. He ordered one of the doormen to get into the hotel's airport van and block our limos from getting out of the circular driveway. We were stuck. When the manager finally caught his breath, he was indignant about the disaster he found in "le chambre de Monsieur Frehley," meaning Ace had ravaged his room. The manager claimed, in broken English, that the room was a wreck. We had to make a plane for Paris. I didn't know anything about what had supposedly happened in Ace's room but I did know we'd never get out of Lyon if we didn't pay the bill. This hotel manager would gladly call in the *gendarmes* next. While Kiss sat stewing in the limos, I forked over $1,500 in francs to settle the bill. Seconds later, the van moved and we were on our way to the airport.

In Brussels, we met some of Kiss's spookiest fans. A group of girls and their boyfriends had been following Kiss all over northern Europe, traveling on motorbikes. They looked barely old enough to get a license. Strangely, they never said a word to anyone, even though they stayed at our hotels and were always backstage. They parked themselves in the hotel lobby beginning at dawn every day and waited until Kiss came down from their rooms. When the band arrived, they just stared at them without blinking, devoid of any expression and with a hollow look in their eyes.

At the Hyatt Regency one night, they sat for hours staring at Kiss without making a sound while the band was at the bar. Kiss left around 1:00 a.m. The next morning at breakfast, also served in the bar area, the fans were already in place, staring from the same seats they'd been in the night before. They became known as the ghouls. Whenever they were spotted, a bodyguard would issue a "ghoul alert." The ghouls continued to follow Kiss on tour. They never did utter a word to anyone.

A fiasco with a promoter awaited us in Holland as the tour headed into its final week in early October. Kiss played a big arena in Leiden, about an hour's drive from Amsterdam. The show only did about half as much business as the promoter expected. We got stiffed for half of our guarantee that night—while the promoter pleaded poverty. It was a particularly embarrassing episode since Leiden had been Kiss's only show in Holland, where Phonogram has its world headquarters. Five years later, we finally made a settlement with the promoter.

When the tour ended, Super Kiss had played twenty-nine shows in Europe and England. Wherever they played, they had made a big impact with the fans and in the press. Photos were splashed across the front pages of newspapers, magazines, and music papers. The press hyped them as an American phenomenon with a fabulous stage show. But Super Kiss suffered from the same bloatedness that plagued the previous year's U.S. tour—too big a production for some venues, too small a turnout at others. Audience sizes varied, from stadiums in Italy with up to 30,000 down to 3,000 in rural France. Crowds in England and Scandinavia were the most consistently large, hitting 10,000 to 20,000 in some cities.

At first, Phonogram was pleased with the tour. Kiss had shown the flag, an important factor in motivating their people to sell more Kiss records. Aart Dalhuisen, Phonogram's president, had become friendly with the group. He'd been a strong supporter of Kiss and was instrumental in keeping them on the label during their contract renegotiation. The tour took on an added importance coming on the heels of Kiss's new worldwide deal, which *Unmasked* kicked off. Previously, Casablanca had licensed the rights to Kiss albums on a territory-by-territory basis whereby different record companies in each country would release the records. Now the overseas market for records was heating up. More top artists were moving in the direction of simultaneous worldwide releases by a single international company. The cumbersome job of coordinating the release of one album on dozens of labels in as many different countries would be streamlined. As Kiss was doing with Phonogram, one company would coordinate worldwide distribution through its own network of company-owned labels in every country with a unified marketing campaign.

Phonogram's enthusiasm for the Kiss tour lasted only until they saw the bill. The tour had cost an unimaginable, unheard-of sum of money. The shortfall was staggering. They were on the hook for up to $500,000, according to the contract, but it was inconceivable to them that a tour could lose that kind of money. They were outraged. They demanded to see back-up invoices, which we provided. It was all there. The seven-week tour of Europe and England added up to a gigantic loss, of which Phonogram bore a substantial share. And the rest came out of Kiss's pockets.

Kiss was about to kick into overdrive in Australia and New Zealand in November and December. We were to fly twenty hours from New York to Los Angeles to Sydney and then to Perth on Australia's west coast to do the first show. Kiss may never have made it south of the border to Mexico, but they would be south of the equator in Australia. It would be the biggest event of their career. The international beat was clicking. And it would be a dream tour: four shows in Perth's new arena followed by outdoor stadium shows across the country including Sydney and Melbourne and then on to New Zealand for a couple of outdoor dates. Bill Aucoin had us panting when he told us the promoter was billing the tour as the biggest since the Beatles. Kissmania was sweeping the country. Australia was then a few years behind the states in catching up with trends and fads so it was logical that Kiss, so hugely popular a few years earlier in America, was now at their zenith down under. The *Unmasked* album had already set sales records and a single, "Shandi," hit #2 in the national charts. Ticket sales were accelerating to record levels. PolyGram/Australia's managing director, Ross Barlow, had geared up to ship hundreds of thousands of Kiss records to stores during the weeks Kiss was on tour.

Pandemonium reigned as we arrived at the international airport in Sydney on November 1 in the broiling sun. Frenzied fans swarmed over the airport, trying to catch a glimpse of Kiss as they emerged from the Pan Am 747. Police battalions held back the mob as we hustled our way into the customs and immigration terminal. Throngs of photographers and cameramen with TV lights were herded outside the terminal, ready to shoot Kiss as they walked through. As we made our way inside, we were nearly blinded by the strobes of flash cameras and high-intensity lamps. Kiss shielded their faces with scarves and sunglasses as reporters shouted questions.

The day after our arrival, Kiss received the keys to the city from Sydney's Lord Mayor. A public ceremony outside Town Hall took place before a sea of fans, filling George Street and the surrounding plaza. We were on the balcony of a stately Victorian building looking out at the thousands of fans who had baked in the sun for hours to catch a three-minute appearance by Kiss, about to be invested as honorary Pooh-Bahs, with all the requisite pomp and circumstance. When Kiss appeared, the crowd erupted.

The *Sydney Morning Herald* carried news and photos about Kiss even before the group landed in Australia, part of the promoter's advance press buildup. Offbeat sidebar stories and features like "Parents: What to do About Kiss" offered advice on how to cope with Kissmania from child psychologists and psychiatrists. The editorial page carried a prominent photo of the group in its "Letters to the Editor" section with an anti-Kiss broadside from a local church official. He thought Kiss to be Satanic.

At the official press conference for Kiss in Sydney, the group clowned it up with a well-known Australian comedian, Norman Gunston. A photo of Kiss with Norman took up nearly half the front page of the *Morning Herald* the next day. Kiss also boosted the career of *Penthouse* Australia's Pet of the Year when she showed up at the press conference and got into a length-of-tongue contest with Gene. Reporters quizzed Paul on what his first sexual experience was like and he replied, "I got blisters on my hand." Ace's whinnying laugh in the background brought down the house as he leaned back in his chair so far that it almost keeled over. It was a media circus gone wild.

Wherever Kiss traveled, they were mobbed by fans who would go berserk at the mere sight of Kiss. It reached such epidemic proportions that whenever our plane landed in the next airport, a fleet of limos pulled onto the tarmac in front of the plane's exit doors to take everyone out of the airport pronto. Kiss was in nirvana. The tour moved with the precision of a Prussian military campaign. Publicity and promotion were at blitzkreig level, with Kiss on the front pages of every major newspaper daily. Radio and TV blurbs about Kiss seemed to appear hourly. Patti Mostyn, a veteran entertainment publicist, had saturated the country with Kiss hype. Even Ansett Airlines, the major domestic carrier, got into the act. They sponsored Kiss's tour and featured them on the cover of their in-flight magazine. Photos of the group were more common than those of world leaders, and news about the recent American election of Ronald Reagan was buried in the back of the newspapers. Even an uneventful news item about a local restaurant that Ace dined at got a front-page mention. Fans were knee-deep on the sidewalks in front of our hotels and record-breaking crowds were reported at every show. More than 40,000 turned out in Melbourne and no one complained about the sweltering summer temperatures which hit 104 degrees.

The after-hours entertainment reached heights that Kiss had never before experienced. A party was thrown in Kiss's honor every night. Kiss was royally feted by VIPs from politics, sports, media, and showbiz, and by a host of local grandees. An invitation to meet Kiss was a coveted distinction. Night after night, it was a steady diet of champagne, caviar, prawns, and girls. Tons of girls. And not groupie types, either. These were girls from an entirely different strata. Penthouse Pets, Playboy Playmates, Miss Worlds, Miss Universes, Miss Australias, Miss New South Waleses, and a passel of runners-up and fashion models flocked to meet Kiss. To fill out the ranks and make sure there was plenty for everybody, one of Sydney's top pimps helped to lasso his best-looking young escorts to see that the parties were always filled to capacity with knockouts. Some of these party girls were from local colleges and modeling agencies who made extra money on the side as call girls and escorts. Kiss had their own universe of wall-to-wall girls each night, beauties with flawless skin, porcelain features, and chestnut and golden streams of hair who sidled up to them, cooing and primping to keep their attention. Walking into a Kiss party was to be bombarded with gorgeous women who looked as if they'd just stepped out of the pages of *Cosmopolitan*. Gene had a well-known cover girl practically glued to him—Diana Ross hadn't made it to Australia.

PolyGram threw its own series of parties, inviting Elton John and his manager John Reid to one bash at a Japanese restaurant in Sydney. They were bemused by all the adulation surrounding Kiss. Ace donned a chef's toque in the restaurant, chopping up shrimps and tossing them onto Elton's plate. Elton was in Australia for a promotional swing and probably hadn't expected a dining adventure with Kiss. To preserve these scenes for posterity, Kiss hired fashion photographer Patrick Jones to travel on tour from start to finish and take pictures. The girls were only too willing to be photographed at Kiss parties and concerts, canted back against the dressing room door backstage or propped up on the bar at an exclusive private disco.

At some point during all this euphoric bliss, Paul came down with a case of lovesickness. He was apparently having the time of his life but suddenly had a yearning to see his latest flame. Paul always had a hard time being happy with anyone or in any place for long. It had been a top secret, but his new paramour was film and TV star Lesley Ann Warren. Paul and Lesley had both grown up in Queens, New York, although she was a few years older than he. It turned out that Lesley was now in that part of the world, shooting a movie near Christ Church, in New Zealand, a mere 1,323 miles from Sydney. The smitten Paul had to see her and the only way he could was to fly to where she was. Due to time constraints, a private jet was the only solution. Paul had the promoter make the arrangements, took a bodyguard with him, and flew to New Zealand on the jet. The bodyguard told me that Paul spent a few hours with Lesley in her trailer and then flew back to Sydney. The next day the story was on the front page of a local tabloid, "Kiss Star Takes $25,000 Love Flight." The romance faded out after that and months later, Lesley had another boyfriend.

Kiss's tour had been a personal triumph for the promoters, Kevin Jacobsen and Michael Edgley. Kevin was emerging as a top rock promoter in Australia and Michael was a successful circus and ice show impresario who came from a wealthy show business family. Michael's magnificent estate, an ultramodern $5 million oceanfront castle in Perth, jutted out onto the sparkling sapphire waters of the Indian Ocean. It was the site, not surprisingly, for another of Kiss's parties. Kevin had been with us since the tour began, a jovial and ruddy-faced Aussie with a tousle of reddish-brown hair who had set up a command post in every hotel to oversee the operation. Kevin and Michael had taken a very big gamble with Kiss but it looked as if it was going to pay off in spades. The shows in Perth all sold out as did most of the stadium shows in the other cities. But New Zealand, the last leg of the tour, came a cropper. Their huge success turned sour when bad weather and intermittent rains decimated the expected turnouts. And production complications muddied the picture. The promoters had to pay for the phenomenally high cost of not only bringing a stadium-caliber Super Kiss show from the U.S. to Australia, but they also got stuck for air freighting everything from Sydney to New Zealand, a crushing expense. New Zealand killed the tour for the promoters, ruining an otherwise unmatched success.

Australia had been Kiss's Emerald City. The tour had shown the group in all their glory and with all the trappings of stardom. It was typically Kiss, big in all the ways which made them the rock phenomenon of the '70s—the big show, the big production, the big promotion, the big spectacle, the big crowds, the big hype, the big media circus—and, as it turned out, the big watershed event for Kiss.

The Super Kiss show in Australia was overpowering, pushing everything to the limits, but some of the authentic *Sturm und Drang* of their earlier concerts was missing. The fiery intensity that had originally characterized Kiss was starting to get lost in all of their space-age hardware. The extravagant costumes designed for their last U.S. tour made the group look cartoonish. The earlier Kiss look of black leather, chains, and silver glitter had projected a harsher, fiercer image, one that meshed with their raucous metal sound. The Kiss shows had a sense of scale that worked best in large settings, but the giant outdoor stadiums could dwarf the show's visual impact.

Kiss was walking on air by the time they got back to the United States for Christmas. Australia had been the event of their career. Eric, the new drummer, had proven his mettle and was rewarded with a flashy new black and silver Porsche from the band. By Kiss standards, the tour was also a resounding financial success. They had been paid one of the highest guarantees ever for a tour of Australia, with the promoter paying for most of the location costs of travel, transportation, hotels, labor, and staging. But being Super Kiss was exorbitantly expensive, and the group managed only to come out a little better than even. The promoters didn't even fare that well. They reportedly lost about $250,000 on the tour.

For Bill Aucoin, neither Europe or Australia was a financial windfall. His pared-down contract agreed to at the Fort Wayne meeting in the summer of '79 would only pay him an equal share with Kiss for any profits from touring. There weren't any. He could no longer commission concert income. Profits from Europe were nonexistent and the Australian surplus was meager after dividing the small take. Merchandising income from Europe was strong, mostly from the shows in England. In Australia, the big merchandising money was made through retail licensing deals put together by Twentieth Century Fox's agent there.

There wouldn't be a U.S. tour for Kiss anytime soon. *Unmasked* had done well in many countries in Europe and was a huge hit in Australia, but didn't do nearly well enough in the United States to build a tour on. As Phonogram had anticipated, Kiss was starting to click internationally. A huge royalty check for old Casablanca records sold overseas had come in for Kiss. And at the same time, the booming international record market of the 1980s was taking off. The compact disc was about to be introduced, signaling the beginning of a massive explosion in recorded music sales around the world. Not long after *Unmasked* was released, Kiss received a letter from Phonogram about the new compact disc they had developed and their plan to make the album one of their first CD releases.

Kiss had settled into recording a new album for most of 1981, but in October, Carlos Spadone came to the fore as the man of the hour. A prosperous businessman from Argentina whose family had made their money in macaroni and food processing, Carlos had some show business experience and owned

Teatro Comico, an elegant theater in Buenos Aires that presented light comedy and drama. And now he wanted Kiss. In Argentina, Kiss was a supergroup. Spadone pitched a proposal to ATI which Bill Aucoin tentatively okayed, provided we could work out the financial arrangements. We jumped on it. Within days, Carlos was in New York.

Carlos was a far more savvy and sophisticated impresario than our bumbling Mexican friends. He arrived with an attorney from Brazil who would act as his counsel and interpreter, Manoel F. W. Salles. Carlos, in his late forties, was a distinguished-looking man with a deep tan and oiled black hair that was brushed back and widowing at the temples. He came to our first meeting in a tailored European suit in a gray woven pattern with a pale blue dress shirt and silk knit tie. Like many Argentinians, he had a prominent nose which had a chiseled quality to it. We sat in the conference room around our large oval table. Harley Lewin, ATI's attorney, came to the meeting along with Mark Phillips, ATI's controller; Marilyn Ford, Wally Meyrowitz's assistant; and Ken Anderson. Manoel did the talking for Carlos. He was a dapper, short man, who spoke carefully enunciated English. His role was both adviser and interpreter. Thanks to a strange fluke, he would later play another role in Kiss's affairs a few years down the road.

Kiss would be paid big money—the proposed deal was worth over $1 million—to come to South America. They would do a tour that included shows in Argentina and Brazil. Carlos's plan was to do several stadiums in Buenos Aires and Mar del Plata and then travel to Rio de Janeiro and São Paulo. These would be big events, broadcast live on local TV. Half a million or more people would be at the shows. He assured us, through Manoel, that the million dollar asking price that had become our standard fee for a Third World expedition was "no problem."

We talked about when the tour would take place and early 1982 seemed the most feasible. Carlos agreed to bring in an experienced production manager from the U.S., Gerry Stickells, to handle the technical side of the tour operation in South America. We told him we wanted a deposit of $100,000, which they agreed to. It looked like an ideal situation for Kiss. With interest in the group waning in the states, they could go to Argentina and Brazil for a few weeks, make a killing, and come back home. Carlos's deal seemed like a gift. We shook hands and agreed to work out the details and prepare contracts. Carlos and Manoel went back home that night.

Weeks later, we reconvened in the conference room at Aucoin Management. Carlos and Manoel had flown to New York and were bringing a certified check for $100,000 drawn on a U.S. bank for the deposit. Aucoin Management and ATI people came over along with Michael Perlstein, a law partner of Paul Marshall. We started around 12 noon, sitting at a round marble-topped table in a

229

room where Kiss gold and platinum albums lined the walls. After more than six hours of haggling and bluster, with stacks of papers circulating around the table, we came to an agreement on terms and on a schedule for the tour.

Fit as a fiddle, Bill Aucoin walked into the room. He would sign on behalf of Kiss. He'd been waiting in his office until all of the negotiations were completed before making his appearance to wrap up everything. Sitting through hours of negotiations with lawyers, agents, and promoters wasn't Bill's strong suit. While most of us were bleary-eyed and rumpled from the long meeting, Bill looked relaxed and fresh-faced. Bill's principal concern was making sure Kiss could bring their own sound mixer to Argentina for the TV audio track so it would be perfectly balanced. In a country which at the time had only black-and-white TV sets with tiny one-inch speakers inside of plastic cabinets, this seemed a peculiar point. But we assured him this was within the realm of possibility. Bill signed the contracts. We then got our bank check. Bill admired it while making a little joke, and then excused himself. It was getting late and we invited Carlos and Manoel to dinner at Il Monello on the Upper East Side. Carlos said he was very tired but agreed to join us. He left for Buenos Aires the next day.

The dinner at Il Monello was the last time any of us ever saw Carlos Spadone. In the days and weeks that followed, we received an increasing number of telexes and unintelligible phone calls. As with the Mexican debacle, dates changed, venues changed, the itinerary was shifted backward and forward, and government permissions were obtained then denied. It was obvious that everything was falling apart at the seams. There also seemed to be a financial problem with Carlos. It got back to us that most of the money for the Kiss venture was being raised through private investors, and Argentina's volatile peso on the world markets was sending them into a tailspin. It appeared that Carlos's financing was in tatters. When the final bell had rung, the deal had been KO'd. But then a new promoter stepped into the ring.

Out of the blue came Jose Rota, a South American promoter who had been a middleman in putting shows together in several Latin countries. He spoke fluent English. Apparently, he knew about Carlos's money troubles. Jose had recently promoted some shows in Venezuela with U.S. and British artists and was known to ATI. Jose would pick up the pieces of the tour that had just disintegrated and make some kind of deal with Carlos to carry on. Jose's idea was to be the front man and use his newly acquired clout as a big-time impresario to get the additional backing for the reconstituted Kiss tour from his own sources.

It sounded fine with us. We went through all the formalities of doing another batch of contracts and schedules. A photo of Rota shaking hands with ATI's head, Jeff Franklin, at the signing appeared in *Billboard*. And then it fell apart again. Jose disappeared. No one knew how to reach him. We heard a rumor he was hiding out in a hotel in Mexico City and we asked our record company there to look into it, but they couldn't find him. We decided to cut and run. The $100,000 deposit was still being held by ATI. Kiss had run up costs to prepare for the tour, as they had for the Mexican tour that never took place. None of us ever heard from Jose again. It's safe to assume he had run into money problems of his own.

Kiss's Third World promoters were disappearing like bodies in an Alfred Hitchcock movie and it seemed we were destined never to get to South America. The group itself had never paid much attention to these negotiations anyway, since they were busy making a new album. As the dust was settling from these botched deals, Kiss was undergoing some dramatic changes of their own. By the end of 1981, they would be whipsawed by more shake-ups—shake-ups that would set them on a radically new course.

13 Crashing Into the '80s

We've done a lot of fuck me suck me songs and we thought we might like to go a slightly different route.

> Paul Stanley talking about Kiss's 1981 concept album in "Kiss Go for Broke," *Hit Parader,* February 1982.

Gene was complaining that he was tired of writing songs about "groupies and getting laid on the road," and being typecast as a hulking monster. Paul once described him as looking like a "walking tree" on stage. Gene was in the middle of his Diana Ross period, now spring 1981. He was frustrated at the prospect of cranking out another Kiss album with his usual smorgasbord of songs with titles like "Plaster Caster," "Room Service," and "Ladies Room," and the kind of heavy-breathing lyrics that were sure to send teen-age boys into paroxysms of sexual excitement. Gene wanted to show a softer, more sensitive side to his music. And so did Paul.

Kiss was portrayed in the press as hucksters, more famous for their monetary achievements than for their music. It was inevitable. For years, they had shown defiance toward their critics by loudly declaiming their superrich status. *People* featured Kiss on the cover of its August 18, 1980 issue with a headline that they were "Rich, Raunchy, and *Not* So Repulsive." The story devoted more space to Kiss's love lives and their supposed wealth —"a nine-digit empire"—than to their music. The *People* article only confirmed what the industry and many of the group's fans already knew. Kiss had made a point of their commercial success as a way of sticking it to the press. But within the music industry, Kiss had become a joke and the snickering wasn't always out of earshot. They were viewed as commercialism run rampant, a bad case of the industry succumbing to its worst instincts. Randy Newman, the singer and composer, recorded a song which parodied Kiss, "It's Money That I Love," released in 1980. The cover of the album, *Born Again,* featured Randy in Kiss-style makeup.

Fans had confided to Kiss that they were worried about Kiss losing their hard-rock edge and becoming "too Hollywood" or "too uncool." Some fans knocked the group for being more concerned with making money than playing on tour. There were murmurs that maybe Kiss had gone overboard with all the merchandising and braggadocio about being rich superstars. Even Kiss's biggest fan, Gene's mother Florence, called me a few times to ask where her "darling sonny boy" was. She lamented that "he's a big star now and gone off to Hollywood," and never called her. Gene eventually reconciled with his mother. But being labeled as "rock aristocrats" in the press had become a stigma.

Kiss was feeling the fallout from their Super Kiss image in other ways. Radio stations shunned any connection to Kiss. The group had become an exaggeration, extreme to the point of comical. Boatloads of unsold toys, games, dolls, and other Kiss paraphernalia was being dumped in closeout stores, discount outlets, and flea markets around the country. Kiss had been overlicensed at the end of the '70s and too many products had flooded the market. Australia was the last big territory where Kiss had been able to cash in on merchandise, and that had just finished. Even with all the Kissmania down under, they were now yesterday's news. The fad was over.

Their 1980 album, *Unmasked,* was a mediocre seller in the United States. They had carried the pop commercial sound and the kiddie image with a cartoon cover as far as anybody could take it. *Unmasked* peaked at #35 in the charts and only reported U.S. sales in the 700,000 range. And the *People* article with its cover photo of a very tarted-up Kiss in garish, Vegas-style costumes fanned the flames of a backlash from their public. Kiss appeared to be losing touch with reality and their own market.

Kiss would do a new album in 1981. At the end of the year, there would be a U.S. tour. It would be their first since the Super Kiss tour two years earlier. Phonogram and its U.S. counterpart, PolyGram Records, suggested to Kiss that now was the time to come back with a hard-rocking album in the traditional Kiss groove. This would counteract some of the damage done by their more recent bubblegum image. It was a message heard even from the executives at PolyGram/Australia, where *Unmasked* had been enormously successful.

At a meeting in 1980 before leaving for Europe, Paul had said Kiss was a "dead issue" in the United States because of their sales slump. In early 1981, Kiss bounced from one studio to the next in New York, recording new tracks that were more hard rock and heavy. But it wasn't working. They didn't like the tracks and there was a lack of cohesiveness to the production.

It was now spring. Kiss was no closer to starting an album than they had been in January. Bill Aucoin met with a number of producers. The group was moping about how dissatisfied they were with the tracks. And then the Super Kiss thinking started to creep back in. Bill and Kiss came to believe that what

Kiss definitely did not need was another traditional, hard-rocking Kiss album. That was old hat. They had done those kinds of albums in the past. True, *Unmasked* wasn't a success, but they wouldn't do another record like that, either. A major career move was called for. The next album would have to be "important," to show the world Kiss was a talented group and capable of producing a stellar record. This album would pull them out of the rut the image of overtly silly superhero comic book fantasy characters had got them into. They wanted to be perceived as artists. At the same time, the album would have to be super in scope and execution.

Everyone conceded that Kiss couldn't do this on their own. It would take a special person to pull off something of this magnitude, someone whose mere association with Kiss would lend credibility to the group. Kiss wanted someone to take the reins who would put them into the pantheon of great rock *artistes* to be honored forever, someone who would unlock the door to a new kind of success and the critical acclaim Kiss deserved. In short, they needed a guru. And the guru would be Bob Ezrin. Kiss liked gurus. Bill had been Kiss's guru for years, reaching that exalted status when Kiss leapfrogged over their competition to become one of the world's biggest bands by the late '70s. But Bill's influence was starting to fade. He was still given credit for the creative touch, but Gene and Paul were becoming more seasoned in the ways of the music business. And Howard Marks was exerting more control over their business and financial affairs, filling a vacuum that Bill had helped to create. Bill was beginning to be squeezed out.

Bill knew that Kiss needed an exceptionally strong album to alter the public perception that the Super Kiss image and the *Unmasked* album had created. He also knew it was critical for him to reinvigorate his relationship with the band and pull off a big coup, or he'd be out of a job. His contract was being extended on a year-to-year basis, not a long lease on life in any business. And the constant carping from Gene, Paul, and to a lesser extent, Ace, about the shifting sands of Kiss's popularity and their sagging morale was becoming worrisome. Relations with the group were mixed. Bill had been partially redeemed by the success of Australia, but after a few months, the glow from that had dimmed. Picking Bob Ezrin as the producer for the new Kiss album could be the bold stroke Kiss needed and could put Bill back in the driver's seat.

Bob Ezrin was a *wunderkind* producer who had worked with Alice Cooper, Lou Reed, and Kiss. At 26, he produced one of Kiss's more critically and commercially successful albums, *Destroyer,* released in 1976. *Destroyer* featured a streamlined Kiss sound where songs were linked together to create an overall aural image. Sound effects like cars zooming along the highway in "Detroit Rock City" were dubbed in to give the record a realism music alone wouldn't convey. It was Kiss's most imaginative album. But the key factor in choosing

Bob wasn't just the creativity of *Destroyer*. Bob had recently produced *The Wall* by Pink Floyd, a double album hailed worldwide as one of the greatest rock records of all time, topping the U.S. charts for 15 weeks. And it had then sold more than 8 million copies. Bob was the kind of guru Kiss needed. Now.

Things moved quickly. Bob's standard producer contract was supplemented by an amendment guaranteeing him a hefty percentage of any merchandising, film, or TV spinoffs from the album in addition to his producer's royalty. It would be a concept album and Bob would be an integral part of extending the concept to other media. Plans were made to record in Toronto, where he lived, and do some sessions at Ace's home studio in Connecticut. These plans later expanded to include sessions at New York studios as well as a mobile recording truck sent to Toronto.

Bob had a well-earned reputation as a virtuoso producer, writing songs, playing keyboards, and arranging music for his albums. He was also a showman, appearing in top hat, tails, and white gloves with Kiss, in makeup and costume, in a recording studio for a publicity photo in the June 1, 1976, issue of *Circus*. Self-assured and voluble, Bob was a take-charge guy who knew how to run the show. His previous work with the band coupled with his stellar track record with other groups gave him considerable clout. He was a producer who could make things happen, something which Kiss coveted. Bob stipulated that he would only communicate with Bill or Kiss. No one else was allowed to contact him. He felt it was essential that he have total privacy and isolation with Kiss without any intrusions or distractions which might upset the delicate creative balance he was trying to maintain. This was, for the most part, a rational and reasonable request, no different than the working conditions a movie director might impose. But Kiss and Bob then created a hermetically sealed existence for themselves, living in a cocoon for the making of the album. It was a radical departure from the way Kiss had recorded in the past and the results would be unusual as well.

Bob wanted a concept album, like The Beatles' *Sgt. Pepper's Lonely Hearts Club Band* with all the songs connected by a common theme. His idea was an album with an underlying story to the music. With Kiss, it would be more of an opera—music and libretto—or as Kiss described it, a movie without pictures where the album would be the soundtrack. Bob's and Kiss's creative machinations were all hush-hush and no one apart from Bill had much of an idea as to what was being dreamed up. Slowly, the story and the album's theme began to dribble out: It was to be a tale of a young boy who confronts good and evil, wanders through darkness and forests, and, in the end, finds his way through perseverance and self-reliance. There was a lot of mumbo jumbo in the Kahlil Gibran leitmotif about "goodness and knowledge," "sacred duty," and "conquering evil" floating around in the original script. There were characters called Morpheus, the Boy, and a kind of secret society called the Order of the Rose. The deep secrecy was designed to imbue the album with a mystical quality; no one in Kiss gave any interviews or even mentioned the project to the press during production.

Paul described the process in a December 12, 1981, interview with *Billboard*, after the record was completed. "We sat around for six to eight hours a day, and we would talk and take notes before we even thought about picking up an instrument," he said. He and Gene saw the album as a way of freeing their image from the shackles imposed on heavy metal groups by their fans. Ace, however, was unconvinced about the concept, and was frequently at logger-heads with Bob Ezrin in the studio.

Bill whipped up enthusiasm within the Kiss organization about what to expect from the record. It would be brilliant, mind-expanding, musically ambitious, and otherworldly. It would enlighten as well as entertain. Of course, no expense would be spared. What Bob was helping to create would be the apotheosis of modern rock music and a milestone for Kiss. It would be their own rock opera in the tradition of The Who's *Tommy*. And avant-garde rock stylist Lou Reed would write three songs. The hype machine was in full swing again. By this time, Poly-Gram Records in New York had taken over the Casablanca label. Apart from funneling the $2 million advances from their overseas company, Phonogram, to Kiss, they had practically no idea what was going on. Bill kept the PolyGram people at a distance until their top execs started making noises about the project.

Most of what was going on in Toronto was kept top secret. Kiss even managed to work around Bob's unconventional scheduling. They would often go into the studio to record all night. Kiss was mesmerized. By late summer, the album was coming together. Now that a script was finished, a narrator was needed for the dialogue to bridge the musical selections. Normally, rock albums don't have narrators but this obviously wasn't going to be a normal album. A veteran actor with a deep, timbrous voice in the style of Orson Welles was flown in. Kiss hired the American Symphony Orchestra in New York to provide a phil-harmonic sound for various pieces that would be integrated into the final tracks, another first for Kiss. Still, no one outside of Kiss, Bill, and Bob had heard a note of the work in progress. Writing songs had been a problem, Bill recalls.

By fall, PolyGram was getting impatient. They wanted to know when the album would be ready. They had to schedule record pressings at their plants along with the printing of the album cover. Six weeks' lead time is usually needed to organize the manufacturing of all the separate parts for records and tapes in facilities around the world. The album was continually being rere-corded, remixed, and rescheduled, but October was targeted as the go-ahead date. There was still no title. Kiss waited until they had almost finished record-ing to decide on what to call the album and to lock up plans for the cover, both critical elements in the marketing of a record.

At last, Kiss announced that the album was to be titled *The Elder.* The name sprung from the story line where a boy confronts a Council of Elders, old wise men with mystical powers, who encourage the boy to use his wits and his faith to come through his ordeal. What Kiss had in mind was an inspirational message for their fans, something very upbeat with a philosophical bent. It seemed a bizarre twist for a group that had previously earned their fame and fortune by pandering to young fans' pent-up urgings of sexual frustration and rebellion against authority. But they had been converted to a vision of Kiss as a mystical force. When Paul and Gene first broke the silence and started talking about the message behind *The Elder,* it was like listening to people who had had an epiphany. Ace was less enthusiastic; he resented the way Paul and Gene had dominated the sessions.

Paul had objected to the cartoon cover of *Unmasked,* which was Gene's brainchild. Paul's inspiration would be used for the new album's cover, which would show the hand of a boy (actually, Paul's hand) grasping an iron door knocker with a rose on it. The door knocker was fastened to a wooden planked door. Picking up the cover, you would simply see a hand holding onto a door knocker set against an expanse of dark brown oak. The record label itself would be an airbrushed photo of Paul's outstretched hand. Kiss felt that all this over-ripe symbolism gave their work the gravitas that it merited.

Kiss demanded a gatefold cover for *The Elder.* Gatefolds, special double covers where the jacket opens up as a separate piece hinged to the sleeve that contains the record, are designed to reveal a dramatic photo inside once the record buyer opens it up. Gatefold covers cost more to manufacture, but can make an attractive package and position the album as something special. Kiss had used a gatefold very successfully with its *Alive!* and *Alive II* records. The gatefold picture in *Alive II* was of a huge Kiss show in full blast, with all of the bombs and smoke and fireworks shooting off, looking like it was shot in wide-screen Cinemascope. Kiss had in mind an equally dramatic photo for *The Elder,* a wide-angle shot of a large, rectangular oak table full of knots and chips. It was the type of table seen in medieval castles with seven ornately carved empty wooden chairs in place around it and a single candle burning in the center. The picture would be darkly lit. And there would be no pictures anywhere of Kiss. They would disappear entirely from the scene and not pollute the proceedings. Kiss would be invisible. The back of the album would feature the credits superimposed on another wooden door.

One more change was made. The title would now be *(Music From) The Elder.* Kiss, Bill, and Bob felt it was inevitable that a feature-length movie or epic would be made before long and this would be the soundtrack to tie in with it. It didn't seem to bother anyone that no one standing in a record store browsing through the racks would understand that. To Kiss, it was the soundtrack to a-yet-to-be-produced movie. The fans' reaction would soon be, "music from *what?*" PolyGram was distraught when they saw the cover. It looked like a big blob of brown with somebody's hand on top. At first, Kiss didn't want their logo or the title on the album cover, either . After a heated debate, Kiss conceded to putting a small logo in the upper left-hand corner of the front cover. The title would appear in the upper right-hand corner.

Kiss had become true believers, seeing the album as the salvation of their career. Not only would it be a serious album to garner the respect they felt they deserved from their critics, but with Bob Ezrin at the helm, it would be a megahit worldwide. *(Music From) The Elder* wouldn't just be their comeback to chart success, it would put them over the top. Soon, Kiss would be in the league of international supergroups like Pink Floyd, The Who, and Led Zeppelin, all of whom had success with high-profile concept albums. Expanding Kiss's audience was the crux of the strategy.

Bill was already toying with ideas about how to promote the new album. A special closed-circuit TV premiere of Kiss performing *(Music From) The Elder* in a stage production was considered. The closed-circuit telecast would be seen in theaters across the country, and tickets would be sold as for boxing championships. We had a meeting with Lou Falcigno, the major producer of closed-circuit boxing promotions at the time, to see if he wanted to promote a live Kiss spectacular. He passed.

In early October, Kiss was finally ready to take off the wraps. Their magnificent obsession was nearing fruition. The moment had arrived when the Kiss organization and the record company people would hear the unedited and unexpurgated *(Music From) The Elder*. Gene and Paul were jubilant, deep in self-congratulatory raptures over what they had accomplished. Bob had already tipped us off about what to expect—a masterpiece and a blockbuster combined that would catapult to the top of the charts in every country around the world. It would be the international superseller that had thus far eluded Kiss. Bob sat in Howard Marks's office to fill in some of the ad agency staffers, cigar smoke from his Montecristo dancing through his fingers. Howard suffered in silence. Brimming with confidence, Bob prepared us for the experience and reminded us of how many more millions *The Wall* had sold as each year passed since its release in 1979.

Bill waxed no less enthusiastic. *(Music From) The Elder* was his passport to take Kiss back to their previously vaunted supergroup status. He was now back in control. The album would burnish the Kiss image, one that had been tarnished by commercial hucksterism, kiddie toys, and the excesses of the end of the '70s. But that was behind us—we were now in the '80s. Big projects like this were important to Bill so that he could act as Kiss's creative maestro. Orchestrating big events was a way for Bill to stroke Kiss's egos and to keep them excited about the Kiss mystique.

Aucoin Management's conference room was packed to standing room only for the listening session. Kiss would be there. And Bill admonished everyone not to talk or make any sounds whatsoever during the session. This was to be on the level of a classical recital, very cerebral and dignified. *(Music From) The Elder* was on a much more elevated plane than any slapdash heavy metal record played through a boom box. We weren't at a party. Everyone did their best to observe the requisite solemnity, despite being jammed elbow to elbow inside a smallish room. Staffers were sitting on the credenzas and leaning against the walls next to the large speaker cabinets. This was to be an occasion for seriousness of the highest order.

For forty minutes, the album played without interruption. It was a strange, almost ethereal experience. No one could believe it was Kiss. No one could compare it with anything they'd heard before. No one could describe it. It was both mystical and eerie, speaking parts mixed with dark, brooding ballads. Some of the songs sounded to me like they were in a dirge tempo. The songs had odd titles like "Just a Boy," "Mr. Blackwell," and "The Oath." There was even an opening orchestral fanfare and background harmonies by the St. Robert's Choir. And there was a lot of talking between some of the songs that sounded like something from Sir Walter Scott. The overall effect was somber and lugubrious. You felt depressed or at least melancholy after listening to it. There were few catchy beats or distinctive refrains and there weren't a lot of melodies that left you humming. The symphonic bridges and string arrangements paid fulsome homage to the operatic concept. *(Music From) The Elder* wasn't so much grand as grandiose. The effect was otherworldly, but also overblown, kind of pompous. It certainly wasn't like anything Kiss had done before.

Kiss was thrilled to pieces. Of course, they had every right to be. It was their work and they had labored long and hard to create it. At the session, everyone was polite and respectful and applauded them loudly at the end of the album. But no one showed signs of embracing the music with any particular enthusiasm. People seemed puzzled about how to react, especially since Gene, Paul, and Eric were darting in and out of the packed room. (Ace was absent from the festivities.) An empty, confused sense prevailed. There were frozen faces and blank expressions. People seemed to be groping for a way to be both deferential to Kiss and to express some reaction to the music. Most people in the room just smiled weakly and offered banalities like "it's great" and "it's really different." Bill congratulated the Kiss members on their opus and tried to keep the occasion upbeat.

Howard Marks wasn't one to mince words. Once Kiss had left the room and only a few of the executives remained, Howard said "the album doesn't sound anything like Kiss and no one is going to buy a Kiss album that doesn't sound like Kiss." He had thought the whole project was, in his words, "asinine" from the start. He made sure the name of his ad agency never appeared in the credits.

"They're scratching their heads over this record at PolyGram. . . .It's certainly a shock when you first put it on," was how Bob described Kiss's new album in a November 21, 1981, interview in *Billboard,* just as the album was hitting the stores. Tearing their hair out was more like it. PolyGram was dumbfounded by the record. Ad agency executive Rosanne Shelnutt recalled the special listening session that was organized for PolyGram in a New York recording studio where the American Symphony Orchestra performed live and Bob played the tracks from the album. "The record company was stunned into silence," Rosanne said, while Bob assured everyone at the session that he knew what kind of music would get played on the radio.

Within days of first hearing the master tapes, PolyGram asked Kiss to remix parts of the album to bring up the guitars so they were more prominent. At the listening session, one record company executive reportedly blurted out, "Where are the guitars?" To some, they apparently sounded like they were underwater, hardly typical for Kiss. The record bore no resemblance to what PolyGram thought a Kiss record should be. Only in their wildest nightmare would Kiss deliver to them a psuedo-rock opera with choirs and symphony orchestras, featuring inspirational lyrics about finding yourself through faith. It was if the Carpenters had decided to go heavy metal and record an album of head-banging hard rock with screaming vocals. It was too much to bear and it would cost PolyGram $2 million to finance Kiss's experiment in musical mysticism.

There was talk of PolyGram not accepting delivery of *(Music From) The Elder,* which was their right under the contract. But rejecting the album would compound their problems. If they didn't release *(Music From) The Elder,* they might have to wait another year to get a new Kiss album. The company was still choking on warehouses full of returned records inherited from Casablanca. Their buyout of the label in early 1980 had opened up a Pandora's box of problems; Casablanca was in far worse shape financially than anyone had realized.

At the end of 1981, PolyGram was sinking from the losses which had piled up. In a profile on the company, *The New York Times* reported on November 3, 1985, that PolyGram's U.S. record operation had lost more than $220 million between 1979 and 1984. Much of that loss was directly attributable to the Casablanca acquisition. They had cut their artist roster by two-thirds, leaving about eighty acts with the company. Kiss had been one of their last, best hopes. It was a major factor in keeping them when the contract was negotiated in 1980. And now on top of PolyGram's woes, the industry was in a trough. Counterfeit albums, at-home taping, and the rise in gas prices which cut into spending by kids on records were all hitting the record business where it hurt the most—at the cash register.

When PolyGram released *(Music From) The Elder* in November, new problems bubbled up to the surface. Some of the overseas companies like Japan, one of Kiss's major territories, were shocked by the album's original cover. They slapped a picture of Kiss in makeup and costumes on top of the official cover. Retailers in the United States complained about customers in the stores not being able to see the album; a brown cover practically disappears in the record racks.

With radio airplay almost nonexistent and the album anchored near the bottom of the charts, it was painfully obvious. *(Music From) The Elder* was a bomb. A huge bomb. It was the biggest bomb in Kiss's history. In a matter of weeks, the album came and went. It was dead in the water. In January 1982, it reached its highest chart position in *Billboard* at #75. By February, it had dropped off the charts. There were no singles and no airplay to give it a breath of life. Returned records in great quantities were reported, a disaster that was mitigated to some extent because the initial pressing had been relatively small. Sales of *(Music From) The Elder* weren't much more than a few hundred thousand in the United States when the album was first released.

Curiously, the public reaction to *(Music From) The Elder* wasn't unanimously negative. Kiss received a favorable notice from *Rolling Stone* in its February 18, 1982, review of the album, which compared the music to Jethro Tull's. But there was scant hope that the good press would offer much of a marketing hook to entice Kiss fans to buy the record. A couple of videos were made from the album, then used primarily for overseas TV. The video for "A World Without Heroes" featured a tight shot of Gene at the end shedding a tear while resting on his sword. "I," one of the few up-tempo songs on the record, was shot on a set that Paul described later as looking like *"American Bandstand on Mars."* The entire project had degenerated into an unsalvagable mess.

There wouldn't be any tour. How could there be? Nobody knew that Kiss had released a new album. If Super Kiss had been a dubious concept that had gone too far, then *(Music From) The Elder* was the nail that sealed the coffin shut. There was no demand for a mystical Kiss, either. And to add insult to injury, the album had been Kiss's most expensive ever, costing several times what *Dynasty* and *Unmasked* had run. Kiss wasn't just adrift, they were in free fall. They had spent nearly a year recording an album that not only didn't sound anything like what their fans expected Kiss to sound like, it didn't even have a picture of Kiss on it. It was as if Kiss was hiding within the album, there but not really there. In fact, Kiss was now in danger of disappearing altogether. A completely unexpected chain reaction had been unleashed. Kiss didn't have to worry about Super Kiss anymore, they had to worry about their being no Kiss.

The failure of *(Music From) The Elder* crashed down on everyone like a ton of bricks. Bill and Bob both took the heat from Kiss on the album's dismal showing. But Bob could go on to record another album with another group. He didn't have to stick around and try to salvage Kiss's career like Bill would.

Overseas, Phonogram reacted quickly. By February 1982, they asked Kiss to record four new songs—hard rock songs were specified—which could be packaged with another eight old Kiss songs to make a compilation album called *Kiss Killers.* The cover would feature Kiss in makeup and costumes, though somewhat toned down from the gaudy Super Kiss look of '79. They hoped that the new record would counter some of the damage from *(Music From) The Elder,* which bombed in many territories overseas as well. *Kiss Killers* would show the faithful that Kiss was still a hard rock band at heart and *(Music From) The Elder* was an aberration. But it wouldn't be released in the states. There were already several live albums and greatest hits collections on the market and another version, even with a couple of new songs hastily recorded in L.A., would make Kiss look like they were milking the back catalogue for every nickel (some of the earlier Kiss compilations on Casablanca were unreleased in foreign markets).

Kiss Killers came together fast. It sold modestly in most countries. It was now spring of 1982. Kiss was scared. Their career was on the rocks. Their record sales had nosedived with *Unmasked,* the Super Kiss image had overexposed them, and *(Music From) The Elder* had practically cratered them. Who knew if they even had a career left? Nothing was working. Kiss was in the pits and Bill had helped put them there. Gene and Paul were crestfallen. They were convinced that Bill had lost his creative touch and didn't have the right instincts to direct Kiss anymore. Since the Fort Wayne meeting in the fall of '79, there had been tension between Kiss and Bill. The big Phonogram deal in early '80 and the later tour of Australia had helped relieve some of the strains. But Kiss had just crash-landed. Bill had to go. By May, he was gone. His contract wasn't renewed. Paul and Gene met with Bill at his office and told him their decision. Bill recalls that it was a tearful farewell as they had been through so much together. Ace wasn't there. His own set of problems was beginning to unfold. Bill soon closed his office at 645 Madison Avenue. He then worked out of his Olympic Tower apartment. There was another exodus of employees. But in the music business, when a major artist releases an album that stiffs, changes are swift and sudden. Kiss was in a landslide and it wasn't going to end soon.

Ace's imminent departure from Kiss was presaged when the band performed on January 28, 1982, at Studio 54 in New York, a live show transmitted via satellite to Europe. It proved to be another first for Kiss on two fronts. More than 20 million viewers on the continent watched this first-ever remote telecast. The show was included as part of the San Remo Music Festival in Italy, and Kiss received a major music award as a result. It was also the first time Kiss performed as a trio.

Ace had never made it to Studio 54. Everyone who had packed into the disco to watch the show waited around for hours. A couple of bodyguards were dispatched to Ace's house in Wilton, Connecticut, to collect him, but when they got there Ace was allegedly in no shape to do the show. And time was becoming a factor. Trucks were parked outside on West 54th Street with satellite dishes on top and miles of looping cables were piled onto the sidewalks. Kiss was to be beamed around the world at a precise time synchronized with the European telecast. At the last minute, Kiss went on without him, having delayed everything as long as they could. Officially, it was announced that Ace was out of action; he had come down with a bout of "the flu."

Car crashes and near-misses had become synonymous with Ace. He had had several crack-ups although, miraculously, no one was ever seriously injured. A police car in high-speed pursuit clocked Ace at 110 miles per hour a few years later in a DeLorean on the Bronx River Parkway. It made a feature story in *The New York Post*. In April 1982, he slammed his Porsche into a wall near his Connecticut home, turning the car into an accordion.

It was time to deal with the Ace problem. Ace was unhappy in the group. It wasn't only *(Music From) The Elder,* it was the whole Kiss setup. Without Peter in the group, the dynamics had radically shifted. It was now the Gene and Paul axis versus Ace. There was no Peter around, a kindred spirit who could ally with Ace to balance against the others. The symmetry of personalities which made Kiss work for so long had disappeared and the chemistry had changed. Peter's replacement, Eric, wasn't a partner. He essentially functioned as a hired musician who worked year-round. Ace's rock 'n' roll lifestyle, his boozing, and his hang-loose attitude were always going against the grain of Gene and Paul's rigidly disciplined work ethic where sobriety was key. He called them "control freaks" who now could dictate all the decisions in the band and easily outvote him.

Fritz Postlethwaite, who had recently left the Kiss organization to finish his college education and start a business career, recalled talking with Ace in 1979 when Peter was on his way out. At the time, Ace told Fritz that without Peter he was unsure how long he would remain in Kiss. The shifting balance of power had now become lopsided with Ace pitted against Gene and Paul.

Ace's wife, Jeanette, had never been enthralled with Ace's life as a rock star. Being isolated in Wilton only worsened the situation and she openly complained about it. And Ace and Jeanette had recently had a baby, Monique. The mounting burdens of dealing with Gene and Paul and his personal life made him want to escape the pressure cooker and do his own thing, like Peter. Ace wanted out. He had become miserable in the band, and now, without Peter, it was even worse.

But Kiss wanted him in. Gene and Paul thought he was an integral part of the Kiss persona and whatever their problems in dealing with him, they could cope with it. Having a second original Kiss member leave when their credibility as a band was an issue with their public was another reason to keep Ace in the fold. And there was the most important point of all: Ace was a signatory to the 1980

Phonogram agreement. The contract was valid only if all three Kiss members remained in the group; Peter's departure had been written into the agreement. Should Gene, Paul, or Ace leave, Kiss would be in breach and Phonogram could cancel the deal. With Kiss's recent string of failures and their tarnished public image, it was highly unlikely that any other record company would offer them a deal that would come close to matching what they had with Phonogram.

In June of 1982, I walked into the conference room at Paul Marshall's office for a meeting that I knew was about Ace's separation from Kiss. Present were Howard Marks, Gene, Paul, and Ace and Ace's lawyer, Bruce Simon, a well-known labor relations expert. Before I got halfway into the room, Howard told me not to sit down. Ace wanted to restrict the meeting to the barest number of participants. At the end of the day back at our offices, Howard Marks and Kiss's lawyers filled me in on what had happened. Ace was leaving Kiss. Kiss would have to take their chances with Phonogram and the contract. The deal struck with Ace stipulated that future royalties owed to him for his past work with Kiss would be reduced proportionately if Kiss's record deal was voided or modified. And Ace would receive royalties only for his past work, the back catalogue of Kiss records. He wouldn't be a partner in Kiss anymore, meaning he would have no financial interest in Kiss's future income. Gene and Paul were to buy out Ace's interest.

Peter's separation terms had been markedly different. He remained a partner in Kiss and maintained a share in Kiss's net income from ongoing activities even though he wasn't an active member any longer. This was a concession to Peter to induce him to leave the group. Since Peter's departure was written into the Phonogram deal, it didn't jeopardize the agreement. He also received his full share of royalties from past work. But Ace was quitting on different terms. His leaving could easily sink Kiss's ship as far as their record deal was concerned. The Ace departure had to remain a secret.

By the summer of 1982, two searches were in full swing: one for a new guitarist to replace Ace and one to find a replacement for Bill Aucoin. Gene and Paul drew up a long list of candidates and contacted them directly or through Howard Marks. They had in mind someone well known in the industry with a solid track record like Shep Gordon, the manager of Alice Cooper; David Krebs, the manager of Ted Nugent and Aerosmith; and Derek Sutton, the manager of Styx. But most of their top picks as managers weren't crazy about the idea of taking on the job. Mostly, they begged off as too busy with other artists or they confided to Howard that they thought Kiss was "over" and there wasn't much anybody could do to revive their career.

Many of the managers saw Kiss as a hopeless proposition while others wanted too rich a deal. Kiss didn't see a need to bring a manager on board with a full commission arrangement, normally 15 to 20 percent of an artist's income. Kiss had long been a known quantity to the public and in spite of their recent flop album, the major elements of their career—record deal, music publishing rights, booking agency, support staff—were already in place. Another full-price manager was unnecessary. Besides, they couldn't afford one.

Kiss was running out of cash. The shortfall had been slowly developing for years, like a virus breeding within the body, but now the symptoms were becoming acute. The last few years had gobbled up so much cash that there was now a severe shortage of it. Kiss had always had a hard time grasping the simple concept that if you keep running up enormous costs in everything, showing big losses on the tours, and spending huge sums to maintain lavish lifestyles on and off the road, the pie—and each member's one-quarter slice of it—keeps getting smaller. The cost of everything connected to Kiss had spiraled out of control.

Even at $2 million a crack for delivering a new album to Phonogram, the records weren't all that profitable. On *(Music From) The Elder,* commissions totaling nearly $500,000 would be paid to Aucoin Management and Glickman/Marks Management for their percentages. Studio and production costs, including the producer's advance on future royalties, would take a huge whack out of the advance. Some portion of Kiss's business overhead—legal and professional fees, client services fees, payroll for staff and musicians (including Eric), advertising, promotion, and publicity costs—would have to be charged against the album. By the time all of these amounts were factored in and a provision was made for taxes, the balance of the advance had shrunk considerably. And what remained was split four ways, including Peter's share. What was left was enough to cover the upkeep on their apartments and homes and make a dent in their personal living expenses, but not much more than that.

Music publishing monies from the song copyrights would be earned, but only in relation to the sale of the new record. Back catalogue albums, always a strong seller for Kiss, would also generate royalties and publishing income, but back albums sell in relation to the success of the latest album. With a dud in the marketplace, back catalogue sales dry up.

(Music From) The Elder had just sent Kiss's career plummeting. And with Ace leaving the group, their principal asset, the record contract with Phonogram, was in jeopardy. As the '80s took hold, everything was backfiring and Kiss was in a tailspin.

14 The $6 Million Solution

They took this outrageous rock 'n' roll image that had been so effective at the beginning and diluted it to the point that it became a cartoon. They had started out being menacing and outrageous, but they got so they were just considered unhip. It was more like the circus than rock 'n' roll.

> Danny Goldberg, creative consultant to Kiss, talking about the group's image problems in the early 1980s, *Billboard*, June 29, 1985.

For over half a century, the Russian Tea Room on West 57th Street was a stomping ground for show business personalities, media bigwigs, and the legions of theatrical agents with offices nearby for whom the landmark establishment functions as a private dining room. The restaurant's celebrity-studded clientele made it a tourist attraction in its own right. The imperial Russian decor of bright red banquettes, green velvet walls, and smartly polished brass samovars conjured up a Christmas-like feeling year round.

One early evening in spring 1982 I walked into the Russian Tea Room with Howard Marks, Rosanne Shelnutt, his ad agency head, Paul Marshall, the band's lawyer, and Robert Cinque (pronounced SIN-cue). Paul was recognized as a regular with table clout and we were whisked to a banquette near the center of the room. We sat under a large oil painting in an ornate gold leaf frame. As if on cue once we were seated, a tall, bushy-haired waiter with a handlebar moustache and a thick Russian accent brought ice-cold Stolichnaya and blini. Waiters passed by in traditional tunics and greeted favored guests at their tables.

We were at the tail end of a discussion that had started hours earlier in Paul's nearby office. The subject was the Kiss lawsuit. Kiss was suing their record company. Bob Cinque, a litigator, brought us up to date on the latest legal wranglings between Kiss and Phonogram. They were exuding confidence about Kiss's chances to win the suit and bring the record company to its knees. By the end of 1982, we would be in court and the group's case against Phonogram was compelling. Taking on a huge record company and winning a court battle would be a victory of giant-killer proportions. Paul began to digress on the evils that record companies perpetrate on artists and how eternal vigilance coupled with the iron fist of a fearless attorney were the artist's only protection against being exploited. Paul delivered this call to arms with typical aplomb.

The gilded setting of the Tea Room seemed an odd place to talk about schlocking. One of the industry's most common business practices at the time was distress sales, selling albums at cut-rate prices to retailers who in turn sell them to the consumer at drastic price reductions. "Schlocking" is what other industries call distress sales. Distress sales are normally provided for in an artist's recording agreement, but artists and their managers regard them as an odious practice, a cancer which has to be controlled.

By the end of the '70s, after the bottom had fallen out of the disco craze, unsold records and the industry's unlimited returns policy were the bane of record companies' existence. Tons of unsold records had accumulated in the record companies' warehouses. Barring a PVC meltdown, the product had to be dumped somewhere. Discount stores, cut-rate retailers, and even flea markets bought the overstock from the record companies at sharp price reductions and then sold them for much less than the normal retail price. Bins of records selling for a few dollars each were the end result of the '70s schlocking.

Artists hate schlocking. They get a much lower royalty rate since the price on which the royalty is based is lower. Or there may be no royalty at all. It can also hurt the artist's public image to have records sold in this kind of tacky retail environment, like buying last year's Gap jeans at a rummage sale. Record companies insisted on some schlocking rights to help them get rid of unsold product, but usually a minimum number of months or even years had to pass after the initial release of the album before it could be unloaded that way.

Kiss claimed that Casablanca goofed by unloading roughly 1.4 million Kiss albums that were in inventory and unsold, most from the four solo albums in 1978. Record stores had returned huge numbers of Kiss albums to Casablanca, which then had an unlimited returns policy. The contract didn't permit schlocking without Kiss's written consent and Kiss said they never granted it. This wasn't simply a technical dispute—it was a potential whopper of a windfall for Kiss. Kiss would be entitled to a full price royalty on the truckloads of Kiss records that Casablanca had sold at schlock prices. And if Kiss went to court and won, Casablanca's successor, Phonogram, would have to cough up the money.

Paul Marshall had been Kiss's attorney since they first began performing in the early '70s. Bill Aucoin introduced him to Kiss. Paul hit it off with Kiss from the start and soon became part of their extended family, referring to them as "the boys." He was the type of colorful person Kiss gravitated to, an articulate and amusing raconteur who could regale them with anecdotes from his long career in theatrical law. Witty, with an ear for jokes, he often traded one-liners with Ace. Born in 1928, Paul was also much older than the Kiss members, another thing they liked about him. He was experienced. Paul, who had wisps of gray hair strewn about his head, cultivated the image of a legal mastermind. He was seldom seen without a cigarette dangling between his fingers and he usually looked a bit rumpled. He had become somewhat world-weary about the music business over the years, intimating that the constant demands of temperamental artists were the price one had to pay in order to stay in business and prosper.

Paul's office at 130 West 57th Street was cavernous. The vaulted double-height ceiling of his paneled office gave it a spacious feel. The room was always a bit gloomy despite the large bay windows overlooking the street. Throughout the office were piles of papers, contracts, letters, and phone messages. Desks, chairs, sofas, and tables were used like an open filing system. But Paul had the perfect chemistry for Kiss.

Paul had a well-earned reputation as a shrewd negotiator who knew everyone from way back when. He was very influential in the affairs of Kiss, typically operating behind the scenes. When Kiss's success exceeded everyone's wildest expectations, Paul had praised Bill Aucoin to the skies. But he started to become concerned about the money Bill was spending to get them there and prompted Kiss to bring in business managers in 1976. He respected Carl Glickman and had sought out his advice on financial matters. His relations with Howard Marks had cooled over the years, particularly as Howard's influence with the Kiss members became stronger.

When artists hit the big time, legal work typically becomes a growth industry. At a meeting in the Glickman/Marks Management offices in 1978, Paul came to meet with Kiss on their finances. He looked over the financial statements to see what Kiss had spent for the past year on legal fees. It came to a very substantial sum then. Paul couldn't believe that Kiss could have spent so much on lawyers and demanded to know what firms were being paid. Who were all these lawyers getting all this money? Paul was seething. We expected to suffer a thunderstorm of criticism from him for paying lawyers' bills for Kiss that he didn't know about. We called in our bookkeeper, a large, matronly woman, to check on the bills right away. She reappeared twenty minutes later, carrying stacks of ledgers and green, column-lined papers. She had done a breakdown of Kiss's legal fees and with the exception of some small amounts paid to a Detroit firm for trademark work, the overwhelming majority had been paid to Paul's firm. The subject of legal fees never came up again.

Paul enjoyed his status as a member of a small fraternity of music business superlawyers in New York and L.A. These are the deal makers and power brokers who represent top artists like Kiss and who number among their clients record labels, music publishers, songwriters, record producers, and executives. The superlawyers who represent the top creative talent have considerable influence in the industry, often acting as éminences grises in their clients' affairs. In a business where power often grows from having your phone calls returned, the superlawyers are always plugged into the latest industry scuttlebutt about record company signings and are at the hub of insider activity about artists and managers. A promising new singer named Whitney Houston became a client of Paul's in the early '80s as she was preparing her debut album for Arista Records.

Paul, Howard, and Carl were in complete agreement about one thing. Kiss spent way too much money on everything. Paul had been adamantly opposed to Ace's recording studio; he thought the tours were wildly excessive in their costs; and he was shocked that *(Music From) The Elder* had run up such a huge bill. He came to most of the financial meetings with Kiss to inveigh against their spending habits, but he was no more successful than anyone else in changing those habits.

By mid-1982, Kiss's financial bind was becoming apparent. *(Music From) The Elder* had triggered a triple whammy: a new album that flopped, weak sales of back catalogue records, and no chance to tour and earn money from merchandise. We proposed a round of cutbacks that was met with predictable indifference. When Kiss's income began to nose-dive, their bloated costs combined with a shrinking income became a lethal combination. There were no easy solutions to this problem.

A glimmer of hope was seen on the horizon. The schlocking case could be Kiss's salvation, now that their treasury was being depleted. It was actually an old dispute between Kiss and Casablanca that had never been settled. It arose from an audit of Casablanca's books that began prior to the absorption of the label into the Phonogram operation. And the case was now on track for a trial in a federal court in New York at the end of 1982. Attempts to settle the dispute with Casablanca had been fruitless. The two sides were too far apart to resolve anything. Paul Marshall and Bob Cinque felt the only course left for Kiss was to file suit against Phonogram to seek the royalties owed plus damages. Kiss would have to consent to this since they would be the plaintiffs. Artists don't make a habit of suing their record companies because of the possible repercussions to their careers. Most artists are scared of their record companies. Without the support and enthusiasm of the record company, the artist can end up slowly twisting in the wind. Even for a major act like Kiss, with all the millions Phonogram had committed to spending to keep them on the roster, suing was a potentially hazardous step. Lawsuits often create bad blood, exacerbating the raw emotions that run at a fever pitch in the music business under normal circumstances. The lawsuit was a very big gamble.

The most bizarre aspect to the unfolding case was that we had come to this point in late 1982 in part due to a red herring that had been waved in front of Kiss's noses the year before. Paul Marshall had come to a business meeting with the Kiss members at our offices on December 16, 1981, laid out the facts of the case, and asked for their consent to go ahead with the lawsuit against Phonogram. Howard Marks, Carl Glickman, and Bill Aucoin were also there along with Paul's partner, Michael Perlstein, a contract lawyer who was now doing much of Kiss's legal work. The meeting had come to order with Howard at the head of the long, oval-shaped conference table. He was always comfortable in his place as the Master Helmsman. Behind Howard was an oil painting of Kiss, the original cover artwork for the *Love Gun* album, which depicted the group in a dark castle dungeon, surrounded by vampire-like slave girls in chains, groveling at their feet. At Howard's right was Bill and to his left was Carl, both seated like proconsuls to Howard. Next to Bill was Paul Marshall. Across the table was Mike Perlstein. Gene, Peter, and Paul took seats at the far end of the table. Ace hadn't made it. I was in the middle. Dick Weidenbaum from the accounting firm was also at the meeting, as was our general manager, Martin Cornbluth.

The doors were closed and the air-conditioning had been turned up. Howard hated stuffy rooms and always had the thermostat set at near-Arctic temperatures to the displeasure of nearly everyone else. An occasional squeak could be heard as the conferees sunk into the deep black leather swivel chairs set around the table. Gene, Paul, and Peter faded in and out as a laundry list of topics were hashed over, things like tax projections, payroll, album budgets, and insurance. The Kiss members were bored easily. Gene and Paul usually made an attempt to be attentive, although their eyes tended to drift to rock magazines with stories and photos of Kiss. Peter didn't say much. Bill was fidgety. Having all of these meetings in Howard's conference room with Howard at the head of the table acting like a suzerain rankled Bill.

After some joking and horseplay, Paul Marshall took the floor. He spoke in a husky, measured baritone, giving a clear and concise précis of the issues at hand concerning the proposed lawsuit. He provided Kiss with a balanced assessment of the risks as well as the potential rewards of the suit and outlined the possible costs of the litigation. The Kiss members were listening but after a few minutes of Paul's presentation, heads began drooping. It was boring. This might be interesting stuff for lawyers and accountants to mull over, but to them, it was dullsville. Paul continued. He went into the issues dealing with the schlocking and said that he had gleaned enough evidence to substantiate Kiss's claim. He reviewed the pertinent clauses of Kiss's 1977 recording agreement with Casablanca that would affect the case. He provided a recap of the 1980 contract negotiations with Phonogram. He cited other cases that had been litigated on similar issues and then ended his summation in typical lawyerly fashion by providing his recommendation. Paul believed Kiss should sue. The merits of the case were compelling.

By this time, most of the Kiss members had tuned out. Gene asked a few questions and there was an exchange between Paul Marshall and Carl. The Kiss members seemed ambivalent. So far, what Paul Marshall had presented was a business dispute. It sounded like something the lawyers and accountants could argue about and come up with a settlement and leave Kiss out of it. They didn't want to have to give depositions and show up in court to testify, things which Paul told them they would have to do if they sued. It sounded like an awful nuisance and a lot of bother. Who needs it? If they're our record company, why should we become the enemy and fight in court? It sounded self-defeating.

Paul Marshall emphasized the amount of money at stake. Kiss's audit claimed $1.7 million was owed them. Potential compensatory and punitive damages would also be sought. Kiss had an excellent case. They would be passing up the opportunity of a lifetime to make a killing. Kiss had been wronged by their record company and this would set things right. Still, there was no real villain in this. It hadn't been framed in a good guys versus bad guys scenario, and the way Kiss thought, the reason you go to court is to fight the bad guys. With Kiss, issues often had to be presented in terms of black and white. Kiss always wanted to be the good guys. Up to now, this case still looked to be something which could be settled in some way without their involvement. Phonogram didn't strike them as being much of a villain, especially since they would have to continue working with them on a daily basis. There hadn't been any emotional spark to set them off and grab their attention, let alone make them go after Phonogram's jugular. And then it came.

Paul started up again. He began talking about how PolyGram, Phonogram's corporate parent, was a European company. That they had started a record business in 1962 by combining a German record company's record operations with a Dutch company's counterpart. And both companies had begun their separate record units after World War II ended. It was now about to roll off Paul's tongue, smoothly and matter-of-factly. *There was a Nazi connection.* Paul launched into a long monologue about the corporate history of PolyGram. How it had been created when two giant companies, Philips of Holland and Siemens of Germany, merged their record units.* Siemens was Germany's

*In 1972, the two units combined and became known as PolyGram. In 1985 and 1987, Philips purchased the 50 percent interest held by Siemens. In 1989, PolyGram became a publicly owned company. PolyGram was also the name used in the United States for the company's record operations.

largest electronics company and one of the major industrial engines which drove the Nazi war machine. It's alleged that some of their top executives at the end of World War II may have been connected to or affiliated with the Nazi party, however loosely. The same was true for many German companies during that era. But Paul's point was that because Siemens was linked to PolyGram, which had started the Phonogram records subsidiary, the connection was real. The connection was tenuous, if it existed at all. But Paul's jeremiad went on. He shifted into high gear and his voice rose in amplitude. He seemed steaming mad. He said he knew that there had been this connection somewhere in the corporate hierarchy and that he would expose it. He would use his knowledge as the club to beat PolyGram into submission and win the case for Kiss. He would ferret out the bad guys and bring them into the light of day. It would be a crusade that Kiss couldn't turn away from. Paul may have believed that he was on to something but it seemed quite a stretch, reaching back nearly forty years to open a dusty chapter in corporate history.

Kiss was galvanized. It was as if a jolt of electricity had gone through them. Paul and Gene sprung to life. Bill was riveted to his chair. Peter looked as if he had just stumbled out of a coma. Their juices were flowing. The rustle of papers ceased and only the quiet hum of the air-conditioning could be heard whenever Paul paused in his discourse. Kiss now had what they wanted, a villain. It was now a good guys versus bad guys melodrama and not just a business dispute. Kiss had their bad guy, PolyGram, the owners of their record company, and now they had something to fight about. And to make the battle even more worthy, there was a potential multimillion dollar bounty they could get if they could claim victory. Kiss was salivating. This could be the answer to their prayers—to defeat a corporate bad guy with links to a murky past and collect a munificent treasure. It might be a long, arduous, and uphill quest, but this was no ordinary journey. They saw it as their Holy Grail.

While the fires were being stoked, Dick and Carl sat pokerfaced. The ashes from the cigar in Carl's hand missed the large marble ashtray and dropped to the floor. Howard appeared to be frozen, as if in a cryogenic state, his jaw dropping and his mouth agape. Mike Perlstein looked as if his eyeballs were about to bulge out of their sockets. He stared at me with a look of total shock on his face. And I had to practically swallow my tongue, almost choking in the process. I couldn't believe that this blather had persuaded Kiss to jump into the lawsuit. Mike recalled being "stunned at Paul's revelation of this information." Martin Cornbluth was amazed by Paul's effectiveness, later recalling that he had "lit a fire where there was none." Kiss was now raring to go. The lawsuit would go forward. Papers and documents would be prepared for signatures. The battle lines had been drawn and Kiss was ready to march and fire the first shot. Carl and Howard later expressed grave reservations about the lawsuit, but Paul Marshall held considerable sway over Kiss in anything to do with legal decisions. If he thought that Kiss should sue their record company, knowing all the risks, Carl and Howard weren't inclined to challenge him. Bill Aucoin recalled the overheated atmosphere of the meeting; he had hoped that a lawsuit could be avoided.

The meeting quickly concluded. It was never actually stated that the real reason that Kiss should sue was because, allegedly, somewhere in the dark and cloudy past, one of PolyGram's original German owners may have once had Nazi links. But this is what had provided the spark that set Kiss's emotions on fire, charging them up to act. The key to persuasion is often knowing how to hit the emotional hot button; Paul Marshall knew which Kiss buttons to hit.

Beginning in early 1982 we spent an incalculable amount of time preparing for the lawsuit. My job was to work with Bob Cinque and his staff to coordinate all of the trial evidence. Reams of documents and contracts were photocopied, files were sifted through, correspondence was sorted out, reports were written, expert witnesses were retained, and depositions were taken. Thousands of pages of depositions from scores of people, including everyone in Kiss, were stacked up in bound volumes in Bob's office. He had done an exhaustive job of researching the case, knowing his opponent was a prestigious New York corporate law firm, Rosenman Colin Freund Lewis & Cohen, whose client was Phonogram.

In December, *Gene Klein, Paul Stanley, Peter Criss, and Paul Frehley v. Phonogram International, B.V.* [82 Civ. 1150] came to trial. We had been able to get on a fast track in the Federal court system since the case was one involving diversity of citizenship between two foreign entities, a U.S. partnership, Kiss, and a Dutch company, Phonogram. The trial took place in early December 1982 at the Federal Court Building at Foley Square and all the Kiss members showed up in suits and ties for each session. A fleet of limos brought them to the courthouse every morning and stood by until late afternoon when court was recessed. Kiss took the case seriously and Bob had advised them every little thing could count in their favor in persuading a jury. Kiss's regular appearance might make a more favorable impression than if they remained in absentia.

Bob Cinque was very effective in the courtroom. Bob was tall, with a thick head of straight gray hair, and wore steel-framed glasses, and his booming voice commanded attention when he spoke. An experienced litigator, he was quick-witted and knew how to poke holes in his opponent's arguments, trotting out sales records that had been introduced as evidence showing huge shipments of Kiss albums that were schlocked and never reported on royalty statements. Howard Marks sat through the whole trial and told Bob how impressive his performance had been.

When both sides rested their cases, it seemed like a sweep for Kiss on all counts. Trial outcomes are impossible to predict, even by seasoned court observers, but everything had gone precisely according to plan. Kiss's case was strong, their witnesses were persuasive in rebutting the record company's claims, and the exhibits buttressed their arguments convincingly.

The jury returned to the courtroom and their verdict was read aloud. The jury had found for the plaintiffs. Kiss had won the case. It was a hard-fought victory. Kiss's claim had been for over $6.7 million, plus possible punitive damages.

Kiss was back on their lucky streak. They had come close to the edge, but at the last moment they had been rescued. It was like 1980, when Casablanca was collapsing and PolyGram took over the company from Neil Bogart and gave them a $15 million contract. Now they were about to hit the jackpot again. All of those unsold schlocked albums from the end of the '70s had to be worth their weight in gold. But then the full verdict was read. Kiss had prevailed, but what was it they had won? $6 million? $5 million? $3 million? Maybe only $1 million? It wasn't any of those amounts. The jury awarded Kiss $520,000. The jury believed that based on the amount of Kiss records proven to have been schlocked and the royalty rate in effect, they were entitled to only that sum.

Kiss was shell-shocked. How could they could have won the case but been awarded so little? In fact, we later learned that the jury thought they had done a good deed for Kiss, paying them what they felt was a substantial award for monies rightfully owed them.

Howard Marks was also stunned. There would be no $6 million solution to Kiss's mounting money problems. The case was a bust for Kiss, despite all the talk from the lawyers about their chances of winning big. When Howard called his secretary from the courthouse, he was incensed. Kiss had won, but only a fraction of what was expected. After investing a year's worth of time, resources, brainpower, and an enormous amount of Kiss's money, they would end up with a drop in the bucket. The legal bill for all of this would be frightening.

The lawsuit had, predictably, created a great deal of enmity and rancor between Kiss and their record company. In the end, the client usually pays a hidden price in such bitter public cases. And *Klein et al. v. Phonogram* had been a very public case. Individual Kiss members and a long list of record company executives, past and present, had taken sides on the stand. No one knew what the final cost of this would be but it didn't look good for Kiss. The paltry sum they were awarded was hardly worth the blood that had been shed. The lawsuit had turned into a Pyrrhic victory for Kiss.

Meanwhile, at 810 Seventh Avenue, the offices of PolyGram Records, champagne corks must have been popping. They saved themselves about half a million dollars by battling it out with Kiss in court. Just prior to the trial, they had reportedly made a potential settlement offer to Kiss for roughly a million dol-

the lawsuit. Kiss declined to accept the offer. Kiss had gambled that the $6 million payoff was within their reach and they went for it.

There was a great deal of backbiting and buck-passing as to who made the recommendation to Kiss that they turn down the settlement. Jury trials are always fraught with hazard. When the plaintiffs are rock musicians with a far-out public image and are presumed to be rich anyway, it becomes even more of a gamble. Right or wrong, a rock group isn't by nature the most sympathetic party in a courtroom. Kiss took the gamble and lost. They were both surprised and dejected about the verdict.

Ordinarily, the jury award would have been commissioned as any income to Kiss would be, with Aucoin Management and Glickman/Marks Management taking their percentages. The award was for back-due royalties. Although Bill Aucoin wasn't Kiss's manager in December 1982, he was entitled to his share of the award since all of the schlocked records were created during his tenure. But if the jury award was commissioned outright, there wouldn't be enough left over to cover the legal bill and for Kiss to get something. The lawyers adjusted their fees and commissions were assessed only after the legal expenses were paid. According to the formula, each Kiss member would end up with a very modest amount.

Now, it was Phonogram that was on the warpath, sharpening their knives. It was time to cut Kiss down to size. They were looking for some scalps. For them, the real battle had just begun. By the time it was over, it would cost Kiss millions, as much as they had hoped to win from Phonogram in the lawsuit.

✢

An unnamed Supergroup was on the lookout for a new guitarist and everyone wanted to audition for the gig. Hundreds of tapes and photos of lead guitarists flooded our offices, everyone from 6-foot-plus Amazons to hirsute mountain men in coveralls. In addition to preparing for the trial, Kiss was also busy recording a new album for release in fall 1982 and holding tryouts for Ace's replacement. Ads had been placed in rock magazines and trade papers for the lead guitarist slot for a Supergroup. Applicants were flown in from all over the country. Gene and Paul insisted on an unknown for the job, as Eric had been, so they could mold and control him according to their wishes.

The new album, *Creatures of the Night,* was mostly recorded in L.A. Michael James Jackson, who produced the new Kiss songs included on the *Kiss Killers* compilation album released overseas, returned to polish Kiss's sound and bring them back to an in-your-face heavy metal style. He helped to pair up songwriters with Gene and Paul to collaborate on the material. Ace performed minimally on the record, doing some sessions in New York, but his picture would be on the cover to maintain the fiction that he was still in Kiss and not rock the boat with Phonogram. After a far-flung search for a new guitarist, Vincent Cusano, an L.A. musician, got the job by default. He was already playing on the record and Gene and Paul couldn't find anyone else they were enthusiastic over. He was rechristened Vinnie Vincent and given his own makeup, and costume design—an Egyptian ankh—and became the second Kiss employee musician.

"That's what we need, Howard. Real good chainsaw rock 'n' roll," Shelly Schultz intoned as he listened in Howard Marks's office to an advance cassette of *Creatures of the Night*. Shelly, then 45, was the senior talent agent in the music division of International Creative Management, a strapping and outspoken man with years of experience. He'd been instrumental in promoting another ICM client, Eddie Murphy, who had been highly successful performing at arenas in addition to his movie career. Shelly came along with Terry Rhodes, an ICM agent who had been booking rock tours for years. But we all knew that a good heavy metal record wouldn't be enough for Kiss to sizzle at the box office; they needed an opening act with name recognition and radio airplay as an insurance policy to sell tickets.

A group called A Flock of Seagulls was big on the charts then. They had a hit single and were selling plenty of tickets on tour. Shelly knew how badly Kiss needed a hot act, but A Flock of Seagulls was too techno-pop for Kiss's crowd. They dressed in space age outfits and their lead singer had a hairstyle sculpted to look like the flight deck of an aircraft carrier. Shelly picked up the phone to ask one of his underlings to look for a strong opening act for Kiss. "See if we've got anymore of those Flocks flyin' around," he ordered. Shelly and Terry tried hard to find a suitable Flock, but there weren't any takers. Managers of up-and-coming acts decided to hold off and take their chances by waiting to hook up with a bigger headline act than what Kiss appeared to be in the fall of 1982.

Kiss's tour was being booked by ICM now that Wally Meyrowitz and ATI were out of the picture. Wally left ATI after a falling-out with Jeff Franklin, the principal owner. He joined ICM and Kiss came along once their ATI agreement expired. He'd been chummy with Bill Aucoin and the Kiss members, especially Paul, but when Wally borrowed Paul's spanking new fire engine red Porsche and cracked it up, their relationship soured. Jeff was not happy about Bill taking Kiss from ATI, since he had helped Bill stay afloat when his company was in trouble financially.

Soon after joining ICM in 1981, Wally had a falling-out there as well. At one point he tried to start his own agency and wanted to bring in Kiss as his key client. He came to a business meeting at our offices to make his pitch to Kiss. Howard Marks and Carl Glickman listened while Wally told the group how much better off they would be signing with his new agency rather than being another act on the roster of a big outfit with hundreds of bands. But Carl thought he was making no sense. Neither he nor Howard could see any reason for Kiss to sign with a fledgling agency when a bigger agency would have more clout with promoters, for the same price Wally wanted to charge Kiss. Wally became enraged at Carl's line of questioning and started screaming at him. Then Carl turned livid and began yelling at Wally, throwing a notebook at him in frustration. Tempers had passed the flashpoint.

A torrent of shouting and swearing back and forth continued, with Carl blaming Wally for constantly overselling the group on doing tours that ended up losing money and Wally blaming Carl for not understanding how the booking business worked. Like everyone else, Wally was always incredulous at how much these Kiss tours cost. Carl ordered Wally out of the office; by this time, both of them were practically hoarse from screaming at each other. Kiss had said nothing during the episode. Wally stormed out of the conference room, carrying on a tirade until he got into the elevator. It was obvious that Wally's erratic behavior had deteriorated to a deplorable state.

Kiss would continue to be booked by ICM, without Wally. And ICM had something to offer Kiss they weren't getting at ATI—big-time connections in the movie world. While ATI specialized in concert bookings, especially on the rock circuit, they didn't represent their acts in movies and TV. It wasn't their bailiwick. But ICM, a much bigger full-service theatrical agency with offices in New York, L.A., and around the world, represented its artists in all areas. Gene and Paul had seen ICM as their shot at Hollywood, which is one reason they left ATI.

Kiss's search for a new manager had reached an impasse. They couldn't find anyone they were keen on who would do the job for a low price. And they certainly weren't going to sign with a manager who was already handling another artist bigger than they were and end up playing second fiddle. By insinuating himself in the selection process, Howard Marks had shrewdly gotten onto the inside track of the deliberations. He proposed an arrangement to Gene and Paul whereby Glickman/Marks Management would take over all the administrative and business aspects of Kiss's career and Gene and Paul would be their own creative managers. They would make all the artistic decisions on music, image, and the show. Glickman/Marks Management would continue as business managers for 5 percent and get an additional 7 1/2 percent to act as Kiss's administrative managers. We would take over the supervision of areas that Bill's organization had handled, like tours, record marketing, record productions, and merchandising. We would get 12 1/2 percent of Kiss's gross monies on entertainment activities. Our deal was always based on commissioning gross monies, not net income. Aucoin Management had been getting 18 1/2 percent and we were being paid 5 percent, taking a total of 23 1/2 percent from Kiss. This new arrangement would save Kiss 11 percent. It was a low-cost solution and Gene and Paul went for it.

By this time, Gene and Paul felt that they knew enough about managing their careers that cutting the umbilical cord to Bill was feasible. Besides, they had grown accustomed to Howard as their business overlord who could deal firmly with the record company, booking agency, and other entities. Howard's seigniorial self-assurance gave them confidence that the business side would be handled properly. To make the setup a little more well-rounded, Kiss brought in Danny Goldberg as a creative consultant who would be a part of the management team. A former publicist for Led Zeppelin, Danny, 32, had managed artists and record labels. He had signed Fleetwood Mac singer Stevie Nicks to record her first solo album in 1981, which went on to sell 4 million copies. He had also had a brief stint doing publicity for Kiss for eight months in the mid-1970s, before Aucoin Management took over that function for the band. Danny would help to rebuild Kiss's public image and plan a marketing campaign to launch the *Creatures of the Night* album and tour. Amiable and well-connected in the music industry, Danny would hopefully shore up support for Kiss in the press and with radio stations.

Kiss staged a press conference on a Hollywood sound stage in October, announcing the upcoming album and tour, their first in the United States since 1979. Hundreds of reporters and guests showed up, but press coverage was minimal except in the usual rock rags. Gene's idea was to have Vincent Price do the intro and act as emcee for the event, but Paul nixed this as being too hokey.

Early sales and chart action of the new album were lukewarm. No one was rushing to call ICM for Kiss dates on the tour to start at the end of 1982. Promoters who'd been loyal to Kiss in the past were starting to fade away. Larry Magid, Philadelphia's top promoter, regarded Kiss as a fad that was over. He had brighter hopes for the Go-Go's, an all-girl singing group with a '60s flavor, as the latest fad that had stripped away some of Kiss's young audience. Don Fox of New Orleans, who had promoted Kiss in their earliest days, was interested in booking the group in Dallas, where they would rehearse for the tour. But he didn't want to put them in an arena. He had in mind a 1,200-seat nightclub. Kiss refused to play any buildings that weren't arenas or big auditoriums. Unless the local promoters would put them in the biggest venue in the market, they would skip that city on the tour. Kiss believed it would be the death knell for their image as a major rock act to be seen in small halls, since for years, they had only been an arena or stadium act. In the entertainment business, reality paces perception.

Booking Kiss had become a struggle for ICM. Promoters were slow to commit to Kiss, fearful that another flop album would almost certainly mean poison at the box office. Record companies need lead time to get the albums into the local record stores and on the radio, along with their own merchandising displays. With promoters gun-shy about booking Kiss and launching their campaigns and the record company thwarted by lack of airplay and slow retail sales, *Creatures of the Night* was looking doomed from the start.

Our friend Cecil Corbett from South Carolina had booked some Kiss shows in small markets in the Southeast on the upcoming tour. I got a call in my office from Michael Piranian, an ICM agent in New York who was booking Cecil's territory for the tour. (Like any sales organization, agencies frequently divide the country geographically and assign certain agents to territories so they get to know their customers.) Mike sounded tired and anxious. His voice was a droning monotone, not at all his usual upbeat tone. I asked him why he sounded so distraught. It was the two dates he'd booked for Kiss with Cecil. Mike had just gotten off the phone with him and the two had, I was told, a nonstop screaming match because Cecil was pulling the shows from the tour. Cecil's cancellations would open up a big hole in the Kiss itinerary that couldn't be filled at the eleventh hour.

Promoters don't have the right to cancel shows once they've agreed to book them. Their commitment to an agent is a binding agreement and agencies collect deposits to forestall abrupt cancellations. But you can't always force people to do things by the book, let alone sue every promoter who causes problems. Cecil had complained to Mike that one of the Kiss shows, only weeks away, had sold just a couple of hundred tickets and the other show looked equally dismal. Mike told me to expect a call from Cecil about his dilemma. When Cecil did call, his familiar high-pitched Southern drawl came through loud and clear. "Hey, Chris! Hey, Chris! I'm real sorry about havin' to cancel those Kiss shows, but I was lookin' to lose $25,000 dollars by doin' em." His delivery quickened as he became more excited. "Ain't *no way* I'm gonna lose that kind of money! No way. Damn!" Cecil liked one-word exclamations. He was adamant about not taking a bath on a couple of shows when a disastrous outcome was a foregone conclusion. Who could blame him, although I certainly didn't tell him that.

The stark reality of how the dynamics work among artists, agents, and promoters is that the artist is really like a chattel. Promoters and agencies have an ongoing relationship since promoters always need acts, the agency's product, to put in shows. Agencies stick around to offer many new acts to promoters since old acts come and go, often with mixed results. Kiss had become an old act. They no longer meant much to promoters since they couldn't sell tickets.

Kiss was making their own heroic efforts to promote *Creatures of the Night*. They began doing in-person appearances at record stores in makeup and costume, signing autographs and posing for pictures. Jim Lewis, a marketing executive at PolyGram, organized the first of these in a suburban record store in

Richmond, Virginia. Ace showed up, still officially in the group. He missed the flight from New York and had to take a shuttle to Washington, D.C., then hopped in a limo, arriving at the store several hours behind schedule. These publicity stunts at record stores would have been unthinkable during the Super Kiss era, but Kiss and the record industry were in a slump and more aggressive promotions were needed.

We arrived in Stockholm for a two-week trip to promote the new album in Europe. Ace came along to carry out the charade that he was still in the lineup. No one wanted to set off any alarm bells with Phonogram. In fact, Ace's photo was on the cover of *Creatures of the Night,* despite the fact the he was out of the band by the time it was released and wouldn't be doing any concerts after Vinnie Vincent was hired. On the European promotion tour, Kiss hit all the major countries—Italy, Germany, Holland, England—meeting the press and appearing on TV shows. Our host for the promotional tour was Kees Van Weijen, a seasoned marketing manager from Phonogram's headquarters in Baarn, Holland, a hamlet nearly an hour's drive from Amsterdam. He confided to me that he expected Kiss to be a horror show. His colleagues had warned him to expect anything with Kiss and that taking them on a promotional tour was like drawing the booby prize. Kees was visibly relieved after a few days that things weren't as bad as he had been led to expect. Peter wasn't around anymore and Ace was relatively restrained. After the European trip, it was back to the states to start the tour.

Kiss's merchandising gold mine had been mined dry. We'd planned on getting a big advance from a merchandiser for the tour rights to help the group's ailing cash flow, but the merchandising companies shared the same sentiment as the promoters. Winterland, the biggest outfit, offered to do the Kiss tour and pay an advance of less than a hundred thousand dollars, but that was a pittance compared to what we expected. Three years earlier, had Kiss not been locked into their deal with Bill Aucoin's company, they could have commanded an advance of ten times that amount. And Kiss needed the money this time around.

A hopeful candidate proposed by Howard Marks, a notorious bootlegger of merchandise at rock concerts from coast to coast, was sure to make a bid. *Bootlegging* is another word for piracy. Our candidate had become one of the premier bootleggers in the rock concert business, manufacturing artists' merchandise with their name and likeness without their permission. During the '70s, bootlegging became a huge business, in some cases generating more sales than the legitimate product authorized by the artists themselves. It was a cleverly run scam where bootlegged products, mostly T-shirts and sweatshirts, were hawked outside of the venues until the police chased the vendors away. By the time the fans entered the building, they'd already bought their goods and had no money left for the official versions sold inside. Artists were ripped off for untold millions of dollars in royalties that the bootleggers never paid.

Bootleggers had another leg up on the artists—their T-shirts were usually much bolder, wilder, and more garish than the official products approved by the acts. Rock fans, especially the younger ones who turn out for heavy metal bands, liked the bootleggers' stuff. The official merchandise that the artists put out was often more subdued, tame by comparison—what the groups themselves might wear, as opposed to what would appeal to the raving, bug-eyed 16-year-olds who are the backbone of the concert business. The bootleggers simply filled a need created by the fans and exploited a situation tailor-made for crooks.

Dick Weidenbaum, Kiss's accountant, sat next to me on a large black leather sofa in Howard's office, waiting for our bootlegger friend, who was flying in to meet with us. He had a reputation as one of the legends of the rock concert business, a fringe character who prospered as the merchandising business was taking off. For years, he'd been the curse of the industry, heavily cutting into the profits of artists and the merchandising companies until court injunctions became effective in curbing the bootleggers. But now, he'd told Howard, he was "going straight." Carl Glickman wouldn't be at the meeting. He left the office early and was on his way to Teteboro Airport in New Jersey where his Cessna Citation jet was parked. Carl had recently bought the jet to cut down on his commuting time between New York, Cleveland, and other locales where he had business interests. Missing the meeting turned out to be a smart move.

Our candidate barged into the room wearing a leather sport jacket, black pants, a flowery shirt, and a fancy tie with an iridescent sheen. He undoubtedly felt the jacket and tie gave him a respectable, businesslike appearance. His black hair was slicked back in a pompadour and there appeared to be some scars on his tanned face. He was friendly and expansive, giving us a firm handshake and a gravelly but enthusiastic "Nice to meet 'ya." He wanted to do the Kiss tour. He told us of his big plans and how he knew how to really "sock it to the buildings" to make sure Kiss got the best concession deals possible. He also knew how to keep the bootleggers "in line" and "whip them into shape" to make sure Kiss got a piece of their action, too. His idea was to have it both ways—handle Kiss's approved merchandise and act as the *capo* of the bootleggers by cutting them in. We were impressed with his aggressive sales tactics but we thought we ought to know how Kiss would be able to verify the actual count for the night, the number of T-shirts, programs, posters, and everything else sold and the amount of money collected. He came right to the point. "That's easy," he assured us. "'Ya just come to me and I tell 'ya. I tell 'ya what the count is." He then unbuttoned his leather sport coat and pulled back the front piece, revealing a .45 automatic securely mounted in a shoulder holster. He let out a hearty laugh as though this was a real riot. We smiled nervously.

We were flummoxed about asking more questions and told him we thought his ideas were great, and hoped to hear some more details on his plan for the Kiss tour. He left our office and went back home. Howard and Dick looked as if they had just witnessed a holdup. But with Kiss strapped for cash, we had to field offers from all possible takers. We went out of our way to keep on good terms with our friend, but none of us felt confident we could survive a Kiss tour with him.

✤

Larry Kravetz was a burly man in his forties with thinning hair and a mustache, very good-humored and likable. I liked working with Larry, whom I'd hired in early 1982 to do Diana Ross's merchandising at Detroit's Joe Louis Arena. Larry had also done the merchandising for REO Speedwagon and Electric Light Orchestra. Since then, he had dabbled in local businesses; he told me he had recently opened a deli restaurant in a Detroit suburb. He was itching to get back in the business. He was perfect for Kiss. And he didn't carry a gun.

Larry and his attorney came to my office to talk about the Kiss merchandising rights for the 1982/83 tour. Mike Perlstein, Kiss's attorney, joined the negotiation. I told Larry he could have the rights if he came up with a $250,000 advance for Kiss. It was a steep price but Kiss needed the money desperately and Larry wanted to get back into the music business. He agreed. But a few weeks later, the deal fell apart when Larry came up short for the full amount. When I told him I would have to pull the plug on the deal, he called me within days to say he'd gotten all the money together. I was told that he had taken out a second mortgage on his house. We would now have our big advance—three times what anyone else would have paid us—and Larry had a deal. He would do the merchandising for the *Creatures of the Night* tour and be back in the rock world.

The Kiss tour rolled out in December 1982 with a much-reduced show and costumes that were sharply trimmed down from the dazzling Vegas look of the Super Kiss period. Three trucks of equipment sufficed this time around, and black leather, chains, and chokers were substituted for rhinestones, feathers, and furs. A military motif was featured on stage, highlighted by a costly rotating tank turret. Turnouts were anemic. Shows were booked, then unbooked. In Sioux Falls, South Dakota, a third-string promoter claimed insolvency on the night of the show and disappeared. Agents call this going "belly up." In San Angelo, Texas, local migrant workers, not the usual union stagehands, put the show up to keep costs down. The promoter skipped the building and stiffed the workers before the night was over. Kiss got stuck with the bill. If we hadn't paid them, the show would never have gotten back into the trucks to make it to the next city.

The tour had begun with a weather-related mess in Denver, when the area was hit by a crippling snowstorm. All the planes were grounded, as were all the passengers. Passengers were stranded for days at Stapleton Airport, many sleeping on the floor of the terminals. Kiss's costumes and the group's wardrobe manager were among them. The band was in Rapid City, South Dakota for the first show, which had to be postponed. But by mid-afternoon, it still looked like no one would be able to get out of Denver, and a backup set of costumes was located in the New York warehouse. A former wardrobe manager was put on a Learjet with the costumes to make it to Bismarck, North Dakota in time for the next show.

At the Mardi Gras in New Orleans in February 1983, promoter Barry Mendelson booked Kiss into the Super Dome. The show was in a cut-down seating configuration and Kiss sold about 10,000 tickets. I'd become friendly with Barry from the Diana Ross tour. He booked a string of Kiss dates that winter. As much as everyone in Kiss liked Barry, it was a sad irony that he would hold the attendance record (for a later Kiss show in Biloxi, Mississippi) for supposedly the lowest turnout ever in the Coliseum for a rock show with a headline act—1,500 tickets sold in a 15,000-seat building. Tropical rains and hurricane winds whipping the Gulf Coast that night didn't help.

In L.A., Kiss played the Universal Amphitheatre and sold out, but to a crowd of only 6,200, a far cry from Anaheim Stadium and the multiple shows at the Forum only a few years earlier. David Lee Roth showed up, slouching against the wall near the backstage artist lounge and looking bored. He was then the lead singer in Van Halen, one of the biggest groups on tour in the early '80s. While Van Halen was tearing up the country and selling out arenas in hours, Kiss was doing a fraction of that business. Ironically, Van Halen had been discovered by Gene. He financed the group in its earliest incarnation in 1977, then called Daddy Longlegs, put them in a New York recording studio, and footed their bill at the nearby Hotel Gorham. The group was later signed to Warner Bros. Records. Gene wanted to manage them, but his partners in Kiss vetoed the idea.

At the Montreal show, promoter Donald K. Donald peered out at the half-filled Forum audience, an arena which holds 17,000. We were standing backstage. He threw up his hands in despair, then put his arm over my shoulder, shaking his head. "Well, it was a great run that Kiss had, but life goes on." I thought he was delivering a eulogy.

Guarantees on the Kiss tour were cut in half and it was getting increasingly difficult to find any buyers. Some of the shows where Kiss had a strong base of fans, particularly in the midwest, did well, but most fell by the wayside. One of

ICM's agents became particularly agitated. He pointedly told me that I should tell the band to stay home and stop wasting everybody's time and money.

Poor ticket sales gave the press ample cause to stick it to Kiss. A review in *The Detroit News* on February 24, 1983, featured the headline, "Controversial Kiss Turns Ordinary." The show was described as no longer holding "thrills and danger," while Kiss performed in a "sparsely populated Cobo Arena," a building where past Kiss shows had overflowed with capacity crowds for as many as three consecutive nights. Even Kiss's claim to be the "world's loudest band" was derided; the reviewer believed he'd heard much louder bands.

Creatures of the Night had gone south in the *Billboard* charts. Despite a hard-edged sound and a striking cover design with the Kiss faces glowing in a luminous blue light,* radio stations avoided Kiss like castor oil. Danny Goldberg, their creative consultant, was shocked at the resistance to playing Kiss. Poly-Gram was equally unsuccessful at getting airplay. The album hit #45 and remained stuck in that position for six weeks before dropping out. Paul would often call Danny from the road to get a progress report on what "the radio people" were doing about playing the new Kiss album. After these conversations, often from airport pay phones as we waited for planes, Paul looked gloomy and depressed. Gene was stoic at the time, shrugging his shoulders and sighing about the sad turn of events in Kiss's career.

The age of MTV had arrived, but strangely, Kiss wasn't a staple on the network even with their obvious visual persona. Kiss, presumably the ideal act for MTV, made a video for their single, "I Love It Loud," hoping it would become their new anthem. Howard Marks had a cameo role in the video, appearing as the father of a Kiss-crazed teenager. It got limited exposure. By this time, Kiss was seen as a '70s act with a '70s image—overblown, outdated, and buffoonish. In its May 31, 1983, story on Kiss, *Circus* said that "The band has not adapted well to the '80s so far, and is perceived by some as a lumbering anachronism trying to stretch a concept—flash, makeup and P.T. Barnum-like concerts—that's outlived itself." While heavy metal was surging in popularity, Kiss was seen by some as a vestige from another era. Nothing was working for Kiss, certainly not the video and definitely not the tour.

Kiss took some action of their own in early 1983 as the tour was in its final weeks. They would leave ICM and go back to ATI. Shelly Schultz fumed that Kiss was leaving on account of "Howard Marks's buddy, Jeff Franklin." Jeff would book the remainder of the Kiss tour in progress even though the ICM contract was still in force and ATI would have to pay ICM their commissions for the shows they booked. Kiss felt ATI had more muscle with rock promoters

---

*Several years later, Kiss replaced the original cover design with a photo of the group's new lineup, without Ace and without makeup.

and would be able to get them a stronger opening act, although there was little reason to think that any agency could have helped Kiss's situation then. But there was a much more pragmatic reason for going back to ATI. There was still the unresolved matter of the $100,000 deposit held by ATI since 1981 from Carlos Spadone, the Argentine promoter whose South American tour had disintegrated. It proved to be a potent bargaining chip to induce Kiss to come back to ATI. Jeff Franklin had been stalling in releasing the monies. Now the deposit dispute could be resolved and Kiss and ATI could take their shares of the monies. Bill Elson at ATI would book Kiss; he would be assisted by Marilyn Ford, who had worked for Wally Meyrowitz.

Kiss was lucky to get the fifty-three shows on the tour that ICM and ATI were eventually able to book. By the end of the tour in April 1983, everyone's worst fears were confirmed—Kiss's popularity had plummeted and their financial underpinnings were crumbling. As Paul put it then in an ominous way, "This wasn't supposed to happen."

But the other shoe was about to drop. Since December 1982, Kiss had been on tour in makeup and costumes. The album cover had featured Kiss, including Ace. But there had been no Ace on tour. He was among the missing. It was no secret that Ace was out of the group since Kiss had gone to great lengths to bring in Vinnie Vincent as his replacement with his own specialized stage persona. Phonogram was now ready to strike. Since the lawsuit ended they had been getting into position for this. They had an inkling some funny business was going on with Kiss and their shuffling of new members for old ones. But Phonogram, and PolyGram in the United States, had been preoccupied with the trial. That was now behind them. The Phonogram agreement called for Kiss to be a threesome and not a twosome of just Gene and Paul and whatever sidemen they decided to bring in. Now that it had been officially acknowledged by Kiss that Ace wasn't in Kiss any longer, Kiss was in breach of the agreement. Phonogram felt it was high time for the group to get their comeuppance. The fact that *Creatures of the Night* had mediocre sales gave the company a strong impetus to act. They demanded that the contract be renegotiated.

Howard Marks was advised of Phonogram's intentions when he cornered Mel Ilberman, then the senior business affairs executive for PolyGram, for an additional advance at the start of the Kiss tour. He told Mel that without more cash, Kiss would have to shut down the tour. They were tapped out. Most of the merchandising money had gone to pay for the start-up costs of the tour like rehearsals, supplier deposits, and production expenses. PolyGram grudgingly coughed up a "general advance" to Kiss to keep the group on the road. Howard had a good rapport with Mel, a tough but fair businessman, and thought he would have a better chance to preserve as much as possible of the original Phonogram contract by dealing directly with him. Howard asked Gene and

Paul and Paul Marshall to allow him to handle the renegotiation since he hadn't been a central figure in the lawsuit, unlike the lawyers. They agreed.

The framework of the new deal emerged. Kiss would be Gene and Paul only. The royalty rates and most of the technical provisions of the contract remained, hammered out by Mike Perlstein and his counterpart at Polygram, Beverly Katz, their general counsel. There would now be some modifications to allow Phonogram to more quickly recoup the millions of dollars in advances they had paid out. The biggest modification concerned the advances. They would be substantially reduced. It was the best Phonogram would offer. Ace's departure from Kiss would be very costly to Gene and Paul, shrinking their guaranteed income from delivering albums. Kiss was now reduced to a more manageable level of financial obligation as far as the record company was concerned. Gene and Paul hunkered down and signed in June 1983. They would stay with Phonogram and live with a deal that was, even in its pared-down version, still far better than what any other record company would have offered. Phonogram had exacted its pound of flesh.

15

Learning to Love the Third World

I flew back to New York from San Francisco with Kiss. We were far more interested in chatting about the plane we were on, one of United's new Boeing 767s, than discussing the tour, which had been a depressing series of sparse turnouts and unhappy promoters in most cities. No one had much to say about the recent album, either. *Creatures of the Night* only sold about 250,000 copies in the United States, a far cry from the multimillion sellers of the late '70s. Kiss was demoralized. Only Paul's gallows humor lightened the mood, suggesting that we book the Holiday Inn circuit on the next tour.

A few weeks after the tour ended in April 1983, Marilyn Ford of ATI called me at my office. She said a Brazilian promoter had just arrived in New York and had already put tickets on sale in Brazil for a stadium tour by Kiss. His promotion was in full swing. What Marilyn was telling me was absurd; I interrupted and asked her to slow down. Marilyn repeated the story. The promoter was advertising Kiss in Brazil and the tickets were on sale all over the country. And nobody at ATI or in Kiss knew anything about this. It sounded far-fetched, even for the music business, but my past experience with South American promoters led me to believe that it was well within the realm of possibility. It could also be the opportunity of a lifetime. I told Marilyn to set up a meeting with the promoter right away. With Kiss's career sinking and the group desperate for cash, we couldn't afford to ignore any possibilities, no matter how bizarre.

The fortyish man with thinning hair and horn-rimmed glasses who had just stepped into my office greeted me cheerfully: "Mister Chris, tuto bene." (As I was to learn later, "tuto bene," loosely translated as "everything is okay," is sort of a national motto, used even when things aren't okay at all.) The man's name was A. Vannucci, Jr., but he was known simply as "Junior" or "Mister Junior." A bit fleshy but not fat, Junior was neatly dressed in a light-colored gray suit and tie. He was a little nervous but smiling. And I came to be known from that point as "Mister Chris." Using the honorific "mister" in front of a person's first name is good manners in Brazil.

Junior didn't speak English but he made all the correct gestures, standing to shake hands firmly and using the word "please" a great deal. To facilitate the language problem, Marilyn came to the meeting with Jorge Quevedo. Jorge, who spoke Portuguese and specialized in international bookings, was an agent with one of ATI's competitors, Premier Talent. Junior had just completed a highly successful tour with Peter Frampton, a Premier artist, and Jorge was doing Junior a favor by acting as his business intermediary to help him nail down the Kiss tour. Jorge, a slender man with a neatly manicured beard, was casually dressed in sport shirt and slacks.

Junior, Jorge, and Marilyn sat in front of my desk and Marilyn brought me up to date. Junior had arranged a huge tour of Brazil for Kiss. They would play stadiums. There would be one show in Rio de Janeiro, two in São Paulo, one in Belo Horizonte, and one in Pôrto Alegre. The tour would be in May. Junior blurted out something which Jorge translated. Promotion and advertising had already begun. Junior was now building a stage for Kiss and ordering tons of sound and lighting equipment to be trucked in from all over Brazil. Kiss was a supergroup in Brazil. Monstrous. Bigger than any group on earth. And Poly-Gram Discos, Kiss's record company in Brazil, was behind his plans all the way. Junior was getting excited, rattling away in Portuguese about the extravaganza he was organizing, making expansive motions with his hands while Jorge translated. We would be crazy not to go ahead with this tour, he said.

He was right. Kiss really needed a shot in the arm by doing something in a big way. Playing in front of stadiums full of cheering fans, even in the Third World, would be a lot better than what we had been through just a few weeks ago, when less than 3,000 people showed up in Kiel Auditorium in St. Louis, a building that holds over 10,000. The only rational thing to do was to start negotiating and make the deal as rich as possible. I'd already spoken to Howard Marks and his instructions were to do it—as long as there was a big profit in the deal for Kiss.

The best way for us to do this was to make sure the promoter picked up as much of the production, travel, and transportation expense as possible and to limit the time Kiss spent in Brazil. We wanted to minimize our costs first and then negotiate the fee for the shows. What I had in mind was a step beyond what's called a "delivered show," where the act pays its way to and from the host country including air travel, cargo, personnel costs. With delivered shows, the promoter only picks up the internal costs in his country. This was too chancy for Kiss. There are too many variables involved with all costs when shows are being staged in remote parts of the world. I told Junior that Kiss would go to Brazil but he would have to pay for everything—get all of us to Brazil, do the tour, set up the Kiss show according to our specs including sound and lights, and get us home—and take all the attendant risks. The only cost we would assume would be for a skeleton crew we would bring along. And Kiss's time commitment couldn't exceed two weeks. The fee might be less doing it this way, but it would limit Kiss's financial risk and reduce their out-of-pocket costs. Commissions would also be lower, leaving more money in Kiss's pocket and a potentially bigger net profit.

We had Junior over a barrel, but only to a degree. For any promoter to bring a big act like Kiss to Brazil with an enormous show was an extremely risky proposition. There was a black hole of unknowns. The last group to play stadiums there was Queen, a British rock group with a big production, but that had been a few years earlier. I doubted there were other promoters waiting in the wings to jump in and make offers to Kiss. It was too big a gamble financially and the logistics of it might not be feasible.

The black market for currency was the only way anyone could pay the money we wanted for our guarantee. A promoter would have to buy U.S. dollars at a huge premium on what was called the parallel market, where private money changers converted Brazilian cruzeiros to U.S. currency. At that time, banks in Brazil, controlled by the government, would never permit such large sums to go through official channels since the amounts exceeded restrictions on exporting currency. And tickets in Brazil could be sold for only about four U.S. dollars. Even with hundreds of thousands of fans, the potential ticket gross wouldn't be in the multimillions of dollars but considerably less. The black market cost of converting the ticket cruzeiros into dollars to pay Kiss would be steep. Eventually, Junior and I came to a tentative deal. I asked him to arrange an advance trip to Brazil for me and Kiss's production manager to see for ourselves that everything was doable and then we would make a final commitment. He agreed and we shook hands. The next day, Junior left for Brazil.

A week later, I waited for Tom Marzullo and Felippe Rodriguez to arrive in the Pan Am lounge at JFK. Tom, Kiss's production manager on the last tour, was short and stocky and had a cheerful expression on his round face most of the time. Junior's U.S. liaison was Felippe, who spoke Spanish and Portuguese and had promoted shows in Latin countries. Once they arrived, we talked for a while until Tom and I boarded the 747. Felippe would be involved in the tour later in the game. We landed in Rio eight hours later after an overnight flight. The pale gray light and haze of the early morning sun was beginning to burn away as baking hot winds blew off the mountains. We walked off the plane and into the customs terminal. Getting through the rows of people assembled in front of scores of little booths with uniformed inspectors inside was no problem since Tom and I were greeted by another of Junior's middlemen, Alfie Soares. A young Brazilian with sad little eyes and a kind of weary, hangdog look, Alfie spoke perfect English, which he had learned while living in the states by watching soap operas on TV. He expedited our way out of the airport chaos.

En route to our hotel, the Rio Palace, Alfie told Tom and me his plan for the trip. He would take us to the stadium in Rio and we would inspect the facilities. We would then fly together to São Paulo where Junior had his offices and look at the stadium there. If everything was okay, we would sign the contract and Tom and I would go back to New York. It was now mid-April. The tour would start at the end of May, based on the dates we had agreed to with Junior at our meeting in New York. Alfie assured us that everything would be "no problem." It had a familiar ring to it, but I was still too groggy from the flight to be worried. At any rate, Junior wasn't kidding about having begun his promotion for Kiss in Brazil already; I caught a few Kiss posters plastered on billboards as we drove into Rio. A sticker with the tour dates and cities was pasted on top.

I was never exactly sure when the tickets were put on sale; I'd understood from Junior that he started selling tickets even before he arrived in New York, but he could have been bluffing. But it really didn't matter. At this point, only an earthquake, a revolution, or a financial calamity would prevent Kiss from coming to Brazil. I didn't know it at the time, but one of those events was looming.

PolyGram was thrilled about Kiss appearing in Brazil. Carlos Celles, the record company's international promotion manager, met me at my hotel the first night to put out the welcome mat. It was rare for a top American or British artist to come to Brazil at that time because of all the technical and financial impediments that made touring next to impossible. A chronic problem had always been the lack of high-quality facilities and well-capitalized promoters. Carlos, who looked to be in his mid-thirties, was lanky and loose-limbed, with brush-cut black hair. He was an engaging host who had been keeping tabs on Junior and the Kiss promotion since he first caught wind of it.

The next day, Tom, Alfie, and I checked out possible sites for the Kiss show in Rio. There were many, owing to the fanatical popularity of soccer in Brazil, with dozens of clubs having their own playing fields. We looked at stadiums, all of which were similar to what I'd seen in Mexico City a few years earlier: gargantuan oval-shaped monoliths built to pack in masses of people. Alfie told us that Junior would meet us in Rio, but then abruptly canceled. We would catch up with him in São Paulo.

Driving around Rio for days scouting concert sites made it clear that the Third World stood in sharp contrast to the places Kiss was used to playing. Rio is in many ways two cities. Immaculate beaches, luxury high-rises, breathtaking contemporary and colonial architecture, tranquil lagoons, and the swirling mosaic-tiled pavement that abuts the beaches stretching for miles—this is the photogenic side. Corcovado Mountain stands majestically in the distant gray granite hills that surround the city, with the statue of Christ the Redeemer at its crest. The other Rio is one of human misery, rundown shacks and great swathes of shantytowns known as *favelas* dotting the hills which ring the bustling downtown district. Beggars and wretches are encamped on street corners and in front of buildings. This eerie duality makes Rio a city of troubling extremes, a small sliver of wealth butting against a huge mass of terrifying poverty.

A few days later, we were off to São Paulo. São Paulo, Brazil's business capital, is also its largest city, with more than six million people. We flew on a shuttle from Rio. From the air, São Paulo appears to be an uncontrollable urban sprawl, spilling out in all directions. We were to meet Junior that afternoon at his office to finalize the tour plans.

We checked into the Maksoud Plaza, an impressive luxury hotel located downtown. A block away were clusters of skyscrapers and office towers rising forty stories or more on wide boulevards not unlike New York's Avenue of the Americas. Alfie and Tom went off to check locations and I waited for Junior to arrive at the hotel. An interpreter was provided to me, a young college student named Frank Duurvoort, a tall, bushy-haired fellow originally from Holland. He was pleased to be making extra money for his college expenses and was even more excited about working in show business. He filled me in on what Junior was doing to promote the Kiss tour and how big an event it promised to be. We waited in the lounge area for Junior to arrive. The phone at the bar rang and Frank answered it. Frank told me Junior was now in Rio. He would be back in São Paulo that night. Frank mentioned something about Junior going to Rio to "work on the advertising" but it didn't really matter. We had lunch, and since a car and a driver were put at my disposal, I asked Frank to take me sightseeing.

The next day the same thing happened. Frank showed up at the Maksoud around noon, the phone rang at the bar, and someone called from Junior's office in São Paulo to cancel his meeting with me. We then had lunch. The third time we went through the same routine, I was annoyed, but then I realized that it was silly for me to be annoyed. Since Junior was paying for my trip to Brazil, I might as well enjoy it. Sooner or later, he would show up but it was obviously something over which I had no control. So I encouraged Frank to become a walking encyclopedia of knowledge about nightlife in São Paulo, which makes Rio pale by comparison. I told Frank to do some research and come up with an itinerary for the next few nights.

I had soon visited nearly every disco, go-go bar, private club, and boîte in the city, including a place called Eduardo's Studio, a kind of converted Playboy mansion where you choose from a book of color photos of girls who are summoned to the mansion by electronic beeper. The most intriguing of these diversions was unfortunately the one I couldn't get to, a private celebrity escort service. Well-known TV stars and media personalities from soap operas, news programs, and game shows were available as escorts through the service for a few

271

hundred dollars a date. It was like being able to ring up the local equivalent of Vanna White for the night. Moonlighting was apparently an economic necessity for even the biggest Brazilian TV stars.

The itinerary of Frank, phone call, lunch, and the pursuit of carnal knowledge went on for nearly a week. It was getting to be an exhausting business trip. One evening I took Frank to dinner at Rodeio, São Paulo's top *churrascaria,* or steak house. The restaurant was done in traditional gaucho style with black leather chairs and brass fixtures in a dark, oak-paneled room. Near the entrance was an open grill where thick steaks and chickens sizzled over fiery coals. A novelty at the time was the cellular phone you could have brought to your table. As we were leaving the restaurant, I did a double take. Passing in front of me was Manoel F. W. Salles, the lawyer for Carlos Spadone, the Argentine promoter who had come to New York to book Kiss. Manoel told me about Carlos's business setbacks. He wasn't able to pay Manoel's legal bill in full but he did get some homemade sausages every Christmas from one of the Spadone family food factories. Manoel was pleased to hear that Kiss was planning to be in Brazil. It didn't seem like a bad idea for Kiss to have an attorney represent them in Brazil, I thought, just to make sure the tour's business matters were handled properly at the local level. I promised to contact him once we finalized the deal.

Junior finally arrived the next day. He sent a car for me and Tom to take us to his offices. We arrived at a handsome-looking private home in an upscale residential section of São Paulo. The house had been converted to a complex of offices on two floors and near the entrance was a prominent sign that read Arteshow, the name of Junior's company. Inside, there were dozens of people running up and down the stairs, in and out of the offices and workstation areas. There seemed to be a lot of people working for the Arteshow organization, but wherever you are in Brazil, you always see several times the number of people needed. The work is spread around so everybody gets a piece of it.

We were accorded the royal treatment as we were escorted into Junior's spacious and stylish office. It was all in white and brown tones with neat little modules of track lighting and vertical blinds. A large glass-topped rectangular table was set in the middle of the office. On top of the glass table was a scale model of an enormous stage with tubular metal pieces girded by crossing steel brackets. A major contractor, Rohr, was building the Kiss stage and the scaffolding. Sound, lighting, and trucking companies had their people sitting around the table to answer questions about the production. Frank was there to help us communicate. Tom went over his checklist and then I talked to Junior. He apologized profusely about not meeting us before and said something about "working on the advertising."

Junior's ad campaign for the Kiss tour was massive. He'd already begun hyping the tour and was locking up plans for a big push in all the media—newspapers, magazines, radio, TV, and posters. We also talked about the *sine qua non* of our contract, which was that all the monies due Kiss had to be paid in advance before anyone or any of our equipment left the United States. He also had to guarantee our air cargo expenses round-trip by prepaying everything. We came to a meeting of the minds and agreed to officially announce the Kiss tour the next day at a press conference.

At the São Paulo Hilton in one of the ballrooms, nearly a hundred press, radio, and TV reporters showed up with an arsenal of cameras, lights, and tape recorders. Posters of Kiss and the scale model of the stage were on display. Junior was supposed to be there to announce the tour with me at his side as the official representative of Kiss. He never made it. It seemed strange to me that the promoter of one of the biggest entertainment events in the history of the country would call a press conference and not show up but we had to go ahead with it anyway. One of Junior's underlings stepped in to help me along with an interpreter. It was another unsettling instance of Junior's odd behavior.

Junior and I met for a final meeting just before Tom and I went back to New York. He apologized for missing the press conference, again saying something about having to be in Rio to "deal with the advertising." Despite Junior's vanishing act, Arteshow seemed to have the organization to stage the Kiss tour successfully. Junior's idiosyncrasies notwithstanding, there would certainly be a lot of advertising for the tour. We all shook hands and exchanged signed contracts. Kiss was coming to Brazil.

Back in New York, I told Kiss the tour of Brazil looked to be a huge success, with sold-out stadium shows, live TV coverage, and a big promotion by Poly-Gram. I thought it would be as big as Australia, but cautioned everyone not to expect things to be as well-ordered as they were there. Tom assured us everything would work and the Kiss show could come off. The group was pleased with the news and started rehearsing. And then the problems began.

Kiss's tour was contingent upon us getting all the monies first in New York. The first installment was now overdue. Days later, it came through. Then the itinerary changed. There wouldn't be any Pôrto Alegre, a large port city in the southern part of the country. That was okay, but we had stipulated in our agreement that Junior only had a two-week period for the tour, for which he had the right to do "up to five shows in total." He could cancel shows, but the guarantee would remain the same. The second installment of the monies was delayed. More problems surfaced. Telexes were coming and going around the clock. There seemed to be some sort of screw-up in Brazil in getting permits for at least one of the shows. It was often hard to understand exactly what was going on since the information was often filtered to me through one of Junior's staff who spoke limited English and who was obviously trying to put a spin on any potentially bad news. It was now mid-May and Kiss was scheduled to leave in a little more than a week. Then the wire transfer came through. There had been a mix-up with a financial intermediary in Miami. Kiss's equipment—the tank turret prop, lighting and sound consoles, costumes, and specialized electronic and pyro gear—was en route to a loading area at JFK where Varig Airlines has a depot. The last installment of the monies was due the next day and once we got the payment in ATI's bank account, the equipment would be put on the 8:00 p.m. Varig flight. Kiss would be on the same plane.

It was Monday. We were all scheduled to leave that night. Paul called me in the late morning to find out if everything was "on schedule." I told him it was, but I would call him later in the day in any case. Our crew was headed for JFK and Gene, Paul, Eric, and Vinnie were at home packing. It was nearly 4:00 p.m. and the last installment of the money hadn't showed up. I was sitting at my desk with my suitcases stacked in a corner of my office. We had two of the three installments but the money never came for the last one. The tour was over, or rather, it wouldn't start. I called one of our production people and told him to send the trucks back to the warehouse and then phoned Kiss to tell them not to leave for the airport. Everything was shut down.

Junior had paid two-thirds of our fee, mounted an extensive promotion in Brazil, and organized a major production, but he didn't have a tour. It looked to be another disaster for a Kiss promoter. Felippe Rodriguez came back into the picture. A few days after the tour fell apart, he showed up at my office. He had discussed everything with Junior. Junior needed more backers. There were all kinds of technical and logistical problems. Costs had escalated, especially the TV advertising, and buying large amounts of dollars on the black market had become very expensive. More telexes and phone calls poured in from Arteshow saying they wanted to reschedule the tour. Money wouldn't be a problem anymore; Junior was on his way to New York bringing a suitcase full of it.

I told Felippe we would try to be flexible to honor our obligation to do the tour, but Junior would have to make Kiss whole. Junior wanted to push the tour back by two weeks, to mid-June. We would agree to that, but we now had two weeks of additional costs for personnel, rehearsal, and a list of related expenses due to the cancellation, not to mention a big bill with Manoel Salles's law firm in São Paulo. I couldn't be sure how much of this would get through to Junior. Overseas promoters often believe that every major artist has brigades of employees on duty year-round and all of the equipment is owned by the artist. In fact, most acts including Kiss lease their equipment and personnel from specialized production suppliers on an as-needed basis.

Within twenty-four hours, Junior was in our conference room. He looked as if he'd just rolled off the plane. He was sweating and nervous, frowning as he took a seat at our conference table, facing the *Love Gun* painting. Marilyn Ford came to the meeting and I brought our own interpreter. After a long tale of woe from Junior, I told him we really did sympathize with his plight. The problems of staging a tour on the scale of Kiss in Brazil must be staggering. Kiss was willing to reschedule provided that Junior covered their additional costs on account of the cancellation. It wasn't fair to penalize them for his problems, no matter how legitimate they were. I explained what our extra costs were and showed him the documentation. The explanation got a flinty reception. He was visibly upset, complaining that he'd been backed into a corner "like an animal" but I told him it had nothing to do with trying to exploit the situation. Kiss wanted to get the same money originally agreed to. They should be reimbursed for the added postponement costs. Junior understood what I was talking about, although he obviously didn't like it. We made a new contract with the modifications and a new itinerary and payment schedule. The guaranteed fee now included the extra payment to Kiss for their recent expenses. Kiss would appear in Brazil for two weeks maximum and do four shows. The next day, Junior left for São Paulo. By coincidence, Carlos Celles was in New York at the time for a meeting with PolyGram. I called him to let him know the tour was back on. He replied, "Everything with this guy [Junior] is so crazy."

We started all over again. Everything was moved back into position—the equipment, the trucks, the crew, the flights—all the myriad details. Junior left us with a certified check drawn on a U.S. bank and not the suitcase of cash as we had originally understood. He would arrange the final payment for the last installment within a week. The day it was due, we were supposed to pick it up from the Stamford, Connecticut, office of Deak Perrera, the foreign exchange firm. There was a long and complicated story about why they had to send the monies there, and Felippe drove me from New York to Stamford.

We sat in his car parked curbside in front of the Deak Perrera office for hours, drinking coffee and reading newspapers. The money never came. It looked like the second incarnation of Kiss's Brazil tour was about to go down the tubes. But next morning, the money transfer arrived at a different Deak Perrera office. It had been wired to the wrong location. The tour was on. Kiss would leave for Brazil in days.

Varig Airlines 861 arrived in Rio early Tuesday morning, June 14. It was a miracle we'd made it. A convoy of sedans and trucks met us at the airport and took us to our hotel, Cesar Park. Fans conducted vigils around the clock outside the hotel and across the Avenida Atlântica which runs parallel to the beach. There was endless coverage on radio, TV, and the press. The record company showed up in full force to meet Kiss and to supervise their own promotions for *Creatures of the Night,* recently released in Brazil. Aart Dalhuisen, the head of Phonogram International, was in Rio for the show. Kiss was fond of Aart, and they always ribbed him about his resemblance to Pope John Paul II. Junior met the band for the first time and was burbling. He told them the TV campaign was the biggest ever for a music event. Full-page ads for the Kiss concerts were in all the major dailies. Things were starting to look up. The only disappointing note was that Alfie, one of Junior's aides, had quit in a dispute with him over his pay, and Frank, my trusty interpreter, wasn't brought back. Junior thought Frank was prejudiced against him and too close to me.

We would play Rio in a few days, then Belo Horizonte, and finally, two shows in São Paulo. At our high-rise hotel in the exclusive Ipanema district, the band spent most of the day sunning themselves on the rooftop, surrounded by muscle-bound bodyguards. June is winter in Rio, typically muggy and humid. Miles of beaches sweep up the coast in a curving arc, facing the jumble of tinted glass-and-steel edifices that comprised Rio's block of beachfront hotels. Eric enjoyed going on tourist excursions, as did Vinnie, who had brought down his wife to make a holiday out of the trip, much to the displeasure of Gene and Paul. The notion of Vinnie having fun on a working trip seemed to bug them.

Gene and Paul weren't overly excited about Brazil. The place seemed too foreign, too Third World, for their more Americanized tastes. The climate was uncomfortably soggy and English wasn't widely spoken. We had at least a dozen bodyguards with us all the time and most of them couldn't converse in English. The Brazilian attitude is very laid back and leisurely, and you hear "tuto bene" a lot. Gene and Paul wanted everything to be more organized and more familiar—in other words, more American—like in Australia. The chaos of getting to Brazil in the first place had made them wary. The spot most to their liking was Hippopotamus, a *soignée* disco frequented by an older, jet-set crowd and owned by a Brazilian who had a sister club in New York, Club "A" on the Upper East Side. Hippopotamus was a plush nightspot featuring zebra-striped banquettes and an indoor rain forest enclosed in a floor-to-ceiling arboretum.

The women weren't to their liking, either. Most didn't speak English, many looked too earthy, others were too sleazy, and some were prostitutes of some kind or another. There wasn't the constellation of Anglo Saxon beauties they had in Australia who flocked around them wherever they went. The colloidal mix of dozens of cultures in Brazil was jolting to Gene and Paul. It was a different vibe here and the samba beat wasn't really their style.

Luckily for Paul, he met another blonde bombshell from the west coast, a vivacious poster girl for a Mexican beer who was in Rio on a modeling assignment and who was around for part of our trip. Gene took up with a Brazilian girl with skin that was scorched bronze in color with onyx black hair that flew back in waves, hanging to her waist. She was usually dressed in what looked like a loincloth around her torso with a bikini top over her grapefruit-sized breasts. She spoke no English and had no name that anyone ever heard her utter. She was always referred to by Gene as "my animal."

Everyone else who came down for the trip, especially the crew, was happy. Rio is crawling with idle young girls who lie on the beaches in thong bikinis during the day and roam the bars and discos on every block of the Copacabana district at night. Hedonism is a national pastime, and the sultry climate and languid pace are conducive to incessant pleasure-seeking.

Eric was always game for nightlife and one night I corraled a couple of bodyguards to go out with us. We made a beeline to what was touted as Rio's hottest club for girls, Barbarela. Barbarela was a seedy dive on the main drag of the Copacabana with a cheap neon sign blinking over the entrance. Just blocks from the beach, sea breezes helped cool off the sidewalk area where a few women with small children slept in hovels pitched against the walls of buildings. We got out of our car and one of the club's doormen ushered us into the entrance as we stood for a moment in the glare of the flickering neon. The club was below street level and we walked down a steep, narrow flight of stairs with photos of local showgirls lining the walls of the staircase. By the time we reached the bottom, I thought we'd need night vision goggles. Barbarela wasn't exactly fancy. It didn't seem to be much more than a big room jam-packed with long rows of tables and chairs pushed together end-to-end with barely enough room to squeeze into. There were hordes of waiters in tattered tuxes, frayed around the coat sleeves, circling the tables covered with torn white tablecloths, some full of cigarette holes. The walls were painted ruby red, and pulsing in the background was a continuous flow of disco hits. Ashtrays were filled with butts smeared with lipstick.

Whatever its shortcomings, Barbarela did have girls. Masses of them, all in their early twenties or younger, circulating throughout the room and lined up shoulder to shoulder all along the back of the place. As the room filled up by midnight, streams of girls ambled down the stairs, dressed in jeans, miniskirts, tight cotton T-shirts, and halter tops. Nearly all of them had meticulously made up faces and carefully arranged hairstyles. Eye shadow and hair mousse were popular with Brazilian girls.

Still more girls were dancing on a tiny disco stage with blinking colored lights above it at the far end of the room. Eric, the bodyguards, and I took a table after an obliging waiter bounced a few girls out of their chairs, and we ordered a round of *caipirinhas,* a potent cachaça-based drink that's the national cocktail of choice. The taped music squawked through a set of speakers that crackled every time the treble frequencies hit a shrill note. Girls would swarm over to the table once you alerted the waiter, who bumptiously snapped his fingers or pointed to whom you were eyeing. This was the land of *machismo.* Claudia sat down to join us, a buxom girl with long, wavy curls of light brown hair who was squeezed into a shimmery nylon miniskirt. She told us that she had recently appeared in the Brazilian edition of *Playboy.* Pretty

277

soon, there were four girls sitting with us and the swirls of cigarette smoke and dense clouds from my cigar made our table look like a chimney. Michael Jackson's "Beat It" must have played a hundred times that night before we left Barbarela around 2:00 a.m. We went back to the hotel with Claudia and her friends in tow.

The next morning, Eric called, sounding downbeat. The girls whom he brought back to his room had expected to be paid. They didn't hustle up front, but waited until afterward. He wasn't aware of this routine. It was a given that anyone who could afford to stay at a top hotel in Rio, no doubt a big spender, could easily cough up the going rate, then about $50 to $100. The girls didn't speak any English, except for how to quote prices in dollars. And as Eric had woefully discovered, rock star status didn't compensate for cash, unlike everywhere else he'd been since joining Kiss a few years ago. He told me how angry the girls were, offended that he was only interested in showing them pictures of Kiss and not having sex. Eric had a hard time understanding that discos in Rio weren't the ideal locale for finding soul mates. In Rio, getting picked up in nightclubs was, for many, a way to make a living.

Reporters and photographers snapped to attention when Kiss, in makeup and costumes, walked into the Cesar Park ballroom for their opening press conference. Radio, TV, and press people jammed inside to record Kiss's first public appearance in Brazil. Kiss would make the cover of *Manchete,* a national weekly magazine that's the local equivalent of *Time* and *Life.* The on-again, off-again tour was now a reality and Kiss launched into their now-routine ballyhoo to hype the tour. Kiss was the perfect act for Brazil, a country where Mardi Gras is a national holiday and the streets become an open carnival of people parading in bizarre costumes and masks.

Kiss did have to quash one bit of hype at the press conference. Rumors had circulated that Kiss performed animal sacrifice during the show, killing chickens on stage. It came up again and Gene fielded the question, assuaging everyone's fears that despite Kiss's demonic image, no such thing took place. In a country almost entirely Catholic, but where voodoo is taken very seriously, we were happy to deny the chicken story.

Maracanã (pronounced ma-ra-ka-NAH) stadium, an enormous concrete shell situated at the foot of the mountains that can hold up to 200,000 people in six tiers of seating, the largest stadium in the world, was the site of Kiss's first show. The Kiss stage was set up at the far end of Maracanã. The tank turret and several tons of lighting and sound equipment had been obtained locally. Pyro was in plentiful supply and the large Kiss electric sign filled the back of the stage. The production wasn't on the same technical level as Super Kiss in Australia, but it did provide the usual panoply of explosions, fog, bombs, smoke, and fireworks.

Any similarity between a stadium show in Brazil and anywhere else in the world is purely coincidental. The audience streamed through the gates and into the stadium all night, even after Kiss went on around 10:30 p.m. Some people obviously had tickets, many didn't. Backstage facilities and amenities were nonexistent. We were lucky to get enough power to do the show at all. Tom Marzullo, our production manager, had to do a juggling act just to keep the generators running through the Kiss performance. The sound was often sludgy, with blotchy patches of feedback cutting into the guitar solos and Paul's vocals fighting to be heard over the racket. But the fans were rabid over Kiss. Crowds of them piled on top of each other in the front section of the stadium grounds, pushing and shoving to get a better view. On stage, cameramen from Globo TV, televising the show live, scampered back and forth to get their shots.

The fans were drenched and exhausted, sweat pouring out of their writhing bodies as Kiss cranked out song after song of pounding rock 'n' roll. Some had removed nearly all of their clothes and were waving T-shirts and scarves, their bodies soaking. Masses of them seemed to move in a wavelike formation as the music throbbed. It was a wild rainbow of skin colors—brown, red, tan, café au lait, black, white—thrown together in a crazy quilt. And there were scores of lusty Brazilian girls with tawny complexions and great, heaving breasts and wide buttocks, sitting on the shoulders of their boyfriends, some even standing on them. Kiss in Rio had a wild air of excitement and strangeness to it, unusual and uninhibited, an atmosphere we'd never experienced before. We were unmistakably in a different world.

Maracanã had sold, according to various estimates, 100,000 or 150,000 or more tickets. No one knew for sure. Ticket counts are whatever your best guess is. It didn't really make much difference because it was by far the biggest show in Kiss's history. They had never played before to so many fans at a show of their own. From the stage, the audience was a vast panorama of people; the fans were stacked in every tier of the stadium. Kiss broke into "I Love It Loud" from their recent album and the crowd reaction was explosive, the ear-splitting roar bouncing off the concrete. Floodlights washed the upper deck of the stadium and created a halo effect against the night sky. The finale of fireworks and bombs brought the Kiss show to a ferocious climax and the stage went dark as Kiss disappeared down the ramps in back and took off in waiting cars and vans.

But Gene and Paul were surprisingly unaffected by it. Yes, they enjoyed the show; yes, the fans were great; yes, the audience was huge; but they were very ho hum about the whole event. It didn't seem to count with them. It wasn't America. Or England. Or Europe. Or Australia. It was the Third World, a stew pot of cultures. It wasn't that important. Besides, what did they know anyway? In Brazil, they're years behind the times. They still think Kiss is a supergroup. And who can understand them, yammering away in that strange tongue of theirs? To Gene and Paul, the Brazil tour was just a business trip and they counted the days until the trip was over and the business was concluded.

After Rio, we moved on to Belo Horizonte, a mining center about 300 miles to the north. Trucks carrying all of the equipment and staging had to cut through jagged mountains on narrow highways to get there. The stadium was shoddy-looking and spartan even by South American standards. Kiss was waiting in the hotel lobby for the cars to take them to the sound check around 5:00 that afternoon. The drivers showed up and Kiss and their bodyguards jumped in, heading toward the stadium. Thousands of fans were now circling the stadium grounds, lining up around the building waiting for the gates to open. The opening band would start the show at 9:00 p.m. As Kiss's fleet of cars approached the backstage gate, one of our technicians came running at them, waving and yelling wildly to turn back. The cars stopped. The technician crouched next to the car Gene was in to tell him the power generator had shut down. There was no electricity. And there wouldn't be any show. The cars made a U-turn and careened back down the hilly road they had come in on.

The Kiss show was rescheduled for the next day. It was a near-miss. A few hours later, the stadium would have been packed and canceling the show and telling everyone to go home would have caused a riot. But another disaster had already occurred. A local judge had issued an edict prohibiting anyone under 16 years old from attending the Kiss show in Belo Horizonte without a parent. Strong conservative sentiment in this part of Brazil allows the judiciary and the police to restrict access to public events if they find the moral content to be objectionable. It was a very bad break for Junior. Only 30,000 people came instead of the 80,000 predicted. During the show, the crowd barrier nearly gave way as mobs of fans began surging toward the stage. Just before the usual encore, Paul said good night and the band tore off stage to their waiting limos. After the show, everyone in the band and the crew ended up in Sagittarius, the hot spot of Belo Horizonte, a glitzy disco done in a zodiac theme with a sunken dance floor and multicolored lights twirling and dilating as the music boomed through giant speakers. Like Barbarela in Rio, the place was bursting at the seams with nubile young girls. Kiss sat at a large table in the back and about a dozen girls circled around them, giggling and jabbering in Portuguese. Gene and Paul were nonplussed, but Eric signed autographs and bought drinks for the girls. Vinnie was with his wife.

Not long after we arrived, I spotted a shapely young girl doing her best to attract our attention. She appeared to be around 18, with a huge mane of long sunbleached brown hair and wearing a bright yellow T-shirt labeled "Dijon" in front that was stretched so tightly across her breasts that she looked as if she were about to explode. The girl eventually found her way to our table, announcing that her name was Giovannia. I ordered a couple of snifters of

Fundodar, the local brandy, while a reedy-voiced DJ saluted Kiss's appearance at the club and played "I Was Made for Lovin' You." Soon after, Gene and Paul got bored and left. We learned from Giovannia that Kiss was seen as devil worshipers by some in that region of Brazil. The group was an easy target for the more conservative clergy, who had been able to pressure the authorities to prohibit children from coming to the show.

Our last stop was São Paulo. The two shows were booked at mammoth Morumbi, the city's biggest stadium where championship soccer matches are played. Junior suffered another major setback. The second show was canceled due to lack of ticket sales. There would only be one show; all the tickets bought for the second show would be honored at the first. Junior was getting clobbered; he had overshot his mark. A couple of go-go girls who were backstage at the Morumbi show put it plainly. Kiss was "very big," they said, but two stadium shows, even in São Paulo, the largest city, was "too big."

Morumbi did about 60,000 or 70,000 people. The two shows originally planned had been expected to do about twice that. São Paulo's doubleheader was to be the home run for the Kiss tour and provide Junior with his profit margin. Instead, he took a drubbing. The turnout was still impressive, but Junior had expected to do nearly double that amount of business. Ticket revenues fell way short of what Arteshow had predicted. It was another case of overreaching.

The Kiss tour of Brazil was over. On June 26, the band and their crew from the states assembled in the lobby of the São Paulo Hilton where we'd been staying. Everyone but me and Tom Marzullo were going directly back to New York. Junior suddenly appeared in the lobby. "Mister Chris! Mister Chris!" he shouted from the front doors of the hotel entrance as he approached me. A secretary trailed behind him to interpret. After we exchanged a few pleasantries, he came right to the point. Would Kiss stay in Brazil to do another show?

I sunk deeper into the leather couch we were sitting on across from the registration desk. Junior, the interpreter, and I were in an alcove, alone. He wanted to talk *mano a mano*. I was startled and reminded Junior of the obvious, that we were hours away from boarding the flight back to New York and Kiss and their people had other commitments. The tour was finished and their job was over. Junior didn't get it. Couldn't Kiss stay another week so he could add a show in Pôrto Alegre? I told him that was impossible. We had faithfully fulfilled our obligations to him and done all the shows he asked in the two-week period. Unfortunately for Junior, it turned out that he was only able to do three shows in that time. But no one could say that was Kiss's fault.

Junior started waving his hands, chopping the air like an Italian tenor delivering a Puccini aria. He desperately wanted Kiss to stay and pleaded with me to make them. Junior apparently thought that I was their boss. I proposed to him that we come back later in the year and do some more shows in the hope that he would be able to recoup some of his losses, but we would have to get paid for the new shows under another contract. He was looking for something a little more immediate, like for us to stay around another week or two, until he could get more shows lined up. No doubt, Junior was scheming to keep Kiss in Brazil until he was able to make enough money to compensate for the losses he had taken under our original contract. Basically, he wanted Kiss to stay and do the additional shows for free. The whole thing sounded crazy, like some sort of Wild West showdown. I couldn't ignore the fact that Junior had booked the tour and promoted the shows before he even negotiated a deal with Kiss. The tour had collapsed on him through a combination of bad luck and poor business judgment. I told Junior politely and in a low-key tone of voice that we couldn't stay. It was impossible. Junior looked downcast. I felt badly that the tour had gone awry, but he was the one who flew to New York and begged Kiss to come down and perform. It's a problem common in the concert promotion business—promoters who go to the ends of the earth to book acts and then learn the hard way that they went overboard, way overextending themselves financially. The results are often ruinous.

Junior left the hotel looking like a man who had been given a death sentence. Kiss took off for the airport along with the crew. Our business was finished. I would stay behind for a week to settle some of the administrative details and make sure that the equipment was expedited back home and then to London for the start of the next Kiss tour in September. Tom and I would take a side trip to Buenos Aires to meet another promoter anxious to book Kiss. Brazil was now behind us, I thought. The problems of Brazil were actually just beginning.

We arrived in Buenos Aires on Aerolineas Argentinas, a 1,052-mile flight from São Paulo, just before the July 4 holiday in the states. At the airport, we were greeted with open arms by our hopeful promoter, Daniel Muñoz, a man in his early thirties with longish hair who favored black, trench-coat-style leather coats with jeans. He spoke little English but his assistant, Carlos Schwab, was fluent. Carlos, a young man with a clean-cut, schoolboy appearance, looked like he'd just graduated from high school. They wanted to take us to dinner, an offer we were happy to accept. I had never been in Buenos Aires before, but I did know the place to eat was La Cabaña and after I suggested it, they nodded approvingly.

We drove out of the airport in Daniel's Mercedes. It was around 9:00 p.m. As we raced closer to downtown from the airport superhighway, it became clear that except for the palm trees, Buenos Aires was completely unlike Rio. B.A. was very European in appearance, with wide boulevards and Renaissance buildings that mirrored the architecture of Paris. At night, the arches and boulevards are illuminated and the huge fountains in the center of the city are lit by floodlamps. Daniel stopped first at our hotel so that Tom and I could leave our bags in the room. I got out of the car and started shivering. It was no more than 40 degrees outside. I'd forgotten how much closer we were to the southern tip of the continent than in Brazil, where we were used to balmy, tropical weather even in winter.

The next morning, I opened the door to the meeting room in our hotel. A long banquet table in the center stretched from the door all the way to the bay windows on the opposite side of the room, a distance of about 30 feet. And on both sides of the table were rows of people sitting like delegates at a U.N. negotiating parley. On either side of the table were two dozen young men, all of whom looked to be still in high school, wearing jackets and ties to project a mature image. I thought they might have been a group of Carlos's school pals. We were there to discuss the Kiss tour of Argentina. I'd expected to meet Daniel, Carlos, and a few others about the tour, not this enormous assembled cast.

Carlos did most of the talking for Daniel. The delegates seemed to be present mainly as a backdrop to impress me with the size of Demorcs Producciones, Daniel's organization. It wasn't convincing, though. Like many promoters, particularly in South America then, Daniel was apparently a hustler who from time to time scraped together enough money to stage a small-scale concert. And when enough profits were accumulated and a local reputation was earned, he would strike out and try to lure a major international artist like Kiss to come to his country. But Kiss's faltering finances obligated us to follow up on every possible opportunity even if it mean bargaining with someone like Daniel, who no doubt operated on a shoestring. It was always possible that with enough backers, he could pull off a big show and pay Kiss a few hundred thousand dollars or more which they badly needed to plug holes in their ship. It had happened in Brazil.

Daniel and Carlos came right to the point. Kiss would play three shows at Boca Juniors, a big soccer stadium in the heart of B.A. The tour would be over within ten days and be spread over two weekends. All of the equipment would be supplied locally, except whatever was in Brazil. The Ford Motor Company of Argentina would sponsor the tour, I was told. It all sounded feasible and while the guarantee offered was on the low side, this could be negotiated upward. When we paused in our discussions after a few hours, I took this as a cue to adjourn for lunch. I misread the situation. Daniel placed a contract in front of me. Would I please sign at the bottom? I told him as courteously as I could that I'd be happy to review the contract, and subject to Kiss's approval, we could then go ahead. But right now, it was premature. I had been under the impression that this was a preliminary negotiation.

Yes, my hosts agreed, the negotiation was preliminary. But, they said, it was standard business procedure in Argentina to sign contracts immediately. I politely begged off. It was crystal clear why he wanted a contract, "preliminary" or not, signed by anybody who could be tied to Kiss. It would give his promotion instant credibility and allow him to put tickets on sale, collect an advance from the box office, negotiate a deal with a sponsor, and possibly get financing from private investors as well. But I was so far from committing Kiss to this tour based on one meeting in a hotel room that even to give Daniel a cocktail napkin with my initials on it would have been crazy, even dangerous.

For the next three days that I remained in Argentina, I was hounded day and night by Daniel and Carlos. Tom had come down to inspect the production facilities and the stadium, which I thought was a show of good faith on our part, but that wasn't good enough for them. They wanted a contract now. Today. Immediately. What about signing a letter of intent with a deposit from them at the signing, I countered. That would be, of course, "no problem," but the deposit monies would have to be arranged later, not now. When? "Soon" was the reply. It all started to sound fishy, and Tom and I finally left to fly back to Rio.

Daniel and Carlos hectored me constantly in Rio with phone calls. Sometimes the phone would ring and when I picked it up, there was dead silence. Telexes, many of which were in mangled English and hard to understand, would be slipped under my hotel room door at all hours. A girl I'd met in Buenos Aires, Regina, was visiting me in Rio. She broke into tears, insisting that these people were out to get me. Regina said she'd seen this kind of threatening behavior before in her country. I didn't doubt that she had, but her worries still seemed to me like paranoia.

After a week, the phone calls stopped. An unexpected silence took hold for several weeks. Then I heard from Carlos. He sounded scared out of his mind, his voice quavering and cracking at times. Static kept interrupting the phone conversation. He had to leave his house in B.A. and was calling from a remote region of the countryside where his family had a vacation home. The house where he'd been living had been threatened by bomb scares; he had run away. Daniel had disappeared. No one knew where he was. Terrorists in Argentina had heard about Daniel's plans to bring Kiss to B.A. and were violently opposed. A radical group of commando terrorists were publicly threatening to blow up Boca Juniors if Kiss appeared. They felt that Kiss were degenerates. American sympathies had been with the British in the Falkland Islands dispute, and Kiss, being American, was tainted as pro-British. Carlos's story was hard to swallow, but it wasn't entirely unbelievable. In any case, the Kiss tour of Argentina was now unthinkable.

The Houston Post carried a UPI dispatch on August 5, 1983, with the headline, "Kiss Group Threatened with Third Death Threat," which confirmed the crux of what Carlos had told me. *The New York Post* had Kiss on its front page eight days later with the same story. I had also gotten some information from the chargé d'affaires at the United States Embassy in Buenos Aires which supported the validity of the death threats. I never heard from Carlos, Daniel, or any of his colleagues again. Hopefully, none of them ended up as *desaparecidoes,* the disappeared ones of Argentina's bloody "dirty wars" that rooted out terrorists and their sympathizers.

A few glitches had come up in getting our equipment out of Rio but nothing out of the ordinary, Tom assured me. Days passed. We still hadn't been able to get the gear out of the trucking company's warehouse to be delivered to the airport staging area. I asked Tom if Felippe Rodriguez could help. He never made it to Brazil and Tom told me that he had had a falling out with Junior. I met with our attorneys to make sure we didn't get bogged down in a lot of procedural delays.

More days passed. The glitches had become roadblocks. It was now the second week of July. Tom and I met for drinks in our hotel bar to talk about what was going on. The situation was starting to come into focus. Transportes Fink, the trucking company which was a big outfit like Bekins in the states, hadn't been paid by Junior. And they had Kiss's equipment in their warehouse. Fink wanted to be paid by somebody. At Fink's offices in Rio, the company's general manager told us the gist of his problem. Fink wouldn't admit to it, but they were doing everything possible to frustrate our efforts to take back our equipment until the balance of their bill was paid.

We now had four lawyers working on Kiss's Brazil affair; at the beginning, Manoel Salles was the point man, along with a commercial specialist, Eduardo Henry, who had worked on the pretour arrangements. Now, two other partners, José Cabello Campos and Cassio Portugal, were handling the negotiations. The firm was a prestigious one which represented many U.S. banks doing business in Brazil; many of the partners had studied law at Harvard and New York University. I wrote out a check for $10,000 to get rid of the Fink problem. The lawyers advised me it was the expedient solution; without payment, it could be months before we obtained a court order to release the goods from their warehouse. And that wasn't a sure thing, either. It might go on for years.

Once they had been paid, Fink released the equipment to a customs depot, sort of a way station where goods are stored until they're inspected by customs officials and cleared to leave the country. But then the most serious problem came to light. Now that the equipment had cleared Fink's warehouse, it was ready for inspection. Nothing more was to be taken out than what had come in originally. Brazil is notoriously strict about controlling imports and exports, and goods imported illegally can be confiscated and the owners hit with severe penalties. We had no intention of leaving anything behind, which is what the government tries to protect against, especially technical equipment and products which aren't manufactured in Brazil. The way their custom system works, whoever puts up the bond to bring the goods in for temporary use—like the Kiss shows—has to sign off on the manifest when they're shipped out. The temporary importer was Arteshow, but Junior wasn't signing off on anything.

Press reports, including a big story that ran in the English-language *Brazil Herald* on July 15, stated that Junior had lost $600,000 promoting Kiss. Other accounts pegged his loss at closer to $300,000. Whatever the exact sum, it was big. Junior had badly hurt himself with Kiss in Brazil. The only possible way he could salvage himself would be to hold Kiss's equipment hostage and make a deal with us to get it back.

A technicality in the law gave Junior the power to withhold the release of the gear. It was a loophole big enough to drive a truck through. Unlike most countries in the western world, Brazil didn't use the carnet system to allow goods being used for a temporary period to flow freely into and out of the host country until they're returned to the country of origin. With a carnet, the owner of the goods retains full legal control as long as they're used for the designated purpose and don't exceed their allotted stay in the country. Brazil used temporary import bonds instead. The temporary importer, Arteshow in this case, posts a bond for the goods and controls them while in the host country. Junior had posted the bond and in Brazil, like anywhere else, possession is nine points of the law. Junior would have to pay a steep tax if he kept the equipment, but he could also try and sell it to cover the tax and make a profit. It's not difficult to figure out why Brazil had a temporary import bond system. It can be a windfall in graft and payoffs for customs inspectors who can finagle with the importer to make sure the goods come in and go out on time. The Kiss gear included sound and lighting consoles leased to us along with pyrotechnic equipment, instruments, costumes, and electronics. It was easily worth several hundred thousand dollars.

We were stuck. The deadlock could go on indefinitely. Howard Marks called me a few times while I was in Rio trying to straighten out the mess. He kept saying, "But I thought we had a foolproof contract." No contract is foolproof. The import bond system in Brazil may have been an extreme case, but every country has its own legal quirks. In this case, a promoter who had suffered a financial calamity could take advantage of those quirks.

Cassio Portugal called me each day to update me on any news. On one occasion, I picked up the phone and was told that Junior was threatening to sue Kiss for criminal behavior. He had retained a lawyer to stir up more trouble for us. They allegedly planned to accuse Kiss's technicians of trying to sell equipment while in Brazil, which is illegal.

The lawyers told me that we needed an influential behind-the-scenes operator to play a different kind of role, someone who knew people at customs and who also had connections in the show business world. At that point, Dr. Antonio Adelizzi entered the picture. A stooped, burly man in his fifties, Dr. Adelizzi was a former agent of Brazil's federal police force, similar to our FBI. As is common for practicing barristers, he was always addressed as "Doctor." He knew people at customs and was also the personal attorney of Manoel Poladian, a well-known promoter in Brazil who knew Junior. Dr. Adelizzi would start immediately on our problem.

My biggest fear was that Junior would either attempt to blackmail us into buying back our equipment or he would sell it to another promoter. It had happened before. Years earlier, Earth, Wind & Fire played Brazil and ran into their own equipment problem, I was told. And the Kiss equipment could be a bonanza since most of it couldn't be obtained anywhere in South America. It was also hard figuring out what was going on much of the time since Dr. Adelizzi, now our key negotiator, didn't speak English.

On the advice of the lawyers and the record company, I called a press conference at PolyGram Discos and appeared on the Manchete TV network, hoping to get some public sympathy for our plight. Nothing happened. I asked Cor Van Dijk, managing director of PolyGram in Brazil, if he would enlist his contacts in the local record industry to try and apply some pressure to get Junior to relent. Again, nothing happened. By this time, the cast of characters in Kiss's Brazilian saga had begun to assume *Doctor Zhivago*-like proportions, and managing the relationships with everyone had become an increasingly onerous task. Cor Van Dijk called me at my hotel. It was now the end of July. Between the time I picked up the phone and heard the voice on the other end, there was usually a pause of at least five seconds and a lot of clicks. Rio's phone system wasn't very modern then. Cor told me a sticking point was that Junior had a very good personal relationship with Roberto Carlos, one of Brazil's top singers who sells millions of records. He's a strong competitor to Julio Iglesias in many Latin countries. Junior had promoted some of Roberto's shows and recently he had done a benefit performance for—of all people—the customs inspectors and their wives. It was some kind of annual gala. Cor said someone would have to get to Roberto, a CBS Discos artist, who would get to Junior or, possibly, directly to the customs people to tell Junior to back off. Cor and Dr. Adelizzi were to work out a strategy.

I decided to go back to New York. Howard Marks called me again and told me to wind up whatever I was doing in Rio and "stop running up more bills." Besides, I was becoming a little too well known in Barbarela. I checked out of my beachfront hotel on an overcast and drizzly day, leaving everything in the hands of our small army of attorneys.

The spider's web of intrigue and influence we were caught in didn't start to break apart until the end of August. Things seemed to be progressing, but then another problem cropped up. Junior's prepaid freight contract to return the gear to the states wouldn't be honored by Varig. Supposedly, Varig had not been paid for Kiss's passenger tickets to and from Brazil. Did Varig technically have the right to do that? There were two entirely separate contracts, one for passenger travel and the other for cargo. Kiss was only the recipient of the services and not a party to either agreement. But Varig is the national airline of Brazil and is owned by the government. To try and resolve this in court would take years. From the outset of this dilemma, we wanted to avoid civil litigation, which would be costly and time-consuming, especially since Kiss was booked in Europe in September. We were already putting together a contingency plan to rent equipment in England. We ended up paying Varig for the air cargo under a new contract.

Cassio Portugal called me late one night at my apartment in New York. It was good news. The logjam had cleared. Varig and Fink, the trucking company, were both satisfied. The Kiss equipment could leave the country. All that was left to do was spread some payoffs around at customs and hire a few expediters. After several false starts and stops, the equipment came back to the United States just before Labor Day. I greeted it at JFK when it arrived in the early morning.

Kiss's foray into Brazil had been costly. The unanticipated expenses came to close to $100,000. Still, the tour showed a decent profit for Kiss and provided them with much-needed cash to pay bills that had piled up back home. It was also a big boost for their record sales. According to PolyGram, Kiss's sales in Brazil, the largest market in South America, rose nearly 600 percent in 1983 alone. *Creatures of the Night* sold more copies there than in any country outside of the United States.

A year later, I heard that Junior was promoting small shows in nightclubs in the Copacabana. The Kiss Brazil tour was another case of a promoter betting the ranch on Kiss, this time on the grandest scale ever. And it also turned out to be a historic footnote for Kiss. Brazil was the last tour where Kiss appeared in makeup and costumes for more than a decade.

6 Staying Alive

When I was in the gear, I felt regal, the most beautiful thing on two legs. But when you take a look at the pictures, I look like a dog at birth, pieces hanging down all over the place, grotesque and hideous. I'd say to myself, what kind of girl would want to be with this guy?

Gene Simmons on Kiss's unmasking, quoted in "Give Us a Kiss!" *Creem*, February 1985.

Kiss's decision to unmask was formalized at a meeting at our offices in August 1983. Howard Marks bluntly told Gene and Paul the obvious, that when something isn't working anymore, you have to change it. Kiss had bottomed out as an act. Their most recent albums had sold a few hundred thousand copies each in the states, not the millions of only a few years earlier. There was little discussion; the decision had already been made by Gene and Paul. The debate was about the mechanics of how to do it. The group wanted to avoid slathering the event with hype, which had been their custom, believing that it was no longer a big deal for the press or the public. By trying to pump it up, they would end up looking foolish. Danny Goldberg, their creative consultant, had prodded them into taking off the makeup but cautioned against the usual Kiss-style hoopla.

They were right. More than two years earlier, *Creem* had published an old photo of the group unmasked in their February 1981 issue with a banner headline—"At Last! Kiss Without Their Makeup On! Or: If We Don't Care, Why Should You?" The Kiss makeup gimmick had become a bad joke. A terse press release with a new, unmasked photo of them to accompany their new album would suffice. *Lick It Up* would be released in September, just before the start of the European tour, with a group shot of Kiss in street clothes, standing in front of a plain white background. Michael James Jackson was brought back to produce the record. On September 18, 1983, Kiss unveiled on MTV and premiered their new video, with little fanfare. Danny Goldberg had reportedly gotten MTV to do the promotion by calling in a favor.

The novelty of Kiss without makeup seemed to be the most promising hype the promoters in Europe and England could generate for the Kiss tour that would start in Portugal. Rod MacSween was now booking Kiss overseas. A genial and sharp-witted Englishman who was steeped in the rock music scene, his agency, International Talent Booking, was one of the major rock booking agencies in London. Agents in the United States frequently farm out their artists' foreign tours, particularly Europe and England, to agencies abroad who have the expertise in dealing with promoters in many countries. Rod, with his mop-top haircut, was a type you expect to find next to you at a local pub for a chat. He told us England and Scandinavia would do big business in the arenas but Germany, Spain, France, and the Benelux countries would be fair to middling.

Portugal reminded everyone of Brazil. It wasn't just the tropical climate, with warm, rainy cloudbursts quickly cooling down the cobbled streets and flagstones that had been scorched in the sunlight. And it wasn't only the common language, although Portuguese spoken in Portugal is more melodic and less harsh-sounding than in Brazil. It was the primitive conditions we were working in, especially at the venue in the environs of Lisbon. Our production manager, Tom Marzullo, put it best—"If I'm with Kiss, I must be in the Third World." We weren't, but it certainly looked it from outward appearances. It was early October and we were playing another hellhole.

Outside Lisbon, Kiss was booked in the boondocks in the Sports Palais, an aging arena nestled in leafy vegetation and enshrouded by palm trees. We had to push back the start of the European tour until the equipment came back from Rio. The mixed memories of Brazil were still vividly etched in my mind when we arrived. Driving through the sun-bleached hills and along the curving coastline of nearby Estoril, a seaside casino resort, I saw Kiss posters tacked up everywhere. Twisted alleyways and the weather-beaten stone walls of buildings were used as billboards for huge Kiss logos pasted on the sides, scores of them linked together, creating an almost hypnotic pattern. The massive postering, commonly used for promotions in Europe, gave the Kiss show a high profile.

But there was a big difference now—Kiss had unmasked. Kiss had nowhere else to go. They could hardly make a living playing stadiums in Rio and São Paulo and parading around in makeup and costumes in the states, looking like a nostalgia act from the '70s. No matter how faithfully they cultivated their old fans with the raw sound and high-energy shows that had made them famous, the makeup and costumes weren't working anymore. We got off to a rocky start in Portugal, but taking off the makeup did create press interest in Kiss and helped to sell tickets for most of their tour dates.

By the end of November, Kiss was back on tour in the United States. Reaction was lukewarm. The shows were hit or miss. Some traditionally strong cities like Cleveland and Detroit did well and others died. It was becoming a skull and crossbones tour, with promoters taking Kiss shows as favors to ATI to maintain their standing with the agency. The agency ploy of pressuring promoters to book acts they don't want—expected losers like Kiss in 1982 and 1983—in order to make sure they'll get to book a money-making act when one becomes available for shows in their market, is standard practice. Most of the promoters had made money with Kiss in their heyday and now it was time to call in a few markers to keep the tour alive. Kiss was cashing in their chips at every turn and promoters were buckling under to pressure from ATI. It was payback time.

Bill Graham had originally booked Kiss into the Civic Auditorium in San Francisco in February 1984. The tour before, still in makeup, the group had a strong showing. But advance sales for the current show were so abysmal that he switched venues and moved Kiss into the Berkeley Community Theater, a small hall normally played by dance troupes and folk singers. I asked Gene how he would explain to the press why Kiss was performing in such a small venue. "We'll just say that the big halls weren't available," was his response.

Radio commercials played up the novelty factor of Kiss without makeup and costumes, announcing that Kiss was "coming to town and taking off the greasepaint." It had a cheap ring to it. It certainly didn't sound big and by this time, it wasn't even interesting. Four years earlier, Kiss unmasking would have been promoted as a three-ring circus in every city. Now, it was just a tag line in a commercial. We had heard that Bill Aucoin, no longer the manager, felt Kiss was going about it in an uninspired and indifferent manner, but the reality was there was very little public interest. Apart from an occasional flurry of gossip about their love lives, Kiss had fallen into a black hole of media nonexistence.

Paul was the most relieved about taking off the makeup and costumes. It was like having a weight lifted from his shoulders, he told me. The makeup routine had become a tiresome ritual and the costumes with all of their accoutrements were like stepping into a suit of armor each night. It had become confining, mentally and physically. Paul was the most self-conscious about the image, particularly since Kiss was no longer in their early twenties. The old Kiss persona had now become silly, especially since the gimmick had worn itself out on a business level.

Gene seemed unsure about his new stage role without his monster getup. He joked in a meeting before the tour began that he would feel naked without it. The disguise had become his alter ego. He wondered aloud what he was going to do in his new outfit "wearing a three-piece suit" instead of portraying a living gargoyle. It took Gene a long time to adapt to not being the center of attention on stage; Paul would now fill that role. Gene had to learn how not to play the monster role—growling, grimacing, prancing, and behaving like a menace on the loose. He was now the bass player and back-up singer.

Paul had been anxious to get rid of the makeup and stage costumes, believing that the "music was strong enough to carry us through." Gene was equally emphatic, telling *Billboard* in its October 15, 1983, story on Kiss's unmasking that "Our calling card is our music." Oddly, there was never much talk about what would fill the void. Kiss's success had for years been based not just on the makeup gimmick but on their overpowering stage show with all the pyrotechnics and their role-playing as a personality group. Ace and Peter were replaced by excellent musicians, but the new additions were afforded few opportunities to promote themselves in the press. When we first set up the stage gear in England for the tour, Paul thought the new drum riser looked like an oversized cigarette filter with stripes on the side; it was hardly on the Super Kiss scale. Getting by strictly on the music seemed like wishful thinking, considering how Kiss had built their reputation.

The *Lick It Up* tour went on the road in the United States with a downsized production, a far cry from the spectacle of the '70s. There was much less of everything. The craziness and lunacy had disappeared from the tour since Peter and Ace had left and Kiss no longer had the wherewithal to support their trademark special effects and lavish production elements. The platoons of technicians, bodyguards, and schedulers weren't around anymore, either.

Fan interest in Kiss without makeup wasn't overwhelming, judging by the crowds we were drawing each night. Paul joked with me on the road that Kiss had become a "brain dead tour." They were going through the motions of performing with very little enthusiasm from the audience or the promoters. Paul was a terrific mimic and I often split my sides watching him do impressions of hapless promoters with nooses around their necks, suffering the grim consequences of booking a brain dead Kiss tour. By New Year's Eve in Jacksonville, Florida, it was body dead as well. Less than 3,000 people showed up in the 10,000-seat Coliseum and the arena looked like a nearly-empty airplane hangar.

Promoters are jammed by the agents to take the cream along with the sour milk. When an act can't sell tickets and the show loses a bundle, the promoter complains to the agency about how badly he was "beaten up." Typically, they ask the agency to negotiate a retroactive reduction in the guarantee for the show. Shows where the promoter really took a beating are described by agents as dates where "a lot of blood was spilled." There was a lot of blood spilled on the Kiss tour.

Booking agencies prey upon the paranoia and weaknesses of some promoters and engage in a kind of perverse psychological game. The promoters are paranoid about not playing ball with the agency, fearing that their phone will stop ringing and they'll be out of the concert business. Agencies fear losing clients. If they can't impress the artist and the manager with big offers coming down the pike from gullible promoters, the artist may decide not to tour or, worse, switch agencies when their contract expires. Big agencies have high overheads and need to hang on to as many artists as possible, sometimes hundreds. Top acts seldom work more than one major tour every two or three years, sometimes even less often. Agencies have to keep scores of acts working all the time, even marginal earners. The big agencies run a volume business like a mass-production operation—getting hall availabilities from promoters and facilities, plotting the open dates on routing sheets, checking travel logistics, negotiating terms with buyers—and without continuous cash flow from commissions year round, they can't stay in business.

Money problems were pinching the Kiss operation. Eric and Vinnie, Kiss's employee musicians, had to take salary cuts. Their combined annual salaries were chopped in half. Replacing Peter and Ace had been an additional, though unavoidable, expense. Until early 1983, the two original Kiss partners were drawing out monies for personal living expenses while Kiss footed the bill for their replacements. *Creatures of the Night* had run up a whopping bill to produce, partly inflated from flying in guitarists from around the country to audition for Ace's job. Since the Phonogram renegotiation, the album advances were sharply cut down and back catalogue sales had diminished.

And now Ace had to be paid off. He had officially left Kiss by this time, a fact made clear when Vinnie appeared on the *Lick It Up* album cover. The terms of his leaving Kiss had previously been negotiated. In March 1983, Ace received an advance against his share of the royalties for past work, to be accounted for twice yearly. Things were so tight that Ace's advance had to be spread out over twelve months and the accountings were always late. Over the next few years, he would receive additional payments for past royalties. Eric and Vinnie didn't share in the advances or the record royalties; if they co-wrote a song, they would get their share of the songwriters' royalties.

Merchandising proved to be the short-term solution to Kiss's money crunch. Larry Kravetz, who did the *Creatures of the Night* tour, originally had a deal to do Kiss's next tour, *Lick It Up*. While in Madrid with the group in October 1983, Howard Marks called me to ask if I knew whether Kiss had signed another contract with Larry. Nobody had actually signed anything, although a contract had been negotiated. The *Lick It Up* tour would start the following month in the states. Howard told me that Winterland Productions, the largest merchandiser in the United States, founded by rock impresario Bill Graham, had dangled in front of him a $350,000 advance for the rights to the Kiss tour. The offer had come to him through Jeff Franklin of ATI, a friend of Dell Furano, Winterland's head. Winterland was gambling that the anticipated lure of Kiss taking off their makeup and costumes would enable them to recoup their advance. Most likely, Kiss would stay on tour for at least fifty to seventy-five shows, increasing their chances. At worst, Winterland could recoup on a subsequent tour after *Lick It Up*. Howard grabbed the offer. Whatever we planned to do with Larry Kravetz would have to be scuttled; Kiss desperately needed the dough. "We'll just have to take our chances down the road in court with Larry," Howard said.

Small operators like Larry Kravetz were being squeezed out of the business by the giants who could offer big advances to artists and produce the merchandise for much less since they handled many acts throughout the year. Larry wasn't able to come close to matching Winterland's offer and claimed he hadn't fully recouped his $250,000 advance from the *Creatures of the Night* tour.*

Jeff Franklin's initiative would earn him a 10 percent commission for his role as an intermediary. In future years, as the deal between Kiss and Winterland was renewed, it would prove to be a very lucrative arrangement for him. Jeff had established himself as a deal maker in the music industry and had many interests, including Riva Records, the original label for John Cougar Mellencamp and for which Rod Stewart also recorded albums. Riva Records was eventually sold to PolyGram. Jeff had also been a middleman and equity owner in putting Neil Bogart and Casablanca together with PolyGram. Jeff's booking agency and his financial interests in record deals, music publishing, TV, and a chain of record stores enabled him to buy an enormous estate on several hundred acres of farmland in upstate New York and an Upper East Side townhouse. A stretch limo chauffered by a personal aide shuttled him around town. Jeff was never reticent about reminding you of his deal-making acumen.

By the end of the *Lick It Up* tour, Vinnie Vincent was on his way out as the lead guitarist for Kiss. He had had a falling out with Gene and Paul over his salary, and had asked Kiss for a better deal. Despite Vinnie's talent as a prolific songwriter and a musician, Gene and Paul had had enough and he was fired. There had always been friction between Vinnie and Gene and Paul, and Vinnie had often carped about his contract and his working conditions. Vinnie was justified in complaining about at least one of those conditions. When Kiss brought him from his home in L.A. to New York to work on the *Lick It Up* record, we scrimped on his lodging expenses by putting him up at a crummy hotel in midtown Manhattan. It was a rundown place, frequented by hookers who paid a weekly rate, with a lobby that stank of rancid cooking odors from the adjoining coffee shop. Vinnie hated the place, calling it a "mutant hotel" because of the weird-looking clientele who congregated in the lobby each night. We moved him to another hotel. Mark Norton, renamed Mark St. John, an L.A. session player and guitar tutor, replaced Vinnie.

Lick It Up quickly went gold, and an award ceremony was organized backstage at the Long Beach Arena in California in late January 1984. Kiss posed for photos with their producer, Michael James Jackson. Later, Gene confided that he felt a little uncomfortable with Michael in the picture, who was short-haired and slender with steel-framed glasses and had been conservatively dressed in a knobby sweater and flannel slacks. "He's not rock 'n' roll looking," said Gene,

---

* Court records. *Rock Tours, Ltd. v. Kiss and Kiss Organization, Ltd.* (1984), 84 Civ. 0011, U.S. District Court, Southern District of New York.

"and some kid picking up *Billboard* might get the wrong impression about Kiss. Kids expect to see us with people who look really rock 'n' roll." I asked Gene what was so "rock 'n' roll looking" about Eddie Kramer, who produced all of Kiss's live records. "At least he had a Vandyke beard," Gene said.

The arithmetic of the record business worked against Kiss despite a gold album, no great shakes for a group that once had the chutzpah to release an album with the title *Double Platinum.* If their advance was recouped, Kiss would be able to collect additional royalties from their record company, assuming their royalty account wasn't in a deficit position.

But Kiss was a long way from getting any more money from Phonogram. Kiss's account had been in arrears since 1980, owing to the unrecouped advances, then $2 million each, for *Unmasked, (Music From) The Elder, Creatures of the Night,* and now, *Lick it Up,* at a lower rate. Kiss was millions of dollars in the hole with Phonogram and would need a lucky streak to dig themselves out. Income from song publishing had shrunk since Vinnie Vincent had co-written eight of *Lick It Up's* ten tracks. The gross profit on the album would quickly disappear when recording costs, overhead, and other expenses were deducted.

Kiss was sitting on top of a cliff. The *Lick It Up* tour was a break-even proposition and once the tour ended in early spring of 1984, their cash flow had dried up. They managed to slog through fifty-eight shows, in large part as a result of ATI's deftness at jamming promoters. But the group needed money fast. Carl Glickman had previously arranged short-term financing through his Cleveland banking connections, but we now had to find another source. A bank in Louisville, Kentucky, was proposed by Dick Weidenbaum, Kiss's accountant; they wanted to get into the business of entertainment financing. The Louisville bank loaned Kiss several hundred thousand dollars until the next album was finished. Kiss and PolyGram's New York office exchanged papers with the bank, pledging the group's recording contract and the master tapes for the new album as collateral for the loan. More money was raised when Kiss sold a parcel of industrial property in Cincinnati and the proceeds were used to prop up their hobbled finances.

With money in the till from the Kentucky bank loan and the Cincinnati land sale, Kiss released a new album, *Animalize,* in September 1984. It reached #19 in *Billboard* and quickly sold over 1 million copies in the United States, the biggest Kiss record in years. Its success was strong confirmation of the wisdom of the group's decision to abandon the makeup and costumes. With a Top Twenty album, more shows could be booked on a U.S. tour. Another tour of England and Europe was planned first.

In Brighton, England, a faded down-at-the-heels seaside community with a long boardwalk running for miles along the English Channel beach, Gene and Paul grilled Rod MacSween, their booking agent, as to why the ticket counts were so meager. We were backstage as the group was getting ready for the show. A busty girl in braided hair with a thick German accent who was hanging around said she was surprised that for "zuch a beeg groop zere vas zo little people." Danny Betesh, a veteran English promoter, was also surprised. He'd done very well on the '83 tour and was now looking at a big loss for Kiss's dates in England and Scotland. Rod couldn't explain it except for the obvious reason—unlike the previous year, there was no novelty factor like taking the makeup off for the first time. Record sales in England were average. Kiss was a silver act, selling well under 100,000 albums with each new release. Paul pointedly asked Rod, "Well, doctor, what's the cure?" There wasn't any. While Kiss could once play the press like a violin and sell gobs of tickets, there wasn't much Kiss could play up anymore. Music papers like *Melody Maker* and *Kerrang!* reported on Kiss but the group was no longer big news.

The Phonogram people assigned to work with Kiss on their press and promotions changed with each tour. Most of them were based in London. As Kiss's popularity declined from their highwater mark in '80, so did the apparent seniority of the record company people working with us. Paul joked about their junior status. "By the next tour, we'll be greeted at the airport by schoolboys in short pants with Phonogram logos on their blazers," he said to me as we rode together to the next show on the schedule in the U.K.

Germany was looking gloomy. I'd been on vacation in Monte Carlo before the tour started when our German promoters, Ossi Hoppe and Tony Joannou, called me at the Hôtel de Paris. Tony had left the employ of our previous German promoter, and was now Ossi's partner. I was in the domed saltwater swimming pool. The phone rang at the patio bar while I was in the water, trying to unclog my arteries from the gastronomic excesses of the previous night's dinner. The attendant put the extension phone down next to my chaise lounge. It was Tony on the line. He told me ticket sales were poor in many of the cities and Kiss would have to cut their guarantee or skip those cities. Otherwise, they'd have no choice but to cancel the tour and pull out. Their company, Top Concerts, wasn't a big outfit and I doubted they could sustain taking a big loss on Kiss. I called Howard Marks in New York and we agreed it was better to play and get some money as opposed to not playing and getting no money. With Kiss barely able to make supplier payments each week to keep the tour on the road, pragmatism took precedence over principle. The tour was already booked and Kiss would be there regardless.

By the time we reached the midpoint of the tour in England, Kiss was strapped. Concert earnings were mostly puny and Winterland's latest merchandising advance was spent paying Kiss's bills. We had to get Phonogram to kick in some money, otherwise we might not be able to finish the tour. Mathieu Vansweevelt had recently taken over the day-to-day operation of the pop music division of the company from Aart Dalhuisen, who had been promoted to a senior post. Mathieu would be coming to see one of the Kiss shows in northern England and it would be the ideal opportunity for me to buttonhole him for an advance. Howard Marks wanted me to ask for $100,000, but I told him we would just get laughed at.

I met Mathieu in his hotel room soon after he arrived. He was in his late thirties, with neatly combed thinning brown hair, and was wearing slacks, slip-ons, and a cable-knit sweater. Basically, it was a shakedown and I tried to finesse it as much as I could, explaining Kiss's problem as a "short-term cash-flow reversal." Mathieu was gracious about helping Kiss with their problem and agreed to an advance, which he would arrange the next day. It was an embarrassing reversal of fortune. Four years earlier in Europe, Kiss was on a spending rampage, keeping a fleet of Daimler limos on 24-hour call, staying in royal suites at the poshest hotels, and flying around a traveling squad of handlers and bodyguards to make sure they got to the gigs on time. By 1984, we were begging the record company for a few crumbs in order to pay our suppliers' bills and keep the tour from sputtering to a halt.

With Phonogram's help and our suppliers' willingness to play ball and let us stretch out their payments, Kiss was able to press on. The band was never crazy about playing Europe, except for England. Many of the venues were then antediluvian relics, outdated and impractical for shows with lots of equipment. In some of the theaters, everything had to be carted up several flights of winding, cramped stairways backstage where there weren't any lifts. Outside the U.K., the changes in language and customs from country to country, sometimes daily, became increasingly annoying to Gene and Paul, who preferred a more homogenized culture.

On both the '83 and '84 tours Kiss was often booked in places far off the beaten track in order to pack enough dates into the itinerary to make the trips economical. Out-of-the-way places like Sindelfingen, Germany; Lund, Sweden; Aarhus, Denmark; St. Austell, England; Clermont-Ferrand, France; and Oulu, Finland were typically on the schedule. Aarhus was a port town where the hotel offered its guests the convenience of an on-premises club filled with local prostitutes. They worked there regularly and shuffled between the bar adjacent to the lobby and guests' hotel rooms.

In Oulu, a small city sitting on a frozen block of tundra about 100 miles south of the Arctic Circle, an enormous subterranean nightclub was built under the city's major hotel. It was clearly a popular spot for locals. On weekends, the nightclub and its multiple bars and dance floors were standing room only, with hundreds of people tottering around drunk, some collapsing on the floor. Alcohol is often used to cope with the icy Nordic climate and the months of perpetual darkness in that part of the world.

The last stop in Paris in November 1984 brought good news from the home front. It was nearly midnight when Jules Belkin, a key promoter in the midwest, tracked me down in the lobby of our hotel, the Meurice. Kiss had just returned from Le Zenith, the big tent-topped venue where they'd played, and I was sitting with Paul and some stragglers from the show. Two young girls, vampish in their low-cut pullovers shorn of sleeves and shiny black hose, were making small talk in halting English. I took Jules's phone call at the reception desk. He asked me what I was doing in the lobby at midnight and I told him, naturally, working overtime. Kiss had gone on sale in Detroit and Cleveland and both were doing well, he told me. He wanted to add more shows in secondary markets like Dayton and Toledo. It was a good sign. Jules is a cautious man who wouldn't stick his neck out too far unless he smelled money. He had started promoting shows in the mid-'60s while running a family business in men's clothing. I told Paul the news. He was thrilled. At least a few of the upcoming shows would do well.

Kiss began their *Animalize* tour in the states right after Europe. The novelty of Kiss without makeup and costume had worn off by now. Reviewers also picked up on the tiredness that had become apparent in the Kiss formula. Kiss drew only 7,000 to the Atlanta Omni, less than half a house, and the *Atlanta Constitution* wrote in its January 10, 1985, review that "Kiss has lost some of its ticket-selling power and seems to be just holding its own in the musical marketplace."

Despite their improved musicianship and a new lineup that produced a tighter, crisper sound than the Super Kiss shows, which often sounded as if they were filtered through a cement mixer, attendance remained spotty. Crowds would range from 2,500 one night to 10,000 the next. Concert earnings were also on a seesaw.

The *Animalize* album, despite its strong showing, wasn't enough for a knock-out tour. Gene always asked me what the attendance was at the shows just before he went on stage. One night I told him the show had really done well, that Kiss had sold over 7,000 tickets in the 10,000-seat arena. "Woop-de-fucking-do," he replied sarcastically, turning to Paul who was standing beside him, ready for the cue to take the stage. "It just shows you how warped things have gotten," Gene said. "Now I'm supposed to get excited about 7,000 tickets being sold. Before, we'd sell out the place and not even get excited about it." Paul, grim-faced, nodded his head slightly.

Gene and Paul's perpetual lament about the mediocre attendance was that the promoters didn't advertise enough, but this is a common complaint from artists. As in any business, some promoters do a better job than others. The more aggressive and imaginative ones did actually promote, creating contests and campaigns to make the Kiss show stand out in their market. Others just ran a batch of commercials on the usual rock radio stations, crossed their fingers, and hoped for the best. There are a lot of variables determining why some shows do well and others bomb. Competition for Kiss's audience from other heavy metal bands like AC/DC, Whitesnake, Iron Maiden, or Def Leppard cut into ticket sales. Other events, including sports, movies, and school functions, can take priority for the entertainment dollar. But Kiss had an additional problem. As one fan put it, the group just wasn't "special" anymore.

Eric Carr had comfortably settled in as the drummer in the group by now. Eric's professional experience had been limited to local bands before joining Kiss in 1980. He'd made his living repairing ovens and other odd jobs. Eric was quite a musical talent, enhancing the band's sound with his mastery of intricate rhythms and metronome-perfect beats. He was 30 when he joined the group but looked far younger. Short, trim, with bulging biceps and large hands, Eric had an enormous mat of frizzy black hair that sprouted from his head forming what looked like a giant helmet. His small facial features seemed to disappear when you saw him from a distance. All you could make out was this huge mass of hair atop the shoulders of his body. Even for Kiss, it was too much hair. Eric was constantly chided about getting haircuts. Paul said he looked like a walking Smurf doll.

Eric was a likable and easygoing guy. His vices were limited to things like margaritas and Harvey Wallbangers, pretty tame stuff compared to Ace and Peter. But Eric revealed some quirks of behavior that suggested a more troubled soul beneath the surface. He had apparently had several anxiety attacks from dealing with Gene and Paul, whom he found overbearing and intimidating. At times, he would get so upset that he went into seclusion for days. At the Mardi Gras in 1983, Eric was invited to a slew of parties and events. He spent the three days we were in New Orleans sequestered in his room at the Royal Orleans with the windows covered and the curtains drawn. When one of the other band members stopped by his room to try and coax him out, Eric, I was told, answered the door stark naked except for a pair of sunglasses. He wanted to be alone.

When Eric first joined Kiss, his longtime girlfriend, Pantera, a Donna Summer look-alike, was a singer in a local band in Brooklyn. Eric stuck by her and tried to promote her group. He was guilt-ridden about having made it into the big time with Kiss while Pantera was still struggling, and this eventually created a rift. He went to great expense to furnish and decorate a spacious apartment for the two of them in Greenwich Village, but they were destined to live there only a short time. They soon split.

Once Pantera was no longer in the picture, Bambi entered his life. Still in her teens when she met Eric, Bambi had a body that would stop traffic. Eric and Bambi stayed together for years but eventually parted ways. Paul tried to introduce Eric to other women, but met with little success. Eric began to spend a lot of time in L.A. and was pulled into the local music orbit, frequenting rock clubs like The Rainbow on Sunset Strip, then a watering hole for musicians and groupies.

His relationship with Paul and Gene became somewhat strained. He felt that he was never accepted as an equal, even after years of performing with Kiss and hearing their unstinting praise of his musical prowess. Eric felt that Gene and Paul kept him in his place. For their part, Gene and Paul liked Eric very much but found him to be immature and unable to make a creative contribution to Kiss beyond the solid musicianship for which he was hired. Eric relished playing drums and being a part of a famous rock group, but he was often unhappy about what he thought was a demeaning role, that of a supporting player.

A tempting offer was received in 1985 for Kiss to appear in Sun City, the resort complex in South Africa. Many top American and British entertainers had performed there and Sun City wanted Kiss to do a series of shows. They were willing to pay all expenses and a fee of $800,000. It would have been a windfall for Kiss but South Africa in general and Sun City in particular had a kind of pariah status at the time. Sun City was located in a racially integrated homeland territory known as Bophuthatswana, but some critics charged that it was a sham state, controlled de facto by the white minority government. Gene and Paul balked. Howard Marks tried to persuade them to go—only because they needed the money so badly—but his approach wasn't very convincing. He said he'd talked with Frank Sinatra's attorney, Mickey Rudin. Sinatra had performed in Sun City. Supposedly, his attorney had made an inspection trip on Sinatra's behalf before agreeing to do the shows there. Gene and Paul weren't overly impressed by this endorsement and it wasn't enough to sway their opinion in light of the brouhaha in the press then about racial turmoil in South Africa. Howard tried another tack, contacting the State Department to find out if Sun City was "safe," in other words, not listed as a country U.S. citizens were cautioned about visiting because of possible dangers to their physical safety. He assured Kiss that the State Department said Sun City was "totally safe." Safety, however, had never been the issue. The tour never took place.

In a strange twist of events, Kiss was now going back to ICM. We were on tour when it happened and Paul greeted me with the news, not yet made public, while checking out of the Hilton in Midland, Texas—"We're working for ICM now." In February 1985, it was announced that Jeff Franklin had sold ATI to ICM. He wanted to get out of the booking agency business and ICM needed rock acts, which ATI had plenty of. ATI's roster of eight-eight artists included Kiss, the Cars, Neil Young, Rush, and John Cougar Mellencamp.

Some of ICM's top acts and agents were defecting to Creative Artists Agency, then an upstart West Coast talent agency that had recently started a music division. ATI's acts, which toured regularly, would bolster ICM's market share. Jeff was also expanding his ATI Video Enterprises unit which had been soaking up cash generated from the booking operation. Jeff would remain a consultant to ICM to help shepherd acts like Kiss with whom he had a relationship. He was then devoting much of his effort to the video company, producing music programs for TV including *Night Flight,* seen for years on the USA Network. *Night Flight* aired from 11 p.m. to 7 a.m. on Friday and Saturday and featured a diverse mix of music, films, and comedy.

By mid-1985, Kiss was off the road. Despite the hard work and dedication to rebuilding their base of fans, it was like climbing a slippery slope. Amassing any significant amount of money from this string of back-to-back tours and albums was next to impossible.

Money was tight. Kiss's income was now half of what it had been, and most of it continued to be eaten up by personal living expenses, touring, recording, and overhead. All of these costs had been slashed, but Kiss had grown used to running their business when much greater sums were coming in. Spending was still high. Business reverses and sagging sales caused income to tumble and earnings to evaporate.

Unpaid bills kept coming out of the woodwork. At one point, huge amounts of bills had stacked up, with payments due suppliers, vendors, and outside royalty participants like songwriters and producers. Our office was fielding phone calls daily from angry creditors. Producer Michael James Jackson was owed royalties from the albums he worked on and hadn't received any royalty checks for nearly a year. Fearful that Kiss might go under, he reportedly filed suit demanding payment.

Claims from the laser company which provided the ill-fated system from the '79 tour were made against Kiss; they claimed that the laser system had worked and Kiss was therefore in breach of contract. A production supplier, which had its equipment on tour in Brazil, sued Kiss. They claimed lost revenues when they couldn't rent their gear to other customers since it was stuck in Brazil for two months.

Vinnie Vincent, the ex-guitarist, was owed songwriter's royalties from Kiss. He managed to gum up the works when his lawyer succeeded in blocking payments from PolyGram to Kiss (for publishing monies) and from ASCAP to Kiss (for performing rights royalties) until the dispute was settled. And Larry Kravetz, Kiss's former merchandiser, sued, claiming he was shafted when Kiss gave the 1983–1984 *Lick It Up* tour to Winterland.

Another key figure from the past returned who had to be reckoned with. Bill Aucoin was owed his percentage from Kiss's record royalties and publishing monies produced during his years as manager. His settlement agreement with Kiss in 1982 paid him a series of advances until 1983. Because of Kiss's shaky finances, he hadn't been paid anything since then. Bill was having money problems of his own, having gone through the staggering sums that he had earned from Kiss since he first began as manager. Bill agreed to have his interest bought out for a one-time payment. In exchange, he would release Kiss from any further obligations to him. By 1986, Bill was paid off and out of the picture.

Bill had just gone through another incredible rise and fall. Following his breakup with Kiss, he became the manager of British singer Billy Idol, an unknown in America who was living in New York. Bill Aucoin skillfully found a niche for Billy Idol, an artist whose visual appeal and musical style were rooted in heavy metal rock but whose records had a strong dance beat with pulsating rhythm tracks. Billy Idol's platinum hair, clenched fist, and sneering rictus meshed perfectly with his stage outfits of leather and chains. With dance music hitting the top of the charts in the mid-80's and heavy metal acts storming through every arena in the United States, Billy Idol became a sensation. He was soon selling millions of records, headlining tours of his own, and was a fixture on MTV. But Billy Idol eventually decided to change managers and bring in a new team of advisers. His father came over from England to help do a house-cleaning while Billy Idol relocated to L.A. Despite his success with Billy Idol, Bill Aucoin was soon gone from the scene. Now, with the settlement from Kiss, he was back at the beginning for the third time.

Changes were under way at ICM. Marsha Vlasic, an ICM agent who'd started with ATI and was one of the few women agents in the music business, would book the Kiss tour. Jeff Franklin introduced her to Howard at our office and everyone was pleased with the new arrangement. Howard soon kicked off the relationship by taking Marsha to lunch at Arcadia, a chic restaurant on East 62nd Street known for its luxury-class club sandwich of homemade brioche chock full of morsels of Maine lobster. It would be a short honeymoon, though.

Bill Elson, the top agent in charge of rock bookings at ICM, was one of the more astute agents in the business. He had long since sized up Kiss's situation in the marketplace. Kiss couldn't understand why other '70s groups like Aerosmith who were back on the road at the same time as Kiss were doing twice the business. As Bill put it, "Aerosmith never had an image problem; Kiss does." Aerosmith had maintained a consistent image as a hard rock band with a raunchy edge and a blues-based sound. Kiss had swung wildly—from hard rock with a striking image created by makeup and costumes, to pop rock/disco with progressively outlandish makeup and costumes, to a mystical image, complete with rock opera and mythic vision, and now back to hard rock, but this time with no makeup and costumes. And half of the original band had been replaced. Kiss had successfully promoted themselves for years as a personality group, but the personalities were now constantly changing. The originals were retiring and the replacements were continually reshuffled. In private, everyone in Kiss joked about needing a scorecard to keep track of who was in the band.

Kiss's continual transmogrifications became too hard to digest, particularly for the fickle youth market. The image was now convoluted and the fans had become confused by all the changes. Kiss had initially seared a powerful image in the public consciousness. But once an image is established, it's no easy feat to blot out the old one and replace it with a new one. In trying to create new images that they deemed more suitable, Kiss had fallen into their own credibility gap.

Howard Marks proved to be a Merlin in keeping the bill collectors at bay and stalling for time. On the strength of *Animalize,* which by 1985 was at over 1.3 million copies in the United States, he was able to get some improvements in Kiss's record contract. There was also the hope of a long-term deal with Winterland. The theory was that as long as Kiss kept working, things could turn around for them. It was a longshot that Kiss would hit the jackpot with a multi-million-selling album or a sold-out arena tour, but it was likely they would tour and deliver a new album each year that sold in the million-unit range. Record companies need steady product flow to fill their distribution pipeline and move back catalogue, and merchandisers need mid-level acts to generate operating income for their business. With superstars only delivering albums every two or three years, some even less often, Kiss could produce two or three albums in the same period and play at least 50 to 100 shows with each new release. The economics worked in their favor.

PolyGram, which had now taken over the responsibility for Kiss's Phonogram contract, would increase Kiss's advances on new albums. Howard was also able to get PolyGram to pay Kiss a big bonus, really an advance on a future series of advances, with no interest charged. Winterland came up with another sizable advance. While Kiss struggled to get out of their cash bind, PolyGram and Winterland became their Household Finance Corporation, a revolving credit plan of loans and advances.

The stacks of unpaid bills were eventually cleared up and most of the lawsuits were settled. Larry Kravetz went to court concerning his merchandising contract but lost. Michael James Jackson received his producer's royalties. Vinnie Vincent was paid back-due royalties, but future monies would be paid to him directly by PolyGram. Paul's electric bill was also paid. (Our office had slipped up. So many bills had been due that Paul's Con Ed bill had been lost in the pile. When Paul came back from an out-of-town trip, his apartment was pitch-black. We put him up for the night at the Parker Meridien Hotel.) Kiss's warehouse bill—where they stored their stage gear and costumes—was also taken care of.

Kiss's investments had been a mixed bag. Their windfall earnings between 1977 and 1981 enabled them to invest millions, but after 1981 there was little cash available to invest. Some of the early investments produced spectacular returns. An oil drilling partnership went public and the original partners, including Kiss, reaped huge profits when their interests were converted to shares on the American Stock Exchange. An interest in an office building in the Gramercy Park section of Manhattan, bought before rents began to spiral upward, was also a big success. Another oil deal was purchased as the price of oil was peaking in 1981. It showed good returns for years but as the price of oil plummeted around the world, the company shut down operations. An apartment complex in Baton Rouge, Louisiana, went under due to high vacancy rates when the oil glut in the south forced many oil companies to lay off workers. Another apartment building in Jacksonville, Florida, suffered a similar fate when market conditions for rentals soured.

The profits from the winning investments in oil and real estate were, for the most part, used to pay for Kiss's homes and apartments and to plow back into the business to keep it running once the shortfalls began to occur. But events had finally caught up with Kiss.

The coal investment from the late 1970s was something that no one liked to talk about in polite company. I had asked Carl and Howard over the years why we just didn't write it off and take the investment off the books. A sullen look would come over their faces, followed by dead silence. The problem was that the value of the investment as a tax shelter had been used up. The coal mines themselves were now of dubious value since the boom in coal exploration had come and gone. In other words, the investment was worthless. After a while, I stopped bringing up the subject. But I always had the dreaded feeling that it was a ticking time bomb.

Even the luckiest and most savvy investors don't hit a bull's-eye each time. Huge profits can be generated from a few deals, so that the clunkers don't matter. Kiss's problems would have been correctable over time if they had been able to keep their original Phonogram deal intact and Ace had stayed in the band. But years of spending every dollar that came in left the group with little more than tax shelter investments, whose value was exhausted. And Kiss's succession of image makeovers, musical shifts, and new members coming and going produced a zigzag pattern of record and ticket sales and shriveling income. Kiss's super-rich image, a reality in the late 1970s, had become a mirage by the mid-'80s.

By the fall of 1985, *Asylum*, Kiss's follow-up to *Animalize*, was released. *Asylum* initially failed to reach platinum status, and overseas sales, even with the much vaunted Phonogram distribution system, would only total in the mid-six figures. Kiss had a new guitarist, their third since Ace left. Bruce Kulick, 32, a New Yorker, was hired after Mark St. John, a lightning-fast guitar player, contracted a rare arthritic ailment which hampered his playing. Kiss was forced to let him go. Bruce was an experienced studio session player who had been in several bands. His brother, Bob, also a session guitarist, was friendly with Gene and Paul and had worked with Kiss on previous studio albums.

Promoters continued to take chances on Kiss. One of Kiss's promoters from the early days, Dave Lucas, stepped up to the plate to promote a Kiss show in San Juan, Puerto Rico, in January 1986. Although his home base was Indiana, Dave had branched out to find new markets and was working with a local impresario in San Juan. I warned Dave not to take the show as the costs and uncertainties were too great, especially with all the air cargo and travel costs he'd have to absorb. We already had an offer from a more experienced local promoter there. Dave kept topping his offer and we finally said yes. But the Catholic church admonished parents to keep their kids away and articles in the press tied Kiss to Satanism. Dave lost a bundle promoting Kiss in Puerto Rico.

Promoters who'd done poorly with Kiss on the last tour were now lining up to renegotiate their deals. Many had lost money on Kiss shows and now it was their turn to get paid back. Frank Russo, one of New England's top promoters and a longtime Kiss supporter, wanted better terms for his shows. We agreed. We needed all the promoters we could lay our hands on. Similar concessions were made to Jules Belkin in Ohio, Jack Boyle in Florida, and Arnie Granat in Illinois, allowing them to keep more of the profits or reducing the guarantees.

Acts that consistently burn promoters with inflexible terms do so at the peril of not having enough shows for a tour. Kiss needed five shows a week to break even; turning down shows because the deals weren't tight enough or the guarantees were too low was like shooting yourself in the foot. We needed all the cash we could grab. Agents can only exert so much pressure. If word gets out among promoters that an act is a "tour of death," pretty soon there won't be any promoters making offers.

The *Asylum* tour, which ran from late 1985 to the spring of 1986, wasn't much different than the last, averaging 5,000 people per night. It was hit and miss. Sacramento would sell 2,600 tickets but Philadelphia would sell 10,000. Ticket prices were stepped up. Arena shows had been priced as low as $12.50 and some were closer to $10.00. These were bargain basement prices. Many promoters hadn't changed their ticket scales by more than a dollar since the late '70s. We stopped leaving ticket pricing to the discretion of the local promoters and set $15.00 as the benchmark. Without the increase, Kiss would never earn percentage monies. We also jettisoned another money-losing practice, giving discounts on advance purchases of tickets. It didn't seem likely that a dollar or two off the regular price would have much stimulus to people not predisposed to seeing Kiss in the first place.

A dollar or two at the box office may seem inconsequential, but in the concert business, these small increments add up to big money very fast. It's a business of small change. If Kiss only did 5,000 tickets each night, an extra two dollars per ticket would bring in an additional $10,000 gross revenue. Over a week with five shows, that's an extra $50,000, and over twenty-five weeks, the length of the *Asylum* tour, it adds up to $1.25 million in extra ticket monies. Once a show's costs are covered, much of this extra revenue flows to the bottom line.

By the time the Kiss tour made it to the West Coast, we were at the midpoint. The *Asylum* tour would do nearly 100 shows before it ended in April 1986. It felt like Kiss was stuck on a treadmill. To Gene and Paul, it must have been drudgery. They'd done it countless times in the past dozen years. It had become a grind, but it was the only way to keep their careers alive and their bills paid. Touring was part of the job requirement for rock groups.

❖

It was after 1:00 a.m. when I pulled my car into the portico of The Beverly Hills Hotel. Kiss had played the San Diego Sports Arena that night and we would be at the L.A. Forum next. The original Forum show had been canceled when Gene came down with bronchitis. It was now February. Three of us got out of the car after a long and boring two-hour drive on the freeway to L.A. The group's assistant tour manager, Wayne Sharp, headed straight for the front desk to get his room key and call it a night. I took Nancy, our other passenger, to the Polo Lounge for a nightcap. A pretty blond 20-year-old with her hair cut in a short shag, Nancy had been squabbling with her family and was only too glad to get out of town. The Polo Lounge was nearly deserted. The hotel was always quiet late at night, a kind of ghostly stillness that's the opposite of the daytime hubbub of people mingling and phones ringing. We sat in one of the booths which were in plentiful supply at this hour. The waiter came by for last call. Nancy wanted to know what Kiss was like "before," meaning in the '70s. I told her that it was a lot different, but it was hard for me to really explain all of the differences. Compressing years of experiences and the complicated personalities of many people into a few pithy remarks isn't easy to do.

Kiss was now a workaday business. The sameness of the routine and the regimen of recording and touring had become cut-and-dried. The excitement, the imagination, the craziness, and the outrageousness that were once the essence of Kiss's mystique had long since dissipated. Kiss was now predictable. There were no more legions of zealous fans beating down the doors to see them at every pit stop in America. Kiss unmasked ultimately settled down to being just another arena rock act with a name and a modest following.

The traveling carnival atmosphere of the old Kiss days on the road had been replaced by a clock-punching order. Stodginess had set in as the *modus vivendi*. Dom Pérignon and Remy Martin were gone and fruit juices, hot soups, and brewed decaf took their place. Wild parties with rooms full of girls gave way to bowling nights. Learjets were seldom if ever seen; the group was spending a lot of time in customized tour buses like those popularized by country stars, with built-in microwaves, bunk beds, and VCR's. And coke and pot were banished from the scene. Kiss on tour in the mid-'80s was virtually hazard-free. Getting rid of many of these things wasn't necessarily a bad idea, but it did change the mood considerably. Kiss was now much more of a corporate rock enterprise. What was left of their self-styled image as rabble rousers and rock 'n' roll rebels was simply a thin veneer to keep the faithful happy. The reality was that feistiness had turned into fustiness.

Rock 'n' roll thrives on excess and extremes. The risk always exists of falling into the danger zone of self-destruction and decadence. But trying to exorcise all of the demons, however well-intentioned, inevitably dilutes the intense, raw appeal of rock. Rock's biggest success stories, including Kiss, have been personalities who projected an image of riskiness and uncertainty to the public. The notion that rock should be safe, sanitized, and antiseptically clean goes against the grain of what its committed believers typically find alluring about it.

In days past, Gene and Paul had to interact with Ace and Peter as equals. Now, there were two bosses giving orders to their charges, Eric and Bruce. The stand-up comedy routines for the press with all four Kiss members sparring with reporters were history. The p.r. function was now handled exclusively by Gene and Paul. The once-snappy repartee became subdued and steeped in clichés. By the mid-'80s, press coverage of Kiss, even in the rock magazines which they once dominated, was limited to an album review and occasional articles when they toured. Their interviews reflected this blasé attitude. Paul told *Circus* in its November 30, 1985, article on Kiss, "To me, making rock music is not making anything except TV dinners. That's what rock music is and that's what people relate to."

Gone were the zaniness and the feeling of living on the edge when Ace and Peter were around. Gene and Paul had looked upon the departure of Ace and Peter as a blessed event. It seemed logical that Kiss could now work harder, produce more, and be more profitable. But it didn't work out that way. In spite of the negatives, the lunacy of Ace and Peter provided the spark that made the chemistry work. That spontaneity, once the catalyst for success, had become a casualty. With rock, as with many things, the whole is often greater than the sum of its parts. When Kiss began to replace the parts, their appeal was blunted and their popularity plunged. They were running on a watery fuel.

A rush of memories raced through my mind and Nancy asked me what I was thinking about. I managed a smile. It was hard to put into words the stream of experiences and feelings that had defined for me what Kiss and the music business were about. I kept telling her, "You had to be there," which was hardly illuminating. I then shifted gears and told her what it was like now with the band.

"We're always scrambling for dollars," I said, and Nancy looked at me incredulously. What I was saying didn't jibe with the perception of Kiss as super-rich megastars, something they'd drummed into the public for years. Events had taken an unforeseen turn. In the Super Kiss era, money came cascading in and even with all the waste and stupidity, there was plenty around to try new and bold ideas. Kiss was now working harder than they had in years, but it was like climbing uphill without ever being able to reach the top. A sense of powerlessness had set in. It was a sea change from the almost fantasyland existence in the late '70s when anything and everything was possible.

The waiter stood patiently behind me after dropping the check next to my cinder-filled ashtray. We were the only guests left in The Polo Lounge. Nancy was starting to nod off and the droning vacuum cleaner in the lobby was putting me to sleep. We left the bar, slipping down the hallway to find our room. The hotel was as quiet as a graveyard.

Collapse of the House of Cards

"Are you in it for the money?"

> Director Penelope Spheeris, interviewing heavy metal bands including Kiss in her film *The Decline of Western Civilization, Part II: The Metal Years* (1988).

"Did you see it? Did you see it?" Paul was screaming at me, as he got out of his limo and saw me walking toward him. I told him I did. He was talking about Gene's movie, *Runaway*. Gene played a mad scientist who sets a team of remote-controlled robots on a path of mayhem and destruction. Paul was panting for my reaction to the movie. "Wasn't it the worst?" he asked. Kiss was on tour when the film opened in December 1984 and I caught it at a local theater in Rochester, New York, where we were doing a show. Paul had been badgering me for days to make sure I saw *Runaway*; he'd gone to a screening in New York and said the movie was "awful." When he flew into Rochester the afternoon of the show, he couldn't wait to find me. There was a glint in his eyes and a gleeful look came across his face. I assured Paul that I didn't think it was a great film and that Gene was hammy. Paul was beaming. "We've got our own Sting in the band," he observed, barely containing his laughter.

Runaway wasn't really Gene's movie but he did have a major co-starring role in it with TV hunk Tom Selleck, then riding high on his hit series *Magnum, P.I.* The movie was directed by best-selling author Michael Crichton and also featured newcomer Kirstie Alley, more recently of *Cheers*. Gene had gotten the part as the rogue scientist through his movie connections. *Runaway* didn't do much business in theaters, but it launched Gene's career as a movie actor. In its December 14, 1984, review, *The New York Times* described his performance as having a "comic book vitality." With characteristic zeal, he milked it for all he could, hyping himself to movie people he often called from airport pay phones while on tour with Kiss. Later, ads appeared in *The Hollywood Reporter* and *Daily*

Variety, trumpeting his performance in *Runaway* for Academy Award consideration as best supporting actor.

Gene had been spending most of his time in L.A. once he sold his New York pad. He bought a ranch-style split-level home in Benedict Canyon, near Beverly Hills. He began actively promoting himself as an actor and after *Runaway,* landed a part in an independent feature, *Never Too Young to Die,* along with ex-Prince backup singer, Vanity. Gene played a hermaphrodite appearing in women's clothes and makeup. The movie only played in a handful of theaters before hitting the video stores. But Gene kept up the high-pressure hype, making round-the-clock phone calls to Hollywood agents, producers, and directors and sending flowers, gifts, personal notes, and Kiss souvenirs to prospective employers.

Whatever Gene's shortcomings as an actor, he certainly knew how to advertise himself. At a postconcert party arranged at a Kiss show at the Long Beach Arena, not long after *Runaway* was released, Gene's personal guest list exceeded 200 people; the remaining three band members had invited a few dozen guests among them. The hors d'oeuvres bill went through the roof that night. Paul was incensed. It wasn't so much a Kiss party honoring the band's performance, but a private reception for Gene and his movie contacts. Anyone Gene knew with even a remote connection to the Hollywood scene was backstage shaking hands with him and talking shop.

None of Gene's movies were critical or commercial successes, but it was an impressive coup to have gotten two major roles in feature films. His relentless self-promotion helped him land the parts. The acting jobs from these two films and some other TV and movie appearances over the years also enabled him to set aside a nice nest egg. Gene adapted well to living in Hollywood, acquiring a Rolls-Royce from Lionel Richie's fleet of cars and appearing on *Lifestyles of the Rich and Famous.* Paul thought all of this was very "jive." Gene's moguling with the movie set became a priority; he saw it as a way to assure a life in the public eye after Kiss.

Having chalked up romantic conquests with Diana Ross and Cher, two of America's most renowned leading ladies, Gene was on the prowl for new blood. His celebrity dating took a serious turn when he met Shannon Tweed, the 1982 Playmate of the Year. A tall, striking woman with luxuriant blonde hair, her stunning good looks bowled Gene over. She had established her credentials as a head turner during her years with Hugh Hefner. In 1982 at the hearings in Atlantic City to consider Playboy's application for a gambling license for their proposed casino hotel, Shannon reportedly appeared at Hef's side in form-fitting sweaters and skin-tight leather pants. It created quite a *frisson.* Shannon showed up at a number of Kiss shows while Gene was on tour. Strong-willed and with a somewhat icy disposition at times, Shannon made it clear to the staff that unless all her traveling arrangements were first class in every respect, Gene shouldn't expect her to show up. They were.

Early in his courtship of Shannon, Gene admiringly described the dimensions of her breasts to some of the touring staff who were huddled around him. He was never bashful when it came to speaking about women and sex. According to Gene, "They're not the biggest, but by far the most perfect in size and shape." Gene cupped his hands for emphasis while talking. Had Shannon been within earshot, she undoubtedly would have slugged him. Once Gene's relationship with Shannon heated up, the two set up house in Gene's Benedict Canyon home.

311

Gene had become accustomed as to how to treat celebrity girlfriends. On one tour, he'd planned to fly actress Carol Wayne out to a Kiss show in Kansas City. When she insisted on limo service from her home in L.A. to the airport, in and out of the hotel and airport in Kansas City, and the same on the return leg back to L.A., the logistics became too much for Gene to cope with—"That bitch was trying to limo me to death." Gene abhorred the idea that anyone should try and gouge him. "Paying for pussy," as he put it, was something that was unthinkable for a rock star, yet the red carpet treatment was often deemed acceptable. Compared to what he spent on Cher, these frills seemed like peanuts.

Gene also produced a few bands in the studio, squeezing them in when he wasn't on tour or acting. Among them were Ezo, a Japanese heavy metal band, and Wendy O. Williams, a punk rocker whose former band was the Plasmatics. Several years earlier Wendy had reportedly been arrested at a Milwaukee concert for "simulating masturbation with a sledge hammer" and pinned to the stage by police. Neither Ezo nor Wendy took off.

He tried to manage some groups and made a pitch to become Van Halen's manager. He and Howard Marks started Monster Management to manage artists outside of Kiss, and they arranged a meeting in our office in 1985 with the two Van Halen brothers, Eddie and Alex. David Lee Roth had recently left the band. Nothing came of it and Van Halen soon found another manager and a new singer. It was Gene's second shot at the group since backing them in the late '70s. Curiously, the new singer turned out to be Sammy Hagar. He'd opened for Kiss years earlier and was thrown off the tour for swearing in front of the audience, something indecorous for Kiss's young fans then.

By this time, Gene had started to give himself a makeover. He had several wigs outfitted which he would wear on stage and in Kiss photos and album covers. Presumably, his hair was thinning, the death knell for a rock star. *Animalize*'s back cover shot featured Gene in his first wig. Not surprisingly, there was a lot of kidding about it from Paul, who lampooned Gene for always needing time to "tighten up his wig." On one flight, I stood up and announced that in the event of air turbulence, passengers wearing wigs should be advised to cover their heads. Gene was livid, but the rest of the band was practically rolling in the aisles. None of the other passengers had the vaguest idea what was so funny.

The wig wasn't a bad idea in theory, but it never looked like the real thing, even in photos with extensive retouching. It wasn't at all like Gene's natural hairstyle, and gave him a Prince Valiant look. One of our promoters in Germany asked me why he wore such a cheap-looking wig and when I told him a set of them had cost thousands, he was floored. Not long after the wig became a fixture, Gene told me that he had had cosmetic surgery where his nose was reshaped.

The dynamics between Gene and Paul were changing. Gene was based in L.A. while Paul split his time between the coasts. Their relationship became less personal and increasingly businesslike. As Kiss receded from the headlines and their influence waned in the music world, Gene was making efforts to develop other avenues for himself. Resuscitating Kiss's career was proving to be an uncertain undertaking. Paul took center stage as the spokesman for Kiss now that the makeup was discarded, and much of the songwriting and creative direction for the group flowed from Paul. Gene resigned himself to a diminished role; without a monster suit and makeup, he couldn't keep playing the part of Godzilla, rampaging across the stage. But Paul seemed jealous of Gene's acting roles. Even though none of the films was much to rave about, Gene had something Paul didn't.

Paul found a new love in the meantime. Lisa Hartman, one of the stars of the TV series *Knots Landing,* became his steady in the mid-'80s. This was Lisa's exposed navel period, when she'd show up at splashy Hollywood parties and restaurants in spiked hair and peek-a-boo outfits that revealed her navel. The outfits also conspicuously displayed her perfectly toned and trainerized curves. Paul loved the attention she created in public when the two would appear together, as photographers jumped in front to snap photo after photo for the tabloids.

A Houston girl, Lisa began her TV career in 1977 when she was just 21 as the star of *Tabitha,* a short-lived series about a pretty young witch. She had pursued a singing career but turned to acting when that didn't get off the ground. In an odd twist, Lisa originally played the part of Ciji, a rock singer, on *Knots Landing.* Lisa and Paul had a whirlwind affair. Paul was on the rebound since the Donna Dixon disaster. But with Lisa, there was more of a geographical obstacle to keeping the relationship in motion than there had been with Donna. Lisa always seemed to be very busy, too busy to come to New York to be with Paul. She once made it to a Kiss show in San Francisco while Paul was on tour. But Paul spared no effort to see Lisa frequently, even when he was barnstorming across the country on tour. He would regularly get up at the crack of dawn whenever there was a day off to make connecting flights to L.A. from wherever Kiss was (the days of private jets were long gone) so he could spend twelve or twenty-four hours at most with Lisa. Lisa seemed to be unbending about the rules of their relationship. If Paul wanted to see her, he would have to fly to California. Period. Her shooting schedule for TV was a major impediment. Once the visit was over, Paul was sent back to the airport for another grueling set of connecting flights. This shuttle romance became a real grind for Paul, but it was the only way he could keep the flame burning.

Paul was always diving in head first to prove himself in a big way. It was the same with Lisa as it had been with Donna Dixon and Lesley Ann Warren. Eventually, the Paul and Lisa affair came to an abrupt end. At our office, he handed a secretary a letter addressed to her with the envelope already sealed and asked to have it sent Federal Express. Paul never mentioned Lisa again to me or anyone else on the staff.

While Gene's forays into acting and producing records weren't exactly earthshaking successes, Paul's attempts never made it off the drawing board. Paul had become an experienced record producer with Kiss and decided to seek out other bands to record. That didn't work out as anticipated. The bands he was offered were usually either too young, too inexperienced, or not important enough. An early meeting with an then-unknown group called Guns n' Roses went nowhere. I was told that the meeting took place in the L.A. apartment of one of the band members, littered with garbage and looking like a crash pad for junkies. Some of the band were half-asleep on one of the couches. Paul seemed lukewarm about working with the group and took a wait-and-see attitude. I had asked him about making a pitch for us to become their business managers if he got the gig. He said, "Let's see what happens."

Guns n' Roses eventually found another producer and went on to make a hugely successful debut album. Paul's corporate moniker, Immaculate Management, remained true to its name—a letterhead company with beautiful engraved stationery. He had formed the company with Howard Marks. Unlike Gene, Paul seldom took chances. He was always leery of the risks involved in being linked with something not already big or prestigious.

Another movie part came Gene's way in 1986, a co-starring role with Rutger Hauer in *Wanted—Dead or Alive*. Gene played an Arab terrorist. Paul described him as looking like a street cart vendor of kabobs. Gene was well on his way to becoming a screen villain, a spinoff from his stage role in Kiss. The movies gave the press a new angle to explore with Gene, something that bugged Paul. It rekindled interest in Kiss, albeit from a different perspective. Kiss was otherwise of very little interest to the press. The '70s were history and a spate of newer bands were emerging on the scene as the rock icons of the '80s. Rock magazines would dutifully interview Kiss, but the media fascination had long since faded away. Gene and Paul contented themselves by expounding on their music, but Kiss was never about music *per se.* Years later, in August 1993, Ace described their dilemma in an interview in *Guitar World,* saying that when he left the band, "Kiss got a musical vasectomy."

"The truth is never good enough for you," Paul once said to Gene. He made the remark on board a flight, after Gene had boasted to a journalist who was interviewing him that Kiss's show in Rio had drawn over 500,000 people. It was a wild exaggeration. No stadium anywhere could hold that many, even if everyone was piled on top of each other like ants. Paul chastised Gene when the reporter returned to his seat. Gene's penchant for chest-thumping proclamations had begun to annoy Paul, even when it was designed to emphasize something positive about Kiss. The problem was that hype and more hype had become second nature to Gene. His public utterances in interviews often revealed a hazy recollection of facts and events that sometimes had little to do with reality.

A temporary halt to the business of Kiss was called in the middle of 1986, after the *Asylum* tour. In the past four years, Kiss had produced four albums and done three overseas concert tours, four U.S. concert tours, and two overseas promotional tours. It had become a Sisyphean task trying to restore their status as a supergroup, and Kiss had only been able to climb back to the middle rungs of the success ladder. Ironically, the sameness that began to undermine the Kiss mystique, and their metamorphosis from trailblazers to followers, could be traced in part to Kiss's 1984 tour in England.

Bon Jovi, newcomers who were having a taste of success in the United States with their first album, were opening for Kiss on the 1984 tour. In the mid-'80s, Bon Jovi were virtually unknown in England and Europe. One acerbic rock critic referred to them as "Bon Jerk Off," denigrating them for their squeaky clean pop-flavored *lite* metal sound. Bon Jovi's ebullient manager, Doc McGhee, had made a deal with PolyGram to get his band on the Kiss tour since they were both on the same record label worldwide. Jon Bon Jovi's pretty boy good looks and ringlets of golden brown hair falling over his shoulders were starting to win the hearts of teenage girls back in the states. Touring with Kiss in Europe would give them the exposure they needed abroad.

I was sitting with Paul in the drawing room of a charming and picturesque country inn somewhere deep in the English countryside near Ipswich, a tiny dot on the map. Kiss played a lot of these small towns in England full of young fans who are passionate about their rock heroes. It was late and the Kiss show had ended well over an hour ago. The small, cozy drawing room was a quaint setting with lace curtains, a fireplace, and Victorian-style couches with embroidered fabrics, the ideal backdrop for a Laura Ashley advertisement. Jon Bon Jovi joined us in the drawing room along with several members of his band. Jon and his group were sitting on one side of the room, clustered around a couch and a coffee table, and Paul and I were on the other side of the room. We were sitting in large wing chairs with footstools in front. Each side kept its distance and chatted amongst themselves, part of the tribal nature of rock groups. Headline acts usually don't mingle with their opening acts.

"So Paul—who're you fucking these days?" broke the ice like a meat cleaver splitting apart a frozen side of beef. One of the Bon Jovi band members asked Paul in his sandpapery voice the burning question of the day. It wasn't intended to offend, it was simply a matter-of-fact inquiry about Paul's latest romantic conquest, but it came off as a bit cheeky. Paul was thrown off guard. He sat immobile for a moment, then fudged a response to deflect more questions on the subject. Paul's private space had been invaded, something which he didn't like. But his trophy case of celebrity paramours—Georganne LaPiere, Donna Dixon, Lisa Hartman—had always been on public display, as had Gene's affairs with Cher, Diana Ross, and Shannon Tweed. Updates on Kiss's celebrity loves had become a major topic of interest both to those in the rock world and to the public.

Eventually, Jon and Paul became friendly, and prior to Bon Jovi's recording of *Slippery When Wet,* Paul recommended a friend of his, Desmond Child, to collaborate with Jon on writing songs for the album. Desmond had co-written Kiss's big disco hit, "I Was Made for Lovin' You." It was a stroke of genius. *Slippery When Wet,* released in 1986, was one of the biggest-selling albums in the history of PolyGram, with U.S. sales of nine million and millions more overseas. Bon Jovi was no longer opening for Kiss, or anyone else for that matter. It was also the second major success for manager Doc McGhee in which Kiss had played a part. Doc had also been the manager of Mötley Crüe, a group of unabashed Kiss imitators from L.A. who had opened for Kiss in 1983, boosting ticket sales for a string of dates on the West Coast. Mötley Crüe went on to become a major headline act, appealing to the same market as Kiss had in the mid-'70s with glittery costumes, makeup, and a flamboyant stage show. Of course all this was still in the future when Bon Jovi first toured with Kiss in 1984. At a stop on the tour in Oslo, Kiss's road manager Mark Adelman had to bail out the group at a local McDonald's when they ran out of money. With the meteoric success of Bon Jovi not far away, the group would soon be able to return the favor to Kiss.

On August 22, 1987, Bon Jovi was the headline act at the Castle Donington rock festival in England, an event that drew upward of 100,000. Kiss was invited to open for Bon Jovi this time around. It was a startling turnabout. Three years earlier, Bon Jovi had been traipsing through Europe and England in a small bus with a broken heater, with everyone in the band bundled up in blankets to ward off the freezing cold at night. They barely made it to the gigs on time to open the shows for Kiss. At one point, Doc McGhee was making rumblings to our mutual booking agent, Rod MacSween, that the Kiss tour had much lower turnouts than expected and he was thinking of pulling Bon Jovi off the tour. Now, Bon Jovi was the main event at one of the biggest outdoor rock shows in the world and Kiss could be their special guests. Kiss politely declined. Gene and Paul felt it would be a humiliating experience for them, an unwelcome reminder of the rough, poetic justice of the ups and downs of the music business.

By coincidence, Gene, Paul, and I ended up in England at the same time as the Castle Donington festival. We were there on a promotional tour for the record company. Jon invited us to their show. We linked up with the group at their London hotel, the venerable St. James's Club, and we were then taken in a convoy of limos to a heliport on the other side of the city. There would be two helicopters taking the Bon Jovi entourage to the festival site. The weather was miserable in London, rain and wind sweeping the central part of the city. A police escort with klaxon blaring led us to the heliport, now encased in fog. After an hour's wait until the fog lifted, we finally took off and made it to Donington Park, a wide open field near the site of an old castle, where the show was held. The weather there wasn't much of an improvement. By dusk, it was cold and damp and the rains had turned much of the ground into mud with puddles of water scattered all around the backstage area. Still, the event was sold out and a new attendance record was set.

Gene and Paul spent most of the day in hospitality tents that had been set up for all the acts. Before taking the stage to close the show at around 9:30 p.m., Jon invited Gene and Paul to join his band at the end of their performance for an encore. Paul snapped up the offer but Gene was put off by it and wanted to mull it over. Jon headed for the stage as a thundering roar from the crowd preceded Bon Jovi breaking into their first song. As Gene put it to me backstage while Bon Jovi was playing, "I don't want to look like the bass player for Bon Jovi, standing in the background." Paul had no compunctions about appearing with what was now one of the biggest bands in the world, and at the end of the show, to the delight of the audience, he jumped on stage with Jon.

In a matter of a few years, Bon Jovi had eclipsed Kiss's success, selling multimillions of records and setting attendance records throughout the world. There wasn't any animosity toward Bon Jovi—but it was an unbelievable shock to Kiss. Bon Jovi had really gone over the top. Worse, they were on the same label as Kiss, and *Slippery When Wet* albums weren't just flying out of the stores, they were shooting out like guided missiles. PolyGram had no problem selling Bon Jovi records by the tens of millions but they had to sweat it out just to get Kiss to the million-mark worldwide. Kiss began to think it might not be a bad idea to copy a few pages from Bon Jovi's book.

The imitation crept up in subtle ways. When presented with a marketing proposal for Kiss's records, Gene and Paul would want to know whether Bon Jovi had used a similar strategy. Their videos were studied and their directors contacted and, in some cases, signed up. Promotional gimmicks like live versions of songs for the B sides of singles released overseas would be quickly okayed if Bon Jovi had done the same. Bon Jovi's strategy became the litmus test. If they had appeared on a particular TV show or released a special version of a record it was safe for Kiss to follow suit. In many respects, Bon Jovi became the model for how Kiss could remold themselves and get back on the success track. I often said to Paul only half-jokingly that "Did Bon Jovi do it?" had become almost a mantra in our office.

Rock groups are rarely as iconoclastic and individualistic as they like to think of themselves, and Kiss's infatuation with Bon Jovi was not the first time they had played follow the leader. Kiss's fawning over Bon Jovi's success was similar to the way they reacted when Van Halen had overtaken them in the early '80s. Kiss admired the Van Halen sonic boom of rapid-fire guitar playing and throbbing bass and their high-energy stage show and hip stage clothes. When Van Halen used synthesizers prominently in their hit single "Jump," at a time when synthesizers weren't widely used by heavy metal bands, it was safe for Kiss to use them. Van Halen's costumer was soon hired as well. Kiss liked the type of outfits Van Halen wore—tights in various colors, slashed T-shirts, fabrics that looked like gauze and fishnetting—and had similar ones made up for their photo sessions. When Van Halen played Madison Square Garden at the time "Jump" was topping the charts, I asked Paul if he was going. He told me the band invited him but he passed. He said it would make him too depressed to see how hugely popular they had become, and to watch their stage show, which rivaled the Super Kiss extravaganza.

Gene and Paul kept a watchful eye on the charts and paid close attention to what was selling. If it could be used by Kiss and adapted in some way to give them a more up-to-date sound with a more contemporary image, they jumped on it. Whatever trends were emerging among heavy metal bands, a genre of music Kiss had helped to invent, they now emulated. Meetings took place at our office with stacks of rock magazines strewn over the conference table, full of photos of what other groups were wearing, how they were photographed, what kind of lighting they used for their shows, and how their album covers looked. Everything was evaluated to see what would "work for Kiss," as Gene and Paul put it. Even concert venues would be approved for Kiss shows based on what other acts of comparable stature had played there recently.

In an interview in *The Miami Herald* on December 30, 1983, shortly after Kiss unmasked, Gene said, "I'd rather sing sexual songs about meeting girls on the road." After the flop of *(Music From) The Elder*, it was back to basics for Gene.

Paul felt the same way, often telling interviewers that *(Music From) The Elder* was a misguided effort to try and prove to the world how "smart" they were. Kiss tried to develop a racier image for themselves in the mid-'80s with songs like "Uh! All Night," "Keep Me Comin'," and later, "Let's Put The 'X' in Sex." The Kiss concept had mutated into a leering sort of sexist rock with Paul spouting a lot of profanity on stage to excite their largely male audience. He told me that he often felt uncomfortable about this since he was old enough to be their father. And at concerts in the New York area he felt even worse since his parents showed up.

At one of Kiss's bigger shows in New Jersey's Meadowlands Arena in April 1986, Paul's raw execrations were in full blast, with hefty doses of expletives in every sentence of his raps. The girl I'd taken to the show, admittedly not a Kiss fan, found it repellant. "Is that all they can say to their audience, talking about getting their pants unzipped and putting their dicks in some girl's mouth?" I tried calming her down with some gibberish about teenage hormones and adolescent angst. Paul thought the rough talk gave Kiss a hard edge and made them more credible as raucous rockers with their young fans.

The new video-age Kiss featured a full-length production, *Kiss Exposed,* with the "X" highlighted in the packaging to make sure you got the point. The video was an endless parade of half-dressed nymphs cozying up to the band and striking sexy poses around the swimming pool of a Beverly Hills mansion. Everyone talked in double entendres. Old Kiss concert footage was interspersed with the band romping with modelesque video starlets. The video was an attempt to revive the raunchiness of Kiss's early days, but by comparison, it seemed hokey and contrived. *Rolling Stone* reviewed *Kiss Exposed* in their March 26, 1987, issue and described the group as "brainless, filthy-rich slobs, reveling in sexism that would floor even David Lee Roth."

Kiss had taken the '70s by storm as trendsetters. They were now dedicated to becoming trend followers. Kiss was metamorphosing into a generic heavy metal band with no particular identity, just one of the pack. This mentality wasn't unique to Kiss. But because they had once led their own parade, it was particularly disheartening to see them running to jump on a bandwagon. Compounding the problem was that Kiss had entered a sort of no-man's-land of rock. They weren't yet over the hill, but middle age was setting in, creating an increasingly wide generation gap between them and their predominantly high school-age fans.

The glory days of Casablanca when Kiss was king of the hill had passed. Changes had swept the record company. The Casablanca label fell into disuse and the L.A. offices, with their ersatz Moroccoan decor and indoor palm trees, were shuttered. The label's new owners, PolyGram, shelved the Casablanca logo featuring a desert castle and the ubiquitous camels, except for a rare movie soundtrack. Kiss was now on the Mercury label, PolyGram's imprint for hard rock artists including Bon Jovi and Def Leppard, a British group that was setting sales records of its own with 7 million copies in the United States for the *Pyromania* album.

All of this created problems for Kiss. The promotion and marketing people who had been key ingredients in the hard-sell success of Kiss were no longer with the company. With PolyGram now based in New York, an entirely new team of executives and support staff were running things. New people filling posts at the restructured PolyGram had no experience working with Kiss. Some came and went so quickly that the company appeared to be a revolving door for record executives. Kiss was seen by many as an old warhorse act, a relic from a bygone era with an uncertain future. It was no easy job to build enthusiasm among the younger ranks and in the music business, enthusiasm is the key to everything. Some of the new hires were too young to even remember when Kiss had been a supergroup. Jim Lewis and Jerry Jaffee, senior marketing and promotion executives, were among the few at PolyGram that kept close tabs on Kiss. For the most part, Gene and Paul stayed at arm's length from the record company except to coordinate album delivery dates, tours, and press interviews.

Howard Marks became increasingly drawn into the daily affairs of Kiss, managing their business activities and dealing with PolyGram. But it was taking its toll on him. His advertising agency coasted along for years on the business generated by a few loyal clients, but new clients to replace the ones that dropped by the wayside were hard to come by. Rosanne Shelnutt was running the agency while Howard had become the titular head. His failing health created additional strains. Howard was totally devoted to Kiss. While once the ad business was his mainstay, his only interest now was Kiss and the possibility of signing up another big-time artist. This proved elusive.

Howard had made inroads with Roberta Flack and Ted Nugent over the years, but they never became clients. Roberta had had a disastrous experience with a previous manager that threw her life into turmoil for years. She wasn't keen on changing her career direction, either, intent on sticking with a familiar formula despite the fact that since her hits in the '70s, record sales were spotty. She was also battling a weight problem, taking yoga classes to try and slim down. Weak record sales gave The William Morris Agency, her agents then, a tough time booking shows. A gifted performer, Roberta was content to do the occasional movie or TV theme song and appear in commercials for Kentucky Fried Chicken. She scored a hit album with Peabo Bryson, teaming up for a duet, that helped to buoy her career.

Ted Nugent was another '70s hard rock warrior whose career had floundered in the '80s. Ted's gonzo-rock style and his self-proclaimed Motor City Madman personality had become dated. Once a multiplatinum-selling artist, his newer releases were considerably less successful. His home base in Detroit and the surrounding towns in Michigan and Ohio were his safest turf for drawing a big crowd. But he did have a name and a reputation. We had been talking on and off with Ted, and I flew to Detroit on New Year's Eve in 1986 to try and sign him as a client. We had lunch at the London Chop House; the manager gave Ted a tie to wear. Ted's mile-a-minute conversation didn't lead us very far. He felt he couldn't afford a manager and was happy plugging away as he was, doing his annual New Year's Eve bash at Cobo Arena, touring when he could get work, and hunting in the wilds of northern Michigan the rest of the year. He'd also had bad experiences with managers. Years later, he joined a few other rock 'n' roll pros in a band called Damn Yankees and had a platinum album.

Howard wasn't widely known in the music industry outside of his relationship with Kiss and, earlier, Diana Ross. These two artists were really special situations. We'd gotten our foot in the door as business managers with an expanded role, not as discoverers or promoters of talent. Our forte was maximizing artists' monetary rewards and managing the business elements of established professional careers.

Getting new clients is basically a referral business. Unless the top record company honchos and superlawyers recommend you to up-and-coming new artists or established ones looking to make a change, getting business is an uphill struggle. Our connection to Kiss wasn't much of a drawing card to attract other music clients. If anything, it was a deterrent. Some thought Kiss was irrelevant and others believed Kiss was our exclusive occupation. Trying to piggyback on Kiss in the hope that they would bring in business was a no-win strategy. Sadly, Howard became fixated on Kiss, often spending hours in his office looking at old videotapes of Kiss concerts and talking to Gene and Paul on the phone a dozen times a day.

Carl Glickman thought that Kiss had become addicted to overspending and there was little that he could do after years of trying to curb their habit. He began to distance himself from the company. Carl made repeated efforts to get Howard to move to less opulent offices and reduce his own overhead since the commissions from Kiss were declining, but Howard resisted. By now, Glickman/Marks Management had become a very small part of Carl's life.

There wouldn't be a new Kiss record in 1986. Even Kiss felt the sameness of their recent releases and the lackluster results of their last album, *Asylum*. Paul was emphatic about coming out with a "great album," something that would light the fire under their career again. Paul's vision wasn't like the grandiose thinking that had been responsible for *(Music From) The Elder*, but he did want something big and important. And it would require a top producer with name recognition who would give Kiss entree to working with top songwriters and getting radio airplay at key stations. In short, they needed a guru.

Gene went along with Paul's plan. He was living in L.A. and left the management of Kiss's creative affairs largely to Paul. A kind of truce had emerged. Gene could devote his time to acting and producing records while Paul would direct the affairs of Kiss. They no longer shared all their income on a 50-50 basis; songwriting royalties would be distributed according to who wrote the song. Paul knew exactly who he wanted as guru, the ideal candidate to turn around the slumping career of rock artists who needed a big record to get back on the fast track—Ron Nevison. Ron had been a friend of Paul's for years. He'd produced one of the most successful albums of Ozzy Osbourne, a heavy metal singer with a similar audience to Kiss's, and had leaped to the top of the charts with a multimillion seller by Heart, a group with two female singers. Heart's career had faltered after initial success in the '70s. An image makeover and a new album produced by Ron turned things around for them. He had had similar success with Jefferson Starship. Ron seemed the perfect choice for Kiss.

But there was a problem. Ron was booked. Like most top producers, Ron had commitments to other acts and wasn't able to start working with Kiss right away. In fact, he was booked for a year in advance and wouldn't be able to start with Kiss until early 1987. This meant that not only wouldn't there be any Kiss record in 1986, it was next to impossible that a new record could be released until the end of 1987. Signing up Ron would idle Kiss for a year and create a two-year gap between the release of *Asylum* in 1985 and the next Kiss album. Seemingly, waiting a year for a top producer to record an album for a group struggling to jump-start their career was a small price to pay. A hit would easily be worth the wait. But to Kiss, it had a serious downside which had nothing to do with Ron. Kiss was running out of money. Once the last tour ended in early 1986, their operation was stitched together with merchandising monies, loans from an ever-changing assortment of banks, and advances from foreign music publishers. With another tour and album at the end of the year, their cash flow would have been adequate to regain their financial footings. But that was now out of the question. As they tried to turn the corner, they faced an unexpected roadblock. They were back behind the eight ball.

Gene and Paul decided to take the gamble. They wanted their next album to be produced by Ron Nevison; they couldn't agree on anyone else. Howard told them that because of the shortfall in income, their finances would be stretched thin. It was a big chance but if the next Kiss record sold millions, it would be worth it many times over. A big success can cover up a lot of mistakes. Ron would start rehearsing with Kiss as soon as he was free in March 1987.

As if on cue once Kiss made their decision, more setbacks arose. Another person from the past with a chit to collect on popped up like a jack-in-the-box. Peter Criss, the estranged member of Kiss for many years, now had to be settled with. He'd been living in the Redondo Beach area in Southern California after selling his home in Darien a few years after his daughter, Jenilee, was born. He'd also been through rehabilitation for his substance abuse problems at a Long Island, New York, hospital. His most recent solo record, *Let Me Rock You,* had been released in 1982 in Europe through a deal with Phonogram; it wasn't released in the states. It sold modestly. Peter's singing career was in limbo except for a few efforts he made to put together bands of his own in the L.A. area.

Peter was still a partner in Kiss and there was the unresolved matter of settling his share in the group. Until 1983, Peter continued to draw monies from Kiss comparable to what Gene and Paul took out. More recently, he hadn't gotten any money owing to Kiss's cash-poor situation. In 1986, lawyers were negotiating a buyout of Peter. Both sides agreed to bring in an outside attorney to independently evaluate Kiss's anticipated income stream to make sure that everyone got a fair shake. Harold Orenstein, one of the deans of theatrical law in New York and in whose firm Paul Marshall had once labored, was retained. Eventually, an agreement was reached. Peter would get a one-time cash payout as the settlement for his interest in Kiss. By 1987, Peter was out of the picture.

We decided to test the waters with one of Winterland's competitors for Kiss's merchandising business. I asked Great Southern Merchandising to make a pitch. Great Southern had earned a reputation as a specialist in hard rock tour merchandising with a knack for eye-popping graphics and aggressive salesmanship. One snowy day in January 1987, Ira Sokoloff, the owner of Great Southern, flew to New York from his headquarters in Macon, Georgia. Ira, a colorful character with long graying hair and a quick smile, was a fast talker, at times almost combative, who could sell ice to Eskimos. Ira was wearing snowboots and a hooded zipper jacket with bold stripes. He and Howard didn't hit it off when we met in our offices. Ira's lively, rock 'n' roll style and Howard's dour Madison Avenue executive image mixed like oil and water. Ira asked how many people Kiss had averaged on the last tour and I told him, "in the range of 6,000 to 7,000 a night," which, of course, was an exaggeration, but that's the business we're in. It was closer to 5,000, although Kiss's take from merchandising was substantial. Ira scoffed and bluntly told Howard that Kiss's current track record couldn't possibly justify the amount of advance money we were asking for. Howard's face reddened. He was visibly offended, thinking that Ira was belittling him. He got up from behind his desk and ordered Ira to get out of the offices. Now. The meeting with Great Southern had concluded. After clearing a few hurdles, the Winterland deal was renegotiated to tide Kiss over until the new album was finished.

Another land mine turned up in our offices one afternoon—an audit report which must have weighed as much as the Manhattan Yellow Pages and looked to be as thick. Vini Poncia, the producer of several Kiss albums, had his accountants audit Kiss's books to see if his royalties were paid in full according to his contract. Producers generally receive a percentage of the record's retail or wholesale price on every copy sold. They're either paid directly by the artist or the record company. His accountants had been doing the audit for years.

"Vini's accountants say in this audit that Kiss owes him a ton of money in back royalties. If that's true, Kiss will have to pay him, or Vini will go to court," Howard told me when he first looked at the report. It sounded astounding to me that Kiss could owe Vini so much money. I spent the better part of the next three weeks analyzing the audit with our controller, Barry Miller.

Luckily for Kiss, Vini's demands were an exaggerated laundry list of puffed up claims, in customary music business mode. Vini's accountants were one of the more well-known firms in the music industry and knew how to play the game. It was the kind of audit designed to impress an artist client, who isn't usually financially sophisticated. Hundreds of pages of photocopied contracts filled up most of the volume along with a lot of royalty statements. Even the addition was wrong on the summary page, in Kiss's favor. Accounting firms like to present inflated claims like these to artist clients to get them steamed up emotionally about how badly they've been treated. The accounting firm becomes the client's savior and by comparison, the firm's huge bill for all the work is a drop in the bucket. In fact, many of these big audits are simply fishing expeditions.

After one meeting with the partner in charge, we settled the audit. Kiss had wanted to keep on good terms with Vini and avoid litigation. We agreed to pay a small part of the claims plus the undisputed monies due Vini that were already in the pipeline. We shook hands after forty minutes.

It was also time to change booking agencies again. Howard had had enough of ICM in its reconstituted form following the ATI acquisition. He had clashed with ICM on several occasions. But Paul provided the most pressing reason to give ICM the axe. At the Live Aid concert in Philadelphia in July 1985, Paul reportedly showed up at the backstage gate at JFK Stadium with four last-minute guests he brought with him from New York. Paul had only asked for two backstage passes, which he was given. Paul and his entourage were kept outside the gate cooling their heels for half an hour while an ICM representative scrambled to find the promoter to get more passes, no simple task at the biggest rock show of all time where hundreds of people were backstage.

To Paul, it was an unpardonable sin to have been kept waiting like a supplicant in front of other rock stars and VIPs. ICM would pay the price when their contract was up. Despite their efforts to keep Kiss on the road, routing and rerouting the tour repeatedly to make sure there were enough shows to make it work financially, Paul's surprise guests at Live Aid had doomed them.

Kiss was also unhappy that ICM couldn't get them stronger opening acts for their tours. They felt that was one of the main reasons they didn't have bigger turnouts. By this time, packaging was emerging as an important marketing tool in the touring business—putting two or more artists together on a bill that would make a value-added package for the concertgoer. A top act has pick of the litter. They'll draw big crowds and many acts will want to be on their tours. A middling act like Kiss without a hit single or a hit album, and in many instances only drawing half-houses, has to take what they can get.

Then there was the other agenda—getting movie roles for Gene and Paul. Gene had gotten a few, but it was largely through his own efforts. Paul hadn't gotten any. And Paul was miffed that Gene was doing movies, no matter what he might have said about them. At least he was on the screen. The solution was simple. They would switch to Creative Artists Agency.

Starting in 1975, CAA began an astonishing rise to become the leading talent agency in Hollywood. By 1986, they were representing a good chunk of Hollywood's top actors, directors, writers, and producers in both movies and TV. A music division was set up in 1984 when Tom Ross, then 37, was wooed away from ICM to start the operation. Tom scored a number of early successes in luring superstars from the music world to CAA, including Prince, Madonna, Michael Jackson, and John Cougar Mellencamp. Kiss thought CAA's superstar clientele would be great company to be in. CAA would have the clout to not only get them a top opening act for the next tour, but with their powerful movie connections, they could also get them acting jobs. Since CAA was the hot agency at the time, Kiss felt they were latching on to a good thing. Despite CAA's star-studded client list, many of the top acts toured infrequently and some were reportedly signed for a reduced-rate commission.

Tom Ross was disarming and affable, a smooth talker. Paul, Gene, and Howard liked his low-key style. At the time, CAA didn't have many heavy metal acts on their roster and Kiss would be a plus for them. And Kiss toured extensively, doing hundreds of shows just in the last four years. Not surprisingly, CAA felt they could do a better job at getting opening acts for Kiss. But all booking agencies work with the same talent pool at any given time—whoever is available to tour—and if the demand exists for an act, the agency is seldom a factor. Kiss also hit it off with Mitch Rose, a young agent at CAA who had worked hard to develop a relationship with them. Signing with CAA went smoothly, much more so than an earlier, aborted meeting at The William Morris Agency in Beverly Hills. Paul told me he had driven into the underground garage in their office building and been chased away by an officious parking attendant.

Crazy Nights, the new Kiss album that Ron Nevison was producing in L.A., would be finished in September 1987, and a tour was to follow in November. Early reports on the record were highly positive and the chemistry seemed to be working between Kiss and Ron. As the release date approached, Kiss's precarious financial situation was becoming a factor. Cash was drying up. Some of the suppliers and studios would have to wait to get paid until the group got the final installment of their advance from PolyGram when the album was completed. Kiss needed a blockbuster record to get massive radio airplay, something they had had for only a couple of singles in their history. With heavy airplay, sold-out arenas would follow on tour. It was a tall order.

Bruce Bird, the former Casablanca president, was brought on board to spearhead the campaign to get Kiss on the airwaves. Since Casablanca folded, Bruce had been running a small record label that MCA distributed, Camel Records, and was one of the top independent record promoters in the country. Danny Goldberg, Kiss's creative consultant, was dropped. (Danny went on to greener pastures and managed several successful artists of his own including Bonnie Raitt and, later, Nirvana.) Bruce would augment PolyGram's promotional efforts.

Independent promotional campaigns are not inexpensive. Major artists frequently hire record promoters at their own expense to supplement what the record company does, to wheedle and cajole radio stations into playing the latest single from the new album. Stations get hundreds of requests each week for new records to be added to their tightly constricted playlists; only a couple of new singles make the cut. And only the top acts can afford this extra help, which can run thousands of dollars per week, sometimes tens of thousands. The independent promoter can focus on one single and tout it to hundreds of key stations around the country. The record company's promotion department has to diffuse its efforts over a roster of artists.

Kiss didn't want to take any chances. Bruce Bird was a veteran at radio promotion and could handle the job. It would be another expense they would have to absorb to make sure every base was covered. Plans started to coalesce for a Kiss tour. It would have to be an impressive stage show, according to Gene and Paul. With the hoped-for success of *Crazy Nights,* Kiss would be on top again. A chintzy show that wasn't in the same league as supergroups like ZZ Top, Def Leppard, Van Halen, and Bon Jovi would be a comedown. Kiss couldn't afford to look cheap. Gene and Paul were intent on ratcheting everything up a few notches. Yet the new album hadn't even been released, and unlike their competitors, Kiss didn't have multimillion-selling records and sold-out tours in the recent past to build on. Their thinking was symptomatic of what happens when you expect success and spend the money before you've earned it.

Paul and Gene arrived at The Record Plant studios in New York in September just before the start of the listening session for *Crazy Nights.* Ron Nevison was there, looking suave and collected in a black silk shirt and jeans, tinkering with the speakers. Record company and press people were seated in a large studio in neat rows of chairs, as if they were at a lecture. Howard Marks acted as the master of ceremonies. He conducted the seating arrangements and made the necessary introductions. It wasn't the solemn ritual of the listening session for *(Music From) The Elder,* but it was hardly a party atmosphere, either. Decorum would prevail.

Ron switched on the record and for forty-three minutes, *Crazy Nights* played. Gene and Paul darted in and out of the studio. The music had the distinctive high-gloss sound and technical polish that Ron as well as Kiss had become known for. If the album was a hit and Ron recouped his advance, he would earn additional royalties. Ron's percentage on the album would make him nearly an equal partner of Gene and Paul on the sale of *Crazy Nights* albums (the producer's points come out of the artist's royalty paid by the record company). This made everything a bigger gamble since in the long run, giving up such a large piece to Ron meant that Kiss would get a smaller share of the royalties. The two-year wait came with a lot of hidden costs.

When the album finished playing, everyone applauded and congratulated the team. The PolyGram people seemed pleased. It was hard rock and in the Kiss groove, but not so overpoweringly heavy metal that it would scare away radio stations from playing it. Paul and Gene were happy with the album. In a conversation with me and Howard, Gene said that much of Ron's contribution had been in the engineering area, getting the right sounds for the guitars and drums and mixing them properly. But he believed that Ron's reputation as a top producer had a certain cachet in the music world, and Kiss needed that desperately in order to be taken seriously.

The tour would rehearse in L.A. and then move to Jackson, Mississippi, for the first show. There would be more trucks, more buses, more lights, more sound, and more pyro. There would also be computerized lighting and a keyboard player to handle the synthesizers. All of this extra start-up expense along with the cost of a new stage would add up substantially over the course of a twenty-five-week tour. That was on top of the average weekly touring expenses. It was a lot of money for Kiss, an act that had barely broken even on the last tour, and another big gamble.

Promoters were buying dates for the tour, but the guarantees offered were about the same as two years earlier. No one was going out on a limb to pay Kiss much money in most markets. No matter how well the agents at CAA hyped the new Kiss album, the promoters wanted to see proof in the sales charts first. Changes had also taken place at CAA. One of their employees, who had been performing yeoman service helping to organize the Kiss tour itinerary, ran afoul of Howard on account of some minor faux pas. Michael Piranian, a former ICM agent who was now with CAA, was brought in to book the shows and oversee the tour.

But the opening act was still a sticking point. There was no miracle solution from CAA. The usual assortment of garden variety new acts with first-time records had been offered to Kiss. They decided that Ted Nugent would open the first leg of the tour. Despite the fact that his recent albums weren't huge sellers, he still commanded a steep guarantee, based on the marquee value of his name. Fearful of ending up with a nobody as their opening act, Kiss signed on with Nugent.

There wasn't much to talk about as far as movie roles for Paul were concerned. Having had little success at ICM as an actor, Paul was now facing the same fate at CAA. Paul was able to get some promising auditions, however. Howard told me that Paul had had a tryout for a Broadway version of *The Three Musketeers* and Paul told me of readings that he'd done for movie directors including William Friedkin. At one point, I suggested to Howard that it might help if Paul had some new publicity shots of himself taken. The ones we had seen showed him with shoulder-length hair and wearing torn T-shirts, looking like a rock musician. He was, undoubtedly, typecast for parts in TV and movies as a rock musician, which he told us wasn't what he was looking for.

The job of advancing Paul's acting career, especially in dealing with the talent agency, largely fell to Howard Marks. Howard had long ago become Gene and Paul's *paterfamilias*. And as their business manager, he was expected to promote their professional careers in whatever direction they chose. From my vantage point, Paul was never able to be the self-promoter that Gene was and it was natural that Howard would have to assume this role for Paul.

Howard told me that he had become despondent. He obviously wanted to keep his client happy and did what he could to pressure CAA to find him a part. He talked with their movie agents and to Tom Ross. When Tom paid a visit to our offices to talk about the Kiss tour, Howard told Tom how disappointed he was about Paul not having any movie offers. It had become a monkey on Howard's back. Howard had been a major impetus in steering Kiss toward CAA and implored Tom to try and pull a few strings when he got back to L.A.

Michael Ovitz was the next person on Howard's list to contact, then head of CAA and the most influential talent agent in Hollywood. Howard believed that all it would take was "one phone call from Mike Ovitz" to a major studio and Paul would be in a movie. Howard couldn't even get a phone call in to Mike Ovitz. He was probably right about Paul's problem being solved with one phone call from the top man at CAA, but the phone call never came. Before long, the Kiss tour would start. Paul's acting career was put on the back burner.

Crazy Nights was being shipped to the stores in early October and the single was getting airplay. Bruce Bird predicted it would be a hit. There was a kind of eerie calm to everything. Kiss may have been teetering from all the bills that had piled up, but you'd never know it from the outside. Kiss was rolling along, hoping that *Crazy Nights* would strike a vein of gold and bring them a mother lode of riches. But money was still tight. It was all part of the surreal world of rock 'n' roll, where the truth is usually an unwelcome intruder in the realm of wishes and dreams.

But as ticket reports came in from CAA for the initial shows, the results were well below expectations. Paul and Gene were apparently getting cold feet about going ahead with the tour. Production rehearsals were in full swing by now in San Bernardino, California, and we'd already sunk hundreds of thousands of dollars into start-up costs for the tour. Howard was trying to talk Paul and Gene out of postponing or even canceling the tour; they were concerned that the tour was off to a disastrous start. As I was leaving the office in New York to go out to the West Coast, Howard warned me to be prepared to shut down everything immediately if Paul and Gene decided not to go ahead with the tour. When I checked into the Four Seasons in L.A. the next day, there was a message at the desk for me. Howard had called to say the tour was back on track.

By December, after a couple of weeks on the road, the familiar pattern had set in. *Crazy Nights* was stalled in the charts. The shows were up and down. A second single was being primed for release in early 1988; the first one had already petered out. But it was clear that if things kept up the way they were going, Kiss would be in dire financial straits. There wouldn't be any more advance money from PolyGram or Winterland; they were already overadvanced. Tour business wasn't generating enough cash to cover the weekly nut. Kiss was being battered.

At an early airport stop in Memphis, I broached the subject to Paul as we changed planes. We would have to start a round of cutbacks. I was probably too indelicate about how I framed the argument, couching it in strictly dollars and cents language. I reminded him that the album wasn't a home run, at least not yet, and the other bands with big tour productions on the road were selling more tickets than Kiss. It was logical but unpersuasive. Paul said, "There's a certain emotional level to this, too." He didn't want to go on tour and perform if it meant that their show had to be skimpy and second-class.

He was right, of course. Even though the economics I was trying to get across made sense, too, I couldn't argue with anything he said. He was the one doing the performing every night and opening his viscera to the public. But without some sense of balance, all of their work would simply end up as a charitable endeavor. We had come to a stalemate.

Just before Christmas, we met in New York at our offices. The tour was leaking money like a sieve. By this time, Kiss had let go of several of their touring staff. Other cuts were approved. The keyboard player was dropped. Some of the elaborate computer lights would go. Pyro was reduced. And a more comprehensive plan would be considered in a few weeks based on how well the album and the tour were holding up. But there was a far more serious crisis to discuss at the meeting, even more important than how to patch Kiss together for the next few months despite having just chewed up a fortune in touring costs. Carl Glickman, Howard Marks, and Dick Weidenbaum started passing some memos around the conference table for everyone to look at. The ticking time bomb was ready to detonate.

In the late '70s, Kiss had invested some monies in coal mines in Kentucky, West Virginia, and Tennessee. The government was then encouraging private investors to put money into natural resource development. It was a policy of the Carter administration to explore new sources of energy. The inducement to investors was that they would be able to legitimately shelter part of their income by taking the risk of investing in natural resources. Investors could deduct amounts three or four times greater than what was allowed with other, less risky investments, and thousands of well-heeled and sophisticated investors took advantage of this policy to reduce their tax bite. In the late '70s and early '80s, tax shelters were a booming business. The four Kiss partners had invested some of their money, too. They were big earners and wanted to hold onto as much of their money as possible. Kiss was very concerned that their tax bill be minimized, something which they impressed upon us repeatedly since that was an important part of the job of business managers. Originally, coal mines were only one of many investments that Kiss had. But by the end of 1987, the coal mines and the apartment complexes in the south were about all they had left, apart from their homes and property and some personal assets.

In the mid-'80s, a dispute was raging over the government's interpretation of the tax laws and how they should be applied to these shelters. The change in administrations from Carter to Reagan put in place an entirely new group of people in the IRS and the Treasury Department. The new group wanted to interpret the rules in a way that would be considerably less generous to the original investors. There wouldn't be any preferential tax benefits for investments in high-risk energy development. The write-offs that had been possible under the Carter policies, which could amount to three or four times the value of the amount originally invested, would no longer be allowed. Basically, the tax benefits would be reduced to the cash value of the original sum put in. The change in the rules would trigger additional taxes due *retroactively* plus interest. Calculated for a period of nearly a decade, as was the case with Kiss, this could amount to an enormous sum. And the dispute was close to being resolved after years of costly litigation and negotiations. If the original tax breaks were reduced, Kiss would owe the government a lot of money, possibly more money than they had originally invested. With Kiss, the additional money due in taxes and interest wouldn't just be another disaster, it would have the impact of a nuclear meltdown.

Kiss would owe *millions*. It couldn't be determined exactly how much since the negotiations were still in progress. But it could be catastrophic. The taxes they'd saved over the past decade had been used in part to pay for their fabulous homes, the Super Kiss productions, their crushing overhead, and their lavish lifestyles. Many investors had used the tax savings from the shelters to make other investments with the freed-up cash. These investments, in many cases, generated profits that would ultimately be able to cover their tax liability. Kiss got the benefit of the tax shelters by deferring the taxes, but used up all the savings from them. They had spent their wad. For years, money came in the front door and went out the back door. Everything was spent as fast as it was earned. Kiss worked hard, but they could never hang onto their money. It was always slipping out of their hands. Once their crash began in the early '80s, Kiss's money troubles grew progressively worse.

At the meeting, the looming tax shelter meltdown was discussed. It wasn't the first time, but now a resolution was closer at hand. Carl, Howard, and Dick brought Kiss up to date on the negotiations. They had invested in the same deals and were in the same boat as Kiss. A team of expert lawyers had been retained by a large group of investors, including Kiss, to try and work out a settlement with the government. The negotiations had become drawn out because of the complexity of the problem and the severity of consequences of the proposed rule change. Gene and Paul sat stone-faced throughout the discussion. A final settlement proposal from the attorneys handling the matter was expected in early 1988. We would then meet to decide what to do. It was just a matter of time until the tax bill came due, but the die had already been cast. The house of cards had collapsed.

18 Aftermath

I waited for the car to arrive in front of my apartment on West 55th Street in New York on a bitter cold day in late January 1988. The sidewalks were slippery with patches of ice still frozen from the cold snap we were suffering. The grating sounds of winter, sidewalks being scraped and streets being shoveled, were all around me. Two attache cases stuffed full of papers and financial reports were stacked next to me on the pavement. The car pulled up to the curb in front of my building and we headed for Newark airport.

I was taking a late-morning flight to Cleveland and would link up with Howard Marks and Dick Weidenbaum at the airport. We were going to meet with Kiss on their day off before the Cleveland show at Richfield Coliseum. Carl Glickman would also be at the meeting. Kiss had asked us to provide them with more details about their financial condition. They wanted us to come to the meeting prepared with estimates on how much the tour was costing, what they were worth individually, and how much they could expect to salt away over the next few years if they kept working.

It was clear that *Crazy Nights* wouldn't be a mega-album. It sold well initially, and shortly after its release in October, spurted to #18 in *Billboard*. The album began drifting downward in the charts and by January, it was sinking fast. No one was holding their breath about the next single's prospects. The tour plodded along, some weeks raking in big money, other weeks just squeaking by. The cuts made in December helped to keep the tour in a break-even position.

Kiss was crushed. The album and tour was a two-year plan on which they'd pinned their hopes. The result wasn't a failure, but it was below expectations. Gene and Paul seemed tremendously let down, not only by the so-so performance of the *Crazy Nights* album and tour, but by the unprecedented success of another group whose album PolyGram had released at about the same time as the Kiss record. Def Leppard's latest album, *Hysteria*, was on its way to selling 11 million copies in the U.S.

At the Marriott Hotel in the Cleveland suburb of Beechwood, we started our meeting with Kiss late in the afternoon. The group had done a show the previous night in a nearby city and arrived at the hotel in one of their tour buses. The meeting was in a small conference room with a bank of sliding glass doors covered by a beige curtain. I put together some tables and chairs and rented a typewriter to do some last-minute work. On the plane, Howard had a brainstorm. He felt if we could come up with a projection showing that Gene and Paul would each be able to amass $5 million over the next two or three years, the meeting would turn out fine. I began digging into all the income estimates to come up with a possible, if not entirely likely, scenario. Dick Weidenbaum helped me with some of the computer runs he'd prepared to sort out Kiss's tangled finances.

When Gene and Paul walked in, the atmosphere was strained. The usual banter and joking were reduced to a few pleasantries. Paul looked drained and anxious. He was normally good-humored and even-tempered at these meetings but not today. Gene was outwardly upbeat, as always. But it was often difficult to tell by looking at him or even listening to him just what he was thinking. He was buoyed by an offer he said he'd gotten for another movie role. Carl Glickman didn't make it. The wife of a close friend in Florida had died and Carl had flown down for the funeral.

I poured some coffee for myself. Howard was sitting at the head of the table and motioned for me to sit down. He looked as if he was about to start talking when Paul made an unusual request. He wanted to tape-record the meeting. We'd never had a meeting recorded before, but Howard didn't object and we proceeded. Dick glanced at me when he heard Paul's request, obviously taken off guard by the idea.

Howard told Gene and Paul that their financial situation had deteriorated, something we'd been telling them for a long time. Years of excessive spending on all fronts were to blame. Their income had decreased sharply over the past few years, and their cash problems had been exacerbated by the two-year hiatus. And unexpected business and legal problems with former partners, producers, their ex-manager, and the Phonogram lawsuit were all jokers in the deck. We had a long list of costs—tour production, album covers, photo sessions, costumes, recording sessions, producer's fees, personal living expenses, professional fees, payroll, monies provided to their families—which delineated what was spent and how each item affected their individual net worth.

What Gene and Paul had were their personal assets of homes, cash savings, and securities. Kiss's principal remaining business asset was the future value of their record contract, if they continued to make albums, and the value of their back catalogue of records and song publishing. It wasn't one big blunder that had torpedoed Kiss, but the accretion of many losses and failures over the years. They had become like a bucket with a slow leak in the bottom. Every time the bucket filled up, it would start to leak and before long, the bucket was empty again.

We came up with a plan as to how they could dig themselves out of this mess. It would mean sharp reductions in the tour production so it would show a net operating profit every week. We'd budgeted a surplus if they cut their recording costs and didn't use outside producers, who command up to 5 points on every record sold. That was nearly a third of Kiss's royalty. We reviewed their personal living costs for what must have been the one thousandth time. We talked about how all of their business activities had to earn money for them. After about an hour of this, Howard, who was doing most of the talking, was getting raspy. He'd come to the meeting looking pale, with large bags under his eyes, and his pallor seemed to be getting worse.

Dick Weidenbaum handed out a chart which summarized the last twelve years of Kiss's income and expenses. Seeing their financial history reduced to a chart was quite a jolt for Gene and Paul. They seemed startled when they looked at it, a single sheet where years of work were compressed into a dozen columns of numbers. The "nine digit empire" touted by *People* magazine eight years earlier had all but vanished. The astonishing sums of money accumulated from 1975 until 1988 were gone. We were now sitting in a stuffy, nondescript hotel conference room in Cleveland to divvy up what was left and start all over again to earn back the money that was frittered away. Not surprisingly, the atmosphere in the room was like a wake.

Paul was asking questions that sounded as if they were for the benefit of the tape recorder. He kept repeating things, like "How much am I actually worth?" and "What do I have in the bank?" He got snappish about a detail concerning his annual car expenses. He was leasing a Porsche, which he had to insure, garage, maintain, and repair, and on top of that he rented luxury cars on his regular trips to L.A., maybe a dozen times a year. Limos were an additional expense. Paul felt that these were trifling sums for a rock star. But his failure to grasp the point we were trying to make was symptomatic of Kiss's problems in general. The costs were way out of line.

Gene asked about the coal investments. There hadn't been any new information since the December meeting, as a settlement was still being hammered out. The tax shelter liability was another wild card in the deck. It was sure to be more bad news. Stacks of financial statements were circulated and we fielded questions for about an hour. At 7:00 p.m., the meeting ended. Kiss didn't decide on anything except that we should send copies of all these documents to their attorney, Paul Marshall.

Later that night, Dick, Howard and I had dinner at Giovanni's, an elegant Northern Italian restaurant near the hotel. They were both weary, and Howard was visibly exhausted. We felt the meeting had gone as well as could be expected, but clearly Kiss was devastated about their grave financial condition. Howard didn't disagree, but he had a stubborn faith that no matter how bad things were, they'd only get better in time. At least, that's how he hoped things would work out. He was much more comfortable in the role of motivator and cheerleader than as the bearer of bad news and Draconian solutions. We discussed our strategy for the next meeting with Gene and Paul, who had asked us to set a date for another meeting in a few weeks to give them time to digest everything. As it turned out, Cleveland would be our last meeting with Kiss.

Over the next few weeks, it became increasingly clear that Glickman/Marks Management was being written out of the script. Paul never called Howard as he used to, sometimes as many as ten times a day. Gene was also incommunicado, except for keeping current on record company business having to do with the album. Gene and Paul vented some of their frustrations when they were in New York on a day off from the tour and were interviewed on a radio program. Talking about the *Crazy Nights* album, they badmouthed PolyGram for not having done more to promote it and laid the blame on them for the record's disappointing performance in the charts. It was a dumb thing to say. A few days later, Gene and Paul signed a letter of apology to Dick Asher, then PolyGram's president, to defuse the situation. The interview had been widely reported at the record company and had stirred up resentment toward Kiss.

Kiss hired an auditing firm to review all twelve years of their books and records. Accountants started showing up at our offices to examine all of Kiss's contracts and financial records. Letters were being messengered to us from Paul Marshall's office with Gene and Paul's signature instructing us not to sign their checks any longer. And they planned to change banks and brokerage firms soon. It was all a prelude to the inevitable. Kiss was telegraphing us that the end was coming.

On March 3, 1988, Paul and Gene called Howard on a cellular phone from the back lounge area of their tour bus. The phone call was short and to the point. We were fired, effective immediately. Howard called me into his office to tell me the news, but there wasn't much he could add since it hadn't been a long conversation. Howard said that Paul sounded very upset and choked up emotionally about their decision. Gene, he said, was composed but distant. After an association that dated back to 1973 when Howard first met the group, we were dumped. And the sad tidings were delivered from the back of a bus, barreling down a highway somewhere in the plains states.

I was sad about what had happened, but the January meeting in Cleveland had made it pretty clear that we were living on borrowed time. I knew that when it finally sank in that Kiss's cupboard was bare, we would undoubtedly end up as the scapegoats. It goes with the turf of being a manager or a business manager in the entertainment business. It was a shabby way to end things, especially since Kiss's money troubles were never concealed from them and they were regularly provided with financial information. Still, I understood how they felt: the emotional shock of having worked so hard and earned so much and having so little to show for it was not to be underestimated. I was always surprised that we'd lasted as long as we did. But as Kiss's finances kept going downhill, and our involvement deepened, it was simply a matter of time until they cut us off. The only mystery was who had persuaded them to finally make the move.

Within days, Kiss did a full-scale housecleaning. Dick Weidenbaum's firm was replaced by Kiss's new auditors. Dick found out that his firm was being dropped when Paul Marshall sent a fax to his office. The advertising agency and the insurance company Kiss used were also discharged. Bruce Bird, the record promoter, was dropped. Even Rod MacSween, their British booking agent, was let go. Paul Marshall's firm would stay on. Kiss's former secretary, an employee of our company, was hired away to function as administrator of their operation. She collected all of the group's files from our office and removed them to Paul Marshall's office. Kiss would be based there temporarily. It was chaotic and disorganized and obviously little thought or planning had been given to the whole arrangement. Kiss was still on tour at the time, and the tour continued to have problems. The L.A. show originally scheduled for the Forum was canceled when advance ticket sales fell flat.

And then we heard the next piece of news. We had been replaced by a guru. Dr. Jesse Hilsen, Paul's longtime psychiatrist, would assume the role of business adviser and financial consultant. His official title and function weren't exactly clear and we never had any direct contact with him. Dr. Hilsen soon installed himself in a penthouse suite on West 58th Street and Avenue of the Americas and hired a full-time staff to manage the group's affairs. He would have an ongoing role in Kiss's business. We later heard that Dr. Hilsen had listened to the tape of the Kiss meeting in Cleveland. We also came to learn that Gene and Paul's principal gripe was not that we hadn't continually advised them over the years that they were spending too much, but that we didn't do it "hard enough." We went wrong by not emphasizing their financial problems more than we had. It was hard to imagine what else we could have done. Sometimes people just get tired of hearing the same thing over and over and at a certain point, they tune out both the message and the messenger. Browbeating the Kiss members was never a very effective strategy; they were all very headstrong and sure of themselves.

Gene and Paul complained that we had failed to set aside money for their retirement. This had been one of their original concerns when they took on a business manager. They were right about that. Entertainers often have a short career span with very large sums being earned in a brief period of time. Kiss should have been able to sock away enough from their high-earning years to carry them through later in life. But the band's gravity-defying spending habits made it impossible to create savings out of thin air. The successful investments were sold in order to pay for all the spending; there wasn't anything left over to provide for retirement. Kiss wanted to have it both ways—spend the money now, but still have it show up in a bank account somewhere. They had a hard time accepting the old adage that you can only spend a dollar once.

Predictably, the Kiss situation became a feeding frenzy for the lawyers. Claims and counterclaims were filed on both sides.* A battery of high-priced legal talent entered the fray. Kiss had a long litany of complaints, alleging that they'd been overcharged on commissions, given bad investment advice, were stuck with risky tax shelters, and been grossly mismanaged. As is always the case in emotionally charged disputes, the great successes and achievements got lost in the shuffle and the mistakes took center stage. The record company deal, the merchandising contract, and the highly profitable investments were soon forgotten.

The main bone of contention for Kiss was the coal deal and its repercussions. When the tax shelter disintegrated, it served as the lightning rod for Gene and Paul's ire and brought their simmering resentment over Kiss's declining fortunes to a boil. The tax bill triggered their decision to throw out nearly everyone who'd been involved in their career for almost twelve years. The only survivor of Kiss's purge was their attorney, Paul Marshall, whose firm had represented the group since their earliest days, including the period in which they made their coal investments.

By 1989, Gene and Paul reportedly had settled their tax problems. Kiss was apparently able to negotiate another extension of their record contract and make a deal with a Japanese company, Hori America, for their music publishing catalog of songs. The 200-plus Kiss songs recorded over the years and the rising value of music copyrights in the late '80s may have helped to bail out the group from their tax woes.

By July 1990, a settlement was reached between Kiss and the various parties they had made claims against. Kiss agreed to drop their claims and end the litigation in exchange for an out-of-court cash settlement. By this time, I'd already given three days' worth of depositions in a conference room with seven lawyers present. Kiss claimed tens of millions of dollars were owed them, including damages, standard stuff for divorces between artists and their managers and advisers. The sum received by Kiss in the settlement was a very small percentage of the amount that had been sought. The matter was then closed.

Not long after the split with Kiss, I ran into Gene walking along West 57th Street. I didn't have much to say to him then. I waved hello and strode by. He seemed a little taken aback that I didn't stop to chat. But I was angry about the way I had been treated, especially since neither Gene nor Paul had ever called me since the breakup. A few months later, I bumped into Paul in the Parker Meridien Hotel, around the block from my apartment. We said hello to each

---

* Court records. *The Kiss Company, et al. v. Glickman/Marks Management Corp.,* et al. (1989), 89 Civ. 1595, U.S. District Court, Southern District of New York.

other and that was all. It was an awkward feeling, like being cut off from something that was once part of your lifeline. They weren't exactly family, but it was a closer relationship than simply "former colleagues" or "ex-clients." Sadly, we no longer had any common bond. It was as if a trap door had suddenly slammed shut, sealing years of memories inside.

The changing of the guard had inevitably caused a rupture in the relations between me and Gene and Paul. Business had taken precedence over the personal. I don't think that their beef was with me. I wasn't a party to the litigation. But my longtime association with the company made me the odd man out. Carl Glickman was surprised that they never asked me to run their new organization when they parted company with us, but I wasn't. They wanted to clear out all the old faces. And there was also the potential problem that I would be called to testify on behalf of Glickman/Marks Management if Kiss's litigation went to court. Kiss probably thought having me around would be like having a mole in their organization. I ended up staying where I was.

Following the split, things didn't go well for Howard Marks. The loss of Kiss was a heavy blow. We took on a German rock group, Accept, that had some success, but by mid-1989, they had broken up. The Madison Avenue offices were kept, with much of the space rented out to other firms. Bank loans and borrowings were needed to keep Glickman/Marks Management afloat, despite the company's earning millions from Kiss since 1976. Howard was always anticipating that a big business deal was just around the corner.

The music business isn't kind to the former managers of artists, especially when they're no longer connected to the business. There really isn't a place for them. I ended up suffering a similar fate. After a long run in a key supporting role, there didn't seem to be a place for me, either. By 1990, there was no money left in the company to keep me on. I'd already taken on some freelance work, including a short stint with Rick Astley, a British crooner, and later, taught at several universities in New York and took on consulting clients.

I basically ended up with very little to show for my years with the company and Kiss, except a treasure trove of experiences. It was a rewarding job but not a lucrative one. I was never in a position to really benefit from Kiss's riches since they were already established as a top act when I joined them as a rookie out of business school in 1976. And my company never had much success with other artists for any length of time. We had overdosed on Kiss. The break-up of the Kiss-Aucoin-Glickman/Marks organization had unfortunate consequences for my career. In a business of relationships, most of mine had been severed.

In many ways, the story of Kiss's crash is unusual. They weren't surrounded by connivers, fast-buck artists, schemers, or courtiers. By the end of the'70s, Bill Aucoin's creative stewardship had made Kiss the success story of the music business. In the course of a few short years, Kiss had become an instantly recognized brand name. Their business managers, Carl Glickman and Howard Marks, were already successful in their own right and didn't need to be in the music business to reap additional financial rewards.

Kiss's success lasted years longer than anyone ever imagined. But once they started to crash, the media shifted from adulation to avoidance. The backlash from disgruntled fans who got turned off by Kiss's overcommercialism, the musical chairs of changing members, the image makeovers, and the mounting money problems had taken their toll. Once renowned for an outrageous image and an unmistakable and overpowering sound, by the end of the '80s they had became known as the rock group that dated a galaxy of movie stars, models, and magazine foldouts. The brand name remained but what it meant to the public had become blurry and barely recognizable.

Public reaction to Kiss did a 180 degree turn. At their peak, the mere mention of being connected to Kiss brought gasps of envy and disbelief from people not even remotely connected to the music business. But by the late 1980s, the reaction was typically, "Are they still together?"

Not long after Kiss took off the makeup, during the dog days of summer 1984, I ran into John Goodhue, an old hand from the Kiss organization. John had directed some of Kiss's first videos from the *Dynasty* album released five years earlier. Crossing Park Avenue at 60th Street, we stared at each other for a moment, blinked, and then our memories must have clicked at the same time. We shook hands and exchanged small talk and John asked me what I was up to. I told him I was still involved with Kiss. He then casually opined, "It's pretty much died down now, hasn't it?" It sounded almost Delphic to me. I got a little defensive, telling him about the huge crowd in Rio, the band's new image, and all the new albums. But what he said stuck in my mind. The obituary might have been premature, but no one could deny that the hype had "died down."

I once asked Paul during the period that they were rebuilding their career in the mid-1980s why it was, at least from my vantage point, that no one in the original foursome listened to all the advice about reining in the spending when they were earning big money. He didn't flinch when he shot back with his response. "We were all out of our minds," he said. Success was evergreen. Kiss thought they would always be able to top themselves and keep one step ahead of the public. The money would always be there. It didn't work out that way.

19 Coda

Nobody's taking the easy way out, which would be to make Son of Destroyer, put on the makeup again, and do the obvious thing. But if we just sit here, resting on our laurels, we might as well build a fireplace, put on our slippers, and say "Yeah, 1974. That was a really good year."

> Gene Simmons commenting on Kiss's future in "Kiss Unfazed," *Creem*, January/February 1993.

Kiss continues to record under a long-term contract with PolyGram. The longevity of Kiss in an industry noted for instability is in itself a remarkable phenomenon. Few artists have had careers spanning three decades; Kiss released its first album on Casablanca in 1974, a label that was later acquired by PolyGram.

Kiss eventually played at the Donington rock festival in August 1988. They were the supporting act for Iron Maiden, a British heavy metal group. Paradoxically, Iron Maiden was one of the many groups which opened for Kiss on tour in the late '70s.

Another package of oldies, *Smashes, Thrashes, & Hits,* was released in 1988 and sold more than two million units. *Hot in the Shade,* an album of new Kiss material, came out in 1989 and spawned a ballad, "Forever," that reached #8 in *Billboard*. The following year, Kiss headlined a "triple header" tour of 127 cities in the states.

Eric Carr, Peter's replacement since 1980, died of cancer in November 1991. He was 41. Eric Singer replaced him on drums.

Kiss reunited with producer Bob Ezrin in 1992 for their *Revenge* album. He had last worked with the band eleven years earlier on *(Music From) The Elder.* *Revenge* reached #6 in *Billboard* but soon dropped out of the Top 40. Following the release of *Revenge,* the band toured the United States at the end of 1992. Turnouts were disappointing, and the tour wrapped up after three months. In 1993, *Alive III,* produced by Eddie Kramer, was released, Kiss's first live album in sixteen years.

Kiss albums in recent years—*Hot in the Shade, Revenge, and Alive III,*—have each sold upwards of 500,000 copies, well below their previous automatic platinum level. *Entertainment Weekly* reported in its June 19, 1992, story on Kiss that PolyGram had hired a marketing research firm to conduct surveys as to why Kiss concertgoers weren't buying albums. Survey results concluded that fans wanted "more headbanging rock and fewer power ballads."

Seeking to reach the current generation of rock fans as well as to pay homage to their own influence on newer artists, Kiss organized a tribute album to themselves in 1994. Self-referentially titled *Kiss My Ass: Classic Kiss Regrooved,* the record featured performances of Kiss songs by an array of notables, including Garth Brooks, Lenny Kravitz, the Gin Blossoms, Anthrax, Toad the Wet Sprocket, and Stevie Wonder.

A traveling Kiss Convention was assembled in the summer of 1995 that featured an exhibit of Kiss memorabilia, souvenir merchandise, shows by Kiss imitator bands who performed in '70s era makeup and costumes, and an appearance by the current Kiss lineup, playing acoustical numbers and fielding questions from fans. The day-long extravaganza, which toured the United States, had an admission price of $100. Peter made a surprise appearance at the convention in Burbank, California; he had called Gene to ask if he could come to the event. Once there, he was invited to sit in with the band and play a few Kiss songs for the fans. This mini-reunion proved to be a harbinger of things to come.

In October 1995, MTV aired an *Unplugged* special featuring Kiss. Ace and Peter joined Paul, Gene, Eric Singer, and Bruce Kulick for several songs. The taping went well and the original four Kiss members agreed to pursue the possibility of working together in the future. PolyGram released an album of the *Unplugged* show in March 1996 and the six Kiss members, past and present, appeared on the album cover.

On April 16, 1996, the original Kiss—Gene, Paul, Ace, and Peter—staged a press conference at the Intrepid Museum in New York to announce a summer reunion tour. Dressed in their classic Kiss costumes and in makeup, the group unveiled plans to recreate their *Love Gun*-era stage show, circa 1977-78, complete with a panoply of updated special effects and bursting with high-tech sound and lights. To further solidify the image of the original hard-edged, heavy metal Kiss, no songs would be performed that were recorded after 1979's *Dynasty* album, the last time all four toured together. This time around, there would be no mistaking what Kiss stood for.

Harking back to the past has proven to be a screaming success for Kiss. Within weeks of the press conference, the kickoff show at Detroit's Tiger Stadium sold nearly 40,000 tickets in under an hour. Cities across the country reported almost instantaneous sellouts at major arenas, many booking multiple shows. Four shows set for July at Madison Square Garden in New York sold out quickly, as did three shows in August at the Great Western Forum in Los Angeles. The band returned to Donington in England where they co-headlined with Ozzy Osbourne and toured Europe in the fall. Plans call for more overseas tours in 1997, including Japan, Australia, and South America, followed by another round of U.S. shows.

The current Kiss show is a faithful note-for-note, bomb-for-bomb re-creation of their trademark shows of the late '70s. It is uncompromising and unwavering from what it was that made them famous. Ticket prices are probably the only item that doesn't hark back to an earlier era: prices in most cities range from $40 to $80.

Yet another package of oldies, including unreleased live tracks from the '70s, was brought out by PolyGram to coincide with the 1996 tour. The album *You Wanted The Best, You Got The Best!!*, one of the band's more memorable slogans, also included a taped interview with Jay Leno. An official discography published in 1996 lists Kiss as having released thirty albums registering more than 33 million copies sold in the United States. Millions more have been sold in dozens of countries around the world.

Burying the hatchet among the original Kiss members promises to reap outsized financial rewards for each of them. In December 1996, music trade publications *Pollstar* and *Performance* reported that the Kiss Reunion Tour was the highest-grossing concert tour of the year, with over $40 million in ticket sales. In fact, they've been selling more tickets in most cities than they did at their zenith nearly twenty years ago. How the four will split the profits is unclear; press interviews with Gene and Paul indicate that, not unexpectedly, they are now firmly in charge of the business of Kiss and will receive the lion's share of the final take. Peter and Ace are apparently being kept on a short leash owing to the problems that wreaked so much havoc in the past.

For Gene and Paul, the reunion of Kiss is a personal triumph. Keeping Kiss alive since their beginnings in the early '70s was at times a tiresome, trying, and unrewarding ordeal, particularly after their gut-wrenching downturns in the '80s. With the resurrection of the original Kiss, contrivances like the Kiss Conventions, where they offered gassy reminiscences of their glory days to fans, can now be mothballed. And for Peter and Ace, the Kiss reunion is a chance to regain the limelight.

Critics have disparaged the Kiss Reunion Tour as a warm bath of nostalgia, a last-ditch effort to make money. But in reality, the tour is an unusual convergence of opportunities. A new generation wants to tap into a legend, and Kiss fans from past decades want to relive an experience that for many of them is at best a hazy memory. For much of the audience, Kiss is an event that is both new and fresh. At the same time, everyone in the original group stands to earn back the money that was blown in their heyday, possibly even making more. Until the Reunion Tour, Kiss had largely been eclipsed in the current era of entertainment marketing, despite the fact that Kiss originated many of these techniques in the music business of the late '70s. Kiss may ultimately have the last laugh, confounding their critics and detractors one more time.

Kiss can now continue to be Kiss. Strangely, they are as original and unique now as when they first seized the public's imagination. Few imitators have attempted to copy or adapt the Kiss formula's obvious appeal, and certainly none have surpassed Kiss's success at capitalizing on that formula. And there now exists a vast audience around the world for whom Kiss is an experience yet to be realized. In time, Kiss may one day be permanently enshrined as a theme park thrill ride, a Las Vegas casino attraction, or some other modern era mass entertainment spectacle—which is what Kiss was all about in the first place. I wouldn't bet against it.

Epilogue

We've outlived our critics.

Paul Stanley, reflecting on Kiss's history in *USA Today,* June 22, 1993.

Gene Simmons lives in Beverly Hills with Shannon Tweed. They have two children, Nicholas and Sophie.

Gene has dropped from sight as an actor and his Simmons Records label, a deal he made in 1988 with RCA Records, folded several years ago. Simmons Records had little success in discovering and promoting new artists. A venture that he began with Howard Marks, managing the recording career of Liza Minnelli, also fizzled. Gene and Howard had landed a deal with Epic Records for Liza to record an album showing off her talents as a pop singer. The album was released in 1989 and sold modestly.

Gene is no longer managing Liza or any other artists. Shannon Tweed, 39, his longtime girlfriend, has enjoyed a successful career as a star of erotic thrillers made for home video, playing steamy seductresses.

Paul Stanley now lives in Los Angeles. In the late '80s he was linked to yet another blonde bombshell, British pop singer Samantha Fox, who reportedly began her career as a topless model for the London tabloids. An article in *The Wall Street Journal* on November 13, 1991, quoted a tabloid gossip who claimed that Samantha had sought a $1.5 million insurance policy for her breasts. Paul put together his own group, The Paul Stanley Band, and performed in clubs for a brief tour while Kiss was off the road. In 1992, he married Pamela Bowen, a TV actress. They have a son, Evan.

Peter Criss lives in Southern California. He is divorced from his second wife, Debra. In January 1991, he created a stir in the national media when an imposter appeared in the headlines of a supermarket tabloid, identifying himself as Peter Criss and claiming to be a homeless alcoholic and panhandler. Peter was subsequently featured in a *People* magazine article and appeared on *Donahue* to deny the reports, which were false.

In 1994, Peter released an album of new songs on Tony Nicole Tony Records, an independent label in L.A. The cover showed half of his face painted as his Kiss character and the other half as he normally appears without makeup.

Ace Frehley has been living in Westchester County, New York. Following his departure from Kiss, he took an extended hiatus from music. In the late '80s, he released several albums with his band, Frehley's Comet, on the Megaforce/Atlantic label. Ace has toured throughout the United States and prior to the Kiss Reunion Tour, he teamed up with Peter for a club tour.

Howard Marks died in June 1990. He was 61. He'd been hospitalized after suffering a series of strokes. For many years, Howard was the glue that held Kiss together. His business prowess enabled the band to weather many setbacks and he engineered the megadeals for Kiss and Diana Ross which made them among the world's highest-paid recording artists. He devoted most of his professional life to the group in later years.

Carl Glickman continues to serve on the board of directors of Bear Stearns. He is active as a private investor as well as in civic and charitable organizations. Shortly after Howard's death, Carl settled the litigation that had been brought against Glickman/Marks Management by Gene and Paul. Carl is no longer involved in the music business.

Bill Aucoin formed a brief association with Howard Marks after his split with Billy Idol. They had hoped to develop new acts to manage, but the partnership didn't last long. More recently, Bill has started a company in New York, Dreamscape Entertainment.

Diana Ross married a wealthy Norwegian shipping magnate, Arne Naess, in February 1986. They have two sons. Diana continues to tour and record for Motown, her original label, which recently came under the umbrella of PolyGram.

Cher has emerged as one of Hollywood's leading actresses since winning the Academy Award in 1988 for Best Actress in *Moonstruck*. Her singing career was revitalized when she switched to rock. Cher has had a run of hit singles and platinum albums on Geffen Records.

The Isley Brothers, now in their fifth decade of making records, released an album on Island Records in 1996.

Lisa Hartman frequently appears on made-for-TV movies and miniseries. In 1991, she married Clint Black, one of country music's biggest stars.

Neil Bogart, who founded Casablanca Records and signed Kiss as one of the label's first artists, died of cancer in 1982. He was 39.

Jeff Franklin, who founded Kiss's original booking agency, ATI, booked an arena tour in 1987 for Jim and Tammy Faye Bakker, the controversial Praise the Lord minister and his wife. Ticket sales were almost nonexistent and the tour was quickly aborted. ATI Video Enterprises closed in 1989. Jeff now runs Franklin/Waterman Entertainment, a TV and movie production company in L.A., which supplies programming to networks including the Family Channel and international markets. Jeff was a co-producer of the feature film *Casper*.

Wally Meyrowitz, Kiss's booking agent from their days as a club act through their most successful years, died in 1984, reportedly of complications from drugs and alcohol.

Paul Marshall, Kiss's longtime attorney, no longer represents the group.

Danny Goldberg, a former publicist for Kiss and later their creative consultant, is now head of Mercury Records, Kiss's label.

Jesse Hilsen, 56, Paul's psychotherapist and, later, Kiss's financial adviser, received national media attention when his former wife appeared on the CBS News program *48 Hours* in December 1993. In a segment on lawsuits in America, she stated that Jesse never paid the alimony and support for their children awarded her by the courts. Following the broadcast, a viewer recognized Jesse from the photo shown as working for Kiss. In an April 1994 update, Dan Rather stated that Jesse was "reportedly earning up to half a million dollars a year" and that a warrant had been issued for his arrest. In *Forbes* magazine's September 23, 1996, issue featuring Kiss on the cover, Jesse was reported to be a "fugitive."

Doc McGhee, who formerly managed Mötley Crüe and Bon Jovi, is now Kiss's manager.

Index

348

349

BillboardBooks

Thank you for buying a Billboard Book.
If you enjoyed this title, you might want
to check out other books in our catalog.

**THE BILLBOARD BOOK OF
NUMBER ONE ALBUMS:**
The Inside Story Behind Pop Music's
Blockbuster Records by Craig Rosen
A behind-the-scenes look at the people
and stories involved in the enormously
popular records that achieved Number
One album status in the Billboard charts.
Inside information on over 400 albums
that have topped the chart since 1956,
plus new interviews with hundreds of
superstar record artists as well as a wealth
of trivia statistics and other facts. 448
pages. 425 photos. Paperback. $21.95.

**THE BILLBOARD BOOK OF
NUMBER ONE HITS,**
**Third Edition, Revised and Enlarged by
Fred Bronson**
The inside story behind the top of the
charts. An indispensable listing of every
single to appear in the top spot on the
Billboard Hot 100 chart from 1955
through 1991, along with anecdotes,
interviews, and chart data. 848 pages.
800 photos. Paperback. $21.95.

**THE BILLBOARD BOOK OF
TOP 40 ALBUMS,**
**Third Edition, Revised and Enlarged by
Joel Whitburn**
The complete guide to every Top 40
album from 1955 to 1994.
Comprehensive information on the most
successful rock, jazz, comedy, country,
classical, Christmas, Broadway, and film
soundtrack albums ever to reach the top
of the Billboard charts. Includes chart
positions, number of weeks on the chart,
and label and catalog number for every
album listed. 416 pages. 150 photos.
Paperback. $21.95.

**THE BILLBOARD BOOK OF
TOP 40 COUNTRY HITS:**
**Country Music's Hottest Records, 1944 to
the Present by Joel Whitburn@$3:**
From the classic recordings of Hank
Williams and Bob Wills, to enduring
artists Patsy Cline and Tammy Wynette,
to today's young superstars Garth Brooks
and Shania Twain, the rich history of
country music is documented in this
comprehensive compilation of Billboard's
Country Singles charts. Provides
exhaustive data on every record to score
at least one Top 40 hit. 562 pages. 96
photos. Paperback. $21.95

**THE BILLBOARD BOOK OF
TOP 40 HITS,**
**Sixth Edition, Revised and Enlarged by
Joel Whitburn**
A perennial favorite, listing every single
to reach the Top 40 of Billboard's weekly
Hot 100 charts since 1955. Includes new
chart data and expanded biographical
information and trivia on artists listed.
800 pages. 300 photos. Paperback. $21.95

THE BILLBOARD BOOK OF ONE-HIT WONDERS,
Second Edition, Revised and Expanded by Wayne Jancik

A one-of-a-kind rock and roll reference guide that charts the flip side of the pop music story. Uncovers the fascinating circumstances surrounding the rise to fame—and occasional rapid return to obscurity—of performers who had only one hit in Billboard's Top 40 charts. Contains over 100 new entries and a wealth of data and entertaining information that just can't be found elsewhere. A must for pop music fans and record collectors. 512 pages. 235 photos. Paperback. $21.95.

BILLBOARD'S HOTTEST HOT 100 HITS,
Revised and Enlarged Edition by Fred Bronson

The Ultimate music trivia book. An illustrated compendium of 40 years of Billboard's chart data broken down into 175 categories, including artists, writers, producers, and record labels. Plus, a definitive list of the Top 5000 hits from 1955 through 1995. 512 pages. 250 photos. Paperback. $21.95

THE REAL DEAL:
How to Get Signed to a Record Label From A to Z by Daylle Deanna Schwartz

A new music industry primer offering crucial information and advice that any musician playing popular music and desiring a record deal needs to have. Includes an explanation of the roles of an agent, attorney, A&R person, producer, and manager; what copyright and music publishing are; the importance of doing live performance; ways to build a following; how to use networking to reach the right people; and the pros and cons of releasing an independent recording. Also contains advice from top creative and business professionals and a resource section. 256 pages. Paperback. $16.95.

THE ROCK AND ROLL READER'S GUIDE by Gary M. Krebs

An indispensable consumer guide for book collectors and music fans alike. The first comprehensive bibliography of books about, and by, rock and pop stars in addition to works written about the music scene itself. Focuses on both selected general reference works—such as artist profiles, chart data, pictorials, concert events, women and rock, and magazines—and all publications on artists A-Z. 464 pages. Paperback. $21.95.

THIS BUSINESS OF MUSIC,
Seventh Edition by M. William Krasilovsky and Sidney Shemel

The bible of the music business, with over 250,000 copies sold. A practical guide to the music industry for publishers, writers, record companies, producers, artists, and agents. Provides detailed information on virtually every economic, legal, and financial aspect of the complex business of music. 736 pages. Hardcover. $29.95.

MORE ABOUT THIS BUSINESS OF MUSIC,
Fifth Edition, Revised and Enlarged by Sidney Shemel and M. William Krasilovsky

A completely updated companion to This Business of Music, this book presents a practical guide to areas of the music business such as jazz, religious music, live performances, the production and sale of printed music, background music and transcriptions, and the impact of technology from CDs and DATs to VCRs. 224 pages. Hardcover. $18.95.

The above titles should all be available from your neighborhood bookseller. If you don't find a copy on the shelf, books can also be ordered either through the store or directly from Watson-Guptill Publications. To order copies by phone or to request information on any of these titles, please call our toll-free number: 1-800-278-8477. To order copies by mail, send a check or money order for the cost of the book, with $2.00 postage and handling for one book and $ .50 for each additional book, plus applicable sales tax in the states of CA, DC, IL, OH, MA, NJ, NY, PA, TN, and VA, to:

WATSON-GUPTILL PUBLICATIONS
PO Box 2013
Lakewood, NJ 08701-9913